METHODS OF BIOCHEMICAL ANALYSIS

Volume XI

METHODS OF
BIOCHEMICAL ANALYSIS

Edited by **DAVID GLICK**

Head, Division of Histochemistry
Professor, Department of Pathology
Stanford University Medical School
Palo Alto, California

VOLUME XI

INTERSCIENCE PUBLISHERS

a division of John Wiley & Sons, Inc., New York · London · Sydney

PREFACE TO THE SERIES

Annual review volumes dealing with many different fields of science have proved their value repeatedly and are now widely used and well established. These reviews have been concerned primarily with the results of the developing fields, rather than with the techniques and methods employed, and they have served to keep the ever-expanding scene within the view of the investigator, the applier, the teacher, and the student.

It is particularly important that review services of this nature should now be extended to cover methods and techniques, because it is becoming increasingly difficult to keep abreast of the manifold experimental innovations and improvements which constitute the limiting factor in many cases for the growth of the experimental sciences. Concepts and vision of creative scientists far outrun that which can actually be attained in present practice. Therefore an emphasis on methodology and instrumentation is a fundamental need in order for material achievement to keep in sight of the advance of useful ideas.

The current volume is another in this series which is designed to try to meet the need in the field of biochemical analysis. The topics to be included are chemical, physical, microbiological, and if necessary, animal assays, as well as basic techniques and instrumentation for the determination of enzymes, vitamins, hormones, lipids, carbohydrates, proteins and their products, minerals, antimetabolites, etc.

Certain chapters will deal with well-established methods or techniques which have undergone sufficient improvement to merit recapitulation, reappraisal, and new recommendations. Other chapters will be concerned with essentially new approaches which bear promise of great usefulness. Relatively few subjects can be included in any single volume, but as they accumulate these volumes should comprise a self-modernizing encyclopedia of methods of biochemical analysis. By judicious selection of topics it is planned that most subjects of current importance will receive treatment in these volumes.

The general plan followed in the organization of the individual chapters is a discussion of the background and previous work, a critical evaluation of the various approaches, and a presentation of the procedural details of the method or methods recommended by the author. The presentation of the experimental details is to be given in a manner that will furnish the laboratory worker with the complete information required to carry out the analyses.

Within this comprehensive scheme the reader may note that the treatments vary widely with respect to taste, style, and point of view. It is the editor's policy to encourage individual expression in these presentations because it is stifling to originality and justifiably annoying to many authors to submerge themselves in a standard mold. Scientific writing need not be as dull and uniform as it too often is. In certain technical details a consistent pattern is followed for the sake of convenience, as in the form used for reference citations and indexing.

The success of the treatment of any topic will depend primarily on the experience, critical ability, and capacity to communicate of the author. Those invited to prepare the respective chapters are scientists who either have originated the methods they discuss or have had intimate personal experience with them.

It is the wish of the Advisory Board and the editor to make this series of volumes as useful as possible and to this end suggestions will always be welcome.

DAVID GLICK

CONTRIBUTORS

OSCAR BODANSKY, *Division of Enzymology and Metabolism, Sloan-Kettering Institute for Cancer Research; Department of Biochemistry, Memorial Hospital for Cancer and Allied Diseases and James Ewing Hospital; and Sloan-Kettering Division of Cornell University Medical College, New York, New York*

I. E. BUSH, *Department of Physiology, University of Birmingham, Birmingham, England*

F. L. CRANE, *Department of Biological Sciences, Purdue University, Lafayette, Indiana*

B. G. CREECH. *Lipid Research Center, Baylor University College of Medicine, Houston, Texas*

ROBERT P. DAVIS, *Albert Einstein College of Medicine, Yeshiva University, New York, New York*

R. A. DILLEY, *Department of Biological Sciences, Purdue University, Lafayette, Indiana*

E. C. HORNING, *Lipid Research Center, Baylor University College of Medicine, Houston, Texas*

IRWIN J. KOPIN, *Laboratory of Clinical Science, National Institute of Mental Health, Bethesda, Maryland*

OTTO H. MÜLLER, *State University of New York Upstate Medical Center, Syracuse, New York*

MORTON K. SCHWARTZ, *Division of Enzymology and Metabolism, Sloan-Kettering Institute for Cancer Research; Department of Biochemistry, Memorial Hospital for Cancer and Allied Diseases and James Ewing Hospital; and Sloan-Kettering Division of Cornell University Medical College, New York, New York*

W. J. A. VANDENHEUVEL, *Lipid Research Center, Baylor University College of Medicine, Houston, Texas*

J. B. WILLIS, *Division of Chemical Physics, C.S.I.R.O. Chemical Research Laboratories, Melbourne, Australia*

CONTENTS

Analysis of Biological Materials by Atomic Absorption Spectroscopy

J. B. WILLIS, *C.S.I.R.O. Chemical Research Laboratories, Melbourne, Australia*

I. INTRODUCTION

Although the average biochemist may not be familiar with the expression "atomic absorption spectroscopy" he will almost certainly have observed the phenomenon of absorption of light by atoms very early in his career. If the sun is viewed through a pocket spectroscope, two black lines (the Fraunhofer lines) can be seen at exactly the same wavelengths as the well-known sodium D lines emitted by a flame containing traces of sodium chloride. The Fraunhofer lines arise from the absorption of radiation from the hot center of the sun by the layers of sodium vapor in the outer parts of its atmosphere.

The first application of atomic absorption spectra to chemical analysis was made just over 100 years ago by Kirchoff (51), who demonstrated the presence of various elements in the solar atmosphere. Together with Bunsen he demonstrated shortly afterwards that atomic spectra, whether in emission or absorption, could be the basis of a powerful method of chemical analysis (52–54).

Since that time emission methods of spectrochemical analysis have been widely developed and have culminated in the direct-reading spectrographs which provide multicomponent analyses at high speed for the metallurgical industries. In biochemical work, where interest until recently has been confined mostly to the elements sodium, potassium, and calcium, emission analysis has generally been carried out with a much simpler instrument, the flame photometer.

Whereas emission methods have been firmly established for many years, absorption methods have been almost completely overlooked except by the astrophysicist in the determination of the compositions of solar and stellar atmospheres. Admittedly, the determination of mercury vapor as a contaminant in laboratory atmospheres has been carried out for more than 20 years by an atomic absorption method (97), but it was not until 1953 that Walsh (84) recognized the potential advantages of the absorption method over emission methods and devised simple and versatile apparatus applicable to the routine analysis of solutions of a wide range of elements.

In 1955 Walsh (85) and Alkemade and Milatz (2,3) published papers describing the application of atomic absorption techniques to chemical analysis. Walsh's paper surveys the theoretical factors involved in atomic absorption analysis and discusses the advantages to be expected in the use of absorption rather than emission measurements. These advantages are that atomic absorption is independent of the excitation potential of the transition involved and that it is less subject to temperature variation and interference from extraneous radiation or energy exchange between atoms.

Several reviews (11b,26,30,42a,55,65,69,72,86,94a) and one book (34) have appeared in recent years describing the rapidly growing volume of work on this topic. The present article will discuss briefly the theoretical basis of atomic absorption spectroscopy, the different types of instrument used, and the factors involved in making absorption measurements, and finally give a detailed account of the work which has been done on the determination of different elements by this method with particular emphasis on determinations of interest to the biochemist.

II. THEORETICAL

The production of atoms from a molecule of a chemical compound requires the absorption of energy, and heat is usually the most convenient form in which to supply this energy. When vaporized by heating in a flame, a compound such as sodium chloride is partially or wholly broken up into its elements in the gaseous form, and some of the atoms are further excited to a state from which they can emit radiation on returning to the unexcited, or ground, state.

The relation between the number of atoms in an excited state and in the ground state is given by

$$N_j/N_0 = (P_j/P_0) \exp \left\{ -E_j/kT \right\} \tag{1}$$

where N_j and N_0 are the numbers of atoms in the excited and ground states, respectively; P_j and P_0, the corresponding statistical weights; E_j, the energy difference of the two states; k, Boltzmann's constant; and T, the absolute temperature. The higher the value of E_j, i.e., the shorter the wavelength of the spectral line corresponding to the transition between the ground and excited state, the smaller will be the fraction of atoms in the excited state. Table I shows the fraction of atoms in the first excited state for several elements at different temperatures.

It can be seen that at any easily attainable temperature only a small fraction of the atoms of even the most easily excited metal (cesium) is raised above the ground state, and that for metals such as zinc only an insignificant fraction of atoms is excited. It is for this reason that flame photometry, while very sensitive for the alkali metals, is unsatisfactory for metals such as magnesium or zinc. If, however, the absorption of light by the atoms in the highly populated ground state is measured, this difficulty disappears, and the same order of sensitivity can be expected for zinc as for cesium. It is this measurement which is the basis of the technique of atomic absorption spectroscopy.

TABLE I

Values of N_j/N_0 for Various Resonance Lines[a]

Resonance, A.	Transition	$\dfrac{P_j}{P_0}$	$T = 2000\ °K.$	$T = 3000\ °K.$	$T = 4000\ °K.$	$T = 5000\ °K.$
Cs 8521	$^2S_{1/2}$–$^2P_{3/2}$	2	4.44×10^{-4}	7.24×10^{-3}	2.98×10^{-2}	6.82×10^{-2}
Na 5890	$^2S_{1/2}$–$^2P_{3/2}$	2	9.86×10^{-6}	5.88×10^{-4}	4.44×10^{-3}	1.51×10^{-2}
Ca 4227	$^1S_0$–$^1P_1$	3	1.21×10^{-7}	3.69×10^{-5}	6.03×10^{-4}	3.33×10^{-3}
Zn 2139	$^1S_0$–$^1P_1$	3	7.29×10^{-15}	5.58×10^{-10}	1.48×10^{-7}	4.32×10^{-6}

[a] Reproduced, by permission of *Spectrochimica Acta*, from reference 85.

Atoms in the ground state can only absorb radiation at a limited number of wavelengths, corresponding to their resonance lines, and Figure 1 shows schematically the resonance lines and energy levels involved for sodium, magnesium, zinc, and phosphorus. In atomic absorption spectroscopy it is nearly always the first resonance line which is used, i.e., the line corresponding to the transition from the ground state to the lowest excited state. For metals with complicated

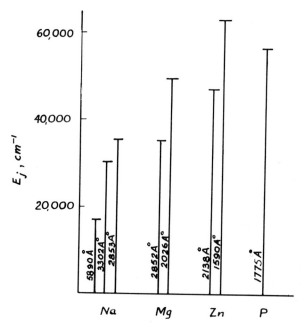

Fig. 1. Energy levels and resonance lines of sodium, magnesium, zinc, and phosphorus.

electronic structures, such as iron and manganese, there are frequently several resonance lines which absorb to a roughly similar degree, but for most metals the choice of absorbing line is simple. In Table II are shown the lines which have been found most useful for the measurement of a large number of metals.

The width of such lines is inherently very small (ca. 10^{-4} A.), and even when the broadening due to various factors (Doppler, pressure,

TABLE II

Optimum Conditions and Limits of Detection of Metal Ions in Solution by a Simple Atomic Absorption Spectrophotometer

Reproduced, by permission of *Spectrochimica Acta*, from reference 41.

Metal	Lamp current, ma	Line, A.	Slit width,* A.	Noise, ±%	Flame†	Concentration (p.p.m.) giving 50% absorption	Concentration (p.p.m.) giving 1% absorption	Notes
Li	12	6708	110	nil	C	2	0.03	1
	30	3233	3	1	C	1000	15	
Na	750	5890	13	0.25	C	2	0.03	a,b,j
	830	3302	3	1	C	350	5	
K	900	7665	30	0.5	C	2	0.03	a,b,j
	900	4044	6	0.25	C	350	5	
Rb	800	7800	150	0.5	C	9	0.1	a,j
	800	4202	6	0.25	C	700	10	
Cs	650	8521	400	1	C	9	0.15	a,j
	900	4556	8	nil	C	1500	20	a,j
Cu	4	3248	3	nil	C	6	0.1	a,l
	18	2228	0.5	2	C	100	2	
Ag	4	3281	3	0.5	C	4	0.05	a,l
	4	3383	3	0.5	C	12	0.15	
Au	6	2428	1	1	C	20	0.3	a,l,n
	6	2676	1	1	C	100	1.3	
Be	20	2349	1	1	A		>100	k
Mg	6	2852	2	0.25	A	0.5	0.01	a,c,l
	6	2796	1	0.25	A	1500	5	
Ca	10	4227	6	0.25	A	5	0.08	c,l
	20	2399	1	1	A	2000	20	
Sr	20	4607	8	nil	A	10	0.15	b,c,l
	20	4078	6	nil	A		3.5	
Ba	36	5536	14	1	A	600	8	c,m
	36	7911 } 3262			A		>1000	
Zn	6	2139	2	1	C	2	0.03	a,d,k,o
	6	3076	2	0.5	C	10,000	150	

Element		λ			Flame			
Cd	2	2288	2		C	1400	20	e
	2	3261	3	1	C	1000	10	k
Hg	20	2537	1	0.5	C		>1000	a,k
Al	4	3962	5	0.25	A	250	3	
Ga	4	2874	1	0.5	A	400	5	
	4	4172	4	0.25	A	300	3	
	4	2944	1	0.5	A	500	7	a,j
	4	4033	4	0.25	A	60	0.8	
Tl	750	2768	7	0.25	C	200	3	
	750	3776	4	0.5	C		>1000	1
Ti	10	4982	10	0.25	A			
Sn	8	2863	3	1	A (very rich)	350	5	a,c,l
Pb	4	2833	2	0.5	C	40	0.5	a,l
	4	2614	1	1	C		50	
V	10	2892	2	0.5	A (very rich)			1
	10	2909	2	0.5	A (very rich)		>1000	
	10	3184	2	0.25	A (very rich)			
	10	4379	7	0.25	A (very rich)			
Nb	10	4059	6	0.25	A (very rich)		>1000	1
	10	4080	6	0.25	A			
	10	4124	6	0.25	A			
	10	4137	6	0.25	A			
Sb	6	2311	4	1	C	100	1.5	b,g,l
Bi	12	2176	1	2	C	75	2	a,b,c,l
	8	3068	2	1	C	150	0.15	c,l
Cr	10	3579	4	nil	A	10	0.5	
	4	4254	7	0.5	A	60	0.5	
Mo	6	3133	4	0.25	A	40	0.5	c,m
W	4	3170	4	1	A (very rich)	150	2	
	20	4294	7	0.25	A		>1000	1
	20	4302	7	0.25	A			

(continued)

TABLE II (*continued*)

Metal	Lamp current, ma.	Line, A.	Slit width,* A.	Noise, ±%	Flame†	Concentration (p.p.m.) giving 50% absorption	Concentration (p.p.m.) giving 1% absorption	Notes
Mn	5	2795	1	0.75	C	4	0 05	a,l
	5	2801	1	1	C	10	0.2	
Fe	5	2483	1	0.75	A	7	0.1	b,f,k
	10	3720	4	0.25	A	75	1	
Co	25	2407	1	1	A	15	0.2	a,b,h,l
	25	3454	3	0.5	A	300	4	
	25	3527	3	0.5	A	400	3	
Ni	29	2320	0.5	1	C	15	0.2	b,d,j,k
	29	3415	3	0.5	C	40	0.5	
Rh	4	3435	3	0.5	A	25	0.3	a,c,l
Pd	6	2476	2	1	C	55	0.8	a,b,l
Pt	7	2659	1	1	A	600	5	a,b,l

* The spectral slit width quoted is the half-intensity bandwidth, which is taken from the dispersion data supplied with the Beckman DU monochromator. The mechanical width was checked for various settings of the slits. † C = coal gas–air; A = acetylene–air. ᵃ Markedly dependent on lamp current. ᵇ Markedly dependent on slit width. ᶜ Markedly dependent on flame type. ᵈ Helium-filled hollow-cathode tube used. ᵉ "Mineralite" mercury lamp used as source. ᶠ Neon-filled hollow-cathode tube used. ᵍ The line at 2176 A. is slightly more sensitive than that at 2311 A. for low concentrations of antimony, but the calibration curve flattens out rapidly above about 100 p.p.m. The noise level is much higher than for 2311 A. ʰ The calibration curve for the line at 2407.3 A. flattens out rapidly above about 50 p.p.m., owing to the presence of a weak line near 2406.7 A. (probably Cu 2406.67 A., arising from the copper cathode containing the pellet of cobalt). ⁱ The calibration curve for the line at 2320.1 A. flattens out rapidly above about 50 p.p.m., owing to the presence of a weak line near 2319.8 A. (probably Ni 2319.76 A.). ʲ Osram or Philips spectral lamp as source. ᵏ Hollow-cathode tube made by W. G. Jones. ˡ Hollow-cathode tube supplied by Ransley Glass Instruments, Melbourne. ᵐ Hollow-cathode tube supplied by D. J. David. ⁿ Lockyer and Hames (59) found that, for a given concentration of gold, the absorption decreased as their Meker-type burner warmed up. This effect does not occur with our burner. ᵒ Gidley and Jones (42) found that halogen acids caused spurious absorption near 2139 A.; this effect does not occur with our equipment.

resonance broadening, etc.) is taken into account, the width is still only 0.01–0.1 A. If a continuous source of radiation were used to measure atomic absorption, as in ordinary spectrophotometry, a spectral slit width of about 0.005 A. would be required. Such high resolution is beyond the powers of most spectrographs and monochromators. However, if a source giving out a strong sharp line of the appropriate wavelength is available, then radiation from this source can be shone through the atomic vapor and into the monochromator, which need now be only good enough to separate the desired line from any others which the source may emit. If the width of the emission line from the source is negligible compared with that of the absorption line in the atomic vapor, and if it is assumed that the shape of the latter is determined entirely by Doppler broadening, then the relation between the absorption coefficient (K_{max}) at the peak of the line and the concentration of atoms in the vapor is given by

$$K_{max} = \frac{2\lambda^2}{D_\lambda} \left(\frac{\ln 2}{\pi}\right)^{1/2} \frac{\pi e^2}{mc^2} Nf \qquad (2)$$

where D_λ is the Doppler width; λ, the wavelength of the line; e and m, the electronic charge and mass, respectively; c, the velocity of light; N, the number of atoms per cm.[3] which are capable of absorbing light of wavelength λ; and f, the oscillator strength, which is the average number of electrons per atom which can be excited by the incident radiation. This implies a linear relationship between absorbance and concentration, which in practice is approached at low concentrations. At high concentrations the width of the line is principally determined by factors other than the Doppler broadening.

Since the effective resolution of the system is determined by the width of the lines emitted by the sharp-line source (ca. 0.01 A.) the use of a sharp-line source containing one isotope of an element may allow the determination of this isotope in the atomic vapor. This requires, however, that the vapor be produced at temperatures sufficiently low that the half-width of the absorption line is less than the peak separation of the isotopic lines. Since for most metals except lithium (Section VI.1), the isotope separation is less than 0.01 A., vaporization of the specimen by means of a flame, which leads to half-widths greater than this (86.99), will usually be impracticable.

10   J. B. WILLIS

III. INSTRUMENTAL

The atomic absorption spectrophotometer, shown schematically
in Figure 2, thus consists of:

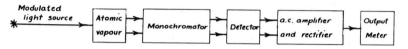

Fig. 2. Schematic diagram illustrating operation of an atomic absorption spectrophotometer.

1. A light source emitting, under conditions which ensure the production of extremely sharp lines, the spectrum of the element to be
determined;

2. A means of producing an atomic vapor of the sample to be
analyzed;

3. A wavelength selector to separate the resonance line required;
and

4. A detector, amplifier, and readout system (meter or recorder).

1. Light Sources

For the more volatile elements such as the alkali metals, mercury
and thallium, the most convenient source is the spectral vapor lamp,
in which an arc is struck between two electrodes in the vapor of the
metal. To minimize self-reversal and consequent broadening of the
resonance line, the lamp current must normally be reduced to the
lowest value which will give a stable discharge. Suitable lamps are
available from Osram and Philips.

For the less volatile elements, hollow-cathode tubes (Fig. 3) are
found to be the most satisfactory sources. A tube of this kind consists of an anode (usually a tungsten rod) and a hollow cylindrical
cathode consisting of or lined with the metal whose spectrum is
desired. The electrodes are mounted in a sealed tube, fitted with a
glass or quartz window, and filled with argon, helium, or neon at low
pressure. When the tube is connected to a source of current providing a starting voltage of about 400 v., the discharge taking place is
concentrated inside the hollow cathode, and bombardment by the
rare-gas ions causes free atoms of the metal to be sputtered off the

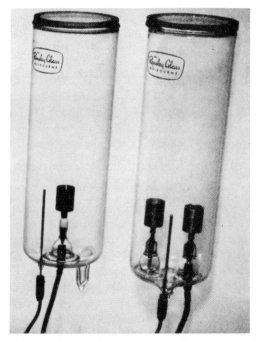

Fig. 3. Hollow-cathode tubes with single and double electrodes (Ransley Glass Instruments).

cathode. These atoms are excited by collision with the rare-gas atoms and emit a strong, sharp line spectrum of the metal.

The early hollow-cathode tubes used in high-resolution spectroscopy required continuous circulation of purified gas, but Jones and Walsh (48) succeeded in making permanently sealed-off tubes, and it is this type which is now made and sold for atomic absorption spectroscopy by several manufacturers (Ransley Glass Instruments, Melbourne, Australia; Hilger and Watts Ltd., London, England; Westinghouse Electric Corporation, Elmira, New York; Micro-Tek Instruments Inc., Baton Rouge, La.; RCA, Camden, N.J.).

In order to reduce the number of tubes required for the analysis of a range of metals it is possible to incorporate two or more hollow cylindrical electrodes of different metals in one tube; any one of these may then be made the cathode, another serving as the anode (48). The metals which can be paired in this way are usually limited to those having fairly similar melting points and volatilities, e.g., calcium and magnesium, silver and gold, copper and iron, zinc and cadmium.

The hollow-cathode tube is run from a stabilized power supply furnishing both filtered and modulated direct current (Section III.4) at a current which can be varied up to a maximum of about 50 ma. It must provide for a starting voltage of about 600 v., though the voltage drop across the tube while running is not more than about 300 v. It is usual to incorporate a ballast resistance in the lamp circuit in order to improve lamp stability.

2. Vaporization of the Sample

Although there are several methods of vaporizing materials directly from the solid state, e.g., the cathodic sputtering technique of Gatehouse and Walsh (40) for alloys and the arc-heated graphite crucible method of L'vov (61), most workers vaporize the sample by spraying a solution of the material into a flame. This is hardly surprising, since convenient and efficient nebulizers* and burners have been developed for flame photometry and are commercially available. However, as will be seen later (Section IV.2), there are several important elements which cannot be efficiently atomized by spraying into a flame, and the development of alternative means of vaporization is one of the outstanding problems to be solved in atomic absorption spectroscopy.

The direct-aspiration type of burner, such as the oxyhydrogen or oxyacetylene burner used in the Beckman DU flame photometer, has been employed for atomic absorption by Robinson (75). It has the disadvantage, however, of being suitable for only one type of fuel mixture and of being the wrong shape for absorption measurements, where a long flame rather than a tall one is desirable. Robinson has recently described a forced-feed burner in which the rate of supply of solution is independent of both the viscosity of the solution and the rates of flow of the fuel gases (78).

Most workers use an indirect nebulizer–burner system, i.e., one in which the air supply aspirates the liquid sample and produces a

---

* The device used for spraying a solution into a flame is commonly called an "atomizer," but in this article it will be referred to as a "nebulizer," since the word "atomization" will be used in its exact sense to mean "production of atoms" rather than in the colloquial sense meaning "production of a fine spray"

cloud of droplets which is mixed with the combustible gas in a spray chamber, where the larger droplets settle out and leave only the finest ones to be carried forward to the burner where the mixture is burnt. With such an arrangement a long burner can be constructed to burn air–coal gas, air–propane, or air–acetylene mixtures interchangeably, the only alteration required being in the size of the gas inlet jet. Furthermore, the burner can be rotated so that the distance traversed by the light beam passing through the flame is reduced up to 20-fold, which provides a convenient way of measuring solutions of widely differing concentrations. Burners of this type have been described by Clinton (21) and by Willis (93); the former is made of aluminum alloy and is provided with a water-cooling jacket, while the latter is made of stainless steel and has not been found to require cooling.

Some workers (42,59) using brass burners have obtained misleading results owing to attack on the material of the burner by solutions containing mineral acids or noble metals, and for this reason the use of brass should be avoided in the nebulizer–burner system. Finkelstein and Jansen (36b) have shown, however, that the use of a brass burner is permissible, even in the presence of $3.5N$ hydrochloric acid solution, provided the temperature of the burner is kept below 130°C. by water cooling.

The nebulizer may be constructed of glass, plastic, or stainless steel, though the latter material becomes corroded if strong acids or halogen-containing solutions are sprayed continually. Under these conditions it is advisable (95) to replace the stainless steel capillary of the nebulizer with one of platinum–iridium alloy and to coat the body of the burner with rhodium.

Herrmann (46a,46b,46c) has recently made a detailed study of the design of nebulizers and spray chambers, with particular attention to the optimum choice of air pressure and size of chamber.

3. The Wavelength Selector

The basic requirement for a wavelength selector is the ability to separate the desired resonance line from the other lines emitted by the sharp-line source. If any background radiation is emitted by the source, a curved calibration graph (absorbance–concentration) will be obtained, but the curvature can be minimized by using a narrow-pass monochromator to reduce the proportion of unabsorbed light.

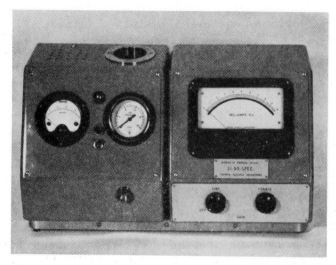

Fig. 4. The SI-RO-SPEC atomic absorption instrument for determination of sodium.

For the alkali metals, whose spectra contain little but the resonance lines, a simple glass or gelatine filter should suffice; indeed, for sodium determinations a very simple instrument (Fig. 4) has been constructed (16) in which no wavelength selector whatsoever is used, since the radiation from a sodium laboratory lamp is concentrated almost entirely in the resonance lines comprising the yellow doublet.

For other metals with comparatively simple spectra, such as the alkaline earths and magnesium, interference filters are satisfactory (87), but the difficulty and expense of making selective interference filters of high transmission in the ultraviolet limits the usefulness of this technique considerably. Interference filters are unsuitable if much background radiation is emitted by the sharp-line source, as this radiation will be transmitted over the bandwidth of the filter. For instance, in the determination of calcium, using an interference filter to isolate the resonance line at 4227 A., a neon-filled hollow cathode tube gives more satisfactory results than an argon-filled tube, as the latter emits numerous argon lines in this neighborhood.

The commonest and most versatile wavelength selector is a monochromator which can be set to pass any wavelength between 2000 and 9000 A., such as that from the Beckman DU or equivalent spectrophotometer. Quartz prism spectrographs have also been successfully adapted for atomic absorption work by placing a pair of slits at the appropriate place in the focal plane (5,23).

4. The Detector, Amplifier, and Readout System

The intensity of the resonance line transmitted by the monochromator is measured, with and without the sample in the flame, by a photoelectric detector such as a vacuum photocell or photomultiplier. Although photocells such as those supplied as standard equipment with most manual spectrophotometers are satisfactory for metals having simple spectra of high intensity, a photomultiplier is essential if the best results are to be achieved in the determination of heavy metals. Most spectrophotometers now have provision for the attachment of a photomultiplier instead of a photocell.

Several workers (5,59,65,82) have satisfactorily carried out atomic absorption measurements on metals whose resonance lines lie below about 3500 A. by using a hollow-cathode tube operated on direct current and feeding the output of the detector to a galvanometer or to a d.c. amplifier and meter. In the ultraviolet the emission from the flame is usually negligible or can be compensated for by "backing-off." For general use, however, it is desirable to modulate the output of the light source, either with a mechanical "chopper" or, more conveniently, by supplying the source with alternating current or modulated direct current, and feeding the output of the detector to an a.c. amplifier whose output is rectified before being fed to a meter. In this way any signal caused by emission from the flame, which of course radiates continuously, is rejected.

Almost all the published work on atomic absorption has been done with a single-beam instrument of the general type described here. However, the accuracy of absorption measurement with such an instrument, particularly for very small absorptions, is limited by fluctuations and drift in the light source, and in principle a double-beam technique is preferable. The first atomic absorption spectrophotometer (79) was in fact a double-beam instrument (Figs. 5 and 6). The light from the hollow-cathode tube was split into a sample beam, modulated at a frequency f, which passed through the flame and a reference beam, modulated at a frequency $2f$, which passed through

Fig. 5. Double-beam atomic absorption spectrophotometer used by Russell, Shelton, and Walsh. Reproduced, by permission of *Spectrochimica Acta*, from reference 79.

Fig. 6. Optical system of the instrument used by Russell, Shelton, and Walsh. Reproduced, by permission of *Spectrochimica Acta*, from reference 79.

an equivalent air path; the two beams were recombined on the entrance slit of the monochromator and the photomultiplier output was fed to a homodyne amplifier. The amplified signals from the two beams were separated and their ratio recorded on a pen recorder. The difficulties encountered in setting up and maintaining in adjustment the optics and electronics of this instrument, however, proved considerable. A somewhat similar instrument, but using null-point detection, has been described by Baker and Garton (13).

When the signal from the hollow-cathode tube shows short-term fluctuations, a single-beam instrument with an integrating system can be used (42). The detector output with no sample sprayed into the flame is fed to a condenser for, say, 30 sec. and the resulting voltage measured, after which the corresponding signal with the sample sprayed is integrated for a similar length of time and the ratio of the two voltages measured. It should be noted that this method does not correct for drift in the hollow-cathode signal over the time taken for the two measurements.

Malmstadt and Chambers (63) have described a null-point instrument in which the concentration of a reference solution is adjusted by addition of known volumes of standard solution until the absorption when sprayed into the flame is the same as that of the sample.

Other double-beam systems have been used in some of the recently introduced commercial instruments (Section III.5.B), but the writer feels that it is too early to say whether the considerable increase in cost and complexity will be justified by greatly improved performance in the applications of interest to the biochemist.

5. Complete Instruments

A. TYPICAL SINGLE-BEAM GENERAL PURPOSE INSTRUMENTS

In Figure 7 is shown the instrument described by Box and Walsh (17), which employs a Beckman DU monochromator and a 5-cm. air–coal gas flame.

The atomic absorption spectrophotometer at present used by the writer is shown in Figure 8, and is typical of a number of instruments in use in Australia and elsewhere. It is basically similar to the Box and Walsh instrument but uses the Zeiss PMQ III monochromator, which is particularly suited to atomic absorption work as it is pro-

TABLE III

Commercially Available Atomic Absorption Equipment

Manufacturer and catalog No.	Type of instrument	Vaporizing system	Dispersing element	Readout	Notes
Hilger and Watts H909	Single-beam, unmodulated	12-cm. air–coal gas or air–propane flame, fed from nebulizer and spray-chamber	Silica prism	Density scale, with null-point meter	Attachment to Hilger Uvispek spectrophotometer
Optica U.K. ATAB I (prototype only)	Single-beam, modulated	Long water-cooled air–acetylene burner, fed from nebulizer and spray-chamber	Low-dispersion grating	Density scale with null-point meter	Designed primarily for determination of Ca and Mg
Optica Milano AT 6	Double-beam	Air–acetylene flame, fed from nebulizer and spray-chamber	Silica prism	Density scale with null-point meter	Atomic absorption attachment for Optica grating spectrophotometer CF4 also available

Perkin-Elmer 214	Double-beam, modulated	10-cm. flame, burning air with hydrogen, acetylene, or petroleum gas; fed from nebulizer	High-dispersion grating	Digital	Recorder can also be attached
Jarrell-Ash	Single-beam, unmodulated	3 Beckman oxy-hydrogen burners in a row, with 5 light passes through the flame	High-dispersion grating	Recorder	
Bausch & Lomb Jobin-Yvon	No information yet available				
Techtron	Single-beam, modulated	10-cm. flame, burning air with coal gas, petroleum gas, or acetylene; fed from nebulizer and spray chamber	Silica prism	Meter	Uses Zeiss PMQ III monochromator. Similar to equipment shown in Figure 8.

vided with a built-in optical rail and has its entrance and exit slits on opposite sides of the instrument housing.

The 10-cm. burner, which will burn either air–coal gas or air–acetylene mixtures, is a commercial version of the massive burner

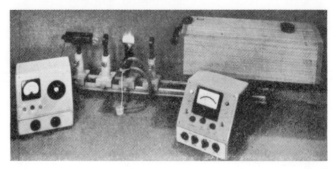

Fig. 7. Atomic absorption spectrophotometer described by Box and Walsh. Reproduced, by permission of *Spectrochimica Acta*, from reference 17.

Fig. 8. Atomic absorption spectrophotometer currently in use at the Division of Chemical Physics, C.S.I.R.O. The lenses, burner, and holders for these components were made by Stuart R. Skinner Pty. Ltd., Malvern, Victoria, Australia.

described by the writer (93). The sample is introduced into the flame by the EEL* nebulizer and spray chamber, as in the Box and Walsh instrument. The nebulizer, which consumes about 3 ml. of solution per minute, uses air at 10–15 p.s.i. (about 4 liters/min.)

* Evans Electroselenium Ltd., London, England.

which is mixed with coal gas (2 liters/min.) or acetylene (about 1.2 liters/min.).

The power supply for the hollow-cathode tube (left) and the combined photomultiplier high-tension supply, a.c. amplifier, and microammeter readout (right) are made to a C.S.I.R.O. design by Techtron Appliances, South Melbourne, Australia. The scale-expansion unit (Section V.2.B) at the extreme right allows higher sensitivity to be attained where necessary.

B. COMMERCIALLY AVAILABLE ATOMIC ABSORPTION EQUIPMENT

Atomic absorption instruments are made under license (84) to C.S.I.R.O., Australia, by several manufacturers. At present licenses are held by the following firms:

Hilger and Watts Ltd., London, England
Optica U.K. Ltd., Gateshead, England
Optica S.p.A., Milan, Italy
Perkin-Elmer Corporation, Norwalk, Conn.
Bausch & Lomb Optical Company, Rochester, N.Y.
Jarrell-Ash Company, Newtonville, Mass.
Messrs. Jobin-Yvon, Arcueil (Seine), France.
Techtron Pty. Ltd., Melbourne, Australia

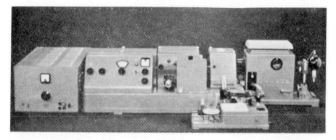

Fig. 9. Hilger atomic absorption attachment H909 with Uvispek spectrophotometer.

Table III and Figures 9–12 show details of instruments now available.

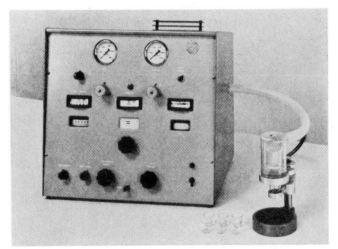

Fig. 10. Optica Milano atomic absorption spectrophotometer AT 6.

Fig. 11. Jarrell-Ash atomic absorption spectrophotometer.

Fig. 12. Perkin-Elmer atomic absorption spectrophotometer.

IV. ATOMIC ABSORPTION SPECTROPHOTOMETRY AND FLAME PHOTOMETRY

Although as mentioned in Section III.2 the use of a flame is not essential to atomic absorption spectrophotometry, it is natural that this technique should be compared with that of flame photometry, since injection of a solution into a flame is such a convenient means of atomization. In general it may be said that almost all analyses which can be carried out by flame photometry can be done at least as well by the atomic absorption method, while the latter technique makes possible many analyses which cannot be carried out at all by flame photometry in its present form.

1. Scope and Limitation of the Two Techniques

The atomic absorption method requires the use of resonance lines, and for most elements there is little choice of line if high sensitivity is required. In flame photometry, particularly if a hot flame is used, there is sometimes a choice of lines, and some metals such as the alkaline earths form compounds in the flame which emit measurable band spectra.

Since the nonmetals mostly have their resonance lines in the vacuum ultraviolet (i.e., below 2000 A.) special difficulties arise in both techniques, as the strong absorption of these wavelengths by the oxygen of the air requires not only a monochromator which can be evacuated or purged with nitrogen but also a means of atomizing the sample which does not introduce absorbing gases into the light path. The sputtering technique of Gatehouse and Walsh (40) has been used for the determination of carbon and phosphorus in steel (83), but this method is not yet applicable to materials of biological interest. In Table IV are shown the wavelengths of the resonance lines of some typical nonmetals.

The limit of detection in flame photometry is set by the ability to distinguish the line emitted by the metal from the background emission of the flame. In atomic absorption spectrophotometry, the limiting factor is the measurement of the small change in the intensity of the sharp-line source caused by absorption by the metal atoms in the flame, which in practice is set by the noise level of the sharp-line source.

TABLE IV

Resonance Lines of Typical Nonmetals

Element	Resonance line, A.
Selenium	1961
Arsenic	1890
Iodine	1830
Sulfur	1807
Phosphorus	1775
Carbon	1657
Bromine	1488

At present, flame photometry is slightly more sensitive than the atomic absorption method for strongly emitting metals such as lithium and sodium, at any rate in the absence of substances which would increase the background emission of the flame.   The sensitivity of the atomic absorption technique, however, should improve considerably with the development of double-beam methods to overcome instability of the sharp-line source and of multipass methods (Section V.2.A) to increase the effective absorption path length in the flame.

2. Effect of Different Flame Types

For metals which are completely atomized in the flame, the sensitivity of the atomic absorption method is usually slightly higher with a cool flame than with a hot one (8,41).   This is probably due to the lower degree of expansion of the flame gases and correspondingly higher concentration of metal atoms per unit volume and also to the smaller Doppler width of the absorbing line, which is inversely proportional to the peak absorption (8).   In flame photometry, of course, the intensity of emission increases with the temperature of the flame, but frequently this advantage of a hot flame is nullified by the higher background radiation and increased interferences by other components of the sample.

Some metals are incompletely atomized when their compounds are sprayed into the flame, and in such cases the degree of atomization varies with the type of flame, for on the temperature and relative proportions of the flame gases depends the metal–metal oxide equilibrium.   With calcium, strontium, barium, tin, bismuth, chromium, molybdenum, ruthenium, and rhodium, the best results are obtained

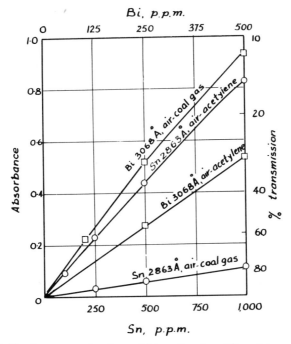

Fig. 13. Calibration curves for tin and bismuth using different types of flame.
Reproduced, by permission of *Spectrochimica Acta*, from reference 41.

in absorption with a fuel-rich air–acetylene flame, and there is, moreover, an optimum height in the flame at which to measure the absorption (24,27,28,41). The effects of flame type on absorption are
shown in Figures 13 and 14.

In flame photometry it is sometimes possible to use the emission
from a band system, e.g., the MgOH band near 3710 A. or the CaOH
bands near 5440 and 6220 A. Although the emission intensity of such
bands is usually critically dependent on flame conditions and is subject to interferences, their use sometimes provides higher sensitivity
in emission than does the use of the resonance line. There is no counterpart to this procedure in atomic absorption spectroscopy.

Metals which form highly refractory oxides may yield only negligible numbers of metal atoms in low-temperature flames, even under
highly reducing conditions. Gatehouse and Willis (41) found no
detectable absorption, even from solutions containing 1000 p.p.m.

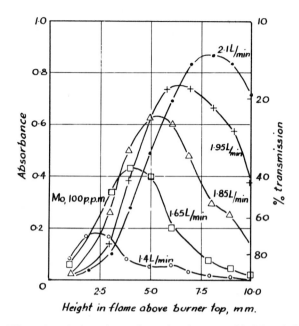

Fig. 14. Effect of variation of acetylene–air mixture and height of absorption path in the flame on the sensitivity for molybdenum. The air flow was kept constant at 5.5 liters/min. and the acetylene flow was varied as shown. Reproduced, by permission of *Spectrochimica Acta*, from reference 41.

in the metals, when salts of aluminum, titanium, vanadium, niobium, and tungsten were sprayed into an air–coal gas flame (ca. 1700°C.) or an air–acetylene flame (ca. 2200°C.). Robinson (75) failed to detect aluminum, tin, molybdenum, tantalum, or tungsten by absorption in the oxyhydrogen flame (ca. 2750°C.) or even in the oxycyanogen flame (ca. 4550°C.), while vanadium was detectable only in the latter flame.

The degree of breakdown of refractory oxides is not merely a function of flame temperature, since both Gatehouse and Willis (41) and David (28) have successfully determined tin and molybdenum by absorption in *rich* air–acetylene flames at relatively low temperatures. Another puzzling aspect of this question arises from the fact that Robinson (75,76) was able to detect aluminum, tin, molybdenum, tantalum, and tungsten in the oxycyanogen flame by emission but not by absorption. If there were sufficient excited atoms present to be detectable in emission, it is difficult to see how there could fail to be an even greater number of ground-state atoms capable of absorption, unless the excited metal ions were produced mainly by the chemi-luminescent processes by Buell (18a) and by Gilbert (42b).

3. Nebulizing Conditions

Since the purpose of the nebulizer in both emission and absorption work is to inject into the flame a fine cloud of droplets of fairly uniform size, from which the metal to be determined can be efficiently con-verted to its atomic vapor, this discussion of the spraying conditions is common to both techniques.

An analysis of the factors influencing drop size is given elsewhere (32,46), but it may be noted that under the conditions prevailing in most flame photometer nebulizers the mean diameter of the droplets is approximately proportional to the square root of the surface ten-sion of the liquid. Thus the average size of the drops and conse-quently of the solid particles formed on evaporation of the drops will be reduced if the surface tension of the solution is lowered, e.g., by the replacement of water by an organic solvent. The effects of the organic solvent will include: (1) increased rate of transfer of solution into the flame (unless the organic solvent is very viscous); (2) a larger fraction of the drops reaching the flame, at any rate in instruments with spray chambers, due to the smaller drop size; and (3) more complete vaporization of the material during the limited time it is in the flame, due again to the smaller particle size.

These effects will lead to enhancement of both emission and absorp-tion by atoms in the flame, but the slight increase of flame tempera-ture caused by spraying an organic solvent instead of water will affect only emission intensity to any marked extent (74). The en-hancement of emission intensities, even with identical experimental conditions and solvent, varies widely both between one metal and another, and between different emission lines of the same metal (32).

The effect of organic solvents on the atomic absorption intensity of metals has been studied by several workers. Robinson (74), using a total consumption burner of the Beckman type which burned oxygen and cyanogen, found for the 3415 A. line of nickel an enhancement relative to water of between 8- and 18-fold for a wide range of sol-vents. Acetone, indeed, gave a 36-fold enhancement. The same system in emission gave enhancements of 4- and 9-fold only. Lockyer et al. (60), using an air–coal gas burner with a spray chamber, found a two- to threefold enhancement for magnesium, nickel, silver, calcium, and zinc in 50% isopropanol–water solutions; iron, however, gave an 8- to 10-fold enhancement. Elwell and Gidley (34), using similar equipment to these authors, found for magnesium, iron, zinc, and lead in 40% isopropanol–water solutions enhancements of between 1.8 and 2.4-fold. Allan (9), using an air–acetylene burner with a spray chamber, made a very careful study of copper in a number of solvents (chiefly ketones and esters). He found enhancements of three-to fivefold, and established that this increase of sensitivity could be accounted for almost quantitatively by the greater rate at which the solutions reached the flame. He obtained similar results for zinc and also for iron and manganese, although these latter elements are incompletely atomized in the flame. Elwell and Gidley support Allan's general finding that the enhancement can be accounted for almost entirely by the greater rate at which solution reaches the flame.

All these authors agree that the change of flame temperature caused by spraying organic solvents is small and contributes little to the increased sensitivity in absorption.

4. Interferences

Interference with the determination of one metal, caused by the presence of another constituent of the sample, is a well-known and troublesome phenomenon in all forms of emission analysis, whether the excitation is affected by the flame, arc, or spark. Several types of interference may be distinguished, and their occurrence differs in emission and absorption.

A. SPECTRAL OR RADIATION INTERFERENCE

In flame photometric measurements, light is emitted not only by the element being determined but also by other elements in the sample and by the flame itself. If the wavelength of this radiation lies close enough to that of the line being used, it will be passed by the filter or monochromator and thus be recorded along with the signal being measured. This type of interference, which causes a positive analytical error, is particularly likely to occur with filter-type flame photometers.

For instance, in the determination of small amounts of magnesium in the presence of large amounts of sodium (a situation which frequently occurs in biological work) the 2852.8 A. line of sodium will make some contribution to the measured intensity of the magnesium line at 2852.1 A., since most monochromators are unable to separate these lines completely (1). Such interference has usually to be corrected for by adding a similar amount of sodium to the calibrating solutions, a procedure which is inconvenient if the approximate composition of the sample is not already known.

In the determination by emission of small amounts of sodium in the presence of large amounts of calcium, the monochromator transmits not only the sodium yellow lines at 5890 and 5896 A. but also the molecular bands of calcium hydroxide which are emitted in this region. Even when using a spectral slit width of 1 A., the total calcium hydroxide emission in this wavelength range may be several times that due to sodium. Under these conditions the background correction needed will be large and to some extent uncertain.

Similar difficulties arise in the determination of copper, using the strong lines at 3247 and 3271 A., from the OH band-emission in this region.

In the atomic absorption method, on the other hand, the only absorption which can be measured is that at the wavelength of the resonance line emitted by the source, which has a width of ca. 0.01 A. This ensures that the effective resolution of the system is far higher than in emission methods and results in correspondingly increased freedom from radiation interference. Of course, if an unmodulated light source is employed, emission from the flame may become important, particularly at wavelengths above about 3000 A., but the use of a modulated system avoids this difficulty.

B. EXCITATION INTERFERENCE

In emission methods many interferences are attributed to "excitation interference," which is due to the change in the number of excited atoms when the introduction of another atomic species produces a change in the effective temperature of the radiating vapor. This type of interference is more commonly encountered in arc and spark work, but it certainly exists also in flame emission, though it has not been identified separately from other types of interference.

As can be seen from Table I, only a small change of temperature is required to produce a large change in the number of excited atoms and thus in the intensity of emitted radiation. The total number of these excited atoms is so small that the number of unexcited atoms can be regarded as constant and equal to the total number of atoms, so that no counterpart to excitation interference is found in atomic absorption.

C. IONIZATION INTERFERENCE

Even a low-temperature flame such as air–coal gas possesses enough energy to ionize an appreciable fraction of the atoms of the alkali metals (37), and in hotter flames the fraction ionized may be very high (Table V). As a result of this ionization there is a reduction in

TABLE V[a]

Per Cent Ionization of Alkali and Alkaline Earth Metals in Flames

Element	Ionization potential, e.v.	Air–propane, 2200°K.	Hydro-gen–oxygen, 2450°K.[b]	Acetylene–oxygen, 2800°K.[b]
Lithium	5.37	<0.01	0.9	16.1
Sodium	5.12	0.3	5.0	26.4
Potassium	4.32	2.5	31.9	82.1
Rubidium	4.16	13.5	44.4	89.6
Cesium	3.87	28.3	69.6	96.4
Calcium	6.11	<0.01	1.0	7.3
Strontium	5.69	<0.1	2.7	17.2
Barium	5.21	1.0	8.6	42.8

[a] Reproduced by permission from "Flame Photometry," by J. A. Dean. Copyright © 1960, McGraw-Hill Book Company, Inc.

[b] From Foster and Hume (37).

the number of neutral atoms which can absorb or emit at the wavelength being measured. In the presence of a second alkali metal, particularly one which loses electrons even more readily than the one being studied, the free electrons produced by the second metal will suppress the ionization of the first, and the intensity of emission or absorption by the neutral atoms will thereby be increased. Such effects have been frequently encountered in flame photometry and have recently been studied in detail by Foster and Hume (37) and by Fukushima (39).

In absorption work a similar enhancement has been noticed by Baker and Garton (13) and by Willis (92), but Figure 15 shows that this type of interference is less pronounced in absorption than in emission. Baker and Garton suggest that this difference arises either from the slightly different gas-flow rates used for their burner in the absorption measurements or, alternatively, from the differing extent of enhancement on the population of atoms in the ground state and

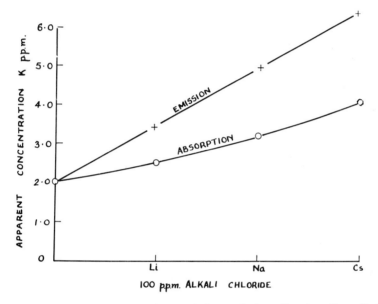

Fig. 15. Enhancement of potassium emission and absorption by other alkali metals. Reproduced, by permission, from reference 13.

excited states. As expected, the enhancement is less in hot than in cool flames, and can in any case be overcome by addition to the standards of the same concentration of interfering elements as in the test solution. Alternatively, a large excess of the interfering element may be added to each. The use of such a "radiation buffer" is open to far less objection in atomic absorption spectrophotometry than in emission flame photometry, since the errors due to increased background emission, etc. do not occur.

D. CHEMICAL INTERFERENCE

Another important type of interference encountered with flame methods of vaporizing the sample is due to chemical combination of the element to be determined with other elements or compounds in the flame. Well-known examples are the combination of calcium with phosphorus and the combination of calcium and of magnesium with aluminum. Clearly, this type of interference will be expected to affect emission and absorption methods in the same way.

A possible method of dealing with many of these interferences is to add the interfering element in excess to both samples and standards, since the intensity of emission or absorption frequently drops to a value which remains constant above a certain concentration of the interfering element. However, this method is frequently unsatisfactory because of the great loss of sensitivity entailed, particularly when a low-temperature flame is used.

Two methods are used to overcome chemical interference in both emission and absorption methods. In the first method there is added a large excess of a metal which can compete with the metal being determined for combination with the interfering element.

For instance, in the determination of calcium in the presence of phosphorus, addition of an excess of lanthanum or strontium is effective in removing the suppression of the calcium radiation in both emission (33,98) and absorption (91,93). Magnesium may also be used for this purpose, but is only really effective in the presence of a large amount of sulfate ion (24).

In the second method a large quantity of a chelating agent such as EDTA is added, normally as the sodium salt (88,91,96). This material has been thought to act by forming a complex which protects the metal from interaction with the anion, and persists long enough in the flame to prevent compound formation taking place there also.

In the last few years some progress has been made towards the understanding of the mechanism of chemical interference and of the methods which are known to overcome it. The subject is complicated by the dependence of the extent of interference on flame type and temperature, so that it becomes very difficult for one investigator to reproduce exactly the experimental conditions used by another. In all cases the interference is least in hot flames, and generally decreases in the upper parts of the flame. It is also dependent on drop size, being least for the finest sprays.

It has been established (4,38) that the nonvolatile compound is formed in the liquid droplet and not by combination of the atoms in the flame itself. If, for instance, a solution containing both calcium and phosphate is sprayed into a flame, there is little emission from calcium atoms; but if the calcium and phosphate solutions are introduced into the flame through separate nebulizers, there is no interference with the calcium emission. Similar results have been obtained for the interference of sulfate, borate, and aluminum with calcium emission.

The first method of removing interference is generally believed to depend on the formation of a more stable or higher melting compound with the interfering element by the excess of competing metal added, whereby the original metal is almost completely liberated. The observation that magnesium is most effective in the presence of sulfate is explained by assuming the formation of two phases in the dried particle, the calcium being present as a readily volatile compound in one phase and the phosphorus, sulfate, and magnesium in the other (24).

The second method is believed by some workers (13,33a) to depend on a physical rather than a chemical mechanism, for the following reasons: (1) the effectiveness of EDTA is not pH dependent; (2) the disodium salt of EDTA is effective, but the diammonium salt is far less so; and (3) other materials, with no specific complexing action, are also effective in removing the suppression, e.g., sucrose, and sodium chloride either alone or in admixture with glycerol.

The explanation suggested to account for these observations is that the particles formed in the flame consist almost entirely of a volatile compound with calcium phosphate homogeneously dispersed within

TABLE VI

Incidence of Different Types of Interference in Emission and Absorption

Type of interference	Emission	Absorption
Spectral (Radiation)	+	−
Excitation	+	−
Ionization	+ +	+
Chemical	+	+

the particles. Since the matrix has a boiling point below the temperature of the flame, its volatilization may still take place rapidly compared with the transit time of the particle through the flame. After volatilization of the matrix, the calcium phosphate may well be present in a form with a large specific surface, which will have a high vapor pressure and will be efficiently vaporized (13).

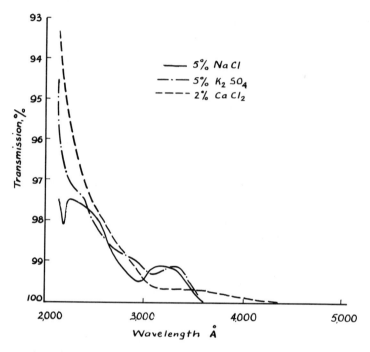

Fig. 16. Apparent absorption due to scattering of light by particles in the flame (reference 95).

The enhancement of calcium emission (20) and of calcium and magnesium absorption (90,91) by protein, and the protection of calcium from phosphate interference by protein-containing solutions may perhaps be explained in the same way.

Table VI summarizes the incidence of different types of interference in atomic emission and absorption measurements.

5. Background Effects

In Section IV.4.A, brief mention was made of the occurrence in flame photometry of spectral interference by the background emission of the flame.   Although this form of interference does not occur in atomic absorption work, there is a small, but in some cases analytically significant, effect due apparently to scattering of light from the sharp-line source by the solid particles of material aspirated into the flame.   This effect, which of course results in higher apparent absorption, is only detectable when trace quantities of a metal are determined in the presence of relatively large concentrations of other salts, and has been independently observed by three workers (11,28,94,95). Correction for it can be made if necessary by measuring the scattering effect using either a nonabsorbing line close to the resonance line (95) or a continuous light source (11), or in special cases by altering the flame type so that the metal being determined is oxidized and so does not absorb (28).

The results of experiments on this effect using a 10-cm. air–coal gas flame are shown in Figure 16.   The light source was a helium-filled brass hollow-cathode lamp, which provided a number of nonabsorbing lines at suitable wavelengths, and the accuracy of measurement was increased by using twofold scale expansion.

It seems that ammonium salts, except for the sulfate and phosphate, and N acids, except for sulfuric and phosphoric, do not show a detectable effect (12).   Calcium and aluminum salts show it to a higher degree than do salts of the alkali metals, and it seems that the more refractory the compound formed in the flame, the greater is the scattering.

The influence of the scattering effect on practical analysis will only become appreciable when trace quantities of heavy metals are being determined in the presence of high concentrations of other salts, e.g., in the determination of zinc and cadmium in urine (94) or in the determination of copper in butter (95).

V. THE TECHNIQUE OF ATOMIC ABSORPTION SPECTROPHOTOMETRY

1. Selection of Optimum Experimental Conditions

The combination of sharp-line source, monochromator, photomultiplier, and amplifier constitutes an optical–electronic system of which several variables can be altered.

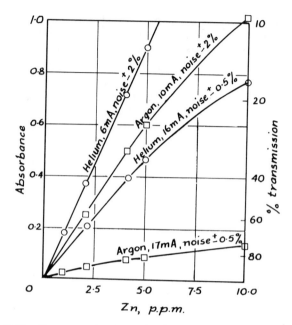

Fig. 17. Calibration curves for zinc, using helium-filled and argon-filled hollow-cathode tubes run at different currents. Reproduced, by permission of *Spectrochimica Acta*, from reference 41.

(1) The current at which the sharp-line source is operated determines not only the intensity of the spectral lines produced but also their width. In order to obtain the highest sensitivity in absorption it is essential that the line whose absorption is to be measured should not exhibit self-reversal or self-absorption. (These effects, which have the effect of broadening the line, are caused by partial reabsorption of the emitted light by the metal vapor in the lamp itself.) For the alkali metals and others such as silver, zinc, and cadmium, which sputter profusely, this can only be achieved by running the lamp on very low currents (sometimes as low as 2 ma. for zinc and cadmium hollow-cathode lamps).

When the sharp-line source is run under such conditions, however, the discharge may become relatively unsteady and the signal-to-noise ratio be reduced to such a level that the advantage of high sensitivity is offset by the uncertainty in reading a fluctuating meter.

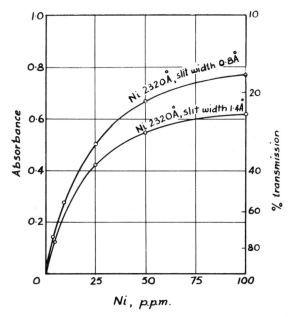

Fig. 18. Calibration curves for nickel 2320 A., showing effect of incomplete separation of resonance line. Reproduced, by permission of *Spectrochimica Acta*, from reference 41.

In such cases it is frequently better to sacrifice some sensitivity in order to achieve higher stability and hence more accurate reading of the scale. The curves in Figure 17 show that with a helium-filled zinc hollow-cathode tube an almost twofold loss in sensitivity caused by increasing the current from 6 to 16 ma. was accompanied by a fourfold improvement in the signal-to-noise level, so that use of the higher current enabled more accurate measurement of absorption in spite of the loss of sensitivity. Similarly, in the determination of copper, the best results are often achieved by running the hollow-cathode tube on a current sufficiently high to result in some self-absorption, but one which gives such a stable signal that the absorption may usefully be magnified fourfold by use of scale expansion (Section V.2.B).

(2) If it is desired to achieve maximum sensitivity for a metal which has a complex spectrum, the use of low hollow-cathode current and narrow slit width may be required. In such a case the high ten-

sion applied to the photomultiplier and the gain of the amplifier must be increased, which may introduce noise from the electronic system. Here again the best conditions of operation must be found by compromise.

(3) The choice of absorbing line may depend on the strength and stability of the emission of different lines by the hollow-cathode lamp and in some cases on the presence of adjacent lines or continuum. For instance, with nickel it is often better to use the 3415-A. line instead of the more sensitive 2320-A. one when absorbances above 0.4 are to be measured, owing to the strong curvature in the absorbance–concentration curve when the 2320-A. line is used (Fig. 18). This curvature, which occurs with several metals having complex spectra, is due to the presence of a nonabsorbing line too close to the 2320-A. line to be separated by the monochromator. Similar effects have been found for the 2176-A. line of antimony and the 2407-A. line of cobalt (41).

(4) Choice of optimum flame conditions has already been discussed (Section IV.2).

In Table II are shown the optimum experimental conditions found by Gatehouse and Willis (41) for the determination of 36 metals.

2. Methods of Increasing Sensitivity

A. OPTICAL MEANS

Russell, Shelton, and Walsh (79), who used a Meker-type air–coal gas flame of circular cross section, achieved an increase in absorption intensity by passing the light beam backwards and forwards through the flame, using an optical system based on that of White (89). The calibration curves shown in Figure 19 show the effect of increasing path length on the sensitivity for iron. Other workers (13,100) have also used multiple-pass systems.

With a long flame it is difficult to achieve effective multiple passes, particularly when determining metals for which the atomic concentration varies considerably from one part of the flame to another. It will be noticed that in Figure 19 a gain of only about sixfold in absorption was obtained by using 12 passes through the flame.

Further limitations on the multiple-pass technique are imposed by the light losses on reflection and by the aberrations involved in off-axis optical systems. The author feels that except in specialized

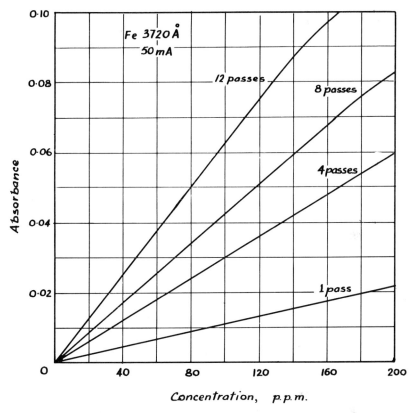

Fig. 19. Calibration curves using multiple traversals of the flame. Reproduced, by permission of *Spectrochimica Acta*, from reference 79.

applications the additional complexity of a multipass system is probably not justified by the increase of sensitivity obtained.

B. ELECTRONIC MEANS

In single-beam instruments the limit of detection is normally set either by the stability of the hollow cathode with regard to drift and noise or by the noise level of the photomultiplier–amplifier system. The stability of the hollow-cathode tube is the more important in cases where the electronic noise can be reduced to a negligible level by opening the slits to give an adequate signal. For a number of metals, scale expansion can profitably be employed, the zero of the meter be-

ing displaced off the scale by applying a potential from a dry battery
through a suitable resistor.   In this way the meter can be used as the
upper end of a much longer scale, and the reading for small absorptions
increased by as much as fivefold.   The useful limit of scale expansion
is reached when the noise level and drift of the hollow-cathode tube,
which of course are magnified to the same extent as the signal, become appreciable.

Some workers have minimized the effect of hollow-cathode noise
by integrating the signal over a period of, say, 30 sec. (Section III.4),
but as yet there is not sufficient evidence to decide whether this
method results in any increase in sensitivity or accuracy.   It seems
that its usefulness will be limited by any drift in the signal from the
hollow-cathode tube over the time required for the two readings necessary to establish the absorption of a sample.

Both noise and drift in the emission of the sharp-line source should
be avoidable by use of a double-beam system, such as the homodyne
amplification technique used by Russell et al. (79) and by Baker and
Garton (13) or the systems used in some of the commercial instruments, of which few details are yet available.   Here again it seems
doubtful whether the full possibilities of the technique have been
utilized.

C. CHEMICAL MEANS

The physical aspects of the use of organic solvents were discussed
in Section IV.3 and it was shown that with the type of nebulizer–
burner system generally used for atomic absorption work an enhancement of about three to fivefold may normally be expected in going
from a solution in water to solution in a suitable organic solvent.
The advantages of this increase in absorption may sometimes be offset by increased unsteadiness of the flame and by correspondingly
decreased accuracy of reading the absorption intensity.

The use of organic solvents has been studied by several workers
(9,60,74).   The most comprehensive study is that of Allan (9), who,
using an air–acetylene flame, studied the enhancement of absorption
intensity of solutions of several metals in various organic solvents.
He concluded that in practical analytical work the small increases of
intensity which can be obtained by using mixtures of water with
miscible solvents such as alcohol or acetone would be more than
counterbalanced by the extra dilution incurred by adding the organic

solvent, though he suggested that dilution with an isobutyl alcohol–acetone mixture would be helpful if the volume of the original sample were too small to spray.

Allan also investigated the use of solvent extraction in atomic absorption work. This valuable technique, which has been extensively applied to flame photometry by Dean and his co-workers (32), is of equal use in atomic absorption spectroscopy, particularly for the determination of trace quantities of heavy metals in biological and agricultural materials (8,94). Allan found the quantitative extraction of such metals from aqueous solution into a nonmiscible ester or ketone by means of a suitable chelating agent could yield concentration factors of 100-fold or more, and of course the sensitivity of the method was increased even further by the enhancement of absorption caused by spraying organic solvent instead of water.

The power of the solvent extraction method is well illustrated in the methods developed by the author for the determination of traces of heavy metals in urine. Although the limit of detection of lead in aqueous solution is about 0.5 p.p.m., the extraction of this metal into methyl n-amyl ketone enables its determination at the 0.01 p.p.m. level in urine with a standard deviation of 0.002 p.p.m. (94).

The chelating agent used by both Allan and the author was ammonium pyrrolidine dithiocarbamate, which is easily prepared from pyrrolidine, carbon bisulfide, and ammonia (62). It chelates with some 30 heavy metals and can be used at pH values as low as 2, though for extraction from very acid solutions other chelating agents may be superior, e.g., the substituted dithiocarbamidates described by Bode and Neumann (15). Since mutual interference between heavy metals is not normally found in atomic absorption spectroscopy, there is probably no advantage in using more specific chelating agents such as proved desirable in colorimetric work. One advantage of the extraction technique is that sodium and other light metals are left behind in the aqueous phase. In the analysis of many biological materials, which may contain relatively high concentrations of sodium, errors due to the scattering effect (Section IV.5) may thereby be avoided.

3. Preparation and Handling of Samples

Most determinations of metals in biological fluids such as blood serum and urine can be carried out on a sample which has been directly diluted with water, containing, if necessary, a suitable material to suppress interference (Section IV.4), though sometimes it is desirable to remove proteins by precipitation with trichloracetic acid (91). For other animal tissues and for plant materials, ashing is required. Wet ashing, using sulfuric–nitric–perchloric acid mixtures, has been used by David (23) and by Allan (8) for plant materials, but for many metals dry ashing followed by solution of the ash in a few drops of hydrochloric acid is satisfactory. Volatile elements such as antimony, arsenic, mercury, and thallium, however, require wet ashing under reflux (81).

TABLE VII

Per Cent Recovery of Metals from Biological Materials by Dry Ashing

Metal	Gorsuch (43)[a]	Pijck et al. (68)[b]
Antimony	96	67
Cadmium	91	—
Chromium	98	99
Cobalt	99	98
Copper	86	100
Gold	—	19
Iron	99	86
Lead	95	103
	99 (at 450°)	
Manganese	—	99
Molybdenum	99	100
Silver	96	65
Strontium	97	—
Vanadium	—	102
Zinc	96	100

[a] Cocoa ashed at 550°C. in silica crucibles.
[b] Blood ashed for 24 hr. at 400°C. in porcelain crucibles.

The optimum conditions for ashing depend not only on the nature of the metal but also on the material in which it is to be determined. In Table VII are summarized the findings of two recent investigators, both using radioactive tracer methods, on the losses of heavy metals during dry ashing of foodstuffs and animal tissues.

The alkali and alkaline earth metals seem to be quantitatively recoverable by dry ashing without critical control of the conditions, though it has recently been pointed out (44) that prolonged heating above 550°C. causes loss of sodium and potassium chlorides.

4. Calibration and Measurement Techniques

Standard solutions containing 100–1000 p.p.m. of the metal to be determined may be prepared from weighed quantities of the metal or of an appropriate stoichiometric salt, and acidified with hydrochloric acid if necessary to prevent hydrolysis. Working standards are made up by dilution as required, and should not be stored longer than a few days, as adsorption of metal ions from very dilute solutions onto the walls of the containing vessel is not uncommon. These working standards will, of course, have added to them any interference-controlling material which has been added to the sample solutions.

Since the concentrations of metals normally measured in atomic absorption work are very low (usually in the p.p.m. range), the precautions to be observed in handling samples and standards are similar to those required with other methods of trace-element analysis, e.g., flame photometry or colorimetry. All glassware should be of Pyrex or other borosilicate glass, and should be acid-washed, particularly when traces of heavy metals are to be determined. Only distilled water from a borosilicate glass still should be used. Solutions for measurement are conveniently held in polythene cups, which should be covered except when the solutions are actually being sprayed.

For most work it is usual to make up about four working standards covering the concentration range expected in the sample solutions and to measure the solutions in the order standards, samples, standards, samples, standards. The three measured absorbances for each standard solution are averaged and plotted against concentration to give a calibration curve, and the concentration of each sample is read off by interpolating on this graph the mean of its two measured absorbances.

The absorbance–concentration curve in many cases will either be a straight line or have at the most a slight curvature towards the concentration axis. Any errors in making up the working standards will be readily detected from points lying off this line. The degree of curvature will also tell the experienced worker whether the operating conditions of the hollow-cathode tube and monochromator are correct (Section V.1).

Some authors (23) plot percentage absorption against concentration, which is satisfactory for most routine work. However, since this method necessarily yields a curve which approximates to a straight line only at very low absorptions, it is less easy to detect any errors in the concentrations of the working standards and to assess the performance of the sharp-line source and monochromator. With scale-expansion methods, where the absorption to be measured is usually not more than 10–15%, it is usual to plot the scale reading directly against the concentration, which results in a calibration curve very close to a straight line.

Another method of drawing calibration curves is by using the Ringbom relationship, i.e., by plotting percentage absorption against the logarithm of the concentration (73). If Beer's law is obeyed, a sigmoidal curve is obtained which approximates closely to a straight line over most of the absorption range. This procedure, however, is no quicker and is less informative than the absorbance–concentration plot.

In some types of experiment it is necessary to measure as accurately as possible the differences between the concentrations of a number of solutions all of approximately the same strength. This can best be done by first verifying that the absorbance–concentration curve is sensibly a straight line over the concentration range covered by the solutions and then preparing a standard of about the same concentration. The sample solutions are measured alternately with the standard and their concentrations calculated directly from the ratio of the absorbances.

In some analyses where interferences cannot be fully controlled, as in the determination of strontium (29), or where the viscosity of sample and standard solutions would differ markedly, the standard addition method may be used. If the absorbance–concentration curve is known to be a straight line, and if the absorbance of the sample solution of concentration x is D_1 and that of a similar solution to which a known concentration a of the metal has been added is D_2, then x can be calculated from the relation

$$x/(x + a) = D_1/D_2 \tag{3}$$

It is advisable to check the result by measuring also the absorbance D_3 of a similar solution with a different added concentration of metal b. If the assumption of linearity holds, the two values of x should agree, and if not, an approximate figure for x may be derived from the three measurements (14,22).

The author feels that the standard addition method is useful as a check on other methods but should be used with great caution if the causes of interference cannot be found and corrected for. The method is based on the assumption that the interfering material alters the absorbance of the added metal to the same extent as it does that of the metal in the original sample. This may not always be so, particularly when only a small amount of interfering material is present (36a).

5. Development and Assessment of Specific Analytical Procedures

When developing a specific procedure for the determination of a given metal in a particular type of biological material, likely causes of interference should be investigated and if possible corrected for by techniques of the type discussed in Section IV.4. Finally, the proposed procedure should be assessed with regard to its accuracy and reliability. The following criteria are suggested for this purpose:

1. The results obtained by atomic absorption spectroscopy should agree, over the widest possible range of sample composition, with those of a reliable and well-tested alternative method.

2. Different variations of the atomic absorption technique should give the same results.

3. Measurements on different quantities of the sample should yield the same final result in terms of concentration.

4. Known quantities of metal added to the sample should be quantitatively recoverable.

5. The standard deviation of the method should be satisfactory for the purposes for which the analysis is required.

Criterion *1* is unfortunately difficult to fulfill in many instances, as for many determinations the atomic absorption technique is likely to yield results which are more accurate than those obtainable by any other convenient method. Frequently, too, study of conventional methods shows that they leave much to be desired in the matter of absolute accuracy even if their reproducibility is satisfactory. In the development of an atomic absorption method for determining calcium and magnesium in blood serum, for instance, it was found that the existing methods of analysis gave discrepant results (Table VIII). Furthermore, the most widely accepted standard method for the determination of calcium (precipitation with oxalate followed by potassium permanganate titration) is known to depend for its accuracy on the cancellation of opposing errors, and the results obtained are therefore influenced by small variations in technique.

Criterion *2* is particularly useful when dealing with biological fluids. In the author's work on the determination of magnesium in blood serum (90), consistent results were obtained using four variations of technique: (*a*) measurement of directly diluted serum with addition of EDTA to control protein interference; (*b*) measurement of directly diluted serum using strontium chloride for the same purpose; (*c*) prior removal of organic material by dry ashing; and (*d*) prior precipitation of proteins by addition of trichloroacetic acid.

TABLE VIII

Mean Calcium and Magnesium Content of Normal Sera[a]

Method	No. of sera measured	Ca, mg./ 100 ml.	Mg, mg./ 100 ml.
Spectrographic	86	8.6	1.90
Removal of Ca and protein followed by colorimetry with Eriochrome Black T	24	—	2.10
Direct titration with EDTA	710	9.7	—
Precipitation with oxalate followed by $KMnO_4$ titration	712	10.5	—
Flame photometry	22	10.8	—
Removal of protein, followed by colorimetry with murexide and Erio-chrome Black T	34	9.5	2.03

[a] Data reproduced, by permission of *Nature*, from reference 47.

Criterion *3* is a rapid means of testing simple methods, particularly those which depend on direct dilution of the sample with water, as interferences normally decrease with dilution. In the author's work on the determination of potassium in blood serum, it was the apparent variation of the potassium content of the serum found by measuring solutions of different dilutions that led to the discovery of the interference caused by the presence of sodium.

Criterion *4* is very commonly applied in the development of all types of analytical methods. Fulfillment of this test is a necessary but not sufficient condition for the reliability of the proposed procedure. For instance, in an atomic absorption method where there is loss of light by scattering (Section IV.5), quantitative recovery of added metal could well be obtained even though the method gave high results for the metal present originally.

Criterion *5* should be applied by carrying out a number of parallel determinations (usually not fewer than six), starting with the original sample in each case. In this way the whole analytical procedure is tested, and not merely the accuracy of measurement of the absorption of the solution. With a single-beam instrument of the type used by the author, the relative standard deviation in reading the absorbance is usually about 0.2–1%, even when a very stable hollow-cathode source is being used, and this variation seems due to fluctuations in the rate of atomization of the sample. The overall standard deviation of methods using direct dilution of biological fluids before spraying into the flame is of the order of 1%, so it appears that the volumetric operations add little to the experimental error. Generally speaking, the accuracy and reproducibility of the atomic absorption method compare very favorably with those of flame photometry and colorimetry.

VI. APPLICATION TO INDIVIDUAL ELEMENTS

Some 40 elements, all metals, have their resonance lines in the spectral range 2000–10,000 A., and most of these can be atomized in the flame. For the metalloid and nonmetallic elements the resonance lines lie below 2000 A. and the use of the atomic absorption method is more difficult (Section IV.1). Table IX lists the limits of detection for a number of metals found by emission flame photometry and by several workers using different types of atomic absorption equipment. In many cases the limit of detection can be further reduced by the methods described in Section V.2.

In the detailed description of the applications of atomic absorption spectroscopy which follows, an attempt has been made to refer at least briefly to all work published up to the time of writing, with special emphasis on the analysis of materials of biological interest.

J. B. WILLIS

TABLE IX. Limits of Detection for Various Metals by Flame Photometry and Atomic Absorption Spectroscopy

Metal	Wavelength, Å	Flame photometry (32)[a]	Russell et al. (79)[b]	Menzies (65)[c]	Atomic absorption spectroscopy			
					Robinson (75)[d]		Allan (11a)[e]	Gatehouse and Willis (41)[f]
					Oxy-hydrogen	Oxy-cyanogen		
Li	6708	0.067	—	—	—	—	—	0.03
Na	5890	0.001	0.1	0.1	1	0.5	—	0.03
K	7665	0.02	0.5	0.1	—	—	—	0.03
Rb	7800	0.6	2	2	—	—	—	0.1
Cs	8521	0.5	10	10	—	—	—	0.15
Cu	3248	0.6	1	1	0.5	0.2	0.1	0.1
Ag	3281	1.0	2	0.1	0.5	0.2	0.1	0.05
	3383	0.6	—	—	—	—	0.2	0.15
Au	2428	—	2	0.5	—	—	0.6	0.3
	2676	(5.0)	—	—	—	—	2.0	1.3
Be	2349	—	—	—	—	—	300	>100
Mg	2852	1.0	0.1	0.1	0.1	—	0.01	0.01
Ca	4227	0.07	—	2	—	—	0.1	0.08
Sr	4607	0.06	—	2	—	—	—	0.15
Ba	5536	1	—	—	—	—	—	8
Zn	2139	500	0.1	0.1	0.3	0.5	0.03	0.03
Cd	2288	10	0.1	2	1	0.3	0.03	0.03
	3261	0.5	—	—	—	—	—	—
Hg	2537	(10)	—	50	100	—	5	20
Al	3962	0.4	—	—	>1000	>1000	—	10
Ga	2874	—	—	—	—	—	1.5	>1000
	4172	0.5	—	—	—	—	8.0	3
In	3040	—	—	—	—	—	0.2	5
	4511	0.07	—	—	—	—	—	—
Tl	2768	—	10	10	0.6	—	0.1	0.8
	3776	0.6	—	—	0.2	—	0.03	3

Element	Wavelength	C1	C2	C3	C4	C5	C6	C7
Ti	4982	—	—	—	—	—	—	>1000
	5180 (band)	10	—	—	—	—	—	—
Sn	2863	—	—	500	>1000	>1000	5	5
Pb	2833	—	—	50	1.5	—	0.3	0.5
	4058	14	—	—	—	—	—	—
V	3184	12	—	—	>1000	300	—	>1000
	5230 (band)	—	—	—	—	—	—	—
Nb	4059 }	—	—	—	—	—	—	>1000
	4080 }							
	4124 }							
	4137 }							
Sb	2068	—	—	—	—	—	0.5	—
	2311	—	—	—	—	—	1.2	1.5
Bi	3068	—	—	—	—	—	0.5	2
Cr	3579	11	40	50	0.5	—	0.05	0.15
	4254	5	—	50	1.0	—	—	0.5
Mo	3133	—	—	—	>1000	—	1.0	0.5
W	4294 }	—	—	—	>1000	>1000	—	>1000
	4302 }							
Se	2040	—	—	—	—	—	5[h]	—
Te	2143	—	—	—	—	—	0.5	0.05
Mn	2795	0.1	—	—	—	—	0.05	—
	4033	—	—	—	—	—	0.1	0.1
Fe	2483	2.5	—	—	—	—	1.0	1
	3720	—	—	—	4.0	—	0.2	0.2
Co	2407	3.4	—	—	—	—	—	4
	3454	—	40	—	10	20	0.13	0.2
Ni	2320	—	—	—	—	—	3.0	0.5
	3415	3.5	20	5	1.0	0.5	2.5	—
	3524	1.6	—	—	10.0	0.5	—	—

(continued)

TABLE IX (continued)

Metal	Wavelength, A.	Flame photometry (32)[a]	Russell et al. (79)[b]	Atomic absorption spectroscopy				
				Menzies (65)[c]	Robinson (75)[d]		Allan (11a)[e]	Gatehouse and Willis (41)[f]
					Oxy-hydrogen	Oxy-cyanogen		
Ru	3499	—	—	—	—	—	1.0	—
	3728	(0.3)	—	—	—	—	0.25	—
Rh	3435	(2.0)	—	2	—	—	1.0	0.3
	3692	(0.7)	—	—	—	—	5	—
Pd	2448	—	—	—	—	—	0.3	—
	2476	(0.1)	—	2	—	—	0.3	0.8
	3635	—	—	—	—	—	—	—
Os	2909	—	—	—	—	—	—	>150[g]
Ir	2544(?)	—	—	—	—	—	—	—
Pt	2659	(13)	—	10	10	—	0.7	5
	2582	—	—	—	10	0.02	—	—

[a] Dean's figures are for sensitivity (p.p.m./% T) obtained with an oxyhydrogen or oxyacetylene flame in a Beckman DU flame photometer.

[b] Russell, Shelton, and Walsh's results were obtained with a Meker-type air–coal gas flame in a double-beam spectrophotometer using a Beckman DU monochromator.

[c] Menzies' results, which include those of Lockyer and Hames (59) for the noble metals, were obtained with the Hilger atomic absorption attachment and a Uvispek spectrophotometer. A 12-cm. air–coal gas flame was used.

[d] Robinson used a Beckman-type burner and a modified Perkin-Elmer model 13 spectrophotometer. The limit of detection was defined as the concentration giving an absorption equivalent to ²/₃ of the noise level of the hollow-cathode signal. Robinson also quotes figures for the corresponding limits of detection with organic solvents.

[e] Allan's figures were obtained with a 12-cm. air-acetylene flame, in some by a photographic technique using a continuous light source.

[f] Gatehouse and Willis used a 10-cm. air–coal gas or air-acetylene flame in a single-beam instrument employing a Beckman DU monochromator. The limit of detection was defined as the concentration of metal which gave 1% absorption, even though in many cases the noise level was as little as ±0.25% (Table II).

[g] Willis, unpublished work.

[h] Using the 1960 A. line of selenium, the limit of detection is about 1 p.p.m. (Robins, unpublished work).

1. Lithium

Although no measurements have yet been published on the determination of lithium in biological materials by atomic absorption spectroscopy, Zaidel and Korennoi have published an interesting paper on the isotopic analysis of mixtures of ^{6}Li and ^{7}Li (99). Using a hollow cathode tube containing pure ^{7}Li, mixtures containing more than 60% of ^{6}Li can be analyzed with a relative standard deviation of 0.6%. The authors point out that in atomic absorption (unlike emission flame photometry) the presence of strontium does not interfere with the determination of lithium.

2. Sodium

Sodium, whose high sensitivity in emission has made possible its determination by very simple flame photometers, also shows high sensitivity in absorption. Owing to the intensity of its emission, modulation of the sharp-line source and use of an a.c. amplifier are essential. Since the spectrum contains few lines other than the D doublet (5890 A., 5896 A.), it is possible to determine sodium with a very simple instrument using an interference filter and a photocell (18). Owing to the strong self-reversal exhibited by the D lines, the source, whether a laboratory discharge lamp or a hollow-cathode tube, must be run on as low a current as possible. A low-temperature (e.g., air–coal gas) flame is best used.

While the flame photometer is suitable for the determination of sodium in most biological materials, the presence of large amounts of calcium can cause interference (Section IV.4.A). With the atomic absorption technique this interference does not occur, and Brownell, measuring the sodium content of the ash from plants grown under almost sodium-free conditions, was able to obtain reliable results with a simple filter-type absorption instrument but not with a filter type flame photometer.

In both flame photometry and atomic absorption spectroscopy it must be remembered that at the 1-p.p.m. level, sodium contamination occurs very readily, and that it is usually better to reduce the sensitivity of the method rather than to dilute the analytical solutions excessively. In flame photometry this is easily enough done by reducing the gain of the amplifier, but in atomic absorption other means must be resorted to.

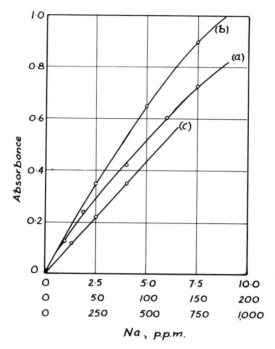

Fig. 20. Typical calibration curves for sodium: (*a*) 10-cm. burner, 5890 A. (*b*) 10-cm. burner at right angles to light path, 5890 A. (*c*) 10-cm. burner, 3302 A. Reproduced, by permission of *Spectrochimica Acta*, from reference 92.

Willis (92) has suggested two methods of reducing the sensitivity. In one the 10-cm. burner is turned through an angle of between 0° and 90°; in the 90° position a 20-fold loss of sensitivity is obtained. The other method makes use of the second resonance doublet of sodium (3302.3 A., 3302.9 A.) for which the oscillator strength, and hence the absorption intensity, is 70 times less than for the D lines. In this way the sodium content of blood serum can be determined on a sample diluted 10-fold to 50-fold instead of 500-fold as required when measuring the absorption in the ordinary way, and more re-producible readings are obtained, owing to the reduction of accidental contamination.   Figure 20 shows typical calibration curves for sodium.

Interference from other materials is not normally experienced in the determination of sodium.   Willis found no interference from the other components of blood serum, and David (25), in determining sodium at the 2–10 p.p.m. level in M ammonium chloride soil extracts, found no interference in the air–acetylene flame from 160 p.p.m. of phosphorus, aluminum, and sulfur and 64 p.p.m. of silicon. Pungor and Thege (70) found no significant interference on the absorption of 23 p.p.m. sodium by $0.5M$ sulfuric acid or ammonium sulfate but a 24% decrease in absorption in the presence of the same concentrations of phosphoric acid or diammonium hydrogen phosphate. Robinson (73), using an oxyhydrogen flame, found no effect with 5000 p.p.m. of either potassium or lithium on the absorption of 10 or 50 p.p.m. of sodium; Malmstadt and Chambers (63), on the other hand, state that with an air–propane flame the sodium absorption fell by 4% when the K/Na ratio rose above 5. Both Robinson and also Malmstadt and Chambers found that "appreciable concentrations" of mineral acids depressed the sodium absorption.

The effect of organic solvents on the absorption intensity of sodium was studied by Pungor and Thege who found that methanol, ethanol, and propanol enhanced the absorption by only about 30%, while Robinson, using an oxyhydrogen flame, found a 10-fold enhancement.

The null-point method of Malmstadt and Chambers (Section III.4), when used for estimating sodium in test solutions in the 1–100 p.p.m. range, gave a precision of better than 0.5% relative standard deviation, while the precision of a direct determination on such solutions was found by Robinson to be about 1–1.5%. In the determination of sodium in blood serum, Willis (92) found a relative standard deviation of 0.7%, and the results agreed to within 2–3% with those obtained using a simple filter-type flame photometer.

3. Potassium

Potassium, unlike sodium, is not completely atomized in the flame, but is present to some extent as molecules of potassium hydroxide. It is also ionized to an appreciable extent, particularly in hot flames (Section IV.4.C). This ionization is repressed by the presence of other alkali metals (37,92) and the resulting increase in the number of neutral atoms leads to high sensitivity in both emission and absorption.

Most metals do not seriously interfere with the determination of potassium by atomic absorption spectroscopy. Malmstadt and Chambers (63) claim that sodium, even at a concentration twenty times that of potassium, has no significant effect, though Willis (92) found a small enhancement, as did Foster and Hume (37) in emission measurements. David (25) found no interference on potassium at the 4–20 p.p.m. level from 160 p.p.m. each of phosphorus, aluminum, and sulfur and 64 p.p.m. of silicon in M ammonium chloride.

David studied the determination of potassium in M ammonium chloride extracts of soils, and found that since there was no interference from other soil constituents standards containing potassium alone in M ammonium chloride could be used. Willis described the determination of potassium in blood serum diluted 50-fold, the sodium interference being overcome either by adding a similar amount of sodium chloride to the standards or by adding a large excess of the disodium salt of EDTA to both sample and standard solutions. Replicate determinations gave a relative standard deviation of about 1.1%.

4. Copper

Allan (8) determined the relative absorption intensities of different copper lines by a simple photographic technique. He placed a burner between a hollow cathode lamp and a spectrograph so that the light passed through the flame before entering the spectrograph. A series of exposures made when spraying copper solutions of different concentrations into the flame, corrected where necessary for flame emission, enabled him to compare quantitatively the absorption intensities of different lines. He found that the line at 3248 A. is the strongest in absorption, though there are about a dozen lines between 2024 and 3274 A. showing appreciable absorption. Copper seems to be completely atomized in an air–coal gas flame.

The sensitivity of the atomic absorption method is rather less for copper than for zinc, but Allan, in developing methods of analysis for agricultural materials, was able to determine copper in acid solutions of fertilizers. With low-copper soils and with soil extracts and plant ash, however, he found it necessary to concentrate the copper by extraction with ammonium pyrrolidine dithiocarbamate into methylisobutyl ketone. Other metals present in agricultural materials apparently did not interfere.

Elwell and Gidley (34) and Strasheim et al. (82) confirm that a 100-fold excess of ten of the more common elements, including silicon, has no effect on the absorption due to copper. Strasheim et al. describe the use of the atomic absorption method for the determination of copper in concentrates and Menzies (65) for its determination in alloys.

5. Noble Metals (Silver, Gold, Ruthenium, Rhodium, Palladium, Osmium, Iridium, Platinum)

Lockyer and Hames (59), using the Hilger atomic absorption spectrophotometer, determined the sensitivity for most of these metals in test solutions.

The high sensitivity of silver in absorption has been used by Rawling et al. (71) in developing a method for the determination of this metal in lead concentrations which it is hoped may replace the classical fire-assay technique.

Lockyer and Hames showed that, although gold could be determined without interference from lead or ferric iron, the absorption decreased as their burner warmed up. This effect, which was apparently connected with the decomposition of gold salts by the brass of the burner, was not found by Gatehouse and Willis (41) with their stainless steel burner.

6. Magnesium

This metal, which is of great biological interest, was very difficult to estimate with speed and accuracy until the advent of atomic absorption spectroscopy. Very recently, methods have been described for its determination using high-performance flame photometers (1,36,66) but the older flame photometric methods, which relied on the band emission of magnesium oxide rather than the emission of the metal itself, were not very satisfactory.

Fortunately, magnesium shows exceptionally high sensitivity in absorption and, providing an air–acetylene flame is used, such interferences as do occur can easily be controlled. The principal interfering substances are elements which form acidic oxides stable at high temperatures, e.g., aluminum, silicon, and titanium, and the interference is most marked in the presence of nitric and sulfuric acids (5,34,65) but can be controlled by adding strontium. The mechanism of this type of interference was investigated by Elwell and Gidey (34) and is discussed in Section IV.4.D. Control of the interference by the addition of strontium or calcium is so effective, however, that magnesium may even be determined in aluminum alloys (57) and in such aluminiferous materials as cement, slags, etc. (56). Its determination in metallic nickel and iron has also been described recently (12a,13a).

Allan, in the first paper (5) to describe the analysis of plant materials by atomic absorption spectroscopy, found that the only interfering element in plant ash was aluminum when present in a concentration comparable with that of the magnesium, and this was confirmed by David (23).

Willis (95) has found that the addition of calcium (if the ash does not already contain sufficient) serves to remove the interference. David (25) has also studied the determination of magnesium in ammonium chloride extracts of soil and finds that the addition of 1500 p.p.m. of strontium effectively removes the interference due to aluminum, silicon, and phosphorus.

The aluminum content of blood serum, urine, and animal tissues is negligible and the phosphorus does not interfere in the analysis (93). However, while urine and solutions of the ash from serum and tissue can be analyzed directly for magnesium, the protein in serum measured directly causes a positive error, sometimes as high as 15% (90) but more usually 2–3% (31,95). The interference may be overcome by adding strontium chloride, EDTA, or hydrochloric acid (31,90), which probably act by liberating the protein-bound magnesium fraction which normally constitutes 35% of the total.

Dawson and Heaton (31) compared the values of the magnesium content obtained for blood serum by atomic absorption spectroscopy (using $0.1N$ hydrochloric acid to liberate the metal) and by the colorimetric magnesium ammonium phosphate method of Simonsen, Westover, and Wertman (80) as modified by Heaton (45). The atomic absorption results were on the average higher by 1.7%, but part of the discrepancy was accounted for by the discovery that there was a net loss of 0.8% of the magnesium in the precipitation stage of the colorimetric method. In urine or in ashed serum, where the net magnesium loss was less, the results of the atomic absorption method were 1.1% higher than the colorimetric ones.

The reproducibility of the magnesium determination by atomic absorption is also good. Allan found a relative standard deviation of 1.7% in a series of measurements on the same solution over a period of a week, and recent work (19) on the magnesium content of the muscle tissue of rats gave a relative standard deviation of 1.3% for the atomic absorption measurement and of 3% for the whole experiment using a group of 18 rats.

7. Calcium

In the past the flame photometric determination of calcium has given rise to many difficulties, chiefly because phosphorus, with which the metal is almost always associated in nature, forms with calcium a highly refractory phosphate in the flame. In atomic absorption spectroscopy the same phenomenon occurs, but since background radiation produces far less interference it is possible to add large quantities of other materials to control this compound formation.

Flame conditions are critical if the highest sensitivity is to be achieved, and the concentration of calcium atoms is highest just above the zone of unburnt gas in a fuel-rich flame (24,91). Phosphorus interference is very pronounced in the air–coal gas flame and its control is more difficult than in the air–acetylene flame. If an air–coal gas flame is used, the phosphorus should be removed from the solution, which may conveniently be done by the anion-exchange process described by Hinson (46d).

David (24) investigated the interferences caused by certain elements and found that if measurements were made in the presence of sulfuric acid (2% v/v) and magnesium (6000 p.p.m.) no interference was caused by the presence of up to 200 p.p.m. of phosphorus, 80 p.p.m. of aluminum, or 40 p.p.m. of silicon. Small amounts of sodium or potassium produced an enhancement of calcium absorption but these effects could be eliminated by adding 200 p.p.m. of sodium and 1500 p.p.m. of potassium. David described the determination of calcium in plant material by wet-ashing followed by atomic absorption measurement after addition of the above quantities of materials to both samples and standards. In a later paper (25) describing the determination of calcium in ammonium chloride extracts of soils he showed that the presence of 1500 p.p.m. of strontium as strontium chloride controlled the interference on 8–40 p.p.m. of calcium of up to 160 p.p.m. of phosphorus, 160 p.p.m. of aluminum, 64 p.p.m. of silicon, and 100 p.p.m. of sulfur.

In the analysis of urine (93), calcium can be determined by atomic absorption measurements using either strontium or lanthanum in the form of the chloride to control the suppression of the calcium absorption by phosphorus, which may be present in concentrations as high as 40 times that of the calcium. This addition also eliminates the slight enhancing effect of large concentrations of sodium and potassium.

With protein-containing materials such as serum or saliva, the situation is more complicated. The effect of the protein is to reduce the suppression of the calcium signal by phosphorus, and in many cases acceptable results can be obtained on specimens of serum diluted directly with water, providing a rich air–acetylene flame is used. More accurate results are obtained, however, if the protein is precipitated by addition of trichloroacetic acid and strontium chloride added to the supernatant liquid to control the phosphorus interference (91). A similar technique has recently been used by Newbrun (67) for the determination of calcium in saliva, though since in this case the protein content is relatively small, satisfactory results may be obtained by simple dilution with EDTA solution to overcome the phosphorus interference.

The relative standard deviation of the calcium determination on test solutions was found by David to be about 1.3%, and on serum and urine solutions is about 1.0–1.1% (93).

8. Strontium

David (27,29) described the determination of this element in soil extracts and in solutions of plant ash using an air–acetylene flame. The high stability of the emission from the strontium hollow-cathode tube enabled him to use fivefold scale expansion. Although neither calcium nor phosphorus by itself seriously depresses the strontium absorption, the two elements together do so, and he found it necessary with plant-ash solutions to remove the phosphorus by passage through an ion-exchange column. Silicon and aluminum were also found to depress the strontium absorption, but their effect could be alleviated by the presence of calcium in the solution. In order to overcome any residual interference, David used the standard addition method.

9. Zinc

The successful determination of zinc at very low concentrations (1 p.p.m. or less) represents one of the triumphs of the atomic absorp-

tion method, since the sensitivity for zinc in emission flame photometry is very low, even if the oxycyanogen flame is used (76). In
absorption, the air–coal gas flame gives the highest sensitivity
(10,41).

Gidley and Jones (42), in developing methods for the determination
of zinc in metallurgical specimens, found that the absorption of 5
p.p.m. of zinc was unaffected by 1000 p.p.m. of 25 other elements,
though it was lowered appreciably by silicon.

David (23) determined zinc in plant materials by measurement of
solutions prepared by wet-ashing, and found that apart from the
residual sulfuric acid from the ashing, which depressed the absorption
a little, the other elements in plant material did not interfere with the
zinc determination. He used standard solutions made up in 5% v/v
sulfuric acid to allow for the effect of the acid in the sample solutions.

Allan (10) confirms David's finding that none of the elements
present in plant digests interfere with the determination of zinc and
that this applies also to soils, soil extracts, and fertilizers. He found
that the determination of 0.4 μg. of zinc in 2 ml. (i.e., 0.2 p.p.m.) can
be carried out with a relative standard deviation of about 5%, which
can be improved where it is convenient to extract the metal into an
organic solvent. In a recent review of chemical methods of determining microquantities of zinc, Margerum and Santacana (64) state
that their preferred method (a colorimetric one) has an operating
range of 3 to 33 μg., with relative standard deviations at the ends of
this range of 6.1 and 1.9%, respectively. The atomic absorption
method thus compares more than favorably with the chemical one
and is probably less liable to errors from contamination.

Willis (94) has shown that zinc in urine can be determined by spraying the sample directly into the flame and using aqueous zinc solutions for calibration. Here again the reproducibility compares very
well with that of the colorimetric method, though for the highest
absolute accuracy it would be necessary to correct for the scattering
effect, as described in Section IV.5.

10. Cadmium

Cadmium, like zinc, shows very high sensitivity in absorption,
and the cadmium hollow-cathode tube, even when run on the very
low currents necessary to prevent self-absorption, gives a more stable
output than does that of zinc. The stability of the emission at the

2288-A. resonance line is such that two or threefold scale expansion can be used, enabling the limit of detection to be set even lower than the 0.03 p.p.m. found by Gatehouse and Willis (41). Concentration of the metal into an organic solvent would allow further improvement in the sensitivity.

Elwell and Gidley (34) found that of twelve common elements only silicon showed any interference, and they described a procedure for the determination of cadmium at concentrations down to 0.1 p.p.m. in zirconium metal.

Willis (94) was able to estimate cadmium in urine by spraying the sample directly into the flame; for the most accurate results, correction for the scattering effect was necessary. Table X shows the

TABLE X

Standard Deviation of the Direct Measurement of Zinc and Cadmium in Urine by Atomic Absorption Spectroscopy (94)

Concentration of metal in urine, p.p.m.	Relative standard deviation, %	
	Zn	Cd
0.05	—	8.6
0.1	—	8.3
0.3	—	7.1
0.6	—	4.3
0.9	—	1.9
1.0	2.6	—

standard deviations for the measurement of zinc and cadmium in urine at different levels by this direct atomic absorption technique.

Kägi and Vallee have recently isolated cadmium-containing proteins (49,50), and if cadmium proves to have a specific biological function, its determination, particularly in minute quantities, will be greatly facilitated by atomic absorption spectroscopy.

11. Mercury

The most sensitive resonance line of mercury lies at 1849 A., but the well-known 2537-A. line, though about 50 times weaker in absorption, is much more convenient to use in the determination of the metal for the reasons outlined in Section IV.1.

The stability of the 2537-A. line emitted by a low-pressure ozonizer lamp is sufficient to enable the use of four- or fivefold scale expansion, and in this way the limit of detection of 10 p.p.m. quoted by Gate-house and Willis (41) can be reduced to about 1 p.p.m. (95). Mercury can be determined in urine by concentrating the metal into an organic solvent and spraying this solution into the flame (94).

It is of interest that a very sensitive method of determining mercury in urine has been developed by Lindström (58). The specimen is sprayed into a flame and the mercury vapor in the products of combustion, after filtration from solid particles of salt, etc., is measured by atomic absorption at 2537 A. in a commercial mercury-vapor meter.

12. Lead

Elwell and Gidley (35), in developing methods for the determination of this metal in alloys, have found negligible interference effects from ten of the more common metals even when present in concentrations 20 times that of lead. Similarly, Robinson, in the determination of lead in gasoline, found no interference on 10 p.p.m. of lead by 900 p.p.m. of tin, sodium, bismuth, copper, zinc, chromium, iron, and nickel, nor from various sulfur and nitrogen compounds occurring in gasoline (77).

Willis (94) has described the determination of lead in urine by the atomic absorption technique. At the levels normally encountered with healthy persons and even with those exposed to lead hazard (0.01—0.7 p.p.m.), it is necessary to concentrate the metal into an organic solvent. Since the degree of extraction is slightly different for water and for urine it is generally desirable to calibrate with a similar specimen of urine to which a known amount of lead has been added. Good agreement was obtained with the results of the classical method (ashing of the urine followed by colorimetry with dithizone), and the atomic absorption method was found particularly suitable for the measurement of low lead levels (<0.1 p.p.m.), as it is specific for lead and yields negligible blank values. It is possible, for instance, to measure a lead concentration of 0.02 p.p.m. with a standard deviation of 0.002 p.p.m.

Zeeman and Butler (100) have described the use of atomic absorption spectroscopy for the determination of lead in wines at the 0.1–0.5 p.p.m. level. To achieve the necessary sensitivity they ash the wine and also use four traversals of the light beam through the flame. Recent work by the writer suggests that it is possible to determine lead in wines at this level with reasonable accuracy by using threefold scale expansion and spraying the wine directly into the flame.

13. Bismuth

Willis (94) found that bismuth added to urine can be quantitatively recovered and determined by atomic absorption measurements after extraction into an organic solvent.

14. Chromium

Williams et al. (89a) have recently developed an atomic absorption method for the determination of chromium in feces. The specimen is dry-ashed and dissolved in a phosphoric acid–manganous sulfate–potassium bromate solution, and the absorption of the 3579 A. line measured in the air–acetylene flame. The interference from aluminum and silicon is overcome by the addition of calcium to the test solution and of silicate to the standards.

15. Molybdenum

David (27,28) found that in the determination of this metal the type of flame is of the utmost importance, as in an oxidizing flame no molybdenum atoms are produced (cf., Section IV.2 and Fig. 14). He found interference from calcium, strontium, manganese, iron, and sulfate ion, which in every case could be controlled by the addition of excess aluminum chloride.

David concluded that atomic absorption spectroscopy in its present form is not quite sensitive enough for the determination of molybdenum in soil extracts or in plant ash, though he was able to determine the metal satisfactorily in molybdenized superphosphate and in stainless steel, using fivefold scale expansion.

16. Manganese

The emission spectrum of manganese is very complex, so that the choice of the best line for atomic absorption is difficult. Using his photographic technique (Section VI.4), Allan (6) found that absorption was greatest for the a^6S–7^6P^0 multiplet, and that of this multiplet the line at 2794.8 A. showed the highest absorption. To obtain maximum sensitivity the monochromator should be able to resolve the 2794.8-A. line completely. Failure to exclude the adjoining line at 2798.3 A. will lead to slightly reduced sensitivity and to increased curvature in the absorbance–concentration graph.

Allan described in detail the determination of this element in plant materials after wet-ashing with a nitric–perchloric acid mixture. He found the absorption of a solution of 10 p.p.m. of manganese to be uninfluenced by the presence of 1000 p.p.m. of sodium, 3000 p.p.m. each of potassium and calcium, 1000 p.p.m. of magnesium, and 500 p.p.m. of phosphorus, which are the concentrations which would occur in a solution obtained by dissolving in 20 ml. the ash from 1 g. of a plant material fairly rich in these elements. The complete lack of spectral interference is in marked contrast to the situation occurring in emission methods, as the most sensitive emission line of manganese (4030 A.) lies in a region where there is strong continuous and band emission from such elements as sodium, potassium, calcium, and magnesium.

Allan obtained recoveries of 99–103% for manganese added to the original plant material before digestion and found a relative standard deviation of 3.3–4.7% for replicate measurements on manganese solutions containing 1.5–25 p.p.m. of the metal. The sensitivity of the atomic absorption method is less than that of colorimetric methods, but Allan claims that its simplicity, speed, and freedom from interference make it particularly convenient and attractive.

In examining the possible application of the atomic absorption method to metallurgical analysis, Elwell and Gidley (34) found that 1000 p.p.m. of sodium, potassium, copper, lead, iron, nickel, tin, and zinc had no significant influence on the absorption of 20 p.p.m. of manganese, but that calcium, magnesium, aluminum, titanium, and zirconium caused a slight, and silicon a marked, lowering of the absorption. The different results obtained by Allan and by Elwell and Gidley for the interfering effect of calcium and magnesium are probably due to the use of different types of flame by the two sets of workers.

17. Iron

The emission spectrum of iron is even more complex than that of manganese, and Allan (6) found that several lines show appreciable absorption, that at 2483.3 A. being the most sensitive. To achieve the best results the slit width of the monochromator must be suffi-

ciently narrow to exclude as far as possible the neighboring line at
2488.1 A., though since the strength of emission of the 2483.3-A. line
by the hollow-cathode tube is low, it is normally necessary to sacrifice
some sensitivity in order to obtain a reasonably high signal-to-noise
ratio (Section V.1).

Allan found that sodium, potassium, calcium, magnesium, and
phosphorus in the same concentrations as he used in his experiments
with manganese had no effect on the absorption of iron in the air–
acetylene flame, but Elwell and Gidley (34) found that the absorption of 50 p.p.m. of iron in the air–coal gas flame was affected by the
presence of 1000 p.p.m. of calcium, copper, aluminum, titanium,
zirconium, or silicon.

The determination of iron in plant ash is described by Allan, and
requires the same quantities of materials as does the determination of
manganese. Recoveries of 97–104% were found for iron added to
the plant material before ashing, and the relative standard deviation
for replicate measurements on the same solution was 1.9–6.5% in
the 2.5–25 p.p.m. range.

18. Cobalt and Nickel

Although no details have yet appeared on the determination of
these metals in biological materials by atomic absorption spectroscopy, Allan (7) has investigated the relative absorption intensities
of different lines in the spectra of these elements. For cobalt the
strongest absorption line is at 2407.2 A. and this line is about 50
times as sensitive in absorption as the strongest emission line at
3527 A. With nickel the strongest absorption is shown by the line at
2320 A., the absorption at this wavelength being about 15 times that
at 3415 A., the wavelength of the strongest emission line.

References

1. Alcock, N., I. MacIntyre, and I. Radde, *J. Clin. Pathol.*, *13*, 506 (1960).
2. Alkemade, C. T. J., and J. M. W. Milatz, *Appl. Sci. Research*, *B4*, 289
   (1955).
3. Alkemade, C. T. J., and J. M. W. Milatz, *J. Opt. Soc. Am.*, *45*, 583 (1955).
4. Alkemade, C. T. J., and M. H. Voorhuis, *Z. Anal. Chem.*, *163*, 91 (1958).
5. Allan, J. E., *Analyst*, *83*, 466 (1958).
6. Allan, J. E., *Spectrochim. Acta*, 800 (1959).
7. Allan, J. E., *Nature*, *187*, 1110 (1960).

8. Allan, J. E., *Spectrochim. Acta, 17,* 459 (1961).
9. Allan, J. E., *Spectrochim. Acta, 17,* 467 (1961).
10. Allan, J. E., *Analyst, 86,* 530 (1961).
11. Allan, J. E., Report of Third Australian Spectroscopy Conference (August 1961), *Nature, 192,* 927 (1961).
11a. Allan, J. E., *Spectrochim. Acta, 18,* 259 (1962).
11b. Allan, J. E., *Spectrochim. Acta, 18,* 605 (1962).
12. Allan, J. E., personal communication.
12a. Andrew, T. R., and P. N. R. Nichols, *Analyst, 87,* 25 (1962).
13. Baker, C. A., and F. W. J. Garton, U.K. Atomic Energy Authority Report AERE-R 3490 (1961).
13a. Belcher, C. B., and H. M. Bray, *Anal. Chim. Acta, 26,* 322 (1962).
14. Beukelman, T. E., and S. S. Lord, *Appl. Spectroscopy, 14,* 12 (1960).
15. Bode, H., and F. Neumann, *Z. Anal. Chem., 172,* 1 (1960).
16. Box, G. F., and A. Walsh, *C.S.I.R.O. Ind. Research News,* No. 17 (1959).
17. Box, G. F., and A. Walsh, *Spectrochim. Acta, 16,* 255 (1960).
18. Brownell, P., Report of Second Australian Spectroscopy Conference (June 1959). *Australian J. Sci., 22,* 64 (1959); *Nature, 184,* 1195 (1959).
18a. Buell, B. E., *Anal. Chem., 34,* 635 (1962).
19. Cheek, D. B., J. E. Graystone, J. B. Willis, and A. B. Holt, *Clin. Soc.,* in the press.
20. Chen, P. S., and T. Y. Toribara, *Anal. Chem., 25,* 1642 (1953).
21. Clinton, O. E., *Spectrochim. Acta, 16,* 985 (1960).
22. Cupr, V., and J. B. Pelikan, *Z. Anal. Chem., 168,* 322 (1959).
23. David, D. J., *Analyst, 83,* 655 (1958).
24. David, D. J., *Analyst, 84,* 536 (1959).
25. David, D. J., *Analyst, 85,* 495 (1960).
26. David, D. J., *Analyst, 85,* 779 (1960).
27. David, D. J., *Nature, 187,* 1109 (1960).
28. David, D. J., *Analyst, 86,* 730 (1961).
29. David, D. J., *Analyst,* in the press.
30. David, D. J., *Rev. Univ. Ind. Santiander,* in the press.
31. Dawson, J. B., and F. W. Heaton, *Biochem. J., 80,* 99 (1961).
32. Dean, J. A., *Flame Photometry,* McGraw-Hill, New York, 1960.
33. Dinnin, J. I., *Anal. Chem., 32,* 1475 (1960).
33a. Dinnin, J. I., personal communication.
34. Elwell, W. T., and J. A. F. Gidley, *Atomic-Absorption Spectrophotometry,* Pergamon Press, Oxford, 1961.
35. Elwell, W. T., and J. A. F. Gidley, *Anal. Chim. Acta, 24,* 71 (1961).
36. Fawcett, J. K., and V. Wynn, *J. Clin. Pathol., 14,* 403 (1961).
36a. Fawcett, J. K., and V. Wynn, *J. Clin. Pathol., 14,* 463 (1961).
36b. Finkelstein, N. P., and A. V. Jansen, *S. African Ind. Chemist,* 106 (1961).
37. Foster, W. H., and D. N. Hume, *Anal. Chem., 31,* 2033 (1959).
38. Fukushima, S., *Mikrochim. Acta,* 596 (1959).
39. Fukushima, S., *Mikrochim. Acta,* 332 (1960).
40. Gatehouse, B. M., and A. Walsh, *Spectrochim. Acta, 16,* 602 (1960), see also Russell, B. J., and A. Walsh, *ibid.,* 883 (1959).

41. Gatehouse, B. M., and J. B. Willis, *Spectrochim. Acta, 17,* 710 (1961).
42. Gidley, J. A. F., and J. T. Jones, *Analyst, 85,* 249 (1960); erratum *ibid., 86,* 271 (1961).
42a. Gilbert, P. T., *Anal. Chem., 34,* 210R (1962).
42b. Gilbert, P. T., *Chemiluminescent Flame Spectrophotometry,* Beckman Research Report No. 37, 1961.
43. Gorsuch, T. T., *Analyst, 84,* 135 (1959).
44. Grove, E. L., R. A. Jones, and W. Matthews, *Anal. Biochem., 2,* 221 (1961).
45. Heaton, F. W., *J. Clin. Pathol., 13,* 358 (1960).
46. Herrmann, R., and C. T. J. Alkemade, *Flammenphotometrie,* 2nd Ed., Springer, Berlin, 1960.
46a. Herrmann, R., *Optik, 18,* 422 (1961).
46b. Herrmann, R., and W. Lang, *Z. ges. exp. Med., 134,* 268 (1961).
46c. Herrmann, R., and W. Lang, *Optik, 19,* 208 (1962).
46d. Hinson, W. H., *Spectrochim. Acta, 18,* 427 (1962).
47. Hunter, G., *Nature, 182,* 263 (1958).
48. Jones, W. G., and A. Walsh, *Spectrochim. Acta, 16,* 249 (1960).
49. Kägi, J. H. R., and B. L. Vallee, *J. Biol. Chem., 235,* 3460 (1960).
50. Kägi, J. H. R., and B. L. Vallee, *J. Biol. Chem., 236,* 2435 (1961).
51. Kirchoff, G., *Pogg. Ann., 109,* 275 (1860).
52. Kirchoff, G., and R. Bunsen, *Pogg. Ann., 110,* 161 (1860).
53. Kirchoff, G., and R. Bunsen, *Pogg. Ann., 113,* 337 (1861).
54. Kirchoff, G., and R. Bunsen, *Phil. Mag., 22,* 329 (1861).
55. Leithe, W., *Angew. Chem., 73,* 488 (1961).
56. Leithe, W., and A. Hofer, *Mikrochim. Acta,* 268 (1961).
57. Leithe, W., and A. Hofer, *Mikrochim. Acta,* 277 (1961).
58. Lindström, O., *Anal. Chem., 31,* 461 (1959).
59. Lockyer, R., and G. E. Hames, *Analyst, 84,* 385 (1959).
60. Lockyer, R., J. E. Scott, and S. Slade, *Nature, 189,* 830 (1961).
61. L'vov, B. V., *Spectrochim. Acta, 17,* 761 (1961).
62. Malissa, H., and E. Schöffmann, *Mikrochim. Acta,* 187 (1955).
63. Malmstadt, H. V., and W. E. Chambers, *Anal. Chem., 32,* 225 (1960).
64. Margerum, D. W., and F. Santacana, *Anal. Chem., 32,* 1157 (1960).
65. Menzies, A. C., *Anal. Chem., 32,* 898 (1960).
66. Montgomery, R. D., *J. Clin. Pathol., 14,* 400 (1961).
67. Newbrun, E., *Nature, 192,* 1182 (1961).
68. Pijck, J., J. Gillis, and J. Hoste, *Intern. J. Appl. Radiation and Isotopes, 10,* 149 (1961).
69. Poluektov, N. S., *Zavodskaya Lab., 27,* 830 (1961); *Ind. Lab., 27,* 834 (1961).
70. Pungor, E., and I. K. Thege, *Acta Chim. Acad. Sci. Hungary, 28,* 133 (1961).
71. Rawling, B. S., M. D. Amos, and M. C. Greaves, *Nature, 188,* 137 (1960); *Proc. Australian Inst. Mining and Met.,* No. 199, p. 1 (1961); *Bull. Inst. Mining and Met.,* No. 662, p. 227 (1962).
72. Robinson, J. W., *Anal. Chem., 32,* 17A (1960).
73. Robinson, J. W., *Anal. Chim. Acta, 23,* 458 (1960).
74. Robinson, J. W., *Anal. Chim. Acta, 23,* 479 (1960).
75. Robinson, J. W., *Anal. Chem., 33,* 1067 (1961).

76. Robinson, J. W., *Anal. Chem.*, *33*, 1266 (1961).
77. Robinson, J. W., *Anal. Chim. Acta*, *24*, 451 (1961).
78. Robinson, J. W., and R. J. Harris, *Anal. Chim. Acta*, *26*, 439 (1962).
79. Russell, B. J., J. P. Shelton, and A. Walsh, *Spectrochim. Acta*, *8*, 317, (1957).
80. Simonsen, D. G., L. M. Westover, and M. Wertman, *J. Biol. Chem.*, *169*, 39 (1947).
81. Society of Analytical Chemistry, Report of Analytical Methods Committee, *Analyst*, *85*, 643 (1960).
82. Strasheim, A., F. W. E. Strelow, and L. R. P. Butler, *J. South African Chem. Inst.*, *13*, 73 (1960).
83. Sullivan, J. V., and A. Walsh, unpublished work.
84. Walsh, A., *Handbook of Third Exhibition of Institute of Physics*, Institute of Physics, Victorian Division, Melbourne, March, 1954, p. 42. Patents: Australia 163,586; U.K. 763,556; U.S.A. 2,847,899; Canada 580,682; France 1,133,308; Germany 1,026,55; Italy 524,989; Netherlands 92,357; Sweden 10436/54.
85. Walsh, A., *Spectrochim. Acta*, *7*, 108 (1955).
86. Walsh, A., "Application of Atomic Absorption Spectra to Chemical Analysis," in H. W. Thompson, ed., *Advances in Spectroscopy*, Vol. II, Interscience, New York, 1961.
87. Walsh, A., and J. B. Willis, unpublished work.
88. West, A. C., and W. D. Cooke, *Anal. Chem.*, *32*, 1471 (1960).
89. White, J. U., *J. Opt. Soc. Am.*, *32*, 285 (1942).
89a. Williams, C. H., D. J. David, and O. Iismaa, *J. Agr. Sci.*, in the press.
90. Willis, J. B., *Nature*, *184*, 186 (1959); *Spectrochim. Acta*, *16*, 273 (1960).
91. Willis, J. B., *Nature*, *186*, 249 (1960); *Spectrochim. Acta*, *16*, 259 (1960).
92. Willis, J. B., *Spectrochim. Acta*, *16*, 551 (1960).
93. Willis, J. B., *Anal. Chem.*, *33*, 556 (1961).
94. Willis. J. B., *Nature*, *191*, 381 (1961); *Anal. Chem.*, *34*, 614 (1962).
94a. Willis, J. B., *Proc. Roy. Australian Chem. Inst.*, *29*, 245 (1962).
95. Willis, J. B., unpublished work.
96. Wirtschafter, J. D., *Science*, *125*, 603 (1957).
97. Woodson, T. T., *Rev. Sci. Instr.*, *10*, 308 (1939).
98. Yofè, J., and R. Finkelstein, *Anal. Chim. Acta*, *19*, 166 (1958).
99. Zaidel, A. N., and E. P. Korennoi, *Optics and Spectroscopy*, *10*, 299 (1961).
100. Zeeman, P. B., and Butler, L. R. P., *Tegnikon*, 96 (1960); *Appl. Spectroscopy*, in the press.

Separation and Determination of Steroids by Gas Chromatography

E. C. HORNING, W. J. A. VANDENHEUVEL, AND B. G. CREECH

Baylor University College of Medicine, Houston, Texas

I. INTRODUCTION

Current procedures for the separation of steroids by gas chromatography for purposes of identification, estimation, or isolation rest upon the use of relatively thin-film column packings prepared with highly thermostable liquid phases. The superb resolution, the ability to obtain qualitative and quantitative data at the same time, the ability to use microgram and submicrogram samples, and the speed of the usual determination suggest that these methods will find many uses. They are particularly valuable in work with complex mixtures of biologic origin, and they are likely to be particularly valuable in research work in biology and medicine. The combination of small sample size, speed, and ability to do multiple determinations in a single run may permit changes in experimental design in some studies, and this may well prove in the future to be the most valuable aspect of these new methods.

The following sections contain a description of current experimental methods and their applications. Thin-film column procedures require somewhat different techniques than those developed for use with fatty acids (see A. T. James, Vol. VIII of this series, pp. 1–59, 1961), although the principles involved in the separation process are unchanged. The limitations and the areas of application of thin-film methods are not yet fully defined, although it is clear that procedures which are useful for steroids are equally satisfactory for work with many alkaloids, drugs, vitamins, derivatives of sugars and amino acids, and many other naturally occurring compounds. This summary should not be regarded as a final account of the methods, but rather as an interim report on current applications in a field that is still undergoing rapid development.

II. HISTORICAL

Development of Gas Chromatography Procedures for Steroid Separations

The first practical demonstration of the separation of steroids by gas chromatography was described by VandenHeuvel et al. in 1960 (60). Prior to this time, several investigators had found that some steroids could be recovered after gas chromatography under conditions involving relatively high temperatures or long retention times or both. Eglinton et al. (14), for example, found that many compounds of relatively high molecular weight (including cholestanone) could be separated by gas chromatography with an ordinary Apiezon column by using high temperatures and long retention times. Short retention times for steroid separations were obtained by Sweeley and Horning (49) using a thermostable polyester phase; however, the temperature was high (270°) and some of the steroids under investigation did not survive these conditions. The work of Beerthuis and Recourt (6) with a thermally stripped silicone phase was particularly valuable in showing that gas chromatographic separations of steroids could be achieved with a nonselective phase when high temperatures were employed. In all three instances there was ample evidence that at least some steroids could be carried through a gas chromatographic procedure. However, the conditions approached the upper limits of temperature suitable for these compounds. A number of investigators recognized at the time that the best way to reduce both temperatures and retention times to useful levels was to decrease the amount of liquid phase. This approach would have been investigated more widely had it not been for a general belief that columns of useful efficiency could not be made with less than about 5% of liquid phase. This belief was supported both by authoritative opinion and by many laboratory results, although the work of Hishta et al. (22) with glass bead columns did not support this view. The problem was resolved by the preparation of relatively thin-film columns after the method of VandenHeuvel et al. (60). Since that time a variety of phases and conditions have been developed for use in specific steroid separation problems. The temperature ranges for general analytical use are now usually 200–220°, although for some work, temperatures up to about 250° may be used. The retention times for many analytical separations are 10–20 minutes, unless temperature programming is used (usually 1–2 hours are taken for wide-range separations). The sample size for analytical applications is at the microgram or submicrogram level. Column efficiencies ranging from about 2000 to 8000 theoretical plates are usually employed.

The conditions which are best for steroid separations are satisfactory for the separation of many classes of compounds of interest in biological and medical studies. These include many drugs and drug metabolites (3), alkaloids (13,33), human skin wax esters (18), vitamins A, E, K, and D (25,68), and derivatives of sugars (54), amino acids (45), and nucleosides (45). Thin-film columns are not restricted in usefulness to any specific class of compounds.

III. PRINCIPLES AND TERMINOLOGY

Gas–liquid chromatography (the name is shortened to gas chromatography in this chapter) is a form of partition chromatography in which the stationary phase is a liquid film held in place on a solid support, and the moving phase is a carrier gas flowing over the surface of the liquid film in a controlled fashion.   The temperature of the chromatographic column is adjusted so that compounds of the mixture undergoing separation or analysis are partitioned between the liquid and gas phases.   The order of elution of components is determined by their respective partition coefficients, and the basic principles of the method are those of partition chromatography.   These principles, particularly as applied to steroid separations, were developed over a period of several years by a number of scientists including Martin (41), Bate-Smith and Westall (5), and Bush (9).   An excellent discussion of these principles, with particular regard to their application in steroid separations by paper chromatography, may be found in the monograph by Bush (9).

The rapid spread of gas chromatographic methods is due to several advantages inherent in the use of a gas–liquid system.   One of these is the very wide range in separating power which may be achieved by changes in the nature of the liquid phase.   Another is the very high resolving power which may be arrived at by appropriate circumstances for the column.   Theoretical plate values for gas chromatographic columns vary from 2000 to 1 million; for steroid separations current practice involves the use of packed columns varying in length from about 6 to 12 feet, and the plate values found with these columns range from about 2000 to 8000.   Theoretical plate values ranging from 30,000 to 100,000 are common for capillary columns, but at the present time packed columns are more satisfactory for steroid work than are capillary columns.   Another advantage of gas chromatographic techniques is the fact that qualitative and quantitative analytical data may be obtained simultaneously.   The ability to analyze microgram and submicrogram quantities of complex mixtures of biologic origin is of great importance in biochemical and biological studies.

Maximum column efficiency with thin-film columns may be attained only when very small samples are used.   For this reason it is customary to use ionization detection systems in steroid work.   Thermal conductivity detection systems are widely used with conventional thick-film columns, but the level of sensitivity attained with these systems is usually not satisfactory for steroid work.

A usual method of operation in gas chromatography is the isothermal separation procedure. Under these circumstances individual components emerge from the column with a distribution which gives rise to one of the few difficulties inherent in partition chromatography. Components emerging early are seen as relatively sharp peaks and as the separation proceeds the peaks become wider; late emergence gives very broad peaks which are not amenable to precise area measurement. Temperature programming is a technique in which the temperature of the column is raised steadily during the separation, and under these circumstances the base widths of the peaks representing each component will be narrower than would be found under isothermal circumstances. When linear temperature programming is employed, members of a homologous series are eluted with a linear time relationship, and when components are separated at constant column efficiency the base widths of the peaks are constant. Since constant column efficiency is not usually observed with all components, the base widths are in fact not equal for all components when this kind of separation is employed. However, this method of operation is often used for separations of mixtures involving compounds with a wide range of molecular weight or functional groups.

Terms and Definitions

Column Specifications

Column size. Column dimensions are usually given in terms of length of packing and inside diameter. Most analytical columns are 3 or 4 mm. in diameter. Lengths vary from 6 to 12 ft. for most applications. Capillary columns are usually 0.01 to 0.04 inches I.D., with lengths from about 50 ft. to 500 ft.; however, capillary columns are not widely used in steroid work.

Column packing. This is specified by type and mesh size of support and kind of liquid phase. Amount of liquid phase is usually given in per cent values on a w/w basis.

Operating Parameters

Temperatures. Temperature values always refer to the column temperature. It is a common practice to maintain the detector compartment or the detector cell at about 20° above the column temperature to avoid condensation. In temperature-programmed separations, the detector cell is usually maintained at the final temperature of the separation or at about 10–20° above this value. Preheaters and flash heaters are normally maintained at higher temperatures than the column; temperatures in the range of 250–270° are commonly used.

Pressure. For packed columns the inlet pressure is usually 10–30 p.s.i. The pressure should be constant throughout the course of the determinations. The outlet pressure is usually atmospheric. It is a common practice to reduce pressures to low levels while columns are not in active use, but in general it is not advisable to reduce the pressure below 5–10 p.s.i. during such periods.

Flow rate. Measurements of the carrier gas flow rate are usually made through use of a soap bubble flowmeter at the end of the system. The flow rate is measured in terms of ml./min. at atmospheric pressure and room temperature.

Sensitivity. This term must be defined in context. The usual use of the term in practice refers to arbitrary instrument settings which provide electrical multiplication of the detector response. In comparisons of detector properties, the term is usually used to indicate the lowest level of response of the system.

Sample size. This is usually specified in microliters (μl.) or micrograms (μg.). The total sample is rarely more than 20 μg. for ionization detection systems; the usual sample size for a mixture of steroids is 5–20 μg., depending upon the nature of the sample. The usual peak seen in steroid separations is 0.1–2 μg. for a single component. The present limit of sensitivity for much work is about 0.01 μg. for a single component.

Chart speed. With the usual differential recording systems a convenient rate is 1 in. in 2 or 3 minutes if the analysis time is short. It is generally undesirable to use very slow chart speeds because of difficulties in measurement of width for narrow peaks.

Bleed adjustment. All gas chromatographic systems include a method for compensation of column bleed. A reference column may be used, or a reference side for the carrier gas may be employed, or the compensation may be entirely electrical in nature.

Definition of Terms

Two recommendations have been made for symbols and terminology in gas chromatography. These are given by Ambrose et al. (1,2), and Johnson and Stross (27). The conventions used in this chapter are those of the International Union of Pure and Applied Chemistry.

Retention time. The uncorrected retention time, t_R, is measured as shown by dimension C in Figure 1. The time of emergence is taken as the time to reach the peak midpoint, and the starting point of measurement is the time of sample injection. If a sample is loaded

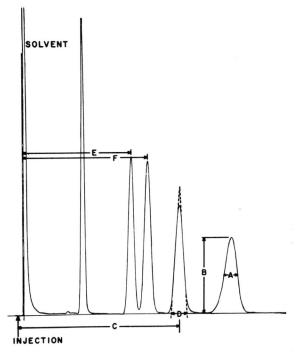

Fig. 1. Isothermal gas chromatographic separation. The compounds are the methyl esters of palmitic, stearic, oleic, linoleic, and linolenic acids. Times E and F are adjusted or corrected retention times, and the ratio F/E is the separation factor for these two components. The retention time C is measured from the point of sample injection, and this value is used in calculations of theoretical plate efficiency. Dimensions A, B, and D represent, respectively, the width at half-height for the peak, the peak height, and the projected base width.

with interruption of the gas flow, it is customary to measure the time from the point of restoration of the gas flow.

The uncorrected retention time is used in calculations of column efficiency.

Retention volume. The uncorrected volume, V_R, is equal to the product of uncorrected retention time and the flow rate of carrier gas; the flow rate is measured at room temperature and at the outlet pressure (usually atmospheric) but it is calculated for the column temperature.

Adjusted retention time. This value is equal to $t_R - t_{gas}$, where t_{gas} is the time for emergence of the front. In instruments where the gas flow is interrupted for sample loading, and where the detector responds to air, this value is measured by using the air peak as a reference point. However, under these circumstances it is more satisfactory to use the method of Peterson and Hirsch (46) for calculation of the adjusted retention time. Most instruments constructed in the U.S. employ conditions where the sample is introduced in solution and without interruption of the gas flow. The retention time of low-boiling solvents under conditions used for steroid work is not measurably different from that of air, and the time for emergence of the solvent front may be used as the reference point. The retention time, t_R', measured in this way is also sometimes called the apparent retention time, and the symbol t is also used for this value. Calculations of relative retention times are made on the basis of retention times measured in this way.

Dimensions E and F in Figure 1 are adjusted or apparent retention times.

Adjusted retention volume. The adjusted or apparent retention volume is equal to the product of the adjusted or apparent retention time and the flow rate of carrier gas calculated for the column temperature and the outlet pressure.

Corrected retention volume. The corrected retention volume is based on a calculation which takes into consideration the pressure drop across the column. This value is given by the equation: $V_r^0 = fV_r$, where f is the pressure correction factor [*J. Chromatography*, *2*, D33 (1959)].

Specific retention volume. The specific retention volume is calculated in terms of unit weight of liquid phase, and this may be used for comparison of liquid phase properties.

Relative retention time and *Relative retention volume.* Experimental data are often reported in terms of relative retention volume or relative retention time. A suitable compound is taken as a reference. The adjusted or apparent retention times of compounds under study are compared with the relative retention time observed for the reference compound. In steroid work, the compound usually chosen as a reference is cholestane. When steroid numbers are calculated, both cholestane and androstane are used as reference compounds.

Separation factor. The adjusted or apparent retention times for any two components may be compared. In Figure 1, for example, the ratio of the distances F/E is the separation factor for the two components. Calculations may be made by using either times or distances measured at constant chart speed.

Theoretical plates. The theoretical plate value for a column is calculated by the following formula:

$$n = 16 \ (t_R/w)^2$$

where w is the base width of the peak with retention time t_R. When these values are calculated in practice it is found that equal values are not obtained for each component. This has led to the custom of using a few selected peaks for comparison purposes; for steroid work it is usually customary to calculate theoretical plates for cholestane or for sterols such as cholestanol or cholesterol.

It should be noted that the retention time value used in this calculation is measured from the injection point.

Area measurements. Several methods for making area measurements are in use. A good method is to calculate areas by the product of the peak height and the width at half height. For example, the product of distances A and B in Figure 1 will give a measure of the peak area.

Triangulation of the peak area, or the use of a planimeter, are among the other methods of area measurement. These methods all have comparable precision when the peak shape approaches the theoretical. In isothermal separations with low resolution columns it must be remembered that a combination of relatively sharp early peaks and flat late peaks makes it difficult to achieve high precision by any of these measurement procedures.

Electronic integration methods may prove valuable in the future. Mechanical integrators have been helpful in some applications but are

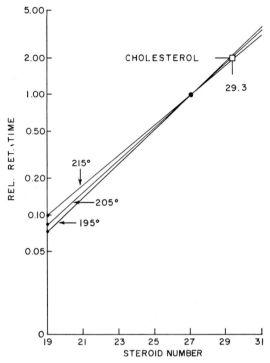

Fig. 2. Steroid number chart showing the relationship between temperature and the slope of the androstane–cholestane line used to determine steroid numbers from relative retention times. The mode of determination of the steroid number (29.3) of cholesterol (relative retention time, 2.06 at 205°) is shown.

generally not useful in work with highly complex mixtures which contain very small amounts of many components.

Steroid numbers. The concept of "carbon number" was introduced into fatty acid work by Woodford and Van Gent (64). "Steroid numbers" may be defined in much the same way for work in the steroid field (55). The steroid number of androstane is taken as 19, and the steroid number for cholestane is taken as 27. The method of determination of steroid numbers with an SE-30 column is illustrated in Figure 2. Cholestane is used as a reference substance, and its relative retention time is established as 1.0. The relative retention time of androstane is determined at a given temperature, and is plotted along with that for cholestane on a logarithmic scale. Relative retention times for the compounds under study are then determined under the same conditions of temperature and flow rate, and with the same column. The relative retention time for a given steroid (cholesterol is used as the example in Fig. 2) is used to determine the intercept along the carbon content scale. This has been termed the "steroid number" (55).

Details of methods for the determination and use of steroid numbers are given in the original paper (55) and they are also discussed in Section IX.

IV. PACKED COLUMN CHROMATOGRAPHY

1. Detection Systems

Ionization detection systems are in wide use; these systems are based on the measurement of changes in conductivity of the flowing gas stream with changes in the composition of the gas. Most of these systems are relatively easily constructed and have high sensitivity. The responses to widely different classes of organic compounds are generally different. These systems also detect the column bleed, and it is generally necessary to use highly thermostable liquid phases. The linear range of these detectors may be exceeded when columns with high bleed rate are employed.

One of the first of the ionization detectors was the argon ionization system developed by Lovelock (34). The cell contains a radioactive source, which is usually a radium-226, strontium-90, or tritium–titanium source. A high potential is applied to the electrodes, and in the presence of α or β radiation, metastable argon atoms are formed. The electrical conductivity of the gas is low, since the argon atoms are not ionized. The metastable argon atoms transfer energy to the organic molecules entering the cell, and a partial ionization of the organic substance occurs. This leads to an increase in the current flow through the cell. This change is amplified and recorded. Argon detection systems are relatively insensitive to temperature and flow rate changes. A triode cell has been described, but the diode cell is most often used in practice.

Flame ionization detectors are based on the measurement of electrical conductivity of gases in a hydrogen flame. The electrical conductivity of hydrogen burning in air is low, but when an organic substance is fed into the flame the conductivity increases.   The detector is reported to be unaffected by water vapor present in the sample, and this is a great advantage when solutions containing water are to be analyzed.   The response of the detector to different kinds of compounds varies in approximately the same fashion as that of the argon ionization detector.   Detailed descriptions of flame ionization detectors may be found in the literature of gas chromatography.

A radio-frequency discharge detector was developed by Karmen and Bowman (28).   This system uses a glow discharge established in helium at atmospheric pressure by the application of an r.f. alternating current field.   The discharge rectifies part of the exciting current, and a direct current signal is provided which is placed on a recorder without preamplification.   When organic substances are present in the helium gas, the current diminishes and the change may be recorded.   Relatively large signals are obtained from low concentrations of organic substances.

Several other types of ionization systems have been used.   A definitive review of ionization detectors has been presented by Lovelock (35).

"Electron capture" or "electron affinity" measurements (36) may be made with a modified argon detection system which contains a tritium–titanium source in the detection cell; a low potential is maintained across the electrodes, either constantly or in pulsed fashion. The ability to capture electrons of thermal energy is limited to specific classes of compounds.   Several groups of steroids have this property (37).

2. Supports and Coating Procedures

A variety of supports have been recommended for gas chromatographic work.   Best results in steroid work are obtained with only a few of the commonly available materials.   Three diatomaceous earth preparations, Celite 545, Gas Chrom, and Anakrom have been used in many applications.   The authors' experience has largely been confined to Gas Chrom P.   The most satisfactory mesh size for general work is 100–120, or 100–140 mesh.   In order to attain maximum column efficiency, it is desirable to screen the support prior to washing and coating, in order to ensure a relatively narrow range of mesh size.   The presence of finely divided particles has a particularly bad effect on column efficiency.

The screened support should be acid washed before use and this process is described in the experimental section.

Three different procedures have been reported to give satisfactory column packings. The first of these involves the use of a support which has undergone base washing. This method was developed in England, and it has been widely used for the preparation of column packings for fatty acid work. Treatment of the support with strong alkali leads to an altered surface, and if the support is washed and dried quickly and coated within a very short time after drying, a satisfactory column packing will be obtained. If the treated and dried support is allowed to stand for a considerable length of time before coating, the surface will revert to the original state and it may be difficult to obtain satisfactory thin-film coatings. Because of a high degree of variability in results, this method is now rarely used.

Polyester phases may usually be coated directly on dry, acid-washed supports without additional treatment. The polar groups saturate active sites on the support. However, it is generally extremely difficult to obtain a satisfactory thin-film column if an acid-washed support is coated directly with a nonselective phase. It has been reported (32) that satisfactory columns may be obtained with nonselective phases if a small amount of polyester is introduced into the phase. The amount of polyester is generally not sufficient to alter the nonselective properties of the column.

In the experience of the authors, the best procedure for obtaining satisfactory thin-film column packings involves the use of a silanized support. The support is deactivated by treatment with hexamethyldisilazane or dichlorodimethylsilane. The dichlorodimethylsilane inactivation process is described in the experimental section.

The coating of the support may be carried out in many different ways. The support and a solution of the phase in a low-boiling solvent may be placed in a rotary evaporator, and evaporation of the solvent will lead to deposition of the phase on the support. This method is widely used, but in the authors' experience it is not entirely suitable for the preparation of thin-film packings. It is difficult to obtain a uniform film of phase on the support, and agitation of the mixture often leads to the production of fine particles. These effects lead to decreased resolution and, with some phases, to active site absorption of steroids. The filtration technique of Horning et al. (24) is satisfactory for all phases, and this method is described in the experimental section. It must be remembered that attention to detail is necessary in order to reproduce packings of uniformly excellent properties, and that variations in the physical and chemical properties of supports which are undergoing continuous manufacture may lead to alterations in the properties of the packings. Test procedures for active site effects and column efficiency are given at the end of the experimental section.

Experimental Procedure. The support (50 g.) is treated with 400 ml. of concentrated hydrochloric acid in a 1-liter beaker with occasional stirring for 12 hours. The acid is removed by the use of a filter stick (coarse porosity). The support is then treated three times with hydrochloric acid in the same fashion, with a contact period of one hour for each washing operation. After the final acid treatment, 750 ml. of deionized water is added to the support and the mixture is stirred. The resulting suspension is allowed to stand for two minutes, and the supernatant liquid is removed by decantation. This procedure removes finely divided particles produced during the washing process. The support is then washed thoroughly with deionized water by repeating this process. After the final decantation the support is washed again on a Buchner funnel with deionized water; the wash should be neutral. The support is then suspended in acetone or methanol to remove most of the water. After filtration and preliminary drying at room temperature, the drying process is completed at 80°.

The dry support (25 g.) is placed in 100 ml. of 5% dichlorodimethylsilane in toluene in a side-arm filter flask. The pressure is reduced in the flask (by an aspirator) for a period of a few minutes. The flask is shaken to dislodge bubbles from the surface of the support, and the pressure is then allowed to return to atmospheric. The treated support is removed by filtration, and washed with 100 ml. of toluene. It is then washed well with methanol, and after preliminary air drying the support is dried at 80°.

The coating procedure is carried out by a filtration process which leads to a uniform deposition of liquid phase on the surface of the support. This is carried out in the following way. A solution of liquid phase in an appropriate solvent is prepared. The concentrations that are used are usually 0.5–4% of phase in solution. The support (20–25 g.) is placed in 100 ml. of solution in a side-arm filter flask. The flask is maintained at a reduced pressure (aspirator) for a few minutes, and the flask is shaken to dislodge bubbles from the surface of the support. The pressure is allowed to return to atmospheric and the mixture is allowed to stand for about five minutes. The slurry is placed on a Buchner funnel with a rapid swirling motion of the flask, and the solution is allowed to drain freely through the bed of support. Reduced pressure is maintained on the filter flask for about five minutes. At the end of this time the filtration process is complete, and the surface of the filter cake usually appears to be damp but not wet. The coated support is spread on a smooth surface for preliminary drying at room temperature. It is then dried in an oven at 80–100°. It is important that preliminary air drying should be carried out before the support is placed in the oven. Column packings prepared in this way should flow freely, and should have the appearance of a powder.

Difficulties may arise from time to time in the behavior of column packings because of inadequate treatment at the inactivation stage or because of development of active sites during use. When this occurs, it may be possible to improve column performance materially by treating the column packing with hexamethyldisilazane. This is best done by the injection of about 20–50 μl. of hexamethyldisilazane into the column maintained at about 100–150° with a relatively low argon or nitrogen pressure (5–10 p.s.i.). This procedure is helpful in ensuring that the column will be free from active sites which may lead to irreversible absorption of compounds undergoing separation.

The preparation of column packings with a specific amount of phase is frequently considered to be a difficult process. When a filtration procedure is used for the preparation of thin-film column packings, the relationship between the concentration of phase in solution and the amount of phase on the support must be determined by experiment. With Gas Chrom P, it has been found that the amount of phase on the support (w/w) is the same (to within about 0.1%) as the concentration of phase in solution. If Celite 545 is used, the amount of phase on the support is approximately two times the concentration of the phase in solution. When these relationships are in doubt, it is best to carry out a determination in a direct way in order to find the amount of phase on the support. A 2- or 3-gram quantity of coated support may be extracted exhaustively in a Soxhlet extractor, and the weight of phase is determined after evaporation of the solvent.

The column packing procedure is important in determining the properties of the final column.   Glass U-tubes are usually packed by gravity flow, but W-tubes and glass coil or "cobra" columns are best packed with the aid of a flowing gas stream.   The column may be attached to a relatively high capacity vacuum pump, and the packing can then be drawn into place through a suction procedure.   Alternatively, a large pipette may be cut at both ends to provide a holding chamber, and the pipette containing the packing may be connected in a horizontal position to the column and to a source of compressed gas at about 20 p.s.i.   When the chamber is tilted the packing will flow into the tube.   During the packing process the tube should be tapped firmly with a rubber-covered rod (an ordinary pencil carrying a section of heavy rubber tubing is satisfactory).   It is also possible to use a mechanical vibrator or a flat-sided wooden or steel rod with a standard electric hand drill.   Excessive vibration should be avoided, since the packing may be partially shattered, but at the same time it is necessary to pack the column so that there are no discontinuities. The procedure is completed while the column is held under about 15–20 p.s.i. of flowing gas.

It is generally believed that glass is inert with regard to the adsorption of organic compounds, but this is not correct.   Glass tubes and glass wool plugs should be silanized before the packing process is carried out.   Further, glass wool plugs in the vaporization zone should be replaced frequently.   Deposits of carbonaceous material, which may accumulate if some decomposition occurs in the vaporizing zone, have a particularly deleterious effect.

TABLE I

Temperature for Conditioning (for 12 hr.) for Steroid Columns with Commonly Used Phases

Phase[a]	Temperature, °C.
SE-30	300
SE-52	300
F-60	300
PhSi	300
QF-1	250
NGS	230–240
NGA	230–240
EGIP	230–240
CNSi	220–230

[a] The composition of these phases is given in Section IV.3.

A conditioning period is necessary for all columns. The optimum temperature and the optimum time are best determined by experiment; the values in Table I are representative of the conditions used in the authors' laboratory for general purpose steroid columns. A conditioning period of 12 hours is usually satisfactory.

In order to characterize a new column in terms of efficiency and absence of absorbing sites, several test procedures may be used. Cholestane is frequently employed in comparisons of column efficiency, and samples of 1–2 μg. or less in 1 μl. of solvent should be employed for this purpose. The solvent volume should not exceed 1 μl. for each sample. Column efficiencies should be determined at several flow rates. In general, rates in the range 30–60 ml./min. are used in much work and other considerations may guide the choice of flow rate for a given separation. The irreversible adsorption of polyfunctional steroids, and the loss of these compounds by thermal degradation, must be kept low by scrupulous attention to the preparation of the packing and the maintenance of good working conditions for the column. (Polyhydroxyl steroids are particularly subject to loss, and for this reason quantitative procedures are often best carried out through the use of trimethylsilyl ethers (38).) A preliminary test of a column may be made with a test mixture containing cholesterol and cholesterol methyl ether in known proportion. The sample volume should be 1 μl., and the peak areas should be compared. A loss of cholesterol will result under several conditions. If the vaporization zone is too hot, or if the packing is unsatisfactory, decomposition or irreversible absorption may result. Liquid phases containing reactive substances or reactive end groups will also cause loss of the sterol. Many samples of EGIP (ethylene glycol isophthalate) phase are unsatisfactory for this reason. Under some circumstances it may also be desirable to determine the end point of sensitivity for the entire system; if appreciable loss of the sterol occurs before the end point of sensitivity for cholestane or cholesterol methyl ether is reached the ratio will change sharply.

3. Liquid Phases

In gas chromatographic work, the ability to vary the nature of a steroid separation is currently largely dependent upon the use of thermostable liquid phases which have different chemical structures, and which show selective retention effects for different functional groups. The terms "nonselective" and "selective" may be used to describe this property. In earlier work the terms "nonpolar" and "polar" were used, but this had the disadvantage of implying that only two kinds of phases are known. There are in fact four distinct sets of properties or characteristics which are recognizable among the many descriptions of liquid phases that have appeared up to the present time. Brown (8) has proposed that liquid phases be classified as nonpolar, electron acceptor, or electron donor phases. A fourth class may act through dipole–dipole interaction. For practical purposes the classification is best made in terms of effects arising from the presence of specific functional groups in the steroids undergoing separation, and this arrangement is used in the following summary of liquid phase properties.

NONSELECTIVE PHASES

Methyl-substituted siloxane polymers, commonly known as methyl silicones, show very little selective retention effects for steroids with different functional groups. This is demonstrated in Figure 3. Retention times are almost the same for cholestane-3α-ol, cholestane-3β-ol, cholesterol, and cholestane-3-one; the figure shows this effect for cholestanol (the 3β isomer) and cholestanone. Cholestanyl acetate is well separated from cholestanol, but this is because of the difference in molecular weight. The order of separation of a group of steroids under these conditions is dependent largely upon the size and shape of the molecules. This is evident in Figure 4. The functional groups which are present contribute to the molecular weight, and they may alter the molecular shape through intramolecular bonding, but they do not lead to separations dependent upon their chemical nature. The general relationship between relative retention times and molecular weight has been noted in many laboratories, and plots of the log retention time or log relative retention time against molecular weight have been made for some groups of steroids (65). This property is also reflected in the relative constancy of the steroid number contributions for different functional groups without regard for the position or stereochemical arrangement of the group.

A number of nonselective phases are available; the code numbers, structure, and origin of these phases are in Table II. The best known, and one of the most useful in packed column separations, is SE-30. This material was used by VandenHeuvel et al. (60) in early studies of

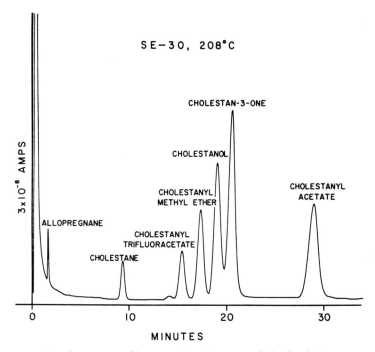

Fig. 3. Gas chromatographic separation of compounds in the cholestane series with a nonselective phase. Column conditions: 6 ft. × 4 mm. glass column, 0.75% SE-30 methyl silicone on 100–140 mesh Gas Chrom P; 208°; 16 p.s.i.

steroid separations and it is still widely used when a high degree of thermal stability is needed together with nonselective properties. Figure 5 shows a separation with an F-60 phase; the properties of this phase are only slightly different from those of SE-30.

TABLE II
Structure and Source of Nonselective Phases

Code	Polymer structure	Source
SE-30	Methyl siloxane	General Electric Co.
SF-96	Methyl siloxane	General Electric Co.
SE-52	Methyl phenyl siloxane (low phenyl content)	General Electric Co.
710	Methyl siloxane	Dow Corning
F-60	Methyl p-chlorophenyl siloxane	Dow Corning

Columns with SE-30 packings are generally conditioned at 300°, and this phase has been used effectively at even higher temperatures. For most steroid work, the chief advantage of siloxane polymers lies in the high degree of thermal stability, leading to a very low bleed rate at 200–250°, and the relatively constant behavior observed over a period of several years with different batches of commercially prepared polymer. The introduction of a low percentage of phenyl

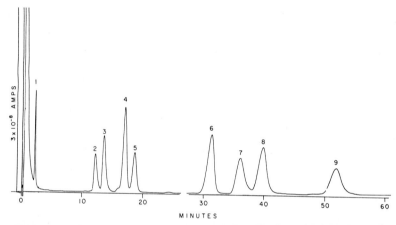

Fig. 4. Gas chromatographic separation of a mixture of steroids with a nonselective phase illustrating the effect of molecular geometry and molecular weight upon retention time. The compounds are (1) androstane; (2) pregnane-3,20-dione; (3) 5α-pregnane-3,20-dione; (4) coprostane; (5) cholestane; (6) stigmastane; (7) cholesterol; (8) cholestane-3-one; (9) stigmasterol. Column conditions: 6 ft. × 4 mm. glass column; 2% SE-30 methyl silicone on 80–100 mesh Chromosorb W; 222°; 10 p.s.i.

groups (SE-52), or the p-chlorophenyl group (F-60, Fig. 5), does not materially alter the phase properties in most separations. It is also possible to use thermally stripped siloxane phases (6), but this offers no advantage over the use of thin-film packings which are made with relatively low amounts of thermostable polymers (43,60).

Hydrocarbon polymers, including Apiezon greases and asphalt fractions, are not widely used in steroid work. These materials are less thermostable than methyl siloxane polymers, and they offer no particular advantages over the siloxanes when nonselective properties are desired. However, an asphalt-containing phase with special

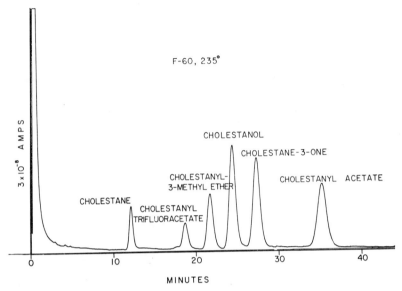

Fig. 5. Gas chromatographic separation of compounds in the cholestane series with a nonselective phase. Column conditions: 6 ft. × 4 mm. glass column; 2% F-60 methyl *p*-chlorophenyl silicone on 100–140 mesh Gas Chrom P; 235°; 17 p.s.i.

properties has been described (Böttcher, C. J. F., and J. W. A. Meijer, *J. Chromatography*, **6,** 535 (1961)).

Methyl siloxane and hydrocarbon polymers are nonpolar solvents, and consequently, polyfunctional compounds have a relatively low solubility even at elevated temperatures when these phases are used. Relatively polar steroids may show association or overloading effects when thin-film analytical columns containing these phases are employed. A greater amount of phase may be used under these circumstances, or less polar derivatives of the steroids may be prepared.

Nonselective phases are used to best advantage when compounds of different molecular size or shape are under study; this generalization is evident from their properties. A major use of these phases is to establish molecular size relationships, but specific examples of useful separations may be cited. Pregnane-3α,20α-diol can be separated readily from 17-ketosteroids with a nonselective phase, and this condition may be used in studies of urinary steroids (a separation of the trimethylsilyl ethers may be preferred for other reasons). The sitosterols may be separated with an SE-30 column (see Section VI) and pyrocalciferol and isopyrocalciferol may also be separated readily (43,68) (see also Section VIII). Steroidal amines (58) and sapogenins (56) may be separated (see Section VIII). A cholesterol–desmosterol separation may be achieved with a relatively high efficiency SE-30 column, but a higher separation factor is found with a methyl phenyl siloxane polymer containing 40% phenyl substituents.   The separation of bile acid methyl esters may also be accomplished with nonselective phases (61); however, recovery of these compounds decreases with increasing hydroxyl substitution.

SELECTIVE PHASES

Phases showing selective retention effects for alcohols, ketones, and esters, but not for carbon–carbon unsaturation.   One of the most useful phases for steroid separations is a methyl fluoralkyl silicone of the type prepared by the Dow Corning Company (QF-10065). The properties of this liquid phase were first described by VandenHeuvel et al. (53).   This phase exhibits a very high degree of stereoselective separating ability.   Ketones are readily separated from the corresponding alcohols, and sterols containing an equatorial hydroxyl group are readily separated from the corresponding isomers containing an axial hydroxyl group.   Figure 6 shows the separation of a number of steroids with this phase.   It will be seen that cholestanone has a retention time which is very much greater than that of cholestanol. Acetyl esters of sterols have retention times which are less than those of the ketones corresponding to the sterol.

This phase is particularly useful in studies involving identification or structural determination of steroids.   Methods which may be used in work of this kind are described by VandenHeuvel and Horning (55); *T* values may be determined by the procedure of Haahti et al. (19). The phase may also be used in separations of sterols, either for identification purposes or purposes of estimation.   It is not useful for the separation of steroids containing a large number of ketone or ester groups, because of the relatively long retention times which result. However, the phase may be used very effectively in some separations of polyfunctional compounds.   For example, acetyl derivatives of sugars are separated with great effectiveness by this phase (54).

QF-1 shows no retention effects for carbon–carbon unsaturation. This can be demonstrated in experiments with long-chain compounds.

Cholesterol has a retention time shorter than that of cholestanol when this phase is used; this is illustrated in Figure 7.

Phases showing selective retention behavior for carbon–carbon unsaturation, but without stereoselective retention properties for hydroxyl-substituted steroids. Methyl phenyl siloxane polymers containing varying amounts of phenyl substituent groups have been used in a

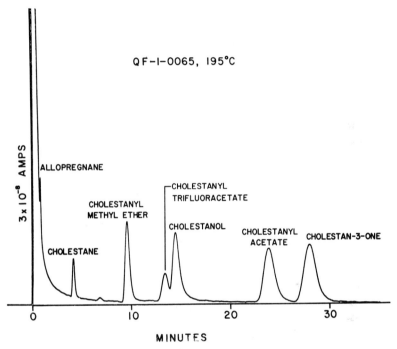

Fig. 6. Gas chromatographic separation of compounds in the cholestane series with a selective phase illustrating the wide separation of cholestanol from the corresponding ketone. Column conditions: 6 ft. × 5 mm. glass column; 1% QF-1 fluoralkyl silicone on 100–140 mesh Gas Chrom P; 195°; 10 p.s.i.

number of experimental studies. These polymers are available both in commercial and research quantities, and they have as their major property the ability to differentiate saturated compounds from the corresponding unsaturated steroids. For example, the separation of desmosterol from cholesterol can be carried out very effectively with relatively low efficiency columns when this phase is used (Fig. 8).

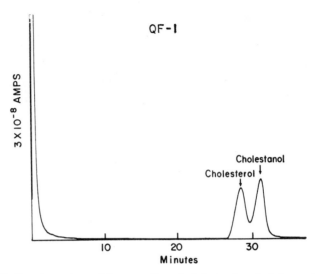

Fig. 7. Gas chromatographic separation of cholesterol and cholestanol with a selective phase. Column conditions: 6 ft. × 4 mm. glass column; 1% QF-1 fluoralkyl silicone on 100–140 mesh Gas Chrom P; 195°; 18 p.s.i.

Phases of this kind have also been used in a number of other applications, including the separation of bile acid methyl esters (47).

Figure 9 shows the separation of a group of steroids with a phenyl methyl silicone containing 40 mole-% of phenyl substituents. The separation of the corresponding alcohol and ketone is quite satisfactory, but in separate experiments it may also be shown that cholestane-3β-ol is not separated from cholestane-3α-ol. This inability to separate stereoisomers makes the phase of relatively little value in steroid identification work.

Phases showing selective retention effects for alcohols, ketones, and esters, and also for carbon–carbon unsaturated bonds. Linear polymers of the polyester class are widely used as liquid phases in gas chromatography. These phases show selective retention effects for a variety of functional groups, including alcohols, ketones, esters, and carbon–carbon unsaturation. For steroid work, they should have sufficient thermal stability so that highly sensitive detection systems are not overloaded when they are used, and the polymerization catalysts should be removed and reactive end groups should not be present. The viscosity at the temperature of the separation should be suitable

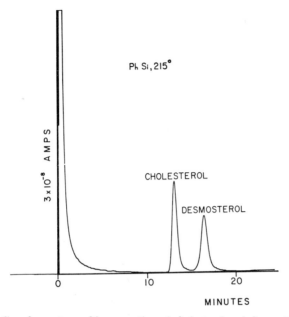

Fig. 8. Gas chromatographic separation of cholesterol and desmosterol with a phase showing selective retention effects for carbon–carbon unsaturation. Column conditions: 6 ft. × 4 mm. glass column; 1% PhSi phenyl methyl silicone on 100–140 mesh Gas Chrom P; 215°; 16 p.s.i.

for partition chromatography. The phase properties of most polyesters have been established by experimental work with commercially available polymers or research samples of polymers made for other reasons.

Polyesters may be classified in terms of polarity and particularly with respect to the ability to separate structurally related compounds differing by a single functional group; the more polar the polymer, the greater the separation. If a separation problem involves compounds containing different numbers of functional groups, the range of choice of polymer may be wide. If positional or stereoisomers are present, it may be necessary to examine a number of phases in order to find a suitable circumstance for a separation. Polyesters of the type used in fatty acid work, including EGS (ethylene glycol succinate), EGA (ethylene glycol adipate), and related polyesters have thermal stabilities which permit their use in steroid separations (20), but these

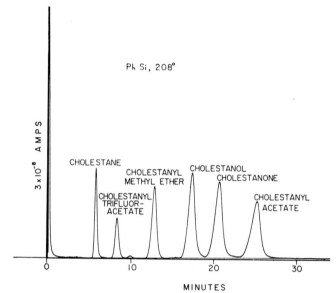

Fig. 9. Gas chromatographic separation of compounds in the cholestane series
Column conditions: 6 ft. × 4 mm. glass column; 1% phenyl methyl silicone on
100–140 mesh Gas Chrom P; 208°; 16 p.s.i.

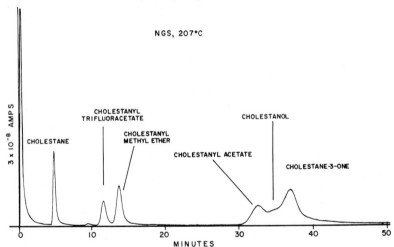

Fig. 10. Gas chromatographic separation of compounds in the cholestane series
with a selective phase illustrating a lack of resolution between the corresponding
hydroxy, keto, and acetoxy compounds. Column conditions: 6 ft. × 4 mm. glass
column; 1% NGS on 100–140 mesh Gas Chrom P; 207°; 18 p.s.i.

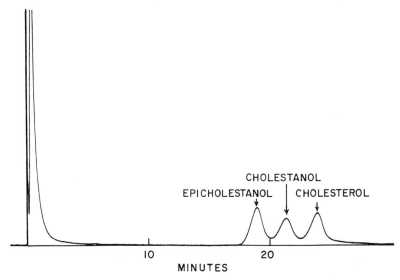

Fig. 11. Gas chromatographic separation of three closely related sterols on a selective phase illustrating the ability of the phase to separate sterols (*a*) differing only in the configuration of the hydroxy group [epicholestanol (3α-ol) and cholestanol (3β-ol)] and (*b*) differing only in the presence of the Δ⁵ bond (cholestanol and cholesterol). Column conditions: 6 ft. × 4 mm. glass column; 1% ethylene glycol succinate–methyl silicone copolymer EGSS on 100–140 mesh Gas Chrom P; 207°; 18 p.s.i.

polyesters are rarely used in practice because polymers of still greater thermal stability are available. Polymers made with neopentyl glycol have been used extensively in steroid work; the observations of Haahti et al. (20) were extended in many studies including that of vitamin D by Ziffer et al. (68). NGS (neopentyl glycol succinate) and NGA (neopentyl glycol adipate) are the most useful of these esters; Lipsky and Landowne (32) have described a number of separations carried out with these polymers. NGS is less polar than EGS, but it has been found useful in both qualitative and quantitative work with steroids containing one or two polyfunctional groups. Figure 10 shows a separation of steroids with an NGS column; it may be seen that alcohols and ketones have very nearly the same retention times (in sharp distinction to the properties of QF-1) and that acetyl esters of sterols are eluted before the parent sterol. Retention times observed for polyfunctional steroids with this phase may be very great.

In general, steroids containing two functional groups are likely to have excessive retention times. Columns made with NGS packings have a long life at 200–220°, and they may be used intermittently at temperatures up to 250°. This phase has been found useful for the determination of urinary 17-ketosteroids according to the procedure of VandenHeuvel et al. (52).

EGIP (ethylene glycol isophthalate) was used in early studies of steroid separations (49), but it has been difficult to obtain samples that do not show a selective absorption of sterols. This disadvantage

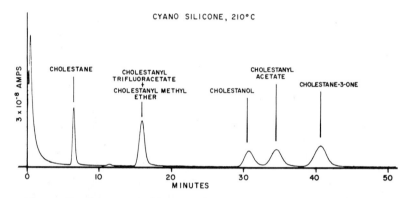

Fig. 12. Gas chromatographic separation of compounds in the cholestane series with a selective phase illustrating the ability of this phase to distinguish between corresponding hydroxy and keto compounds. The properties of this phase are intermediate between those of QF-1 and NGS. Column conditions: 6 ft. × 4 mm. glass column; 1% 50 mole-% β-cyanoethyl methyl silicone on 100–140 mesh Gas Chrom P; 210°; 16 p.s.i.

has restricted the uses of the polymer to studies where very high thermal stability is needed, and where quantitative work is not involved. An example is the study of Haahti et al. (19) with two-component phases.

The separation of epimers of hydroxyl-substituted steroids may generally be accomplished with polyester and modified polyester columns. Since a selective retention effect is also present for carbon–carbon unsaturation, Δ^5 sterols have retention times longer than the corresponding sterol with a saturated B ring. An example of this effect is shown in Figure 11. The separation of the three closely related sterols—cholesterol, cholestane-3β-ol, and cholestane-3α-ol—

may be carried out very effectively with this recently discovered phase (EGSS, a siloxane–ethylene glycol succinate phase).

The separation properties of polyesters are shared by cyanoethyl methyl siloxane polymers (CNSi) containing more than about 50 mole-% of cyanoethyl groups. This is shown in Figure 12. An advantage of CNSi phases is that columns prepared with this material generally show higher plate efficiencies than NGS columns containing the same amount of liquid phase, and ketones are sharply differentiated from alcohols.

4. Operating Procedures

A wide choice usually exists with respect to the conditions which may be used for a specific gas chromatographic separation. The limiting conditions are dependent upon the nature of the compounds undergoing separation, the stability of the liquid phase, the physical nature of the column packing, the solubility of the sample in a suitable solvent, and factors arising from the design of the chromatographic equipment and recording apparatus.

It is desirable to restrict column temperatures to the range 190–220° for 0.5–2% columns, although higher temperatures will be required if very large or highly polar molecules are under study, or if the amount of liquid phase is 3–5%. For example, the separations illustrated in Figures 6, 7, and 25 were carried out at 195°; the separations shown in Figures 3, 9, 10, 11, and 12 were carried out between 205 and 210°; and those shown in Figures 33 and 36 (bile acid methyl esters and sapogenins) at 235°. The vaporizer zone temperature is usually 20–40° above the column temperature, and the detection chamber is usually held at about 10–20° above the column temperature. The usual flow rate limits are about 30–100 ml./min., and 40–60 ml./min. is a usual range in many separations. The latter flow rate range may be obtained with pressures of 15–25 p.s.i. when Gas Chrom P, 100–120 mesh, is used as a support in 6–12 ft. columns. (If conventional thick-film columns are used, the size should be 80–100 mesh.)

Suitable solvents are tetrahydrofuran, acetone, isooctane, hexane, or benzene. Redistilled or purified solvents should be used, and it is usually desirable to concentrate 100–500 ml. of solvent to a few ml., and to examine the residue for evidence of high-boiling impurities which might be evident in a gas chromatographic separation. Methanol and chlorinated hydrocarbons are usually unsatisfactory solvents. The amount of sample is dependent upon the conditions chosen for the operation of the detection system, but in general the concentration of solution should be 0.5–2%, depending upon the nature of the mixture. The volume of solution used for a single separation should be small; 1–3 μl. may usually be used. In studies involving precise measurements of retention times or peak areas, it is desirable to use a small and constant volume of solution. Retention times are affected if large volumes of solvents are used. Instruments are seldom operated under conditions of maximum sensitivity, or at the upper end of the linear range of the detection system, and 0.1–2 μg. of compound is a common range for peaks seen in steroid separations. Larger samples of polar steroids may lead to column overloading for nonselective phases.

The time required for a separation is usually 10–60 minutes depending upon the nature of the mixture under study; 10–20-minute separations are not uncommon. Longer periods of time may be used (for example, it may be desirable to use a low flow rate or a lower temperature in a specific problem) but unless high-efficiency columns are employed, the late peaks will be flat and difficult to use in quantitative work. Temperature-programmed separations usually require 1–2 hours if the mixture contains many components. The recorder chart speed is not usually considered a variable of any consequence, but recorder characteristics differ and several chart speeds should be tried when area measurements are required in order to determine the optimum conditions for recording.

V. CAPILLARY COLUMN CHROMATOGRAPHY

Capillary columns are widely used for the separation of compounds of low molecular weight; they are not ordinarily used for the separation of steroids and other compounds of high molecular weight. This circumstance is due to several factors. Perhaps the most important is that packed columns have been used under many different conditions and with many classes of steroids, and no example of a pair of thermally stable, naturally occurring steroids has yet been found which cannot be separated by a suitable packed column. A second factor arises from problems concerned with the introduction of the sample. Most steroids have a limited solubility in organic solvents, and they are best introduced into the column in relatively dilute solution. This is frequently difficult to accomplish when capillary columns are used. Further, capillary columns are not yet widely available with the variety of liquid phases used in packed column chromatography for steroids. These circumstances may change; the fact that capillary column separations of steroids are possible has been demonstrated (10), and it is possible that capillary techniques will be used very widely in the future. For the present, monographs describing capillary techniques should be consulted if it is desired to carry out a steroid separation by this method.

VI. SEPARATION METHODS

1. Choice of Phase

The versatility and adaptability of gas chromatographic techniques is so great that there are frequently several different methods that can be used for the separation of the components of a given steroid mixture. The first consideration, however, is usually given to the choice of phase. This is particularly important in identification studies and in separations for qualitative purposes, and it is also important for work with steroid derivatives in quantitative studies. In the absence of an established procedure, it is usually best to determine the nature of the separation obtained with a nonselective phase, and to follow this with comparisons of separations accomplished with other phases. If the compounds under study are different in molecular size or shape, the use of a nonselective phase may provide a satisfactory separation. For example, Figure 13 shows the separation of the components of a sterol fraction obtained from soybeans. The phase was SE-30, and β-sitosterol was separated from two other sterols present in smaller quantity. When positional or stereoisomers are present in a mixture, the problem of separation may be more difficult and a selective phase may be required. Figure 14 compares the separating ability of an SE-30 phase with that of a QF-1 phase for a mixture of five closely related compounds in the 5α-pregnane series. SE-30 usually lacks the ability to separate positional and stereoisomers of polyhydroxy steroids, and this effect is apparent in the figure. However, all five compounds may be separated readily with a QF-1 column. It is apparent from this example that an SE-30 phase is not always satisfactory for identification or determination purposes.

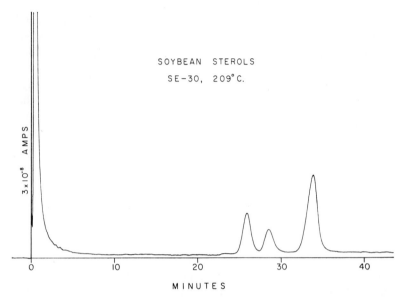

Fig. 13. Gas chromatographic separation of a mixture of sterols from soybeans; the major peak is β-sitosterol. Column conditions: 6 ft. × 4 mm. glass column; 1% SE-30 methyl silicone on 100–140 mesh Gas Chrom P; 209°; 17 p.s.i.

Another example is the desmosterol–cholesterol separation which is of interest in a number of biological studies. The difference in structure between these compounds lies in the presence of the Δ^{24} double bond in desmosterol, and a PhSi phase is indicated if a large separation factor is desired. This view was confirmed by a comparison of phase properties; the largest separation factor observed with 1% column packings was 1.27 for a phenyl silicone phase. A separation with this phase is shown in Figure 8; a low-efficiency column is quite satisfactory for this separation.

When complex mixtures of natural origin are under study, it is generally desirable to examine the result of a separation with one of each of the four kinds of liquid phases described in Section Ib. If it is not possible to find a condition which will provide a satisfactory separation, consideration should be given to the use of columns of higher efficiency and to the possibility of converting the components to derivatives. Much quantitative work is best carried out with derivatives, and derivatives may be studied in the same way as the

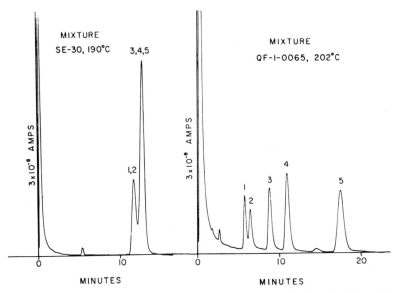

Fig. 14. Comparison of separations for a mixture of five closely related steroids with a nonselective and a selective phase illustrating the greater separating ability of the selective phase. The compounds in the SE-30 separation are (1) 5α-pregnane-3β,20β-diol; (2) 5α-pregnane-3β-ol-20-one; (3) 5α-pregnane-3β,20α-diol; (4) 5α-pregnane-20β-ol-3-one; (5) 5α-pregnane-3,20-dione. The compounds in the QF-1 separation are (1) 5α-pregnane-3β,20β-diol; (2) 5α-pregnane-3β,20α-diol; (3) 5α-pregnane-3β-ol-20-one; (4) 5α-pregnane-20β-ol-3-one; (5) 5α-pregnane-3,20-dione. Column conditions (SE-30): 6 ft. × 4 mm. glass column; 0.75% methyl silicone SE-30 on 100–140 mesh Gas Chrom P; 190°; 16 p.s.i. Column conditions (QF-1): 6 ft. × 5 mm. glass column; 1% fluoralkyl silicone QF-1 on 100–140 mesh Gas Chrom P; 202°; 14 p.s.i.

parent steroids. Opinions differ with regard to the best selection of columns for exploratory work, but phases SE-30, QF-1, PhSi and NGS used in 1% packings will usually provide a great deal of information useful in many steroid separation problems.

2. Column Efficiency

Difficult separation problems usually require consideration of column efficiencies and separation factors. The theoretical plate efficiency of a column is given by the equation:

$$n = 16 \ (t_R/w)^2$$

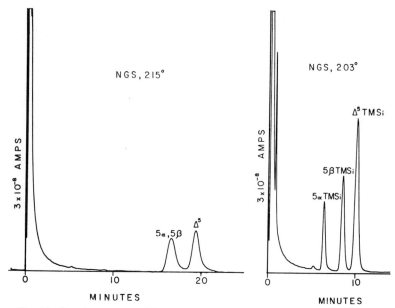

Fig. 15. Gas chromatographic separation of androsterone (5α), etiocholanolone
(5β), and dehydroisoandrosterone (Δ⁵) as the free steroids and as the trimethylsilyl ether derivatives.   Column conditions: 6 ft. × 4 mm. glass column; 1%
NGS on 100–140 mesh Gas Chrom P; 17 p.s.i.; 215° and 203°.

where t_r is the uncorrected retention time and w is the projected base
width for the peak observed for the compound.   A separation factor
near 1 indicates that a column of high efficiency will be needed to
achieve the separation, while a separation factor of 1.2 or higher indicates that a relatively low efficiency column will be adequate for the
separation.   The relationship between theoretical plate efficiency,
separation factor and effectiveness of separation for a pair of components was determined by Glueckauf (16), and the Glueckauf graph
(29) is very valuable in predicting the column efficiency needed for a
given separation.

   The nature of the general problem, and the reason for measuring
separation factors in separate runs rather than in a mixture is illustrated in a practical example in Figure 15.   It may be shown in
separate experiments that androsterone, etiocholanolone, and dehydroisoandrosterone (5α, 5β, and Δ⁵, respectively, in the figure) have
different retention times with an NGS phase.   The 5α/5β separation

factor is very nearly 1, and when both compounds are present an ordinary NGS column is not capable of achieving a separation of the two components. Under these circumstances, as indicated in the figure, a single peak of theoretical shape is obtained and the retention time for the peak is between the two values for each component. It is clear that this condition cannot be used for identification or determination purposes when both components are present, unless an additional column condition can be found which will permit suitable cal-

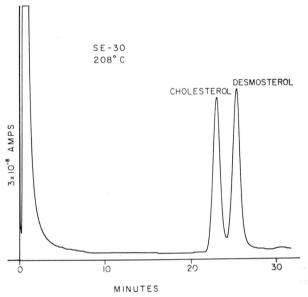

Fig. 16. Gas chromatographic separation of cholesterol and desmosterol. Column conditions: 6 ft. × 4 mm. glass column; 1% methyl silicone SE-30 on 100–140 mesh Gas Chrom P; 208°; 16 p.s.i.

culations (21). The best solution in this instance is to prepare derivatives which can be separated with a column of the same general type. The figure also shows a separation for the trimethylsilyl ethers of these three steroids. This condition is satisfactory for both identification purposes and for the quantitative estimation of the steroids. Since it is usually difficult to prepare NGS columns with high plate efficiency, the preparation of suitable derivatives was more satisfactory in this problem than a solution depending upon the separation of androsterone and etiocholanolone with a high-efficiency column containing an NGS phase.

The desmosterol–cholesterol separation problem may be solved in another way. These compounds may be separated with an SE-30 phase, but the separation factor is low and consequently a column of relatively high plate efficiency is needed to provide a satisfactory separation. SE-30 column packings have been used in columns 12 ft. in length, with theoretical plate efficiencies up to 6000–8000. For this separation, about 3000–4000 theoretical plates are desirable; this can be achieved with a 6-ft. column, as shown in Figure 16.

In studies with complex mixtures of biologic origin, it is best to use columns of relatively high plate efficiency. The reason for this recommendation is evident when an examination is made of separations of this kind. Many components are usually seen as small peaks, and peaks representing major components may obscure many minor components (with a corresponding distortion in quantitative relationships) if columns of low efficiency are used. It is usually possible to prepare satisfactory 12-ft. columns, and these have been valuable in many studies.

3. Derivatives

Steroids with multiple polar functional groups tend to undergo thermal decomposition or irreversible adsorption on active sites of the column to a greater extent than nonpolar steroids. For this reason it is often desirable, particularly when quantitative work is attempted, to convert mixtures of steroids to relatively nonpolar derivatives. Derivatives may also be used to increase separation factors and to provide more satisfactory separations in this way. They are also extremely valuable in studies involving the identification or structural determination of steroids. Derivatives which have a classical foundation in organic chemistry are rarely of value in gas chromatographic work, since these derivatives were usually chosen for reasons of solubility, melting point, or color. The chief requirement for a derivative of a steroid for gas chromatographic work is that it should have an appropriate degree of volatility, and that it should be thermostable and should have polar properties which are preferably less strongly marked than those of the parent compound. The following sections summarize current information for several kinds of derivatives.

TRIFLUORACETYL ESTERS

The gas chromatographic properties of trifluoracetyl derivatives of steroids were investigated by VandenHeuvel et al. (59,62). These esters have retention times shorter than those for the corresponding hydroxy steroids. This effect may be seen in Figure 17 which also illustrates one of the very effective ways in which derivatives may be

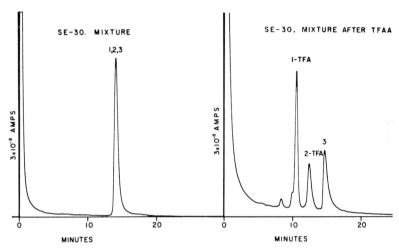

Fig. 17. Gas chromatographic separations of a mixture of (1) 5α-pregnane-3β,20α-diol; (2) 5α-pregnane-20β-ol-3-one; (3) 5α-pregnane-3,20-dione, before and after treatment with trifluoracetic anhydride, illustrating the improved separation for the trifluoracetates. Column conditions: 6 ft. × 4 mm. glass column; 1% methyl silicone on 100–140 mesh Gas Chrom P; 200°; 18 p.s.i.

used. The first panel of the figure shows the failure to separate a mixture of three closely related 5α-pregnane derivatives with an SE-30 column. After treatment of the mixture with trifluoracetic anhydride (59) the same column conditions may be used to accomplish a separation of all three compounds. The esters have retention times shorter than those of the parent compounds, and the presence of two impurities not seen in the original mixture is also clearly evident in the second panel. Figure 18 shows a related separation with an NGS column. The first panel shows that the three components cannot be separated with this phase; the second panel shows that the three components are separated readily after treatment with tri-

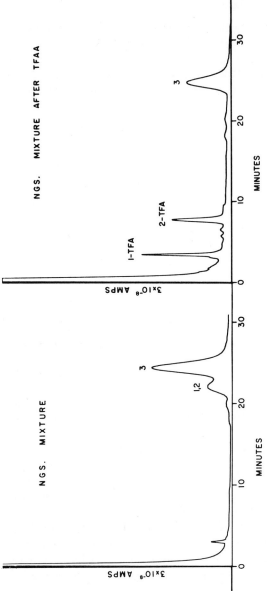

Fig. 18. Gas chromatographic separation of (1) 5α-pregnane-3β,20β-diol, (2) 5α-pregnane-3,20-dione, before and after treatment with trifluoracetic anhydride, illustrating the improved separation for the trifluoracetates. Column conditions: 6 ft. × 4 mm. glass column; 1% NGS on 100–140 mesh Gas Chrom P; 210°; 22 p.s.i.

fluoracetic anhydride.   Figure 19 demonstrates the increase in separation factor that is sometimes achieved when closely related compounds are converted to trifluoracetyl esters.   Although the separation of cholesterol from cholestanol can be achieved with a QF-1
column (Section IV), the separation factor of the trifluoracetyl derivatives is greater and the separation may be carried out at a considerably
lower temperature.

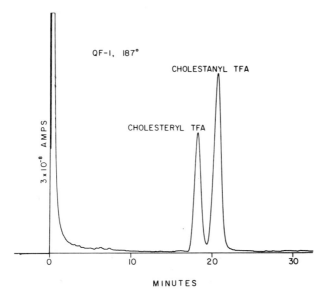

Fig. 19. Gas chromatographic separation of the trifluoracetyl derivatives of
cholesterol and cholestanol.   The separation factor for these derivatives is greater
than that for the parent sterols.   Column conditions: 6 ft. × 5 mm. glass column;
1% fluoralkyl silicone QF-1 on 100–140 mesh Gas Chrom P; 187°; 10 p.s.i.

The esters may be prepared and purified by the usual methods, but
it is also possible to prepare these derivatives by an abbreviated procedure (59), and the entire reaction mixture can be placed on the gas
chromatographic column.   The reagents are removed in the solvent
front.   This is a particularly convenient procedure.
It is necessary to avoid conditions of thermal decomposition for trifluoracetyl esters (62).   If the column packing is permitted to approach the vaporizing zone, conditions are created under which the
ester group will be eliminated during gas chromatography.   The

same effect may be encountered if very high column temperatures are employed.

TRIMETHYLSILYL ETHERS

The gas chromatographic properties of trimethylsilyl ethers of hydroxyl-substituted steroids were described by Luukkainen et al. (38).

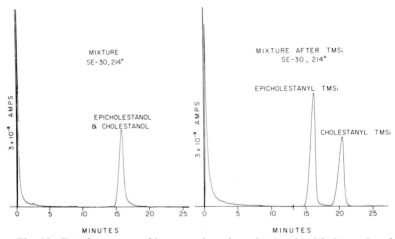

Fig. 20. Gas chromatographic separation of a mixture of epicholestanol and cholestanol before and after formation of trimethylsilyl ethers. No separation was found for the sterols with a nonselective phase, but the trimethylsilyl ethers are separated readily under the same conditions. Column conditions: 6 ft. × 4 mm. glass column; 1% methyl silicone SE-30 on 100–140 mesh Gas Chrom P; 214°; 14 p.s.i.

These derivatives are useful in many applications (39,52). Figure 20 shows the effect of preparing trimethylsilyl ethers for a pair of epimers. Epicholestanol and cholestanol are not separated with an SE-30 column. However, the trimethylsilyl ethers have a very large separation factor when an SE-30 column is employed, and the second panel of the figure shows the separation of the trimethylsilyl ethers of these two sterols. Figure 21 shows the corresponding separation with an NGS column.

Trimethylsilyl ethers are particularly valuable in quantitative studies. Figure 22 illustrates the difficulty of obtaining a satisfactory separation for quantitative purposes of the classic estrogens and

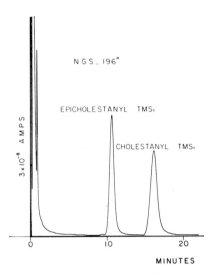

Fig. 21. Gas chromatographic separation of epicholestanyl trimethylsilyl ether and cholestanyl trimethylsilyl ether with a selective phase. Column conditions: 6 ft. × 4 mm. glass column; 1% NGS on 100–140 mesh Gas Chrom P; 196°; 18 p.s.i.

several related compounds. When an NGS column is used, estrone may be separated in satisfactory fashion, but estradiol and estriol undergo irreversible adsorption to a considerable extent. Further, the retention time for estriol is extremely long, and the over-all results are such that it is impossible to use this procedure for quantitative purposes. The lower panel of the figure shows the separation obtained after conversion of the mixture to trimethylsilyl ethers. Progesterone and androstenedione are unaffected by the reagents, but pregnenolone and the three classic estrogens are converted to trimethylsilyl ethers. These may be separated readily with an NGS column and this condition may be used for the estimation of the three classic estrogens in mixtures of biologic origin. The procedures used for this work were developed by Luukkainen et al. (39). Trimethylsilyl ethers of androsterone, etiocholanolone, dehydroisoandrosterone, and pregnanediol are illustrated in Figure 23. The separation illustrated in the figure was carried out with a cyanoethyl methyl silicone phase, and the same kind of separation may be obtained with an NGS phase.

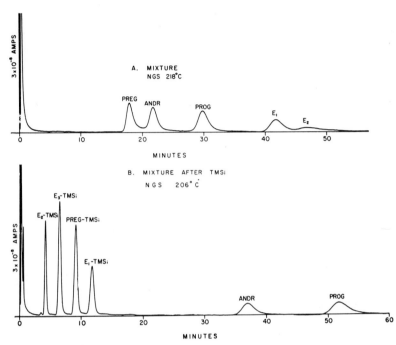

Fig. 22. Gas chromatographic separation of a mixture of steroids. (*A*) Mixture of steroids; (*B*) same mixture after conversion to trimethylsilyl ether derivatives (TMSi). E_1, estrone; E_2, 17β-estradiol; E_3, estriol; *PREG.*, pregnenolone; *PROG.*, progesterone; *ANDR.*, 4-androstene-3,17-dione. Column conditions: 6 ft. × 4 mm. glass column; 0.75% NGS on 100–140 mesh Gas Chrom P; 15 p.s.i.; temperatures as indicated.

Trimethylsilyl ethers are particularly satisfactory compounds for gas chromatographic work. Their properties resemble those of hydrocarbons; they are rarely adsorbed on column packings or column walls and they have a high degree of thermal stability. The reaction conditions are mild, and other functional groups are not affected by the reagents. They are, however, hydrolyzed with great ease and they should be used immediately after preparation.

ACETYL DERIVATIVES

Acetyl derivatives of hydroxyl-substituted steroids are generally stable compounds which can be readily separated by gas chromato-

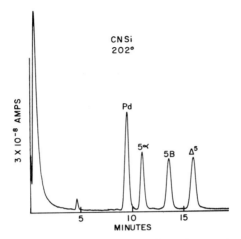

Fig. 23. Gas chromatographic separation of a mixture of pregnanediol di-(trimethylsilyl) ether, *Pd;* androsterone trimethylsilyl ether, *5α;* etiocholanolone trimethylsilyl ether, *5β;* dehydroisoandrosterone trimethylsilyl ether, Δ⁵. Column conditions: 9 ft. × 4 mm. glass column; 2% 65 mole-% cyanoethyl methyl silicone CNSi; 202°; 20 p.s.i.

graphic procedures. These derivatives have been recommended by Wotiz and Martin (65,66) for the estimation of the classic estrogens. It is necessary to choose between a relatively high temperature for the column or a relatively long retention time for the acetyl derivative of estriol, but the separation of the derivatives is excellent.

No particular advantage is usually gained for gas chromatographic purposes by the conversion of sterols to acetyl derivatives in preference to trifluoracetyl esters or trimethylsilyl ethers. However, acetyl esters are useful in identification studies, and they may be prepared easily. The entire reaction mixture, usually containing acetic anhydride and pyridine, may be placed directly on most gas chromatographic columns.

METHYL ETHERS

Methyl ethers of hydroxyl substituted steroids have been studied by Clayton (11). Ethers have gas chromatographic properties very similar to those of hydrocarbons, but the conditions for the preparation of methyl ethers are not generally satisfactory for steroids which also contain ester or ketone functional groups. For this reason the use of methyl ethers in studies of steroid mixtures of natural origin is not likely to be helpful. In a few instances it may be desirable to demonstrate structural differences in the way proposed by Clayton (11).

ENEAMINES

Steroid ketones show marked differences in reactivity with N,N-dimethylhydrazine, depending upon the position of the ketone group, and this effect may be exploited in connection with gas chromatographic techniques in order to study structural effects. The forma-

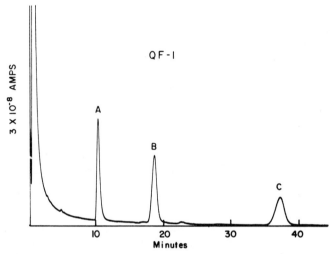

Fig. 24. Gas chromatographic separation of a mixture of androstane-3,17-dione and two of its derivatives. The compound at A is the 3,17-di-dimethylhydrazone (dimethylhydrazine and acid catalyst); the peak at B is due to the 3-dimethyl-hydrazone (dimethylhydrazine alone); the peak at C is due to androstane-3,17-dione. Column conditions: 6 ft. × 4 mm. glass column; 1% fluoralkyl silicone QF-1 on 100-140 mesh Gas Chrom P; 202°; 19 p.s.i.

tion of the corresponding eneamine occurs readily for an unconjugated 3-one group, but a Δ^4-3-one group will react only if an acid catalyst is used. Both a 17-one and a 16-one group will react with N,N-dimethylhydrazine after the addition of acetic acid, but an 11-one group will not undergo reaction even after the addition of the acid catalyst. The eneamines may be separated readily from the corresponding ketones by gas chromatography.   Figure 24 shows a separation of two eneamines and the parent diketone (androstane-3,17-dione) (25).

VII. PROBLEMS OF QUANTIFICATION

Problems of quantification may usually be separated into one of three categories.   These are (1) the establishment of a suitable extraction or isolation procedure in order to obtain a representative sample containing the compounds under study; (2) the establishment of a satisfactory gas chromatographic condition for the separation of components in quantitative fashion, with or without conversion to derivatives; and (3) the interpretation or conversion of the gas chromatographic information into analytical data.   Unless appropriate methods can be established at every stage, the final result will be unsatisfactory.

EXTRACTION OR ISOLATION PROCEDURES

Many gas chromatographic analytical procedures can be used with existing extraction or isolation methods; a representative sample containing the compound or compounds under study is required.   The usual practice is to assume that a solution of the sample, usually 0.5 to 2% in total concentration, can be prepared in an acceptable solvent (hexane, isooctane, tetrahydrofuran, and acetone are among the commonly used solvents).   The usual sample volume for a single determination is 1 μl., and about 5–10 μl. of solution are usually needed in order to permit manipulation of the sample and to carry out replicate analyses if desired.   Changes in existing procedures may therefore amount only to adjustment of the final sample in terms of volume and concentration.   On the other hand, there are many class or group determinations which depend upon colorimetric methods, and these are often used for samples of highly complex composition.   In some of these instances it has been very difficult to evaluate isolation procedures in terms of specific compounds or to estimate individual components with adequate precision.   When a satisfactory gas chromatographic procedure has been developed for members of a steroid group, it is usually possible to reexamine isolation procedures.   For example, procedures for the isolation of urinary steroids may now be reviewed through the use of gas chromatographic methods.   The chief problem in this respect is to determine that peaks in the recorder record which are taken to represent pure compounds are in fact due to a single component, and to establish the gas chromatographic conditions needed for quantitative work.

PROBLEMS ARISING FROM THE COLUMN AND DETECTION SYSTEMS

Two problems involving detector and column properties require consideration. All ionization detection systems have a relatively low upper limit for the linear range, and it is necessary to determine both the limit of sensitivity and the upper limit of linearity for any proposed condition of operation. The sensitivity limit (defined here as a signal five times the nose level) is usually around 0.01 μg. for argon ionization detection systems when a Ra-226 source is used with an imposed voltage of 600–800. This may be extended downward under special conditions. The upper limit of the linear range depends very much upon the characteristics of both the detector and the column. Values of 30–50 μg. or more for a single component are often found. Since the amount of a single component in an estimation rarely exceeds a few micrograms, there is usually no danger of exceeding the linear range under these conditions.

These estimates are valid only when highly thermostable phases are used. In earlier work in gas chromatography, it was a common practice to find that ionization detection systems were overloaded by excessive column bleed before the sample was applied, and under these circumstances it was difficult or impossible to carry out quantitative studies.

It is known that ionization detection systems do not invariably show the same response to different classes of organic compounds. An extreme example of this behavior lies in the responses seen with an argon detection system for compounds which have an extremely high electron affinity coefficient. Under some circumstances a very small signal or an inverted signal may be obtained. For most steroids this effect is not present, but yet the detector responses seen in practice are not identical. This problem was studied by Sweeley and Chang (48), and it was found that the response obtained for polyfunctional steroids was lower than that obtained with hydrocarbons of the steroid group. Estriol and methyl cholate show very low responses, and the work of Sweeley and Chang contains additional examples of compounds showing this effect. This result was interpreted as being due to differences in detector response based on the structure of the steroid; the decreased response may also be due wholly or in part to irreversible absorption or decomposition of polyfunctional steroids by the column. When this phenomenon occurs, it is usually best to turn to the preparation of derivatives which are less polar and which have more satisfactory properties in gas chromatographic separation conditions. For example, it has been found that the trimethylsilyl ethers of the major human urinary estrogens and of urinary 17-ketosteroids show equal responses on a mass basis within each group when an argon detection system is used. In separate studies (26) it may be shown that the limit of sensitivity for these derivatives is about 0.01 μg. It is evident that the loss by decomposition or by irreversible absorption is below this level, and as might be expected from this degree of stability it is usually found that trimethylsilyl ethers give separations which do not show trailing effects and which resemble separations of hydrocarbons. It has also been found that acetyl derivatives are satisfactory for analytical separations of estrogens, as described by Wotiz and Martin (65,66). These examples suggest that when a marked lowering of the detector response is observed for a group of steroids, it is desirable to turn to the use of thermostable and less polar derivatives. The origin of these effects can be studied in detail only when a reference detection system, whose response is unaffected by changes in structure of the compounds under study, becomes generally available.

CONVERSION OF DETECTOR RESPONSE TO ANALYTICAL DATA

Much analytical work is carried out by measurement of peak areas on recorder chart records. It is usually assumed that any recorder will provide an accurate and useful record under all circumstances, but this is not entirely correct. Reference mixtures should be used to determine the optimum chart speed for the recorder and for the conditions of the separation, and the precision of the method of calculation should be determined. It is the usual practice to calculate peak areas from the product of the height and the width at half height of a peak. Other methods of calculation include triangulation and the use of planimeter readings. Electronic integration methods may ultimately supplant these methods, but at the present time the usual procedure is to make chart measurements by hand for each component under study.

It is possible to carry out analytical work through the use of samples of measured volume, but when highest precision is required the use of an internal standard is to be recommended. The sample size should be kept constant throughout an analytical study in order to maintain reproducible retention times.

Numerous examples of quantitative separations of steroids have been published. Difficulties in repeating published work are often due to the use of unsatisfactory columns.

EXAMPLE OF APPLICATION TO URINARY 17-KETOSTEROIDS

A practical example of a problem in quantification is presented by the determination of the major human urinary 17-ketosteroids. Two gas chromatographic procedures have been described for this purpose. The method of Haahti, VandenHeuvel, and Horning (21) required the use of two columns (SE-30 and NGS), and the free 17-ketosteroids were used. A second procedure was developed by VandenHeuvel, Creech, and Horning (52); the trimethylsilyl ethers of the 17-ketosteroids were used and the separation was carried out with an NGS or CNSi column. Cholesterol methyl ether may be used as an internal standard in the first determination, and β-sitosterol may be used as an internal standard in the second (26). The results of a comparison of the two procedures when applied to a mixture containing all three components in approximately equal amount is shown in Table III. Both methods give satisfactory results. When the trimethylsilyl ether procedure was applied to the analysis of urinary samples, the precision was satisfactory. Table IV shows the

TABLE III

Comparison of Composition Data for a Mixture of Three 17-Ketosteroids by Two Gas Chromatographic Methods

Compound, calc. %	Free steroids[a]	Trimethylsilyl ethers[b]
Androsterone, 37.8%	36.7%	38.8%
Etiocholanolone, 36.2%	37.8%	35.0%
Dehydroisoandrosterone, 26.0%	25.5%	26.2%

[a] Average of three determinations by the method of Haahti, VandenHeuvel, and Horning (21).

[b] Average of three determinations by the method of VandenHeuvel, Creech, and Horning (52).

TABLE IV

Daily Excretion Values[a] for 17-Ketosteroids and Pregnanediol
(Present as glucuronosides or sulfates)

	Glucuronosides (mg./24 hr.)		
Replicate	Pregnanediol	Androsterone	Etiocholanolone
1	0.6	1.4	6.5
2	0.6	1.5	6.5
3	0.6	1.4	6.6
4	0.6	1.4	6.7

	Sulfates (mg./24 hr.)		
Replicate	Androsterone	Etiocholanolone	Dehydro-isoandrosterone
1	0.7	Trace[b]	1.3
2	0.8	Trace	1.1
3	0.7	Trace	1.2
4	0.8	Trace	1.3

[a] A sample of normal male urine was used.
[b] "Trace" is less than 0.1 mg./24 hr.

results of replicate analyses for steroids present as glucuronosides and for those present as sulfates. The glucuronic acid-conjugated steroids were extracted after hydrolysis with β-glucuronidase of bacterial origin (Sigma), and the sulfate-conjugated steroids were extracted continuously during hydrolysis at pH 1 and at room temperature. Pregnanediol was estimated at the same time.

VIII. APPLICATIONS

1. Sterols

Sterols may be separated and estimated under a variety of circumstances. If the structural differences between the components are due to different carbon content, the sterols may usually be separated with a nonselective phase. If the differences in structure are due to varying degrees of unsaturation, leading to differences in molecular shape, a separation may usually also be achieved with a nonselective phase. For example, the sitosterol separation shown in Figure 13, and the cholesterol–desmosterol separation shown in Figure 16 were carried out with an SE-30 phase. When the differences in structure

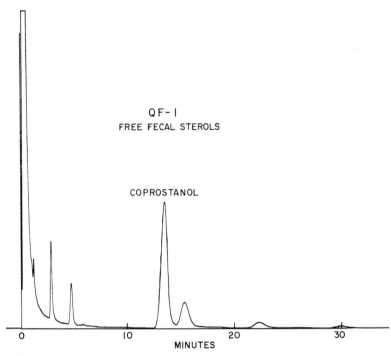

Fig. 25. Gas chromatographic separation of a sample of human fecal sterols. Column conditions: 6 ft. × 4 mm. glass column; 1% fluoralkyl silicone QF-1 on 100–140 mesh Gas Chrom P; 195°; 17 p.s.i.

involve positional or stereochemical isomerism, a selective phase may be required.   For purposes of identification, it is, of course, best to use both selective and nonselective phases.

A number of examples of sterol separations of mixtures of biologic origin have been described.   The work of Holmes and Stack (23) and Kritchevsky and Holmes (23) on the intermediates in cholesterol biosynthesis and of Wilson (63) on rat fecal sterols are examples of this kind.   It is also possible to use a gas chromatographic procedure for the direct determination of cholesterol; this was demonstrated by O'Neill and Gershbein (44).   Algae sterols were studied by Tsudi et al. (50).   Gower and Haslewood (17) studied the biosynthesis of 16-androstene-3α-ol in testicular tissue; the sterol was isolated by gas chromatographic methods, and these were investigated by Baker and Gower (4).

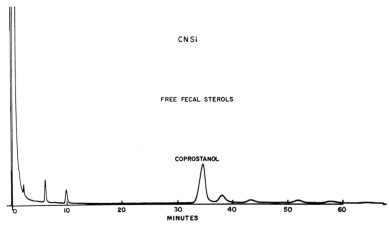

Fig. 26. Gas chromatographic separation of the same sample of human fecal sterols as in Figure 25. Column conditions: 9 ft. × 4 mm. glass column; 2% 65 mole-% cyanoethyl methyl silicone CNSi on 100–140 mesh Gas Chrom P; 205°; 22 p.s.i.

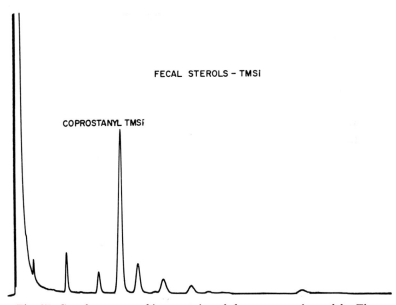

Fig. 27. Gas chromatographic separation of the same sample used for Figures 25 and 26 after conversion to the trimethylsilyl ether derivatives. Column conditions: same as in Figure 26.

It may be helpful for purposes of identification or estimation to convert sterols into suitable derivatives. Trifluoracetyl esters (59) are excellent in identification work and trimethylsilyl ethers (38,39) are particularly satisfactory in quantitative work. A separation of human fecal sterols with CNSi and QF-1 columns is shown in Figures 25 and 26. While these conditions can be used for quantitative studies, it may be more satisfactory to convert the sterols to tri-methylsilyl ethers before chromatography when a high degree of precision is required. Figure 27 shows the separation of the same sample used for Figures 25 and 26 after conversion to the trimethyl-silyl ethers; the phase was CNSi. The separation of trimethylsilyl ethers with a selective phase (CNSi or NGS are particularly ap-propriate) provides a very satisfactory method for work with sterol mixtures from human tissues (25).

2. Urinary 17-Ketosteroids

Urinary 17-ketosteroids may be separated and estimated in several ways. The problem has been studied most thoroughly for the three

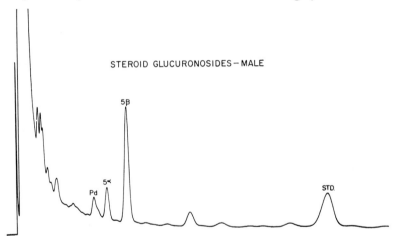

Fig. 28. Gas chromatographic separation of trimethylsilyl ethers of human male urinary steroids occurring as glucuronosides. The steroids were obtained by hydrolysis with bacterial glucuronidase. The compounds shown are pregnanediol (Pd), androsterone (5α), etiocholanolone (5β), and β-sitosterol (STD). Column conditions: 12 ft. × 4 mm. glass column; 2% 65 mole-% cyanoethyl methyl silicone CMSi on 80–100 mesh Gas Chrom P; 220°; Time to internal standard, 25 min. The internal standard was added before formation of the derivatives in order to permit calculations of daily excretion rates.

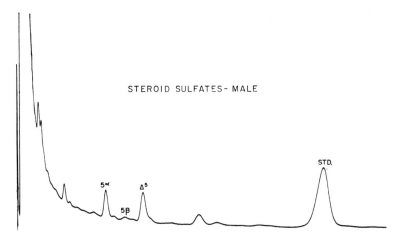

Fig. 29. Gas chromatographic separation of trimethylsilyl ethers of human male urinary steroids occurring as sulfates. The steroid sample was obtained by continuous ether extraction at pH 1. The compounds shown are androsterone (5α), etiocholanolone (5β), dehydroisoandrosterone (Δ⁵), and β-sitosterol (STD) added as an internal standard. The column conditions were the same as for Figure 28.

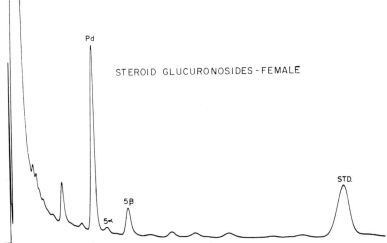

Fig. 30. Gas chromatographic separation of trimethylsilyl ethers of human female urinary steroids occurring as glucuronosides. The steroid sample was obtained in the same way as that shown in Figure 28, and the conditions of separation were also the same. The compounds shown are pregnanediol (Pd), androsterone (5α), etiocholanolone (5β), and β-sitosterol (STD) added as an internal standard.

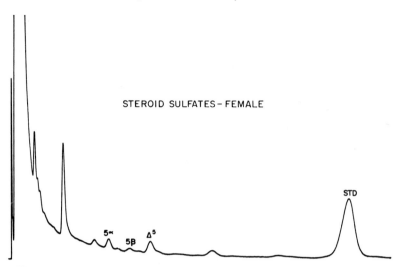

Fig. 31. Gas chromatographic separation of trimethylsilyl ethers of human female urinary steroids occurring as sulfates. The method of isolation of the sample and the conditions of the separation were the same as those used for Figure 29. The compounds shown are androsterone (5α), etiocholanolone (5β), dehydroisoandrosterone (Δ^5), and β-sitosterol (STD) added as an internal standard.

major 17-ketosteroids found as human excretion products: androsterone, etiocholanolone, and dehydroisoandrosterone. Individual steroids may be identified by their characteristic behavior with both selective and nonselective phases, and a method for determining the three major steroids was developed by Haahti et al. (21). This procedure rested upon the use of two columns with different phases. The procedure was satisfactory for much work, and it was used by Cooper and Creech (12) in a study of excretion patterns in examples of steroid endocrine abnormalities. However, it is clear that a procedure which would permit the separation of each component in a single run, would be more satisfactory, and for this reason a different method was developed by VandenHeuvel et al. (52). This was based upon the use of trimethylsilyl ethers and Figures 28 to 31 show examples of applications of this procedure. An internal standard (β-sitosterol which is converted to the trimethylsilyl ether) was introduced for purposes of quantification. This procedure may be used for determining a total 17-ketosteroid value (expressed as the sum of the three major components) and it may also be used to determine the amount of each steroid excreted as the sulfate or glucuronoside as indicated in the figures.

3. Pregnanediol and Progesterone

Progesterone and its metabolites, including pregnanediol, may be separated and estimated in several ways. Steroids of the pregnane group containing two or three functional groups may be separated readily with selective or nonselective phases, depending upon the nature of the mixture. For example, Figure 14 illustrates the separating ability of a QF-1 phase for a group of 3,20-substituted-5α-pregnanes. The problem of estimation is generally concerned with urinary or tissue determinations, and in these instances two courses are open. It is possible to determine progesterone and pregnanediol by a direct separation procedure; this has been established by Turner and his associates (51). For the determination of small amounts of pregnanediol, it is perhaps best to convert the mixture of sterols to trimethylsilyl ether derivatives. Pregnanediol may be estimated in urine according to the method illustrated in Figures 28 and 30. These methods may be useful in pregnancy studies.

4. Estrogens

Estrogen separations were first described by VandenHeuvel et al. (61). The identification of individual estrogens may be accomplished through the use of both selective and nonselective phases. A special problem, however, is presented by the polyfunctional steroids of this group. Estradiol and estriol, for example, are subject to partial decomposition or irreversible absorption on gas chromatographic columns. This effect is evident in Figure 22, and when quantitative studies are undertaken it is best to convert estrogens to derivatives. Acetates and trimethylsilyl ethers have been used for this purpose.

Wotiz and Martin (65,66) advocated the use of estrogen acetates in studies of human pregnancy urine. These esters are stable and they can be separated readily, but it is usually necessary to choose between a long retention time for a determination including estriol triacetate, or to use a high temperature.

Trimethylsilyl ether derivatives are particularly satisfactory for the separation and estimation of estrogens. This method was developed (39) following preliminary investigation of the properties of trimethylsilyl ethers in steroid separations (38).   The procedure may be used in studies of human estrogen excretion during pregnancy.

Synthetic estrogens of the diethylstilbesterol type have been separated and estimated by gas chromatographic procedures by McGregor et al. (40).

5. Adrenocortical Hormones

It is not possible to carry out a direct separation of all the known adrenocortical steroid hormones by gas chromatography.   Hormones of this group containing the 17α-hydroxyl group (cortisol, cortisone, and cortexolone) undergo loss the side chain when carried through a gas chromatographic separation condition.   The products are the

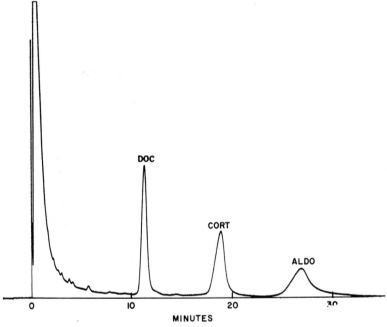

Fig. 32. Gas chromatographic separation of a mixture of adrenocortical hormones following periodate oxidation and treatment with diazomethane.   The derivatives are the methyl esters of 4-androstene-3-one-17β-carboxylic acid (DOC); the methyl ester of 4-androstene-3,11-dione-17α-ol-17β-carboxylic acid (CORT); and the hemiacetal-lactone from 4-androstene-3-one-11β-ol-18-al-17β-carboxylic acid (ALDO).   Column conditions: 6 ft. × 4 mm. glass column;   1% methyl silicone SE-30 on 100–140 mesh Gas Chrom P;   205°;   18 p.s.i.

corresponding 17-ketosteroids; this was demonstrated by Vanden-Heuvel and Horning (57). The inference in the work of Chen and Lantz (10) that cortisol could be subjected to gas chromatographic conditions without change is not correct. A number of derivatives of the steroid hormones have excellent gas chromatographic properties. Merits (42) proposed that adrenocortical hormones be converted to the corresponding 17β-carbomethoxy compounds by a reaction sequence involving periodate oxidation and treatment with diazomethane to form the methyl ester. This procedure gives excellent results for the major adrenocortical steroids. Aldosterone is converted to a hemiacetallactone by periodate oxidation. The separation of a mixture of these derivatives is demonstrated for three examples in Figure 32. The phase was SE-30 and the compounds used for illustration are the methyl ester of 4-androstene-3-one-17β-carboxylic acid (from deoxycorticosterone), the methyl ester of 4-androstene-3,11-dione-17α-ol-17β-carboxylic acid (from cortisone), and the hemiacetal-lactone of 4-androstene-3-one-11β-ol-18-al-17β-carboxylic acid (from aldosterone). The quantitative aspects of this procedure are under investigation in several laboratories.

The bis-methylenedioxy derivative of cortisone is stable to gas chromatographic conditions, and it is possible that derivatives of this kind may also be useful in studies of the separation of adrenocortical hormones (25).

It has been reported by Wotiz, et al. (67) that the 18,21-diacetate of aldosterone can be carried through a gas chromatographic condition without change. However, Kliman and Foster (30) found that the product obtained after gas chromatography was not aldosterone diacetate but a product of thermal alteration which had lost one acetyl group.

6. Bile Acids

Bile acid methyl esters may be separated by gas chromatography with a nonselective phase or a phase which has very little selective retention effects for hydroxyl groups. The first demonstration of a bile acid separation was by VandenHeuvel et al. (61). The separation problem was studied, with a larger group of bile acids, by Sjövall and co-workers (47), who recommended the use of a methyl phenyl siloxane polymer (20 and 35 mole-% phenyl) as a liquid phase. Additional studies were made by Blomstrand (7), who used area correction

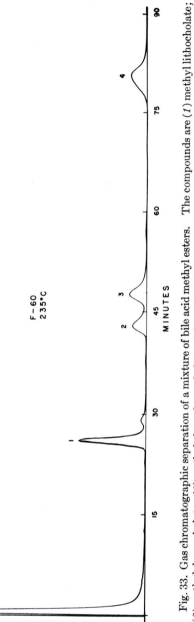

Fig. 33. Gas chromatographic separation of a mixture of bile acid methyl esters. The compounds are (1) methyl lithocholate; (2) methyl deoxycholate; (3) methyl chenodeoxycholate; (4) methyl cholate. Column conditions: 6 ft. × 4 mm. glass column; 2% methyl p-chlorophenyl silicone F-60 on 100–140 mesh Gas Chrom P; 235°; 21 p.s.i.

factors for quantitative work, and by Holmes and Stack (23) (SE-52 column).

The separation of bile acid methyl esters for purposes of identification can be carried out by extensions of present methods. The quantitative determination of compounds of this class is difficult because of increasing loss of the esters on the column with increasing degree of hydroxyl-substitution. Methyl cholate, for example, undergoes extensive loss by absorption or decomposition under gas chromatographic conditions. In order to reduce the polarity of these steroids, with a view to obtaining both shorter retention times and decreasing the loss on the column, VandenHeuvel et al. (59) prepared the trifluoracetoxy derivatives of bile acid methyl esters. Although trifluoracetyl esters may undergo thermal elimination of the ester group (62), the bile acid derivatives were stable under the conditions employed. Further studies of derivatives are needed in order to establish a suitable procedure involving quantitative recovery from the chromatographic column.

Figure 33 shows the separation of four common bile acids as methyl esters with an F-60 column. The fact that methyl cholate is partially lost during the separation is perhaps less surprising than the fact that gas chromatographic procedures can be used for the identification of these highly polar steroids.

7. Vitamins D

Sterols of the vitamin D group are converted by thermal cyclization to a mixture of tetracyclic sterols; the products of cyclization of vitamin D_2 are pyrocalciferol and isopyrocalciferol. The gas chromatographic result when a sample of vitamin D_2 is studied is shown in Figure 34; this illustration is from the work of Ziffer, et al. (68). Although the parent compound is not obtained, the appearance of the two derived sterols may be taken as evidence for the presence in the original mixture of the vitamin. (This is true if the mixture is of biologic origin, since pyrocalciferol and isopyrocalciferol do not occur naturally. If these components are present in the original mixture, this procedure is, of course, inapplicable.)

This method, while suitable for the identification of the vitamins D (vitamin D_3 undergoes a similar reaction) has not yet been evaluated for quantitative work. It is possible that derivatives of the parent

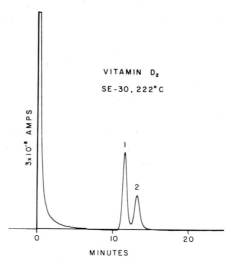

Fig. 34. Gas chromatographic behavior of vitamin D₂, showing (*1*) pyrocalciferol and (*2*) isopyrocalciferol. Column conditions: 6 ft. × 4 mm. glass column; 0.75% methyl silicone SE-30 on 100–140 mesh Gas Chrom P; 222°; 19 p.s.i.

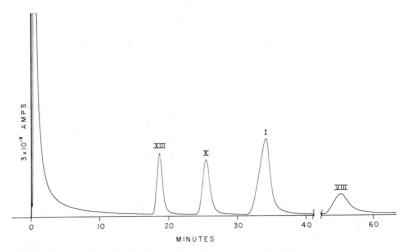

Fig. 35. Gas chromatographic separation of a mixture of steroidal amines. The compounds are solanidane-3-one (XIII); C-25L, 22-isosolanidane-3-one (X); tomatidine (I); tetrahydrosolasodine (VIII). Column conditions: 6 ft. × 4 mm. glass column; 1% methyl silicone SF-96 on 100–140 mesh Gas Chrom P; 222°; 18 p.s.i.

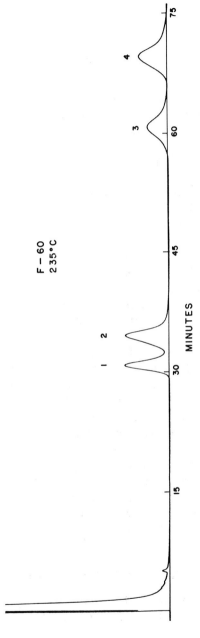

Fig. 36. Gas chromatographic separation of a mixture of sapogenins. The compounds are (1) smilagenin, (2) tigogenin, (3) gitogenin, (4) chlorogenin. Column conditions: 6 ft. × 4 mm. glass column; 2% methyl p-chlorophenyl silicone F-60 on 100–140 mesh Gas Chrom P; 245°; 21 p.s.i.

sterols might be more satisfactory in this connection than the products of thermal reaction.

8. Other Steroids

Steroidal amines may be separated through use of a nonselective phase. Figure 35 shows the separation of a series of steroidal amines according to the work of VandenHeuvel et al. (58). Quantitative aspects of the separation have not been studied. At the present time the method is chiefly useful for purposes of identification and qualitative examination of reaction mixtures or samples isolated from natural sources.

Sapogenins may be separated in the same way (56). The ketal group presents no special problem in a gas chromatographic analysis and it is possible that additional conditions for the separation of these compounds may be found. Figure 36 illustrates the separation of representative sapogenins. The procedure is used largely for identification purposes and for the qualitative examination of reaction mixtures and mixtures of natural origin.

Several investigations of the steroids of the digitalis and toad poison groups have been carried out, but the results of these investigations are not yet available for publication. Evidence of decomposition or alteration in structure is frequently seen, and it may be necessary to convert the compounds to derivatives before attempting a separation.

A variety of synthetic steroids have been carried through gas chromatographic conditions. For example, the presence of a fluorine atom does not usually alter the gas chromatographic properties of a steroid in a marked way, although the retention time will be different from that of the parent steroid. 17-Ethynyl compounds are usually stable under gas chromatographic conditions, and many steroid degradation products are amenable to separation or estimation by gas chromatographic procedures. In general, the same methods that are used for the study of steroids may be used in work with steroid degradation products and compounds prepared through elaboration of the steroid nucleus.

IX. IDENTIFICATION OF STEROIDS

The use of gas chromatographic techniques for the identification of steroids, and for obtaining structural information about steroids of unknown structure, provides a new approach to steroid isolation and identification problems that has great potential value. At the present time there is a widespread belief that these techniques have very limited application in such work, in part because of experimental shortcomings, and in part because only a few structural correlations have been established so far. The problems associated with structural and identification work are discussed in the following sections.

RETENTION TIMES AND STEROID NUMBERS

It is a common experience in gas chromatographic work to find that relative retention times cannot be duplicated in interlaboratory comparisons. The magnitude of the values is rarely different, but variations of from 10 to 20% are common, and this is currently regarded as a reflection of experimental difficulties which are not likely to be overcome very soon. Day-to-day variations are also seen in some laboratories, and this effect has contributed to the view that retention time data are inherently of little value for the deduction of structural information and possibly for identification purposes. The problems present in this situation were studied by VandenHeuvel and Horning (55). It was found that by using suitable techniques, and the same instrument, that the relative retention time of a typical steroid (cholesterol) could be duplicated to better than 1% with a thin-film (1%) SE-30 column over a period of five days with intervening changes in temperature and flow rate. A more detailed investigation indicated that small variations in flow rate led to less than 1% variation in relative retention time for an SE-30 column; with a selective phase (CNSi) the variation was less than 2%. The effect of variation in the amount of phase was studied, and it was found that an increase in phase from 2% to 3% led to only small changes in the relative retention times for representative steroids. The greatest variation was observed for compounds with very short retention times. The effect of temperature change, on the other hand, was found to be a marked one. Since different kinds of instruments and different instruments of a single design have been found to vary considerably in actual temperature of the column compartment when the same instrumental temperature settings are employed, this circumstance is perhaps the chief cause of lack of reproducibility of relative retention time data.

Problems arising from these effects have been resolved in major part by the development of a "steroid number" concept following the work of Woodford and Van Gent (64) in the fatty acid field.   These values are obtained by carrying out three determinations of retention times.   Androstane and cholestane are used as reference compounds, and the retention time for the steroid under study is determined with the same column and under the same conditions of temperature and flow rate as those used for androstane and cholestane.   A plot of log relative retention time against carbon content or steroid number is then made; androstane and cholestane have steroid numbers of 19 and 27, respectively.   The steroid number of the compound is de-

TABLE V

Determination of Steroid Number at Three Different Temperatures with a Nonselective Phase (SE-30)[a]

	RRT[b]	Steroid number
Temperature: 195°		
Androstane	0.07	
Androstane-17-one	0.15	21.2
5α-Pregnane-3,20-dione	0.61	25.5
Cholestane	1.00	
Cholestanyl methyl ether	1.99	29.1
Temperature: 205°		
Androstane	0.08	
Androstane-17-one	0.17	21.2
5α-Pregnane-3,20-dione	0.63	25.5
Cholestane	1.00	
Cholestanyl methyl ether	1.90	29.1
Temperature: 215°		
Androstane	0.10	
Androstane-17-one	0.19	21.3
5α-Pregnane-3,20-dione	0.66	25.6
Cholestane	1.00	
Cholestanyl methyl ether	1.83	29.2

[a] Conditions: 6 ft. × 4 mm. glass U-tube; 1% SE-30 on 100–120 mesh Gas-Chrom P; 20 p.s.i.   Cholestane times: at 195°, 33.0 min.; at 205°, 20.0 min.; at 215°, 12.7 min.

[b] Retention time relative to cholestane.

termined by the intercept along the carbon content scale, as described in Figure 2. These values are determined with a nonselective phase and the work so far has been carried out with SE-30. Table V shows the relative independence of the steroid number with respect to temperature changes for a group of representative steroids. It may be seen that the variation in steroid number is less than 1% over a temperature range of 20°.

Steroid numbers for a variety of compounds are in Table VI. These values may have greater usefulness than relative retention times in interlaboratory comparison of data.

The hypothesis that steroids, when separated by gas chromatography, have retention time relationships that may be expressed in additive form, in terms of functional group values, on a logarithmic basis was studied by Knights and Thomas (31). Following Bate-Smith and Westall (5), Knights and Thomas proposed that equations

$$R_M = \log\left(\frac{1}{R_f} - 1\right)$$

where

$$t_R = t\left(\frac{1}{R_f} - 1\right)$$

and

$$\log r = \sum \Delta R_{Mg} + \log r_N$$

be used in gas chromatographic work by analogy with paper chromatographic separations. A detailed study of these relationships was made by Bush (9) for steroid separations by paper chromatography, and the Bush monograph contains an excellent discussion of basic principles and of problems involved in correlations of steroid structure and behavior in partition chromatography. Clayton's proposals (11) for retention time correlations are based on the same type of logarithmic relationship.

The work of Knights and Thomas (31) and Clayton's observations (11) are valuable in establishing the fact that the basic principles of partition chromatography, as developed earlier for steroid separations by paper partition chromatography, are valid for the gas chromatographic separation of steroids. This conclusion is an important one.

In practice, difficulties may arise when these principles are applied. Temperature differences lead to wide variations in relative retention times, and correlations based on literature data are difficult because of variations in instrument design with regard to the placing of thermocouples and in the control of column compartment temperatures. Further, while the principles apply both to the use of selective phases and nonselective phases, the approach of Knights and Thomas and of Clayton was based on the use of selective phases. A nonselective phase provides less information about the positional and stereochemical arrangement of substituents, but correlations based on the use of a nonselective phase may be very valuable because the molecular size can be defined rather exactly in this way.

TABLE VI

Steroid Numbers and Relative Retention Times for Representative Steroids Determined at 211° with an SE-30 Phase[a]

Steroid	RRT[b]	Steroid number (SN)
Androstane-17-one	0.18	21.3
Androstane-3,17-dione	0.39	23.9
4-Androstene-3,17-dione	0.48	24.6
4-Androstene-17β-ol-3-one	0.49	24.7
Androstane-3,16-dione	0.40	23.9
4-Androstene-3,16-dione	0.48	24.6
4-Androstene-3,11,17-trione	0.57	25.1
4-Androstene-11α-ol-3,17-dione	0.85	26.5
4-Androstene-11β-ol-3,17-dione	0.81	26.3
19-Nor-4-androstene-3,17-dione	0.38	23.8
Androstane-3β,17β-diol	0.38	23.8
Androstane-3α,17β-diol	0.37	23.7
Androstane-3β-ol-17-one	0.37	23.7
Androstane-3α-ol-17-one	0.36	23.6
5-Androstene-3β,17β-diol	0.37	23.7
5-Androstene-3β-ol-17-one	0.36	23.6
17α-Methyl-5-androstene-3β,17β-diol	0.41	24.1
Androstane-3β,16β-diol	0.37	23.7
Estrone	0.46	24.4
Estradiol	0.48	24.6
Equilenin	0.61	25.4
Pregnane-3,20-dione	0.60	25.3
Pregnane-21-ol-3,20-dione	1.10	27.4
5α-Pregnane-3,20-dione	0.66	25.6

The steroid number approach of VandenHeuvel and Horning (55) is not different in principle, but it has several inherent advantages. The relative independence of steroid numbers to temperature variations is helpful in interlaboratory use of gas chromatographic data. An experimentally determinated steroid number, obtained with a nonselective phase, may be expressed as a summation of values relating to the carbon content of the steroid skeleton and values characteristic of the functional groups of the steroid. The equation

$$SN = S + F_1 \ldots + F_n$$

will be useful and valid to the extent that the values $F_1 \ldots F_n$ are in fact found to be characteristic of functional groups commonly occurring in steroids. Table VII contains the steroid number values

TABLE VI (*continued*)

Steroid	RRT[b]	Steroid number (SN)
5α-Pregnane-3,11,20-trione	0.89	26.7
5α-Pregnane-3β,20α-diol	0.66	25.6
5α-Pregnane-3β,20β-diol	0.62	25.4
5α-Pregnane-20β-ol-3-one	0.66	25.6
5α-Pregnane-3β-ol-20-one	0.62	25.4
5α-Pregnane-3β-ol-11,20-dione	0.86	26.6
4-Pregnene-3,20-dione	0.78	26.2
Cholestanol	2.00	29.4
Epicholestanol	1.98	29.4
Coprostanol	1.80	29.1
Cholestane-3-one	2.14	29.6
4-Cholestene-3-one	2.64	30.3
Cholestanyl acetate	3.12	30.9
Cholestanyl methyl ether	1.88	29.2
Cholestanyl trifluoroacetate	1.66	28.8
Cholestanyl trimethylsilyl ether	2.61	30.3
Tigogenin	2.71	30.5
Solanidane-3β-ol	2.24	29.8
7-Cholestene-3β-ol	2.21	29.8
Desmosterol	2.12	29.6
Cholesterol	1.95	29.3

[a] Conditions: Same as for Table V; 211°; cholestane time, 13.5 min.
[b] Retention time relative to cholestane.

TABLE VII

Steroid Number Contributions for Representative Functional Groups Determined with a Nonselective Phase (SE-30)

Functional group	Steroid parent[a]	Steroid number (F)[b]
Δ^5	(Cholestanol/cholesterol)	0.1
Δ^5	(Cholestane/Δ^5-cholestene)	0.0
Δ^7	(Cholestanol/7-cholestene-3β-ol)	0.4
Δ^{24}	(Cholesterol/desmosterol)	0.3
3-one	(Androstane)	2.6
3-one	(5α-Pregnane)	2.6
3-one	(Cholestane)	2.6
3-one-Δ^4	(Androstane)	3.3
3-one-Δ^4	(Cholestane)	3.3
11-one	(Δ^4-Androstene)	0.5
11-one	(5α-Pregnane)	1.1
16-one	(Androstane)	2.3
17-one	(Androstane)	2.3
20-one	(5α-Pregnane)	2.0
3α-ol (ax)	(Androstane)	2.3
3β-ol (eq)	(Androstane)	2.4
3β-ol (eq)	(5α-Pregnane)	2.4
3β-ol (eq)	(Cholestane)	2.4
11α-ol (eq)	(Androstane)	1.9
11β-ol (ax)	(Androstane)	1.7
16β-ol	(Androstane)	2.3
17β-ol (secondary)	(Androstane)	2.4
17β-ol (tertiary)	(17α-Methylandrostane)	1.7
20α-ol	(5α-Pregnane)	2.2
20β-ol	(5α-Pregnane)	2.0
21-ol	(5α-Pregnane)	2.1
Aromatic B ring	(Estrone/equilenin)	1.0
N	(Solanidane-3β-ol)	0.4
Spiroketal	(Tigogenin)	1.1
3β-Trifluoroacetoxy (eq)	(Cholestane)	1.8
3β-Methoxy (eq)	(Cholestane)	2.2
3α-Trimethylsilyloxy (ax)	(Cholestane)	2.5
3β-Trimethylsilyloxy (eq)	(Cholestane)	3.3
3β-Acetoxy (eq)	(Cholestane)	3.9
A/B *cis*	(Coprostane/cholestane)	−0.2
A/B *cis*	(Coprostanol/cholestanol)	−0.3

[a] Structure of the steroid nucleus for the reference compound used in the determination of the SN value.

[b] Determined with the column and conditions described in Table VI.

(F) for functional groups found in naturally occurring steroids and in derivatives which are frequently used in gas chromatographic work. It may be seen that there is a relatively high degree of constancy of functional group values. It is evident that an additive logarithmic relationship for relative retention times, or an additive relationship for steroid numbers, presupposes an absence of intramolecular interaction between functional groups, and unusual or unexpected steroid numbers should be examined to determine if intramolecular effects are involved.

An example of the way in which steroid numbers may be used in identification studies may be found in VandenHeuvel and Horning (55); Tables VI and VII are from this study.

STRUCTURAL CORRELATIONS (T-VALUES)

Structural differences in the steroid skeleton for a group of steroids leads to retention time changes that are much the same for both selective and nonselective phases. An extreme example of this effect is illustrated in Figure 37. i-Steroids have shorter retention times than the corresponding steroids with the usual tetracyclic structure, and

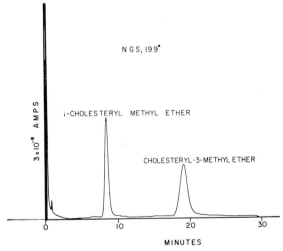

Fig. 37. Gas chromatographic separation of i-cholesteryl-6-methyl ether and cholesteryl-3-methyl ether illustrating the effect of molecular geometry upon gas chromatographic behavior. Column conditions: 6 ft. × 4 mm. glass column; 1% NGS on 100–140 mesh Gas Chrom P; 199°; 18 p.s.i.

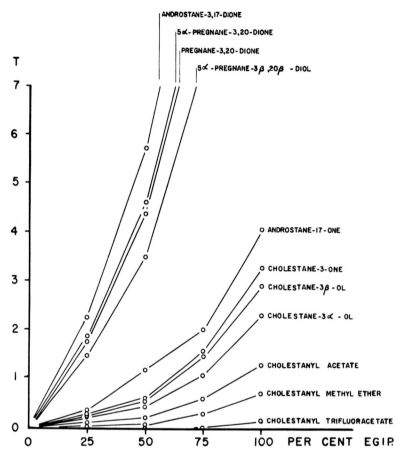

Fig. 38. Effect of polarity of the stationary phase on the retention times of several steroids given as relative to cholestane and SE-30 values (for definition of T, see p. 140). A marked selective retention effect may be observed for various functional groups. The liquid phase was a mixture of 25, 50, and 75% EGIP with SE-30; the 100% values are for EGIP alone.

this effect holds for both selective and nonselective phases. The observation that 5β-H steroids are eluted before the corresponding 5α-H steroids has been made in many laboratories. These effects can be measured in terms of steroid numbers. Correlations between the positional and stereochemical arrangement of functional groups

TABLE VIII

Values of T Determined at 211° for Representative Functional Groups with NGS and QF-1 Phases

Functional group	Steroid	NGS	QF-1
		\multicolumn{2}{c}{T Values}	
3-one	Cholestane-3-one	2.1	2.0
3-one-Δ^4	4-Cholestene-3-one	2.9	2.9
17-one	Androstane-17-one	2.5	2.6
3α-ol (ax)	Cholestane-3α-ol	1.9	0.4
3β-ol (eq)	Cholestane-3β-ol	2.2	0.7
3β-ol-Δ^5 (eq)	Cholesterol	2.5	0.6
3,17-dione	Androstane-3,17-dione	12.1	10.7
3,17-dione-Δ^4	4-Androstene-3,17-dione	15.6	13.5
3,20-dione (A/B cis)	Pregnane-3,20-dione	9.7	8.2
3,20-dione (A/B $trans$)	5α-Pregnane-3,20-dione	9.9	7.8
3β,17β-diol	Androstane-3β,17β-diol	11.8	2.5
3α,17β-diol	Androstane-3α,17β-diol	10.7	2.3
3β,17β-diol-Δ^5	5-Androstene-3β,17β-diol	12.5	2.3
3β,20β-diol	5α-Pregnane-3β,20β-diol	9.4	2.1
3α,20α-diol	5α-Pregnane-3α,20α-diol	10.6	2.5
3β-ol-17-one	Androstane-3β-ol-17-one	11.0	5.1
3α-ol-17-one	Androstane-3α-ol-17-one	10.0	4.4
3β-ol-17-one-Δ^5	5-Androstene-3β-ol-17-one	12.1	4.5
3β-ol-20-one	5α-Pregnane-3β-ol-20-one	9.5	3.8
17β-ol-3-one-Δ^4	4-Androstene-17β-ol-3-one	16.5	7.1
20β-ol-3-one	5α-Pregnane-20β-ol-3-one	10.6	4.6
3,17-dione-Δ^4-11β-ol	4-Androstene-11β-ol-3,17-dione	42.0	15.0
3,11,20-trione (A/B $trans$)	5α-Pregnane-3,11,20-trione	—	15.1
3-ol-17-one, A aromatic	Estrone	34.0	4.9
3-ol-17β-ol, A aromatic	Estradiol	37.2	2.5
3α-Trimethylsilyloxy (ax)	Epicholestanyl TMSi	−0.4	−0.2
3β-Trimethylsilyloxy (eq)	Cholestanyl TMSi	−0.2	−0.1
3β-Trifluoroacetoxy (eq)	Cholestanyl TFA	0.3	0.8
3β-Trifluoroacetoxy-Δ^5 (eq)	Cholesteryl TFA	0.3	0.7
3β-Methoxy (eq)	Cholestanyl ME	0.4	0.2
3β-Acetoxy (eq)	Cholestanyl acetate	0.8	0.7
A/B cis	5α- and Pregnane-3,20-dione	−0.2	0.4

and retention times require the use of selective phases, and for this purpose Haahti et al. (19) explored the use of T values.

The T value for a steroid may be expressed as

$$T = (t_s' - t_n')/t_n'$$

where the relative retention times are those observed with equal amounts of a selective phase and a nonselective phase when both are used at the same temperature. The effect of increasing the polarity of the selective phase on the retention times of several steroids is shown in Figure 38. It is clear that the behavior of the steroid with a specific selective phase will be dependent upon the number, kind, position, and stereochemical arrangement of the functional groups, and that the phases which are likely to be of greatest value include QF-1 and the polyesters (or CNSi). VandenHeuvel and Horning (55) used QF-1 and NGS, and a number of T values taken from this study are in Table VIII. These values are temperature dependent (55).

The number and the nature of the functional groups of a steroid can usually be deduced from SE-30 and QF-1 retention times; the difference in behavior between alcohols and ketones with QF-1 is particularly marked. Positional isomers usually have different retention times with a selective phase, and in general an increase in steric hindrance for the group leads to a drop in retention time. Equatorial and axial isomers of hydroxyl-substituted steroids follow this behavior; the equatorial isomer usually has a longer retention time than the corresponding axial compound. It is advisable to confirm experimental observations made with a QF-1 phase by repeating the T determination with an NGS phase. Structural conclusions from data obtained through the use of either phase should be in agreement.

Ways in which T values may be used are described by VandenHeuvel and Horning (55). These methods should not be regarded as leading to a proof of structure, but they may be employed to provide a tentative structural hypothesis that can be used as a starting point for the application of conventional structural studies. If an authentic sample is available which corresponds to the tentative structure, a direct gas chromatographic confirmation may be made.

X. PREPARATIVE SEPARATIONS

Much work has been done on the development of apparatus and techniques for preparative gas chromatography, and a number of instruments are available which have been designed for preparative work. However, the objective has been to attain a high capacity, and "preparative work" has come to mean the separation of relatively large amounts of volatile compounds through the use of conventional thick-film column packings with either large diameter columns or repetitive programming with analytical columns. At the present time this work has very little relevance to the problems encountered in steroid separations. It is frequently necessary to isolate small quantities, usually milligram or submilligram, of specific compounds from highly complex mixtures of biologic origin, and this problem requires high resolution but not high capacity. Procedures which are based on low resolution but high capacity have no significance in this connection. Further, conventional thick-film analytical columns which are useful for many separations with compounds of low molecular weight are not satisfactory in steroid work.

The use of thin-film column packings in steroid separations is now well established, and the possibility of using these columns for milligram-scale preparative separations was studied by Fales et al. (15). The specific problems which were investigated included those involved in sample injection and vaporization, column behavior under near overload or overload conditions, and sample collection. A 9 ft. × 12.4 mm. I.D. glass U-tube was used as the chromatographic column. Figure 39 shows the loss in column efficiency which occurs when the column diameter is increased. This effect has been noted in many laboratories, and while it is believed that columns of still greater diameter may be used effectively in preparative work, current experience suggests that relatively narrow columns should be used in steroid separations in order to attain column efficiencies of better than 1000 theoretical plates. It was also found in this investigation that temperature-programmed separations gave the same or better resolution than an isothermal condition when a nonselective phase (SE-30) was used. This result was helpful in permitting a study of rates of sample injection. No loss of column efficiency was found when the steroid sample in solution was injected over 15–20 seconds in an ordinary vaporizing zone. A high heat capacity "instan-

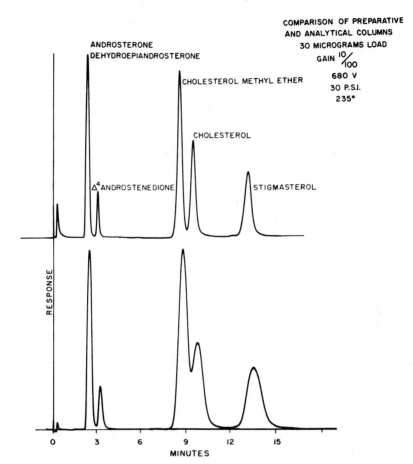

Fig. 39. Comparison of separations of a mixture of steroids obtained with the same column packing (0.75% SE-30 on 100–140 mesh Gas Chrom P) with 9 ft. × 4 mm. I.D. (top) and 9 ft. × 12.4 mm. I.D. (bottom) columns illustrating the effect of column diameter upon column efficiency. The conditions were chosen to give maximum efficiency for the larger diameter column.

taneous'' vaporizer was not needed, and this was very helpful both in simplifying the sample injection problem and in avoiding possible decomposition by excessive heating of the sample.

The behavior of a column under overload conditions was also studied. This is an undesirable circumstance in analytical work, since the column efficiency is decreased and the peak shape is dis-

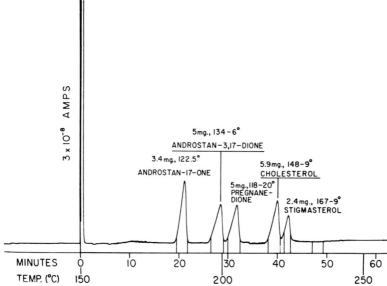

Fig. 40. Separation of a mixture of steroids with a preparative column (9 ft. ✕ 12.4 mm. I.D.). The times and temperatures for the temperature programmed (2.1°/min., 30 p.s.i.) procedure are indicated. The vertical lines indicate the "fraction cutting" operation. The amounts and melting points for each major fraction are shown. The identification of each component was completed by infrared spectra comparisons.

torted from the theoretical. However, thin-film columns have low overload points, and it is virtually a necessity to overload columns used in milligram-scale preparative work. Figure 40 shows this effect. In spite of the evident overload, the separation was still excellent for preparative purposes.

The collection of samples eluted from the column is particularly difficult in steroid work. Many steroids are relatively high melting solids, and when the gas stream is cooled a smoke-like fog is formed. This aerosol containing suspended solids presents a difficult problem in condensation. In many laboratories efforts have been made to develop electrostatic precipitators, and a variety of scrubbing devices have also been developed. From a theoretical point of view, the way to obtain condensation of the steroid is to introduce a component which will condense at the same time and provide sufficient material so that the aerosol represents only a transient phase in the precipitation process. In experiments carried out by Luukkainen and Fales and described in the paper by Fales et al. (15) it was found that the use of a glass U-tube chilled in liquid nitrogen gave excellent results in the collection of steroid samples. The effectiveness of the procedure may be due to the fact that part of the argon carrier gas stream is condensed, and the tubes contain liquid argon along with the organic compounds. The evaporation of the argon in each tube, without special precaution, provides each fraction as a solid adhering to the wall of the tube. The fact that organic solvents are not involved is a considerable aid in further identification work; physical methods of identification involving infrared and ultraviolet spectroscopy may be carried out directly with samples obtained in this way. It is usually also desirable to determine the composition of each fraction by analytical gas chromatography.

The melting points given in Figure 40 are those for the steroid fractions obtained directly and without further purification. The same technique may be used for the separation of alkaloids and other compounds of comparable structural complexity.

Current studies of milligram-scale separations indicate that best results are obtained with nonselective phases. This effect is due in part to the high degree of temperature stability of the silicones. The use of selective phases in preparative separations is equally possible, and the limiting factor at the present time lies in the decreased thermal stability of these phases. The development of phases with a higher degree of thermal stability will undoubtedly make it possible to carry out highly effective milligram-scale separations with a variety of phases. Fractions collected after a separation with a nonselective phase may in turn be submitted to separation with a selective phase, and this should make it possible to obtain small amounts of pure substances from highly complex mixtures in a matter of a few hours. It is also possible to convert mixtures to derivatives before carrying out preparative work, if this is considered desirable.

References

1. Ambrose, D. A., A. T. James, A. I. M. Keulemans, E. Kovats, H. Röck, C. Rouit, and F. H. Stross, in R. P. W. Scott, ed., *Gas Chromatography, 1960*, Butterworths, London, p. 423.
2. Ambrose, D. A., A. I. M. Keulemans, and J. H. Purnell, *Anal. Chem., 30* 1582 (1958).

3. Anders, M. W., and G. J. Mannering, *J. Chromatog.*, *7*, 258 (1962); Haahti, E. O. A., and W. J. A. VandenHeuvel, *Clin. Chem.*, *7*, 305 (1961); Vanden-Heuvel, W. J. A., E. O. A. Haahti, and E. C. Horning, *Clin. Chem.*, *8*, 351 (1962).
4. Baker, R. W. R., and D. B. Gower, *Nature*, *192*, 1074 (1961).
5. Bate-Smith, E. C., and R. G. Westall, *Biochim. Biophys. Acta*, *4*, 427 (1950).
6. Beerthuis, R. K., and J. H. Recourt, *Nature*, *186*, 372 (1960).
7. Blomstrand, R., *Proc. Soc. Exptl. Biol. Med.*, *107*, 126 (1961).
8. Brown, I., *Nature*, *188*, 1021 (1961).
9. Bush, I. E., *The Chromatography of Steroids*, Pergamon Press, Oxford, 1961, Chapters I, II, and V.
10. Chen, C., and C. D. Lantz, *Biochem. Biophys. Research Communications*, *3*, 182 (1960).
11. Clayton, R. B., *Biochemistry*, *1*, 357 (1962); *Nature*, *192*, 524 (1961); *190*, 1071 (1961).
12. Cooper, J. A., and B. G. Creech, *Anal. Biochem.*, *2*, 502 (1961).
13. Eddy, N. B., H. M. Fales, E. O. A. Haahti, P. F. Highet, E. C. Horning, E. L. May, and W. C. Wildman, *Series K of the Economic and Social Council of the United Nations Secretariat*, October, 1961; Fales, H. M., and J. J. Pisano, *Anal. Biochem.*, *3*, 337 (1962).
14. Eglinton, G., R. J. Hamilton, R. Hodges, and R. A. Raphael, *Chem. & Ind. (London)*, *1959*, 955.
15. Fales, H. M., E. O. A. Haahti, T. Luukkainen, W. J. A. VandenHeuvel, and E. C. Horning, *Anal. Biochem.*, *4*, 296 (1962).
16. Glueckauf, E., *Trans. Faraday Soc.*, *51*, 34 (1955).
17. Gower, D. B., and G. A. D. Haslewood, *J. Endocrinol.*, *23*, 253 (1961).
18. Haahti, E. O. A., and E. C. Horning, *Acta Chem. Scand.*, *15*, 930 (1961); Nicolaides, N., *J. Invest. Dermatol.*, *37*, 507 (1961).
19. Haahti, E. O. A., W. J. A. VandenHeuvel, and E. C. Horning, *Anal. Biochem.*, *2*, 344 (1961).
20. Haahti, E. O. A., W. J. A. VandenHeuvel, and E. C. Horning, *J. Org. Chem.*, *26*, 626 (1961).
21. Haahti, E. O. A., W. J. A. VandenHeuvel, and E. C. Horning, *Anal. Biochem.*, *2*, 182 (1961).
22. Hishta, C., J. P. Messerly, R. F. Reschke, D. H. Fredericks, and W. D. Cooke, *Anal. Chem.*, *32*, 880 (1960).
23. Holmes, W. L., and E. Stack, *Biochim. Biophys. Acta*, *56*, 163 (1962); Kritchevsky, D., and W. L. Holmes, *Biochem. Biophys. Research Communications*, *7*, 128 (1962).
24. Horning, E. C., E. A. Moscatelli, and C. C. Sweeley, *Chem. & Ind. (London)*, *1959*, 751.
25. Horning, E. C., and W. J. A. VandenHeuvel, unpublished results.
26. Horning, E. C., W. J. A. VandenHeuvel, and B. G. Creech, unpublished results.
27. Johnson, H. W., and F. H. Stross, *Anal. Chem.*, *30*, 1586 (1958).
28. Karmen, A., and R. L. Bowman, *Ann. N.Y. Acad. Sci.*, *72*, 714 (1959); *Proc. Instr. Soc. Am.*, *2*, 33 (1958).

29. Keulemans, A. I. M., *Gas Chromatography*, 2nd Ed., Reinhold, New York, 1959, p. 128.
30. Kliman, B., and D. W. Foster, *Anal. Biochem., 3*, 403 (1962).
31. Knights, B. A., and G. H. Thomas, *Nature, 194*, 833 (1962).
32. Lipsky, S. R., and R. A. Landowne, *Anal. Chem., 33*, 818 (1961).
33. Lloyd, H. A., H. M. Fales, P. F. Highet, W. J. A. VandenHeuvel, and W. C. Wildman, *J. Am. Chem. Soc., 82*, 3791 (1960).
34. Lovelock, J. E., *J. Chromatography, 1*, 35 (1958); *Nature, 181*, 1460 (1958); in R. P. W. Scott, ed., *Gas Chromatography, 1960*, Butterworths, London, p. 16.
35. Lovelock, J. E., *Anal. Chem., 33*, 162 (1961).
36. Lovelock, J. E., and N. L. Gregory, in N. Brenner, J. E. Callen, and M. D. Weiss, eds., *Gas Chromatography*, Academic Press, New York, 1962, p. 219.
37. Lovelock, J. E., P. G. Simmonds, and W. J. A. VandenHeuvel, unpublished results.
38. Luukkainen, T., W. J. A. VandenHeuvel, E. O. A. Haahti, and E. C. Horning, *Biochim. Biophys. Acta, 52*, 599 (1961).
39. Luukkainen, T., W. J. A. VandenHeuvel, and E. C. Horning, *Biochim. Biophys. Acta, 62*, 153 (1962).
40. McGregor, R. F., D. N. Ward, J. A. Cooper, and B. G. Creech, *Anal. Biochem., 2*, 441 (1961).
41. Martin, A. J. P., *Biochem. Soc. Symposia, 3*, 4 (1949); *Ann. Rev. Biochem., 19*, 517 (1950).
42. Merits, I., *J. Lipid Research, 3*, 126 (1962).
43. Nicolaides, N., *J. Chromatography, 4*, 496 (1960).
44. O'Neill, H. J., and L. L. Gershbein, *Anal. Chem., 33*, 182 (1961).
45. Pisano, J. J., W. J. A. VandenHeuvel, and E. C. Horning, *Biochem. Biophys. Research Communications, 7*, 82 (1962) (amino acids); Miles, H. T., and H. M. Fales, *Anal. Chem., 34*, 860 (1962) (nucleosides).
46. Peterson, M. L., and J. Hirsch, *J. Lipid Research, 1*, 132 (1960).
47. Sjövall, J., C. R. Meloni, and D. A. Turner, *J. Lipid Research, 2*, 317 (1961).
48. Sweeley, C. C., and Ta-Chuang Lo Chang, *Anal. Chem., 33*, 1860 (1961).
49. Sweeley, C. C., and E. C. Horning, *Nature, 187*, 144 (1960).
50. Tsudi, K., K. Sakae, and N. Ikekawa, *Chem. Pharm. Bull. (Tokyo), 9*, 835 (1961).
51. Turner, D. A., private communication.
52. VandenHeuvel, W. J. A., B. G. Creech, and E. C. Horning, *Anal. Biochem., 4*, 191 (1962).
53. VandenHeuvel, W. J. A., E. O. A. Haahti, and E. C. Horning, *J. Am. Chem. Soc., 83*, 1513 (1961).
54. VandenHeuvel, W. J. A., and E. C. Horning, *Biochem. Biophys. Research Communications, 4*, 399 (1961).
55. VandenHeuvel, W. J. A., and E. C. Horning, *Biochim. Biophys. Acta*, in press.
56. VandenHeuvel, W. J. A., and E. C. Horning, *J. Org. Chem., 26*, 634 (1961).
57. VandenHeuvel, W. J. A., and E. C. Horning, *Biochem. Biophys. Research Communications, 3*, 356 (1960).

58. VandenHeuvel, W. J. A., E. C. Horning, Y. Satò, and N. Ikekawa, *J. Org. Chem.*, *26*, 628 (1961).
59. VandenHeuvel, W. J. A., J. Sjövall, and E. C. Horning, *Biochim. Biophys. Acta*, *48*, 596 (1961).
60. VandenHeuvel, W. J. A., C. C. Sweeley, and E. C. Horning, *J. Am. Chem. Soc.*, *82*, 3481 (1960).
61. VandenHeuvel, W. J. A., C. C. Sweeley, and E. C. Horning, *Biochem. Biophys. Research Communications*, *3*, 33 (1960).
62. VandenHeuvel, W. J. A., C. C. Sweeley, and E. C. Horning, in S. Garattini and R. Paoletti, eds., *Symposium on Drugs Affecting Lipid Metabolism, Milan, Italy, June 2–4, 1960*, Elsevier, Amsterdam, 1961, p. 196.
63. Wilson, J. D., *J. Lipid Research*, *2*, 350 (1961).
64. Woodford, F. P., and C. M. Van Gent, *J. Lipid Research*, *1*, 188 (1960).
65. Wotiz, H. H., and H. F. Martin, *J. Biol. Chem.*, *236*, 1312 (1961).
66. Wotiz, H. H., and H. F. Martin, *Anal. Biochem.*, *3*, 97 (1962).
67. Wotiz, H. H., T. Naukkarinen, and H. E. Carr, *Biochim. Biophys. Acta*, *53*, 449 (1961).
68. Ziffer, H., W. J. A. VandenHeuvel, E. O. A. Haahti, and E. C. Horning, *J. Am. Chem. Soc.*, *82*, 6411 (1960).

Advances in Direct Scanning of Paper Chromatograms for Quantitative Estimations

I. E. Bush, *University of Birmingham, Birmingham, U. K.*

149

I. INTRODUCTION

1. Quantitative Estimation Using Chromatography

Chromatographic methods have not only revolutionized the scope of quantitative methods of estimation but have also modified the operational characteristics of such methods. Since all methods of determination depend for their specificity on the combination of selective methods of determination with selective methods of separating the substance to be determined, the revolutionary improvement in the selectivity of separation that can be obtained with chromatography has affected greatly the type of procedure that can be used for determination itself. Thus, for instance, the exceptionally good resolution of closely similar substances that can be achieved with gas–liquid columns enables chemists to use highly sensitive but almost totally unspecific methods of detection and determination with reasonable confidence.

In this article, one particular method of determination is under review but, first of all, one must consider the other methods with which it might reasonably be compared. Two general methods of chromatographic separation can be distinguished. In the first, the separated substances are left in the chromatographic region proper and either detected *in situ* or extracted after breaking up the supporting material into serial sections. In the second, the separated substances are detected in the mobile phase after being allowed to emerge from the system; that is, in the "effluent" from the system. In the latter method, detection can often be performed continuously, or else by collecting the effluent in serial fractions which are treated separately. Most of the procedures using paper or other thin layers of porous material fall into the first class of methods, while all those using columns nowadays come into the second class.

The second class of methods has been the more successful for quantitative work because the substances to be determined are presented in solution, and orthodox methods of determination can be employed with confidence. Furthermore, the materials used for the porous medium of the chromatogram are commonly powders which are relatively easily purified. In contrast, paper, which is used most widely in the first class of methods, is difficult to purify and contains impurities which interfere with many methods of detection. The great practical advantage of the use of paper is that large numbers of samples can be examined with relatively simple techniques using apparatus which takes up a relatively small amount of room.

Within these classes of methods, the following general procedures have been employed for quantitative determination in conjunction with chromatographic separation:

1. *Substances determined in effluent.*

   (*a*) Continuous recording.

   (*b*) Serial fractionation of effluent.

2. *Substances remaining in chromatogram.*

   (*a*) Serial sectioning of extruded column and elution of material from the sections.

   (*b*) Serial sectioning of paper and elution of material.

   (*c*) Incomplete chemical treatment of paper or column (i.e., incomplete reaction), followed by serial sectioning and elution of materials and reaction products, followed by completion of the method of determination in solution.

   (*d*) Complete chemical treatment of paper (i.e., complete reaction) prior to serial section and elution of reaction products for determination.

   (*e*) Serial scanning of paper for pre-existent property of substances to be detected.

   (*f*) Serial scanning of paper after complete chemical treatment to reveal the substances to be determined.

For convenience, methods of class 1 will be referred to as "effluent" estimations or methods; methods of class 2, types *a*, *b*, *c*, and *d* will be called "eluate" estimations of methods; and methods of class 2, types *e* and *f* will be called "scanning" estimations or methods. We shall be concerned here mainly with scanning methods but some of the problems and techniques to be discussed will bear on the other methods, and the latter will have to be considered for purposes of comparison.

2. Logistics

A. EFFLUENT METHODS

Most methods of this type involve the collection of from $8n$ to $12n$ fractions where n substances are to be separated and determined, or else some automatic apparatus for continuous monitoring of the effluent.   With efficient design of the method, such as the use of automatically controlled gradient-elution, and with the usual dimensions that are required for micro- or ultramicrodetermination, it is not usually feasible to reduce the time taken for the complete separation procedure to less than $0.5n$ hours and much longer periods may be necessary.   With automatic and continuous recording methods [e.g., Spackman et al. (58)], it usually requires only a further $0.07n$ to $0.1n$ hours to calculate the results from the record of the chromatogram, and this figure could be improved by using suitable electronic apparatus for integration and registration.   When collected fractions are subjected to separate procedures, much more labor is involved in the determinations.   Although this time can overlap the running of the chromatogram when the customary automatic fraction-collector is employed, it is all "working time" and the worker is not free for other tasks.

The apparatus used for effluent methods is relatively bulky and expensive.   Thus, a typical fraction-collector and columns take up the full depth of about two feet (0.6 m.) of bench and an apparatus using a continuous effluent recorder (e.g., Beckman-Spinco or Technicon amino acid analyzer) may require six to ten square feet (0.6–1.0 m.²) of floor space.   Such apparatus will usually be capable of providing a complete fractionation in 8–18 hours of one or two samples containing 10 to 20 substances.

Much more rapid analyses can be carried out with gas–liquid chromatograms.   With capillary columns, only 0.5–$1.0n$ minutes, or even seconds with volatile substances, may be needed for the separation of the mixture. On the other hand, such methods still require considerable technical development and at present they cannot be applied to the routine determination of certain important classes of substances *in samples of biological origin*. Granted that such technical development is possible, one can reasonably expect, in the next few years, to have available a variety of gas–liquid methods capable of providing quantitative analyses of samples containing n substances in about $0.5n$ minutes. This means that full-time working could provide analyses of about 80 ten-component mixtures every 8 hours.

B. ELUATE METHODS

These methods are carried out nowadays using paper chromatograms or "thin-layer" chromatograms. The latter are extremely rapidly run (15–40 minutes), and fractionation and elution are easily carried out by scraping or sucking the supporting medium off the glass plate. This sort of method is very tedious with paper chromatograms, however, whenever more than two or three substances have to be eluted. Here the chromatogram must be cut into pieces with scissors and the pieces extracted with a suitable solvent. Considerable care is needed to see that contamination is avoided, and the fractions have to be identified by some system of labeling which is usually tedious with large numbers of samples or fractions. Both methods depend critically on the location of the zones to be eluted and rather long runs are needed to reduce the overlap of zones to acceptable proportions (10,45).

Most methods of this type involve quantitative determination in the final eluate—that is, in solution—and are thus both as reliable and as tedious as effluent methods based on serially collected fractions. A large number of samples can be run in tanks occupying a relatively small space, but the elution procedure demands a lot of space if contamination and occasional muddling of eluates are to be avoided.

Many reliable procedures of this sort have been devised but they are undoubtedly tedious, and involve a large number of technical problems. They require painstaking and meticulous work if they are to be reliable (41,56).

C. SCANNING METHODS

The logistics of the chromatographic stages are similar to those of the eluate methods. The same standards of cleanliness are required and the space occupied is the same. However, rather shorter runs are needed to provide separations which are adequate, since overlapping peaks are reliably dealt with by simple geometrical techniques applied to the record (23,45).

The calculation of results from the scanning record takes the same time and involves the same techniques as are needed for continuously recorded effluent methods. On the other hand, the preparation of the record and the treatment of the chromatograms can be made extremely rapid by the use of automatic machinery (17,18). Although most commercial scanners take several minutes to produce a complete scan of a 40-cm. strip of paper (3–10 minutes), this is not essential and relatively simple apparatus enables a complete scan to be made in about 40 seconds.

Most ten-component mixtures can be separated adequately on paper with runs of 12 to 24 hours, all of which is "waiting time" in which the worker is free for other tasks (or else out of the laboratory). Such mixtures usually need strips of 50–60 cm. for really good separation. With the majority of color reactions such strips can be processed at the rate of one every 50–60 seconds with a delay of 3–10 minutes in the appearance of the first record from the chart-recorder. With full-time working, therefore, it is possible to obtain records of about 300 chromatograms every 8 hours, allowing about 7% of the time for mishaps, warming up, and adjustments.

A further advantage is that such apparatus can be readjusted to cope with different classes of substances relatively quickly. The relatively crude apparatus of the author only needs from 10 to 15 minutes to change from conditions suitable for the Zimmerman reaction for 17-ketosteroids to those needed for the use of ninhydrin for amino acids. One apparatus can therefore serve the needs of several research groups every day.

D. SUMMARY

There seems little doubt that existing effluent methods are far less productive than scanning methods for a given expenditure of time, energy, and financial resources. The position is likely to be ameliorated very considerably by the further development of gas–liquid methods but is unlikely to be reversed even if the most optimistic assumptions are made as to the extent of future developments. On the other hand, the great advantage of the latter methods is the *immediacy* of the results, a feature which has already shown its value in a number of fields, such as automatic process control in the petroleum industry, and the analysis of anesthetic and respiratory gases in human patients.

Eluate methods are far less productive than scanning methods but are more productive at present than liquid–liquid effluent methods in the case of simple mixtures (1 to 4 components).

3. Reliability and Analytical Value

A. INFORMATION PROVIDED

Eluate methods are inferior to both effluent and scanning methods in one respect. Thus, it is not feasible in routine practice to take a sufficient number of fractions to enable the construction of a detailed "profile" of the chromatogram. In contrast, slight inhomogeneities in the "peaks" can readily be seen on the chart records of scanned chromatograms or continuously recorded effluents. Further sophistication of the latter methods also provides extra information such as the optical density at several wavelengths, and further developments are obviously possible. Most eluate methods in fact do not, in routine practice, provide an accurate location of the peak concentrations on the chromatogram.

Similarly, there is usually no check on the degree of overlap of zones when using eluate methods. The overlap of commonly occurring substances on standard chromatograms can be assessed and allowed for (e.g., 10) but there is no way of checking this, or of excluding the presence of other substances during the course of routine work. The best that can be done is to use part of the extract for running an additional paper chromatogram which is examined by qualitative methods. This, although often useful, is sometimes a nuisance and is usually not as sensitive as the inspection of the quantitatively recorded profiles obtained with effluent or scanning methods.

B. QUALITY OF SEPARATION

The efficiency of liquid–liquid column methods in this respect has usually been superior to that of paper systems. This, however, is a matter of design and not due to any insuperable defects of paper. There is, of course, little hope in practice of either form of liquid–liquid chromatography competing with gas–liquid methods on this score.

It is still commonly believed, however, that separations on paper chromatograms are inherently bound to be worse than those achieved by column-effluent methods. The apparent inferiority of paper methods is due to the fact that most paper methods are designed to give *convenient* rather than *optimal* separations, because they are used mostly for qualitative analysis. Again, the technique required for such work is not usually as meticulous as is possible when good quantitative results are required (7,17,18). Tait and Tait (61) compared the scanning records of some routine paper chromatograms of reducing steroids, run by the author, with their records obtained from kieselguhr columns using the same solvent systems. They showed that for small quantities of steroid, the height of one theoretical plate on a 1-in. wide (2.5 cm.) strip of Whatman No. 2 paper was 0.26 mm. and for a kieselguhr column was 0.75 mm. This held for amounts up to 50 μg. (1.38 μmole) per centimeter width of paper. With quantities larger than this, the performance of paper fell off rapidly while that of the columns was maintained up to quantities of the order of 3 mg. (0.83 mmole) per square centimeter of cross section of column. Tait and Tait (61) calculated that separations on overrun paper chromatograms (40 cm.) of substances with R_f values around 0.2 were equivalent to those achieved by effluent methods on 60-cm. kieselguhr columns. On the other hand, separations on single-length chromatograms (40 cm.) of substances with R_f values around 0.5 were only as good as those achieved in effluents from 10-cm. columns. Bush and Willoughby (23) emphasized that good quantitative results were achieved only by using solvent systems giving R_f values in the range 0.15–0.3 and overrunning them two or three times (i.e., the solvent is allowed to overrun the paper until one obtains the equivalent of a single-length run on a strip 2 to 3 times as long as the strip itself).

In summary, there is no inherent inferiority of typical paper chromatograms in comparison with columns when the former are designed to achieve optimal conditions. It is not, in practice, difficult to design methods which achieve such conditions, and the quantities compatible with such conditions are well within the range that is easily detected and scanned using conventional color or fluorescence reactions. Such conditions, however, will usually differ quite considerably from those customarily used for single-length qualitative paper chromatograms.

C. SENSITIVITY

It will be seen later that the apparent optical density of absorbing zones on dry paper strips is greater than might be expected. Partly due to this, the sensitivity achieved by such methods is usually a good deal larger than can be achieved with liquid–liquid effluent methods (61). Neither class of method can compete with the exceptionally high sensitivity that can be achieved with gas–liquid effluent methods.

The direct scanning of radioactively labeled substances is usually far less sensitive than other methods when weak emitters such as ^{14}C or ^{3}H are to be estimated, but we shall not be concerned with this problem here.

D. PRECISION OF QUANTITATIVE DETERMINATION

Many early attempts were made to determine substances by scanning methods [see Block et al. (9) for a full review], and with few exceptions the precision that was obtained was low, being of the order of ± 10–15%. This is undoubtedly greatly inferior to the precision that can be achieved with column effluent methods. It will be seen later, however, that with proper attention to the conditions necessary for scanning methods, it is possible to achieve results of considerable precision, and that in some fields such methods already equal the best published effluent methods.

For equivalent time and effort, eluate methods seem to suffer from all the disadvantages and few of the advantages of both effluent and scanning methods. Good results have only been obtained with relatively simple mixtures (e.g., 1 to 4 components) or by extremely painstaking techniques which have taken considerable time for their development (10,47,56,59,63).

The methods for the automatic quantitative analysis of mixtures of amino acids based on the work of Spackman et al. (58) are probably the most highly developed effluent methods in existence. The precision with synthetic mixtures of pure amino acids is about ±3%, a figure which does not appear to have been improved upon in recent years. Scanning methods for reducing steroids and 17-ketosteroids have been developed with precisions of ±2 to ±5% and have been used for several years in the author's laboratory. Recently, it has been possible to achieve a precision of ±5% with a scanning method for amino acids (see below) and further improvement is likely. It should be emphasized that the effort required for the development of such scanning methods has not been any greater than appears to have been needed for the development of comparable effluent methods.

II. CHEMICAL REQUIREMENTS

1. Methods of Manipulation

A. CLEANLINESS

One of the main problems to be overcome is that of "dirt." Suitable strips of paper are large objects and special attention to detail is needed if they are to be kept clean during the various stages of preparation, running, and scanning chromatograms. This problem is analogous to that of performing aseptic surgery and demands rather similar procedures for its solution. Rather like patients, strips of paper have to be cleaned before the operation, kept clean and handled with clean instruments during the operation, and maintained clean until all essential processes have been completed. To open a bottle of an amine in a laboratory in which chromatograms of amino acids are drying in a fume cupboard is rather like a nurse sneezing while a patient's wound is being dressed.

In our laboratory, it has been found useful to adopt a "no-touch" technique which overcomes the major source of chemical contamination—the human hand. It is best, if possible, to set aside a room for the preparation of chromatograms and to have this adjacent to the chromatography room proper. This room should contain the minimum of solvents and reagents necessary for preparing the chromatograms and should be air-conditioned if possible. The worker should wear a clean laboratory coat or smock and, as in surgery, should avoid using his pockets during the procedure. Smoking or extensive nose-blowing should be taboo and the hair should be remembered as an important source of contaminating material. The precautions to be adopted are little, if anything, short of those used in work with radioactive materials or in bacteriology: Special care is needed in order to deal with the rather large areas which have to be kept clean when paper chromatograms are being handled.

B. PREPARATION OF WASHED PAPER

Despite a considerable amount of work, there is no agreed method of washing filter paper for chromatography. Nor is it likely that a universal washing procedure suitable for all problems will ever be practicable or even desirable. The two main purposes of washing filter paper are, first, to remove materials which interfere with the chemical reactions that may be used to detect and determine the substances of interest; and, second, to remove or render harmless those impurities in the paper which interfere with the chromatographic process proper. The procedures needed for these purposes may, in favorable circumstances, reinforce one another even to the extent that the process for one fulfills the function of the other. More often, however, they are inclined to conflict, and careful work is necessary to see that a convenient sequence of washes is devised so that both purposes are achieved.

Thus, for instance, many metallic impurities causing imperfections in the chromatographic separation of organic phosphates and amino acids are removed by washing filter paper with acetic acid (24,35,41). If this acid is not completely removed, however, any ammonia used in subsequent washing, or in chromatographic solvents, becomes trapped in the paper as the acetate. This is nearly impossible to remove after running a chromatogram and will ruin the background color when using ninhydrin to determine amino acids.

The magnitude of this problem is perhaps best indicated by the procedure of Connell et al. (24) for amino acids which falls in class 2c (see Section I.1). These authors use a chromatographic procedure of $2N$ acetic acid, water, $0.5N$ lithium hydroxide, water, 0.1% (w/v) calcium acetate, water, and 95% (v/v) ethanol, in succession. A total of 52 liters of solvents are passed chromatographically through blocks of 60 sheets of filter paper and the process takes about 50 days to complete.

After many years of experimenting with methods of cleaning filter paper for the chromatography of steroids, the author has come to the conclusion that as a general rule the washing of filter paper should be kept to a minimum. Filter paper supplied for chromatography is now available, thanks to the continuing and imaginative efforts of manufacturers, in grades of very considerable purity and reproducibility. In the author's experience of recent years, more background "dirt" is likely to be introduced by impurities in chromatographic solvents, reagents, or in the ambient air, than is present in the paper itself, if this is *kept* clean after opening the packet and is handled with clean instruments. The expense and labor of preparing solvents which are themselves sufficiently pure to be useful in washing paper is very considerable and the return is small. This was not so four or five years ago, when many batches of paper were quite unusable for quantitative work unless thoroughly washed. An entirely similar experience is recorded by Hanes (33).

Three main methods have been used to wash filter paper for chromatography. Hanes and his group first made a large perforated Perspex tray which sucked washing solvents through 10–40 sheets of filter paper, much as with a Buchner funnel. Others [e.g., Neher (50)] coiled strips of paper in a large Soxhlet extractor and extracted them with hot organic solvents. Hanes and others found that "chromatographic washing" was the most efficient (e.g., 33,35,41).

The Soxhlet method is not suitable for washes with aqueous acids or bases, and even with organic solvents the elevated temperature may lead to continuous slow chemical alterations of the paper which themselves contribute to background with color reagents.

When using "chromatographic washing," however, it is sometimes forgotten that the process is indeed *chromatographic*. Much of the "dirt" that is removed during washing behaves, as might be expected, like material with a low R_f value on a chromatogram. For this reason, relatively moderate periods of washing will remove most of the "dirt" from the proximal zones of the strip, but the distal end of the strip will now be occupied by the "dirt" that has been eluted from the proximal zones. In order to ensure that such material is removed from *the whole* of the strip, prolonged chromatographic washing is usually necessary.

Since relatively narrow strips can be used for the scanning method, the author developed the technique of washing strips of paper chro-

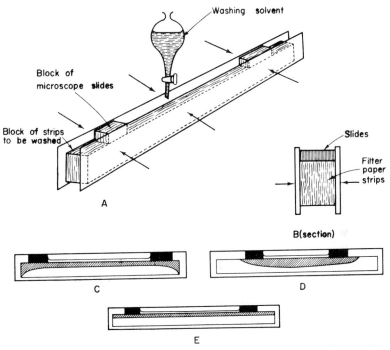

Fig. 1. Cross-washing of paper strips. The strips (2 × 22½ in.) are laid in packs of about 200 (Whatman No. 2) on a plate-glass sheet (4 × 24 in.) and a second glass placed on top. The block is compressed by springs (arrows) in a frame in the position shown and two packs of microscope slides laid on top to form a trough. Gaps between the slides and side-plates are filled with ½ × 2 in. strips of Whatman 3MM paper. The solvent is allowed to drip on to the strips fast enough to form a fluid layer 0.3–0.8 cm. deep between the two packs of microscope slides. The microscope slides are moved along the top edge of the block of paper strips until the leakage past them just produces a straight solvent front at the ends of the block of paper strips. The block and its supporting frame are mounted on a trough with suitable drainage, in the fume cupboard. *C:* microscope slides too close to ends. *D:* slides too far from ends. *E:* correct position of slides. Shaded area represents solvent area in early stages of washing. With aqueous solvents the microscope slides are best replaced by filter paper packs which match the swelling of the main block of paper strips.

matographically in the direction perpendicular to their main axis, that is, across the strips (18). This technique is relatively easy to master once a simple apparatus has been made, and takes up less space than methods in which strips are washed longitudinally. For a given *volume* of solvent passed through the paper, the efficiency of this method of washing equals that of the longitudinal method of irrigation. The *time* taken, however, is very much shorter because of the much shorter effective "length" of the chromatographic system.

The apparatus, and its method of operation, is shown in Figure 1. A further advantage of this method is that one avoids the gradients often found in papers that are washed longitudinally. Such gradients may alter the background or efficiency of color reactions in different zones of the strips. With "cross-washed" strips, such gradients will be less likely to occur and will affect all zones of the strips equally. They will thus be less likely to affect the eventual scanning procedure.

It is best to finish any washing procedure with a volatile organic solvent which will remove most of the water from the strips. Connell et al. (24) used 95% ethanol; the author uses ethanol/ether, 1:1 (v/v). The strips are removed from the washing frame and laid on glass or polythene sheets, in batches of 6–9, to dry in a fume cupboard.

The strips are then collected and packed in foil, polyethylene, or between glass strips, and kept in a dust-proof box. Alternatively, they can be stored in a "dispenser" (18, p. 159) which is itself kept in a box when not in use.

C. APPARATUS FOR MOUNTING AND HANDLING CHROMATOGRAMS

The paper strips are best handled entirely with chromium-plated dissecting forceps from the moment that they have been washed. During the later stages of preparations, the distal ends (e.g., furthest from the origin of the chromatogram) can be handled, if necessary, since this area of the chromatogram is not a part of the strip which will be occupied by any important substance on the final chromatogram.

Special flat-bladed forceps are used for marking and bending the strips (Fig. 2). Pencil marks are made with a hard graphite pencil and are kept to a minimum. Care should be taken to keep the point clean by rubbing it down on a clean piece of filter paper before use.

It is not easy to mount more than a few strips in tanks with conventional troughs, and the use of slotted sheets [e.g., Neher (50)] is not as convenient as the use of separate strips. For instance, the former are difficult to wash conveniently. When many separate

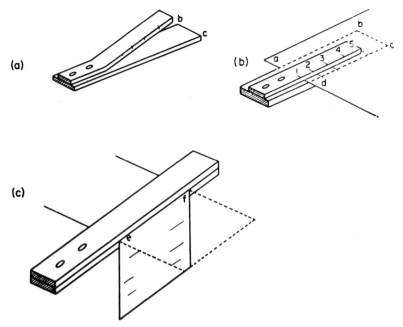

Fig. 2. Marking and bending forceps. (*a*) The marking forceps in open position. (*b*) Being used to mark a sheet of paper. The numbers show the standard marks for the folds for the trough (*2, 3*), the fold over the anti-syphoning rod (*4*), and the origin of the chromatogram (*5*). Note that *bc* is well beyond the upper blade to allow firm code letters to be written on the paper. (*c*) The bending forceps in use. The fold *ef* is made by firm pressure with the outer surface of a pair of large dissecting forceps. For cleanliness the folds can be lightly scored rather than pencilled.

strips have to be hung in a conventional tank, it will be found that it takes a considerable time to get them uniformly arranged, and with none of them touching each other or the walls of the tank. With volatile solvent systems, the worker will inhale dangerous amounts of vapor and the tank will take a considerable time to reach equilibrium after it is closed. To overcome this problem, the author devised a simple frame on which the strips are mounted (Fig. 3). After depositing the materials to be run on the strips, the strips are threaded on to the frame with forceps and aligned. The frame can then be placed rapidly in the tank where its trunnions sit in grooves in a second frame within the tank. In this way, all the strips are oriented

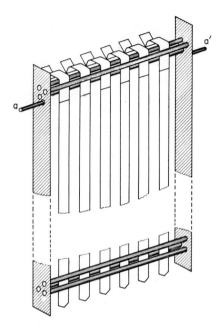

Fig. 3. Frame for mounting strips, made of light aluminum and six glass rods. The two side members are rigidly connected by a stainless steel or aluminum rod at their bottom ends. These have been omitted to make the arrangement of the strips and glass rods clear. The pins (a, a') engage with notches cut in the supporting frame inside the chromatography tank.

correctly and the only task remaining is to press their upper ends into the trough, and secure them with one or two heavy glass rods in the usual way. This technique has been used in the author's laboratory for the last eight years and has increased greatly both the quality of the results and the convenience of the method as a whole.

After the chromatograms have been run, the frames are removed rapidly from the tanks and placed in a fume cupboard. The strips are removed from the frames as soon as they are ready for treatment with color reagents or for passage through the scanner.

With this technique, it is possible to carry out the whole procedure without ever touching the strips by hand, and without an excessive expenditure of time and effort. In the subsequent paragraphs, it will be understood that all procedures are carried out using these manipulative methods.

2. Preparation of Chromatograms

Unless a cross-scanning device is in use (see Section III.2.A and reference 66), the material must be deposited evenly across the full width of the strip that is to be scanned. In any event, the material should be deposited across as large a fraction of the width of the strip as possible. In this way, the concentration of the substances under study in the effective volume of the chromatographic system is kept

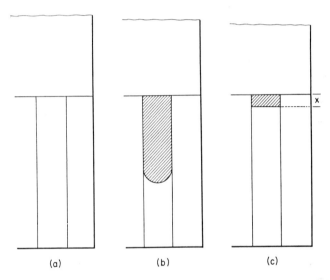

(a)   (b)   (c)

Fig. 4. Concentration of 0.02–0.2 ml. of extract for chromatography by a preliminary chromatogram. "Running up" technique. (a) Marked sheet. (b) After depositing extract. (c) After running up to the origin. (By kind permission of the Editors of the *Biochemical Journal*.)

at a minimum, thus ensuring that the conditions approximate as closely as possible to the ideal and that the maximum number of theoretical plates in the system is achieved (see Section I.3.B). The disadvantages of the conventional "spotting" technique have been discussed before (18, p. 139).

The aim in preparing a chromatogram for scanning methods is thus to finish with the material deposited at the origin of the chromatogram in the form of a thin line or "bar" across the strip. This can be done either by pipetting carefully a solution of the material along a marked line, or by the "running up" technique (15). The technique is shown in Figure 4 as used for sheets of paper but is entirely similar for strips, except, of course, that the vertical lines do not need marking.

The "running up" technique is the best we have found for achieving an even and narrow band of material at the origin of a chromatogram. It is quick and reliable when the substances of interest are soluble in volatile organic solvents. It is less convenient when very polar substances are being "run up" because the solvent employed may have to contain a considerable proportion of water. This makes the "running up" slow, and the solvent takes longer to evaporate before the strips can be mounted and put in the tanks. The efficiency of solvents for "running up" a new class of substances can, however, easily be tested, and the aim is to find the lowest content of water which will achieve a reliable concentration of the material at the origin.

Some of the problems of depositing materials quantitatively on paper chromatograms have been discussed before (18, p. 138). It is important, for example, to avoid premature evaporation when pipetting very volatile solvents on to paper. Again, the danger of irreversible adsorption of materials at the origin is considerable with many classes of compounds and greatly increased by using warm air to evaporate the solvent in which they are deposited. Cold air or nitrogen should always be used.

In summary, the technique of preparing the chromatograms for quantitative work must be more sophisticated than would be sufficient for qualitative work. The crucial importance of securing a really narrow starting band of material at the origin of a chromatogram has been emphasized by Glueckauf (1955) in connection with columns, but the same principles hold for paper strips.

3. Equilibrating and Running the Chromatograms

A. EQUILIBRATION OR CONDITIONING

The importance of this phase of carrying out paper chromatography has been emphasized by several workers (7,33,35). It has sometimes been overlooked, however, since reasonable qualitative results have been achieved in certain fields either without much difficulty, or by running systems under very closely specified conditions in which equilibrium is never achieved. Unless there are specific reasons for neglecting it, however, equilibration should be very carefully considered when quantitative work is undertaken.

Hanes and his group have shown that convection in the tank is the rate-limiting factor in the equilibration of paper chromatograms. He has described a number of devices for increasing the efficiency of equilibration (33). This paper also contains details of several other techniques and pieces of apparatus which are of considerable value when results of high quality are necessary. Hanes also lays considerable emphasis on a valuable technique for achieving reproducible conditions when miscible or "one-phase" solvents are used. He points out that true equilibrium is often neither achieved nor desirable for the best separations. It should be noted, however, that his remarks apply mainly to this type of solvent system. In many other types of system, true equilibrium both can and should be achieved before starting the run.

B. RUNNING THE CHROMATOGRAMS

After the period of equilibration, the mobile phase must be introduced in a way that disturbs the equilibrium in the tank as little as possible. Various devices have been described for doing this at convenient predetermined times, which do not require the worker's presence in the laboratory when this is inconvenient (e.g., 29).

The only special feature of quantitative work is that, for the best results, solvent systems giving low R_f values (0.05–0.30) should be used and the chromatograms "overrun" for a period in which the fastest moving substance to be determined will move to within a short distance of the bottom of the strip (see Section I.3.B). In order to ensure that the rate of flow of solvent is maintained after the front has reached the bottom of the strip, Hanes and Isherwood (35) fitted absorbent pads of thick filter paper to the bottom of paper sheets. The latest details of this technique are given by Hanes (33). With some solvents, this technique is not necessary.

The design of suitable solvent systems, and sequences of such systems, will not be discussed here. An excellent discussion of the rationale involved in this problem is given by Wade et al. (64) and the author has given a more general account of the theoretical problem (18, pp. 201–218).

4. Removal and Pretreatment of the Chromatograms

After the chromatograms have been run, they are removed from the tanks and placed to dry. With volatile solvents, complete evaporation is usually achieved in a fume cupboard within 5–15 minutes and the strips are then ready for scanning.

In many cases, however, some difficulty will be found in securing the complete, or at least uniform, removal of components of the solvent system that has been employed, which interfere with subsequent treatment of the strips. Traces of ammonia, volatile amines, acids, or high-boiling impurities may be extremely difficult to remove to an extent which avoids their interference with color reactions, or even with scanning if the ultraviolet region of the spectrum is being used.

In the event of trouble of this sort—which usually manifests itself as an excessively large or variable amount of background absorption or fluorescence—it is best to concentrate first on deciding what is the source of the trouble. This is easily done by treating suitable control strips of paper to various parts of the procedure. The main sources of interfering material to be examined are:

(a) Impurities in the original paper.

(b) Impurities in the solvents used to wash the paper.

(c) Impurities in the vapor of the tank or in solvents used to impregnate the paper.

(d) Impurities in the solvent used to run the chromatograms.

(e) Impurities in the reagents used to treat the chromatograms.

(f) Impurities in the extracts, or their solvents, that were deposited on the chromatograms.

(g) Contaminants of the air in the room, fume cupboard, or drying oven.

(h) Essential components of the paper or running solvents which have not been, or cannot be, completely removed before treatment with color reagents, etc.

If the results of the investigation suggest that it is impracticable or impossible to avoid the presence of the undesirable material before and during chromatography, then various means can be tried to remove it from the paper after the run. The first is to heat the paper in the presence of steam or water vapor in generous amounts (40); alternatively, the strips can be dipped over (see Section II.5.A), or sprayed with, water, and dried in an oven. This procedure uses water as a displacing or desorbing agent.   It is very effective with ammonia and volatile acids.

In some cases (e.g., chromatograms of amino acids run in phenol systems) the impurities can be washed out of the paper by immersion in a solvent in which the substances of interest are quite insoluble. This step is greatly improved if the washing solvent is run through the strip chromatographically (33,34).   For very involatile solvents, such as glycols, prolonged exposure to a high vacuum in large tanks may be necessary (3).

On the whole, it is undesirable to get involved in lengthy or expensive methods for this part of the procedure.   If relatively simple techniques are unsuccessful in removing interfering material, then it is usually better in the long run to change one's procedure so that the offending substances are avoided altogether.   One of the main reasons for adopting this general policy is that tenaciously retained impurities are usually only removed by drastic conditions which are likely to cause partial destruction of the substances to be determined.

It should be noted that these problems effect all types of quantitative chromatography using paper and are not confined to those in which the final measurement is made by scanning.

5. Treatment of Chromatograms with Reagents

In most cases the substances to be determined must be rendered measurable by some reaction giving light-absorbing or fluorescent products.   The aim of scanning methods is to secure a quantitative, or at least a reliably controlled, reaction in this important stage of the procedure.   In early work with steroids, the author found that existing methods were deficient mainly in their *failure to get a sufficient quantity of reagent* on to the paper strip (17,18).   It was also necessary to control numerous minor effects, such as the influence of gravity, which would cause little or no trouble in qualitative work (23).

A. APPLICATION OF REAGENTS

Many workers have concluded independently that the most even deposition of reagent on paper chromatograms is secured by dipping the latter through the reagent in a shallow vessel (18,34,55).   The author found that with aqueous reagents a slow and steady movement was necessary at a rate of 1–2 cm./sec.   To secure reproducible re-

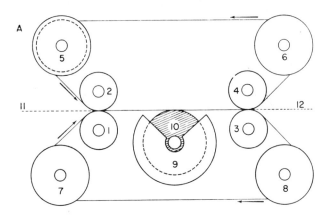

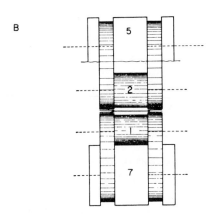

Fig. 5. Mechanical reagent applicator. Stainless-steel or PTFE tapes run continuously over the raised faces of the rollers *1, 2, 3,* and *4* and the grooved pulleys *5, 6, 7, 8.* The drive is to roller *1, 2, 3,* or *4.* *1* and *3* are in fixed bearings; *2* and *4* press down on *1* and *3.* *9* is the reagent trough fed from a small constant-level reservoir. *10* is a roller of adjustable speed of rotation feeding reagent as a film on to the paper strip. The paper is fed in on grooved guides at *11* and meshes with the free edges of the tapes. It emerges at *12.* For aqueous reagents (which weaken the paper considerably) the bottom tape is taken over a third roller to the right of *12* before returning via pulley *8.* (*A*) Elevation. (*B*) Section through and around rollers *1* and *2* and pulleys *5* and *7.*

sults, the movement was controlled by observing a watch with a second hand placed on the bench near the watch-glass containing the reagent. During this process, the cellulose fibers swell so that more reagent can be taken up on dipping the strip a second time. Because of the slow rate of swelling, however, the second dip must be in the same direction as the first so that each zone of the strip will have swelled to an equal extent by the time it is exposed to the reagent at the second dip (17). This is one of several details of technique which are easily controlled once their significance is realized but which can otherwise be overlooked very easily.

Some reagents are affected by the heterogeneous nature of the system in which the reaction is taking place. Thus the use of different chromatographic solvent systems, or even the exposure of the strips to different solvent vapors can affect greatly the efficiency of such reactions (14,17).

In order to overcome human error with the manual technique, several mechanical methods of applying reagents have been developed. The author's machine uses a roller dipping into a trough of reagent which is maintained at a constant level either by a drip-feed or a syringe-injection apparatus. The paper is pressed into light contact with the roller by a polytetrafluoroethylene (PTFE) roller which remains dry and clean by engaging with the paper just before it touches the reagent roller. The paper is supported by its edges with two pairs of belts which pass it continuously forward over the reagent roller at 1 cm./sec. (Fig. 5). Hrubant (39) has devised a similar apparatus for large sheets of paper in which the reagent roller is of plastic sponge and the paper is pressed against it rather firmly by an upper solid roller. This arrangement would not be suitable for quantitative work unless the substances being determined were completely insoluble in the reagent, since the reagent would become progressively contaminated with material from the chromatograms. In the author's apparatus there is little danger of this, since the speed of rotation of the roller, and of the paper over it, can be adjusted to ensure that the film of reagent is sucked up into the paper strip as it meets the paper.

B. FURTHER TREATMENT OF STRIPS

Following the application of the reagent, the strips must be treated in such a way that a complete, or at least a reliably controlled degree

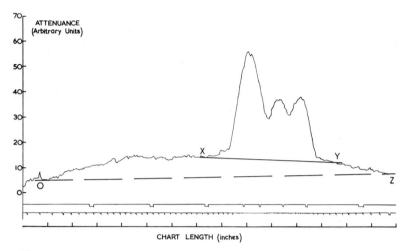

Fig. 6. Effect of uneven distribution of heat. The scanning record of a chromatogram of three partially separated 17-ketosteroids, treated with alkaline *m*-dinitrobenzene. The background is "humped" due to overheating of the central zones of the strip (see Fig. 7*A*). The ideal background should be close to *OZ* (dashed). The background for the steroid zones would have to be taken as *XY* on this scanning record (solid line).

of reaction takes place. In some cases specific measures must be taken to stop the reaction, or to ensure that the colored or fluorescent products do not deteriorate. Again, one must be on one's guard against apparently trivial factors which may completely upset an apparently promising procedure. Most reagents used in qualitative work are not only inadequate in concentration, but are made up in solvents which evaporate long before a complete reaction has been obtained. In such cases, most of the reaction takes place in the polysaccharide gel phase of the paper, whose properties will be very greatly influenced by the original water content of the paper and by atmospheric humidity.

These factors and the problems involved in the even heating of paper strips have been discussed fully before (17,18). An improved apparatus for heating chromatograms has been described by Ough et al. (51). Most of the existing methods, however, obtain only a very imprecise control of the rate of evaporation of the reagent vehicle. It would seem desirable to ensure that reactions taking more than a few minutes for their completion are carried out in a way such

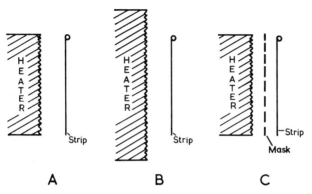

Fig. 7. Arrangements of radiant heaters. (A) Strip some distance (10–15 cm.) from a heater having the same length as the strip. The central zones will be overheated (see Fig. 6). (B) Strip close (1–4 cm.) to a heater which is longer than the strip. Central overheating is minimal. (C) Strip some distance from heater as in (A) but with a mask interposed. The mask contains slots cut in a pattern which reduces heat reaching central zones of paper. These and other arrangements can be tested conveniently with strips of heat-sensitive paper. Alternatively, filter paper dipped through 10% (w/v) phosphomolybdic acid in ethanol can be used.

that either the humidity of the paper and of the surrounding air is properly controlled, or the reagent vehicle does not evaporate to any great extent while the reaction is progressing. During such procedures, it will usually be found essential to mount the strips *horizontally* so as to avoid gravitational movement of the reagent through the paper (23).

If the reaction is carried out in a strongly acid or alkaline medium, it will usually be necessary to stop the reaction, and untoward deterioration of the paper, by neutralizing the paper before drying and scanning it. This can be done quickly and evenly by using a gaseous reagent in a glass or plastic tank in a fume cupboard (e.g., SO_2, CO_2, NH_3, or volatile amines). The use of aqueous neutralizing agents is rarely, if ever, free from difficulties of one sort or another and should be avoided where possible.

The heating of chromatograms presents many difficulties if they are of any size. Figure 6 shows an example of the difficulty of avoiding overheating of the central zones of strips when using a typical battery of electric-fire elements. This can be overcome by two means

(Fig. 7). In the first (Fig. 7C), a mask is constructed which obscures a larger area of the radiating surface in the central zones; its efficiency can be tested with thermocouples or a bolometer. In the second (Fig. 7B), the relative position and size of heater and strip are modified so that the heater is a good deal longer than the strip and the latter is placed close to the heater.

Again, the best method seems to be to make the procedure continuous and automatic by feeding the strip continuously through a heating chamber (see Section III.5, below).

C. THE DESIGN OF REAGENTS

The failure to achieve reliable or complete reactions on paper chromatograms, which has been common experience since early attempts at quantitative scanning were made, can be attributed to various factors, but by far the most important seems to be the quantity of reagent taken up by the paper. The author calculated that the molar ratio reagent/reactant in the conventional Zimmermann reaction for 17-ketosteroids was usually in the range 20–40. With the reagent usually used for paper chromatograms, this ratio would be only 5–8 at the peaks of typical zones of 10–20 μg. steroid per centimeter width of Whatman No. 2 paper, and would be reduced by sublimation of the m-dinitrobenzene during the heating of the chromatograms.

The same general rule has been found to hold for 17-ketosteroids (with Zimmermann's reagent), reducing steroids (with alkaline blue tetrazolium), and amino acids (with ninhydrin). Calibration curves obtained by scanning strips which have been treated with conventional reagents were linear only up to small quantities of substances on the chromatograms, and the "sharper" the zone being scanned, the smaller the quantity at which nonlinearity appeared in the calibration curve. If the concentration of the main component of the reagent were increased, it was found that linearity was obtained up to larger quantities. Judging by our experience, the concentration of typical color reagents used for paper chromatograms may have to be increased as much as five- or tenfold, in order to obtain quantitative reactions over a useful range of quantities of the substances that are being determined.

The reagent vehicle may also be of great importance. The conventional reagent is usually made up in a volatile solvent and the reaction starts in a complicated system of free solvent + water from paper; water–polysaccharide gel + solvent; surface of gel; surface of crystalline regions of cellulose.   As the solvent evaporates, the concentration of water in the reaction medium rises and, finally, the reaction may be completed in phases approximating to gel or solid solution.   In some cases this may actually be desirable.   In all cases, however, the reagent and the conditions in which it is used should be designed to obtain the optimum reproducibility of those factors known or suspected to be of importance.   This task will be much easier, of course, if the color reaction is one in which the mechanism is simple or well understood.

It appears impossible to lay down any hard and fast rules.   For instance, it would seem that the ideal to be achieved would be a reagent vehicle which desorbed the reactants from the cellulose, dissolved the reactants rapidly, and which remained in the paper substantially unchanged in volume until the reaction was completed. While this is a good working hypothesis in many cases, especially where the mechanism of the reaction is understood, it may well be that the efficiency of certain reactions is greatly increased if they take place in surface or gel phases after rapid evaporation of the vehicle.   In some cases, for instance, the colored (or fluorescent) product of the reaction may be soluble in the vehicle but rapidly and strongly "adsorbed" by the cellulose when the vehicle is removed. The rate of a reversible reaction would be greatly increased by this trapping process when the vehicle had evaporated.

Alkaline   "blue   tetrazolium"   (BT: 3,3'-dianisole-bis-4,4'-3,5-diphenyltetrazolium chloride) is a good example of a reagent showing this sort of complexity.   The reagent is used conventionally for determining reducing steroids, using room temperature and 95% ethanol as vehicle.   In pure solution, the presence of other tetrazolium salts as impurities is often not noticeable.   In contrast, the best reagent for treating paper chromatograms is largely aqueous (ethanol <20% v/v) and a reagent made up in 95% ethanol fails to give more than one tenth of the sensitivity obtained with predominantly aqueous reagent.   This is true even for relatively nonpolar reducing steroids which are extremely insoluble in water.   Similarly, the presence of impurities is revealed when the reagent is used on paper chromatograms, and reddish formazans are formed, giving pink or purple "halos" at the edges of the resulting blue zones (17).   Burstein and Kimball (14) have found that this is reduced or prevented by treating the paper with 20% o-dichlorobenzene in hexane and allowing the hexane to evaporate before dipping the strip through alkaline BT. A considerable increase in sensitivity is obtained (14) and the rate of the reaction is increased (21). It seems likely that the residual o-dichlorobenzene is increasing the proportion of "true blue formazan" (19) that is formed from impure BT, by trapping it in solution. This would be in accord with the properties of these formazans described by Bush and Gale (19).

D. TESTING THE SUITABILITY OF REAGENTS

Rees and Laurence (53) and Bush (17) have described the general procedure for testing the suitability of scanning methods. Briefly, there are two stages:

(i) Demonstration that the optical requirements are satisfied (see Sections III.1 and III.2, below).

(ii) Demonstration that a controlled stoichiometric reaction is being achieved.

If (i) has been achieved, then (ii) can be carried out by scanning the strips directly after testing various procedures for carrying out the color reaction. This is the most convenient way of investigating the new procedure. It is often valuable, however, to check the results by eluting the colored product from the paper and determining it spectrophotometrically in solution in the usual way. These tests are best carried out with strips of paper dipped carefully through solutions of the substance of interest at varying concentrations. The "surface concentration" of the substance is calculated from the weight of solution absorbed by the paper under standard conditions. It is far less satisfactory to use "spots" of known quantity deposited over limited areas of paper, since these are invariably irregular and an accurate estimate cannot be obtained of the maximum surface concentration at which complete reaction can be assured.

If the substances of interest are rare or expensive, then a satisfactory compromise is achieved by trying out different reagents and conditions with chromatograms of different amounts of the standard substance. This test is quite valid when the optical requirements have been shown to be satisfied. If the colored products of the reaction are to be eluted for a final check in cuvettes, care must be taken to see that the *whole of the zone is* eluted and compared with a suitable blank eluate (e.g., 2,17).

III. OPTICAL AND INSTRUMENTAL REQUIREMENTS

1. The Optics of Scanning

Optical measurements on inhomogeneous materials have been made in several industries for half a century or more, and their application to chromatograms occurred quite soon after the introduction of paper chromatography [see, e.g., Block et al. (9), Bull (13), Grassmann (32). Most of the information in this field, however, is either not generally available or else of an entirely empirical nature. The author drew attention to some of the complications that were not adequately allowed for in certain commercial densitometers used for filter paper strips (17), and recently Shibata (57) has given a very full account of the problem, particularly in connection with spectrophotometric measurements on biological tissues. Since much of his treatment is directly applicable to the problems of densitometry (and fluorometry) of paper chromatograms, it will be used as the basis of a brief discussion here.

For various reasons the measurement of light transmitted through the filter paper is preferred to measurements of reflectance (see, e.g., 67). For instance, reflectance measurements are likely to be upset more seriously by variations in the distribution of material across the thickness of the paper. The problem is to find an analog of optical density for filter paper, that is, a parameter of the transmitted light which bears a linear relationship to the quantity of any colored material lying in each infinitesimal zone of paper (25,26). Shibata uses the term "attenuance" for what is sometimes called the "effective optical density" of inhomogeneous materials. This term is useful and can be extended to suit different methods of measurement. Thus, attenuance for transmitted light is given by $\log(I_0/I_t)$, and for reflected light by $\log(I_0/I_r)$. In biological tissues, most of the light is transmitted as diffused light (I_d), while in dilute suspensions of cells most of the light transmitted is undiffused, or parallel (I_p). Filter paper lacking pinholes approximates the case of a typical biological tissue where $I_d \gg I_p$.

For translucent (diffusing) materials,

$$I_0 = I_a + I_t + I_r$$

where 0 signifies incident, a absorbed, t transmitted, and r reflected. Shibata (57) distinguishes six types of attenuance, and interested readers will find his discussion of their correspondence with different techniques a valuable basis for comparing the various instruments that have been used for scanning paper chromatograms.

An exact theoretical treatment of the densitometry of absorbing materials irregularly deposited in inhomogeneous media is not available. Some workers (32,53), have got over the problem of inhomogeneity by rendering the paper as nearly optically homogeneous as possible, by impregnating it with an oil with a refractive index close to that of cellulose. They found that a linear relationship between transmission attenuance and surface concentration of colored material (dye + protein) could be obtained in this way. With untreated paper the attenuance was increased considerably but a nonlinear relationship to surface concentration was obtained. This method involves an extra step in the scanning procedure and, in any event, does not solve the problem of uneven distribution of the absorbing material across the thickness of the paper. The author has concentrated on the alternative approach of securing conditions in which linear calibration curves can be obtained while using dry paper. This has the advantage of obtaining from two to three times the sensitivity that is found with clarified paper. The importance of securing linear calibrations (the equivalent on paper chromatograms of obedience to the Beer-Lambert law) is that this is the simplest way of ensuring that the area of a peak on the scanning record will be linearly related to the quantity of material responsible for that peak (see Section III.2.A).

The author found that a linear relationship between attenuance and surface concentration could be obtained if a narrow beam of well-collimated light were used to illuminate the paper. The transmitted light was then limited by a narrow slit before passing to the photosensitive element (selenium cell or photomultiplier tube) (17,18). It was argued that the diffused light most likely to interfere with a quasi Beer-Lambert relationship would be the light scattered at the largest angle from the axis of the incident light. It should be noted that this approach conflicts with the one most usual for dealing with cell suspensions (57). The reason for this is that, in the absence of pinholes or gross irregularities of the light-absorbing zones, filter paper approximates closely to the case in which all transmitted light is diffused (i.e., $I_p \to 0$). Under these conditions, coaxial transmitted light is likely to contain a minimum of light that has suffered scattering at large angles off axis, and a maximum proportion that has passed rectilinearly through the fibers of the paper, that is to say, light which will simulate most closely the passage of light through an optical cell or cuvette.

It is clear, however, that this arrangement does not provide an exact analog of the conventional optical cuvette for the spectrophotometry of homogeneous solutions. In the first place, the distribution of absorbing material is uneven through the paper even for coaxial light, and "on-scattered" light will be measured. Further, the observed attenuance is still much greater than with partially (water), or wholly (oil) clarified paper (17). It is, however, an empirical observation that this optical arrangement secures a much closer correspondence with quasi Beer-Lambert behavior than the more usual instrumental design, in which the photosensitive element collects light over a wide angle. Deviation from linearity has been less than $\pm 2\%$ over a range of attenuance which is more than adequate for the purposes of quantitative absorptiometry.

The increased attenuance observed with inhomogeneous media is a prefectly general phenomenon which occurs in both the visual (17,-53) and ultraviolet (52), regions of the spectrum. It was first investigated thoroughly by Keilin and Hartree (42,43) who observed sharpening of the absorption bands of cytochromes when tissues were frozen, or when kieselguhr was added to the tissue suspension. The apparent optical density was increased up to fifteen-fold in their experiments. The phenomenon is attributed to multiple reflections in the scattering medium. With the usual grades of filter paper, the intensification observed is between two- and threefold. It seems likely that this factor is an important potential source of error when scanning dry filter paper, and that it should be less variable with thick than with thin grades of paper.

A more rigorous treatment of this subject is needed and might yield profitable results. The use of polarized light is one possible line of improvement (17).

2. The Elimination of Optical Errors

A. INFINITESIMAL SCANNING

The accurate densitometry of light-absorbing material unevenly distributed over a sheet depends upon the integration of the attenuances of elements which are small enough to be regarded as having no variation of attenuance within their boundaries. Most scanners, in fact, provide integration of such elements in the direction of the main axis of the strip, but not across the width of the strip. Reasonably good results are obtained with such instruments if the chromatogram is in the form of regular bands across the strip, and as long as the bands extend right to the edge of the strip (17). In order to avoid light bypassing the edge of the strip, the collimating slits are usually arranged so as to exclude the outer 2–3 mm. of the strip from the incident light. This technique depends, therefore, upon a fair degree of manual skill in securing an even deposition of material at the origin of the chromatogram (see above) and upon conditions of running the chromatograms which ensure the absence of "edging" or other irregularities of the resultant bands.

Wieme (66) has in fact tackled this problem and built a scanner which provides cross-scanning by means of linked rotating slits. With this type of instrument, it should be possible to obtain quantitative densitometry with spots or other types of zone, as long as the extensions of any two zones do not overlap in the direction of the main axis of the strip. This device should be well worth incorporating in future instruments since it will reduce the degree of manual skill and the time required for the initial preparation of the chromatograms.

A variety of methods have been tried which avoid the use of infinitesimal scanning. Thus, Block (8) measured the maximum attenuance at the peak of a zone of an amino acid after treatment with ninhydrin, and Rockland (54) used the "total" attenuance of the zone or spot compared with blank paper under an aperture large enough to include a complete spot. McFarren (45) used Block's method with sugars. Such methods depend critically upon the shape and size of the zone or spot and a different calibration curve is needed for each position on a chromatogram. Reproducibility of these parameters is poor with many natural extracts, as distinct from synthetic mixtures

of pure compounds, unless very considerable purification is carried
out before the final chromatogram.

B. BACKGROUND CORRECTION AND DIFFERENTIAL ATTENUANCE

A large part of the total attenuance of a dry paper chromatogram
is due to the opacity of the paper itself and represents "background"
even in the absence of background color due to impurities in reagents

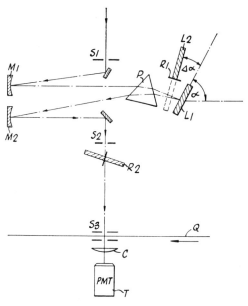

Fig. 8. Background compensator (optics).   Plan view (diagrammatic) of the
optical train of the monochromator of the Unicam S.P.900 flame photometer
modified to include a background compensator and to be used as a differential
absorptiometer.   See text for full description.   (S_1, S_2) Monochromator's entry
and exit slits.   (M_1, M_2) Primary collimating mirrors.   (P) Prism.   (L_1) Original
Littrow mirror of monochromator.   (R_1) Rotor carrying L.   (L_2) Secondary
rotating Littrow mirror (semicircular).   (R_2) Beam shifter synchronizer with R_1.
(S_3) Collimating slits of paper scanner.   (Q) Paper strip.   (C, T) Lens, photomultiplier.

or paper.   It is a commonplace that scanning records of paper chromatograms or of electrophoretograms show considerable irregularity
of the background unless the record is artificially smoothed due to the

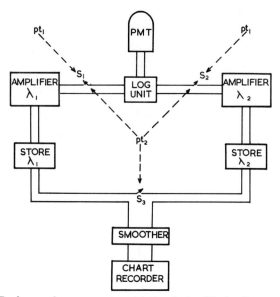

Fig. 9. Background compensator (electronics). Block diagram of system employed by author. The photomultiplier (PMT) is arranged in the logarithmic photometer circuit of Sweet (60). The output of the log unit is fed to one of two amplifier and storage units via electronic relays S_1 and S_2 controlled by a phototransistor (pt_1) actuated by the rotating Littrow mirror (R_1 and L_2, Fig. 8). A second phototransistor (pt_2) actuated by a sector stop on R_1 opens S_1 and S_2 and closes S_3 at the end of each cycle.

		Cycle	(O = open: C = closed)			
t, msec.	S_1	S_2	S_3	Littrow	Light	Electronic operation
	O	Opens	O	—	—	Cutoff signal
	O	O	Closes	—	—	—
0–10	O	O	C	—	—	Discharge difference of stored charges ($\lambda_1 - \lambda_2$) to recorder
	O	O	Opens	—	—	Cutoff store output
	Closes	O	O	—	—	Signal to store (λ_1)
10–50	C	O	O	L_1	1	Integrate signal (λ_1)
50–60	Opens	O	O	—	—	Cutoff signal (λ_1)
	O	Closes	O	—	—	Signal to store (λ_2)
60–100	O	C	O	L_2	2	Integrate signal (λ_2)

characteristics of the electronic recording system, or is one of low sensitivity. Some workers have tried to reduce this source of error, either by scanning a blank strip of paper, by repeating the scan at a second wavelength, or by scanning at the same wavelength after removing the colored material (27).

The author found that, although the irregularities were larger in the ultraviolet than in the visual regions of the spectrum, the attenuance spectrum of untreated filter paper was a relatively smooth undifferentiated curve (18). It seemed likely therefore that scanning the paper with light of a wavelength distant from that of the absorption maximum of the substances being determined should provide a useful means of reducing this source of error. It was thought desirable, however, to carry out the scan at the second wavelength simultaneously with that at the principal wavelength of absorption. Thus, it is not convenient or easy to secure exact mechanical correspondence of the two scans with conventional chart recorders unless low speeds of scanning are used. Further, repetitive scanning would interrupt a continuous process for scanning numerous chromatograms in succession, the process which was envisaged as the most suitable for automation (see Section III.5).

The arrangement chosen is shown in Figure 8. It was designed to fit the existing monochromator of the author's scanner and is probably not the most efficient way of providing background correction at the present time. A semicircular mirror (L_2) mounted in a counterweighted frame (R_1), rotates at 600 r.p.m. in front of the Littrow mirror of the monochromator. It can be set at any angle ($\Delta\alpha$) so as to secure any desired second ("compensating") wavelength. The dimensions of the mirror and its mounting are such that each rotation provides nearly square pulses of light at the two desired wavelengths lasting 40 msec., separated by a "dark" gap of 10 msec. and succeeded by another of the same duration. The rotation of the mirror interrupts a beam of light falling on a phototransistor (not shown in Fig. 8) thus activating an electronic relay which switches the output of the logarithmic photometer (see Section III.3.A, below) into one of two identical storage units (Fig. 9). At the end of each cycle, an 18° sector stop on the outer rim of the mirror mounting interrupts another beam of light activating a second phototransistor and electronic relay. The latter cuts off the input to store λ_1 and store λ_2 and discharges them in subtraction through a smoother to the chart recorder.

A second rotor (R_2) holds a semicircular plate of thin glass whose rotation is synchronized with that of the rotating Littrow mirror. This deflects the incident light in the second half-cycle so as to illuminate the same zone of the (moving) strip of paper (Q) that was illuminated in the first half-cycle. The gain on the two storage units is adjusted so as to correct for the variation of sensitivity of the photomultiplier to different wavelengths of light.

In this way, each 1-mm. zone of the strip moving at 1 cm./sec. is illuminated in rapid succession at two wavelengths and the attenuances are subtracted to provide a differential attenuance. Further development of this device is required, but evidence has already been obtained that serious fluctuations in background due to irregularities of the paper strip are reduced to between 1% and 10% of their attenuance observed when the strip is scanned without the compensator being used. Since the potential sensitivity of the instrument is about 100 times the background fluctuation obtained without the compensator, the device, by eliminating the main source of "noise," should provide a considerable increase in the sensitivity that can be obtained. The device should also provide a considerable degree of correction of errors due to impurities which give rise to anomalous spectral characteristics.

C. FUTURE DEVELOPMENTS

The information contained on a good chromatogram is very considerable. Present instruments are capable of further extension so as to collect extra information. A simpler "chopping" device would enable simultaneous scanning at more than two wavelengths, for instance. Similarly, the scanning records for all the wavelengths used could be recorded as such, and several differential attenuances could be used for the integral records from which quantitative results are obtained (see Section III.3.B, below). A second photomultiplier and source of incident light would enable the fluorescence record to be obtained almost simultaneously, with a time lag that could be eliminated on the chart recorder by suitable placing of the pens.

3. Electronics and Methods of Recording

A. PHOTOMETRY

Most commercial instruments produced in the last ten years use a relatively simple photosensitive device and electronic recording apparatus with a slow speed of response.   The output of the photosensitive element is usually directly proportional to the intensity of the transmitted light and, hence, is related nonlinearly to the surface concentration of material in the element being scanned.   A logarithmic conversion is provided electronically or by a variety of mechanical arrangements; for example, by using a logarithmic scale and manual recording of the results on linearly scaled graph paper (Evans Electroselenium Ltd. Scanner); by suitably shaped balancing neutral wedge filters; by cams regulating the pen movement of the recorder; or by cams regulating the movement of a linear balancing wedge filter in a null-point instrument (Joyce, Loebl & Co. Ltd. Chromoscan). The advantages of such instruments lie in the simplicity and low cost of the photosensitive element and the electronic recording system. The main disadvantage is a rather slow response and hence slow speed of scanning.   A minor advantage of such arrangements is that nonlinear relationships between attenuance and surface concentration can be allowed for by the use of specially shaped cams or linkages.   In the author's view, however, such circumventions of the two basic technical problems of the scanning method are unlikely to achieve the most reliable methods in the long run.

The most valuable design of photometer at present seems to be that due to Sweet (60) in which a photomultiplier is used in a feedback-circuit, which maintains a constant anode current at different intensities of transmitted (or reflected) light by varying the dynode voltages.   The change in dynode voltage is very nearly proportional to the logarithm of the change in light intensity and is measured after correction for residual nonlinearity by means of a suitable resistance and selenium rectifier network.   The advantage of this system is not only that the output is directly proportional to attenuance (or optical density) but that the photomultiplier is run at a constant anode current.   This enables a very wide range of optical densities to be measured accurately without trouble from variations in the performance of the photomultiplier, which are very prone to occur when a constant dynode voltage and varying anode current are used over a wide range of light intensities (60).

Laurence (44) used a simplified version of Sweet's circuit in a scanner for paper electrophoretograms.   The author used a similar circuit for scanning paper chromatograms and obtained a scanning speed of 1 cm./sec. by using a modified Sunvic (now A.E.I.) RSP2 recording millivoltmeter with a full scale deflection time of 0.5 sec.

The response of Sweet's circuit to changes in light intensity is instantaneous, so that it is entirely suitable for use with background compensating systems such as that described earlier.

B. RECORDING AND REGISTRATION

Quantitative work requires at least a chart record of attenuance along the axis of the chromatogram, and preferably a record of the integral of this function. If no integral record is available, the attenuance record must be sufficiently large and accurate to allow the

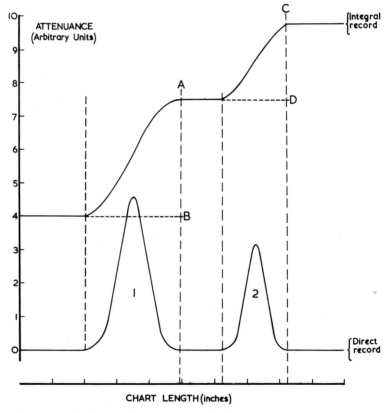

Fig. 10. Continuous integral record. The type of integral record used by Durrum and Gilford [(28); see text]. The area of peak *1* is given by *AB*, and that of peak *2* by *CD*.

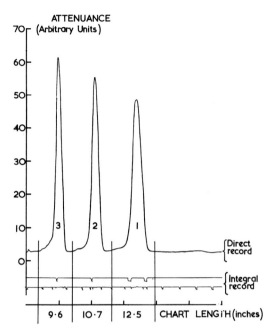

Fig. 11. Digital integral record. The type of record given by the two-pen integrator of the A.E.I. (Sunvic) RSP2 recording potentiometer as modified by the author. The record is taken from a chromatogram of valine (*1*), alanine (*2*), and lysine (*3*) in propanol–2*N* ammonium hydroxide [100:26 v/v; Hanes, (33)]. The upper line of the integral record is of tens, and the lower line of units. The areas of the peaks are proportional to the figures between the vertical projections of their limits, in each case minus a background correction. The third significant figure has to be found by measuring the fraction of the unit that is cut off on the lower integral line.

measurement of peak areas by one of the usual methods, such as triangulation, planimetry, cutting out and weighing, or counting squares on graph paper. A detailed discussion has been given elsewhere of the geometrical methods employed for fixing the base-line and resolving overlapping peaks (18). Closely similar methods are used for the analysis of records obtained with continuously recorded effluent chromatograms [e.g., Spackman et al. (58)].

Most modern instruments, however, now incorporate some sort of integral record. In such cases, the record of attenuance need only be sufficiently large and accurate to allow the precise determination of the start and finish of each peak. Durrum and Gilford (28) devised an instrument for paper electrophoretograms giving a continuous integral record (Fig. 10) (see also Zeiss Extinction Recorder Type II). On reaching full scale deflection, the pen was rapidly driven back to the base-line so as to continue with the record. More recent instruments (e.g., A.E.I. (Sunvic); Joyce, Loebl Co. Ltd.; Beckman Instruments Inc.) use a digital form of integral record which has numerous advantages. For gas–liquid chromatograms, both A.E.I. (Sunvic) and the Perkin-Elmer Corporation have produced recorders given an integral record in the form of printed figures. This can be either cumulative, or triggered so as to integrate separately the area under each peak. Examples of the digital records given by the first A.E.I. (Sunvic) system, used in the author's instrument, are given in Figures 11, 13, 14, and 16. The integrating system employed in the recorder of the automatic amino acid analyzer [Spackman et al., (58); Beckman-Spinco] would not be suitable for rapid scanning of paper chromatograms.

The existing instruments allow of several lines of improvement but are already capable of providing all that is necessary for reliable semi-automatic quantitative determinations on paper chromatograms. Integral records reproducible to within $\pm 1\%$ are provided by the better commercial recorders available at present.

C. HIGH-SPEED RECORDING

Most commercial scanners use a moving carriage to hold the paper strip, which is scanned at speeds of 0.02–0.2 cm./sec. The author's instrument was designed to be combined with the automatic reagent applicator and reaction simulator described below (Section III.5) and has a scanning speed of 1 cm./sec. Furthermore, the paper strip (dry or oiled) is fed directly into the machine without being mounted on a frame. The reason for this high speed of scanning is that 1 cm./sec. is just greater than the maximum initial speed of capillary penetration of filter paper (see Section III.5).

Most chart recorders have full scale deflection (f.s.d.) times of 1–2 sec. It is not, however, difficult to obtain modified recorders with f.s.d. times of 0.5 sec. Such recorders, and their integrators, will give results reproducible to within ± 0.7–1.0% with peaks giving 70–90% of full scale deflection, as long as they are adjusted to maximum sensitivity and are critically damped. There is no reason why much higher speeds of scanning could not be achieved by using fast-response recorders of the type commonly used in electrophysiological work.

4. Fluorometric Scanning

Successful quantitative fluorometry of paper chromatograms has been achieved with steroid (4,31) and indole derivatives (62). Suitable instruments have been devised by Brown and Marsh (12) among others, and Takemoto (62) has described an ingenious modification of a commercial spectrophotofluorometer which provides a continuous scanning record.

This field involves many of the same problems that are met in absorptiometric scanning methods and will not be discussed in detail here. It is worthy of further development due to its great potential sensitivity.

5. The Automation of Scanning Procedures

In the preceding paragraphs, it has been suggested how each of the steps involved in a typical scanning procedure can be carried out by mechanical apparatus. There are various ways in which this can be done, but the methods suggested above have been selected because they can all handle a continuous succession of paper strips if necessary —it is thus not difficult to link them together to provide automation of the complete procedure. The feasibility of this has been confirmed with the Zimmermann reaction for 17-ketosteroids (18, p. 243) and with ninhydrin for amino acids (Bush and Hood, unpublished). The author's present machine is under further development to improve its mechanical stability and durability.

The existing machine (CASSANDRA—Chromatogram Automatic Soaking Scanning ANd Digital Recording Apparatus) carries the strips on continuous belts at a speed of 1 cm./sec.—the minimum speed at which the application of reagent will not distort the chromatographic zones (Fig. 12). The reagent applicator (see Section II.5.A) is followed by a heating and drying tunnel 70 cm. long. The distance from the roller of the reagent applicator to the beginning of the tunnel is 12 cm. The tunnel is supplied with an air blast from two industrial drying blowers, delivered symmetrically via an entry port on each side. The temperature of the air blast is controlled by a heavy-duty variable transformer, and its velocity by a light-duty variable transformer in the supply line to the fan motors of the blowers. The tunnel is heated in addition, when necessary, by one or two strip elements (1 kw.) mounted above and below the path taken by the paper strips.

The belts from the reagent applicator pass through the tunnel and are taken back over pulleys to return to the inlet of the reagent applicator. On the return journey, they dip under pulleys and are

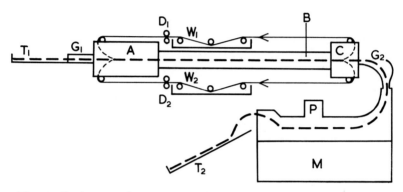

Fig. 12. Semi-automatic treatment and scanning apparatus. Paper strips are fed continuously into the reagent applicator A via the guide G_1 from the storage tray T_1. They then pass through the treatment tunnel B to be treated, dried, etc.; disengage from the belts at C and pass via the guide G_2 into the scanner (P, photomultiplier unit; M, monochromator). The strips are collected in the tray T_2. The belts carrying the paper engage in A, disengage in C and are returned to A via the washing troughs W_1 and W_2 and the drying pads D_1 and D_2. Track of paper, heavy dashed line. Tracks of belts, fine solid or dashed lines. The curved track of the paper through the scanner facilitates the elimination of stray light when scanning unmounted paper strips.

washed by jets of hot water. Excess moisture is removed by absorbent pads following the washing troughs. The belts are of stainless steel $^7/_8$ in. (2.22 cm.) wide and $^5/_{1000}$ in. (0.00127 cm.) thick.

By appropriate variations in the air velocity and temperature in the treatment tunnel, the majority of color reactions can be carried out with the existing machine. In subsequent models it is intended to lengthen the "treatment path" so as to provide a longer interval of time between application of the reagent and completion of the reaction.

The advantages of the continuous nature of this process are as follows:

1. All parts of the apparatus are in a steady state during operation.

2. The mechanical parts are simpler than with discontinuous movements.

3. It is suited admirably to the roller method of applying the reagent.

4. The control of important variables is easier, since their control over moderate periods of time is more easily achieved than over large volumes or areas.

5. The time intervals between the various stages of the process, including the all-important interval between completing the color reaction and densitometry, are constant not only for each chromatogram as a whole but *for each infinitesimal zone* of each chromatogram.

IV. SOME SPECIFIC PROCEDURES

1. General

In the following section some specific procedures of proved value will be described.   The description will include any modifications of published methods which have proved of value.   It is entirely possible, and in some cases known, that equally good results can be obtained with modifications of these procedures.   On the other hand, such modifications can only be expected to be successful if they fulfill the general requirements described in earlier sections of this article.

2. Reducing Steroids

Reagents.   *Blue tetrazolium* (BT; 1% w/v) in absolute ethanol. Aqueous *sodium hydroxide* (A.R., $4N$).
Sulfur dioxide (siphon).
These solutions are stable for weeks or months.   BT should be kept at 1–3°C. and exposed to light as little as possible.   Analytical reagent quality is essential but organic bases may be used instead of NaOH, and 95% ethanol would almost certainly be quite suitable for the BT solution.

Procedure.   Hang the chromatograms for 30–60 minutes in a fume cupboard with the fan on.

For 10 ml. reagent add 2 ml. BT solution to 5 ml. glass-distilled water and mix. Make up to 10 ml. with 4N NaOH. For Whatman No. 2 paper make up 5 ml. reagent per 100 cm.[2] of paper strip to be treated. This reagent should be made up immediately before use and should last about 40 minutes at 16–20°C.

Decant reagent into a watch glass of 14–30 cm. diameter. Holding the strip at each end, allow it to bow downwards and place one end in contact with the watch glass just above the level of the pool of reagent. "Roll" the point of contact down the glass until the reagent wets the strip, and immediately pull the strip *over* the surface of the reagent using the glass at the edge of the pool of reagent as a guide if necessary.

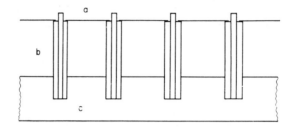

Fig. 13. Supporting strips for even drying. A section through part of the apparatus is shown. (*a*) Section through strips. (*b*) Glass plates in triplets. (*c*) Baseboard.

The speed of movement should be 1.5–3 cm./sec. and controlled with a clock or watch with a second hand. A lamp should be placed over the watch glass, giving a strong reflection from the surface of the reagent. The correct speed is that which ensures that a maximal sheen is obtained on the piece of the strip that has just left the surface of the reagent. For a given speed of movement, this also depends on the length of the strip in contact with the pool at any one moment, and this must be controlled. When the strip has been wetted along its whole length (15–25 sec.) it is moved back to its original position and dipped again over the reagent at the same speed and in the *same* direction. The interval between the end of the first and the beginning of the second dip should be 3–5 seconds.

Each strip is now laid flat on a clean glass plate or supported by its edges in the apparatus shown in Figure 13 for 10–20 minutes according to the room temperature (16–23°C.). The strips are laid in batches of 5 or 6 so that they can be placed in the sulfur dioxide tank in batches without varying the time interval between these stages by more than 5–6 minutes for any one strip. At higher room temperatures, smaller batches must be used so that this variation is reduced to match the shorter time needed for completion of the reaction.

A drop of Universal indicator is now placed on each strip just behind the origin, and a glass chromatography tank is filled with SO_2 from the siphon. This is a heavy gas and a generous quantity is needed to fill the tank. The strips are then hung in the tank from a glass rod with their origins upwards. A sufficient quantity of SO_2 is indicated by an *immediate* change of color of the spot of indicator due to acidification of the reagent on the strip. After 10 minutes exposure to SO_2, the strips are dried by hanging in a fume cupboard with a powerful draft.

After this treatment, the colored formazans given by reducing substances are stable for about 24 hours if the strips are kept dry and in the dark. Exposure to light produces fading of the zones, and a considerable increase in the background coloration before neutralization with SO_2.

It is best to scan the strips within 1–3 hours of their becoming completely dry. The wavelength of maximum absorption is 5840 A. but if a monochromator is not available, a variety of yellow filters will give satisfactory results (e.g., Ilford gelatine "Minus Blue").

Three or four standards should be run to obtain a calibration curve, and they should be treated together with the strips containing the unknowns in random order. This gives a better (i.e., less optimistic) idea of the error of the method and will avoid systematic errors.

Sensitivity. For optimum results the working range of this method is 1–10 μg. (0.002–0.02 μmoles) of reducing steroid per centimeter width of strip. The minimum detectable quantity is about 0.2 μg. (0.0004 μmole) per centimeter with zones of typical length.

Error. In seven years of routine use by research workers and trained technicians, this method (with slight variations) has had a maximum error of $\pm 5\%$ as judged by deviations of standards from the best linear regression line. Over limited periods of time in the hands of skillful workers, the 95% fiducial limits have been $\pm 3\%$. Calibration curves will be found in reference 17.

Notes. It is likely that this or closely similar methods could be used for many types of reducing substances. The initial drying of the strips is that needed for volatile solvent systems. In recent years, it has been possible to use unwashed Whatman No. 2 paper. Other grades of paper could be used (e.g., No. 20) but the softer grades are dangerously weakened by the alkaline reagent. Very pure BT is needed for reliable results (17,19). Pretreatment of the strips with 20% (v/v) o-dichlorobenzene in hexane avoids most of the errors caused by impure BT (14).

3. 17-Ketosteroids

Reagents.   *m-Dinitrobenzene.*
Potassium hydroxide (A.R.)
Absolute ethanol (A.R.)
It is best to purify the *m*-dinitrobenzene by sublimation but in recent months we have found that, despite its yellow color, B.D.H. "*m*-Dinitrobenzene for 17-ketosteroid determination" can be used without purification. When necessary, the *m*-dinitrobenzene is placed in an evaporating basin and a large watch glass containing a wad of cotton wool soaked in cold water is placed on top of the latter. The basin is heated gently with a Bunsen burner and the reagent sublimes onto the lower surface of the watch glass from which it is scraped off from time to time.

Procedure.   The chromatograms are dried in a fume cupboard. If trouble is experienced with a brownish background color, it may be necessary to adopt one or some of the following steps.

(*a*) Washed paper should be used [ethanol–ammonia (19:1 (v/v); 0.880 sp.gr.) → 80% (v/v); aqueous ethanol → ethanol–ether 1:1 (v/v)].

(*b*) The partially dried strips are dipped quickly through 80% (v/v) aqueous methanol and redried before treating them with reagent. Drying is completed in an oven at 80–100°C.

(*c*) The partially dried strips are dried at 80–100°C. in an oven containing a large shallow dish of water.

(*d*) The purity of the chromatographic solvents is improved.

(*e*) Interfering substances (e.g., aldehydes, ketones) are eliminated more completely from the atmosphere of the room.

The reagents are made up shortly before use. If sticks of KOH cannot be obtained, a generous amount of pellets is mixed quickly with 50–70% aqueous ethanol and the solvent decanted after 30–60 sec. The pellets are then rinsed twice with absolute ethanol. Sufficient absolute ethanol is now added to give an approximately $3.5N$ solution. When the reagent is fully dissolved, it is titrated and diluted with ethanol to give a $3.0N$ solution which is placed in an ice bath. The m-dinitrobenzene is dissolved in absolute ethanol to give a solution of 2% (w/v).

These solutions should be kept cool and they should not, at any stage, be warmed to hasten their preparation.

Immediately before use, 1 vol. of $3.0N$ KOH is added to 2 vol. 2% m-dinitrobenzene, mixed rapidly and decanted into a watch glass.

Each strip is dipped over the reagent as described in Section IV.2 except that only one dip is used and the movement needs to be rather faster (approx. 3–5 cm./sec.). The strip is then held horizontally in the draft of an almost closed fume cupboard until the sheen of the soaked paper has been reduced to an even matte appearance (approximately 40 sec.), following which it is hung in front of a radiant heater at a distance such that an ordinary mercury thermometer reads 42–46°C. The strip is removed when the background is just beginning to go brown, and laid horizontally on a clean sheet of filter paper. This takes about 90 seconds and the actual time is measured with a watch. After the first, all subsequent strips are heated for this length of time ±2 seconds.

After 5–7 strips have been done, the reagent will have become dark and some precipitation of solid will have occurred. Fresh reagent is mixed and the procedure is continued until all the strips have been treated. At the end of each batch of 5–7 strips, a clean strip of filter paper is treated with the reagent and heated until dry. This is used as a "protective blanket" for the chromatograms.

During the sequence it will be found that after about 5 minutes the background of the recently treated strips will have faded to a light tan or yellow color. At this point they are piled *in order* on top of one another and a protecting strip placed at the top and bottom of the pile. In this way, the colored zones will be prevented from fading, while the optimum background is achieved by allowing the preliminary period for fading to take place.

Scanning is carried out at 5400 A. in a monochromator or with a suitable green filter. The strips should be scanned in the order that they have been treated with reagent, since slight fading occurs even when protecting strips are used.

Sensitivity. The reaction is occasionally capricious and success depends on a very large number of variables. The best reagent will secure a working range of from 1 to 10 μg. (0.003–0.03 μmole) steroid per centimeter width of paper, and a minimum detectable quantity of 0.1 μg. (0.0003 μmole) per centimeter. Quite reliable results will be obtained with less satisfactory reagents which may only achieve a minimum detectable quantity of 0.3–0.4 μg. (0.0009–0.0012 μmole) per centimeter. A reagent with any less sensitivity than this, however, should be rejected.

Error. With the above manual method, the 95% fiducial limits have been about ±7% during 6 years of routine use by research workers and technicians. Certain workers have been able to achieve a value of ±4% over considerable periods of time. These figures can be improved very considerably by the use of the automatic apparatus for the treatment of strips with the reagent described above. Calibration curves will be found in reference 17.

Notes. A wide variety of procedures have been described for the qualitative use of this reaction on paper chromatograms (18,50). The description above is based on Bush and Mahesh (22) and subsequent unpublished work.

4. Fluorometry of Δ^4-3-Ketosteroids

Reagents. 2.0–2.2N $NaOH$.

Procedure. The sodium hydroxide is made up in glass-distilled water and can be used for 2–3 weeks. Sensitivity falls off after this, probably due to the accumulation of carbonate, which must be avoided.

The dried chromatogram is dipped over the reagent at 2–3 cm./sec. with as large an area of the strip in contact with the reagent as possible. The light reflected from the strip as it leaves the surface of the reagent should show the maximum possible brilliance or "sheen." The wet strip is laid carefully on a clean glass sheet, avoiding trapped bubbles of air by "rolling" it on to the glass. The ends of the strips are clipped to the plate with plastic-coated spring clips. The strips are then placed in a large, completely closed oven at 60–65°C. and left for 50 minutes. At the end of this time, they are dried either by opening the ports of the oven and raising the temperature to 85°C. or by a draft of warm air from a blower. The strips should then be a very light yellow or tan color and should be inspected under ultraviolet light (predominantly the 3660-A. Hg line or the 3600–4000-A. range with other sources). The background color should be an even *light* blue and the zones of steroid should be *light* primrose yellow. If the background is dark or violet, or if the zones are red or orange, the strips need further drying. A greenish color indicates overheating.

The strips are then subjected to fluorometry using exciting light in the range 3600–4000 A. (optimum approx. 3850 A.) and emitted light at 5500–5800 A. A variety of methods can be used. Either the strip is scanned (61), or the piece containing the zone is cut out and compared with a suitable blank in an adaptation of a commercial fluorimeter [e.g., 4, 31; cf. Takemoto, ref. 62].

Sensitivity. With adrenocortical steroids such as cortisol, a working range of 0.20–4.0 µg. (0.00056–0.011 µmole) per centimeter width of paper can be used. More polar steroids such as 9α-fluoro-cortisol and 6β-hydroxycortisol give from 2 to 4 times the intensity given by cortisol. Less polar steroids such as 11β-hydroxyproges-terone give much lower intensities of fluorescence and can only be determined in the range 0.0028–0.056 µmole/cm. Aldosterone di-acetate gives an exceptionally high intensity of fluorescence for reasons which are not understood (J. F. Tait, personal communication).

Error. Ayres et al.(4) and Tait and Tait(61) found that the range of error was approximately ±10% when working near the limits of sensitivity. With somewhat larger quantities, both Ayres et al. (4) and Gowenlock (31) found a coefficient of variation of ±7.3% over 18 determinations. The tests of Gowenlock (31) with a fluorescent dye, however, suggest that much of the error is due to variations in the paper or to instrumental errors. This should be amenable to considerable improvement.

Notes. A wide variety of methods seem to be satisfactory for carrying out the reaction with sodium hydroxide (11,15,18,22,31). The main point of all of them is to ensure that the reaction is carried on for at least 50–60 minutes before completing the drying of the paper (cf. ref. 4). Balfour (4a) found that the fluorescence can be produced by ultraviolet irradiation of the alkali-soaked paper for 50–60 minutes at room temperature followed by quick drying with a heater. Tait (60a) has found that even the ultraviolet irradiation is unnecessary. In the author's experience, however, treatment with alkali at room temperature, prior to drying with a heater, leads to very considerable loss of sensitivity with less polar steroids.

Both Ayres et al. (4) and Gowenlock (31) obtained excellent linearity (S.E. approx. ±0.5%) of their calibration curves up to 4 μg. of aldosterone diacetate (spots ≤ 2 cm. diameter).

In later work Tait and Tait (61) were able to reach a sensitivity of 0.04 μg. aldosterone diacetate (approx. 0.0001 μmole) and the limit to *visual* detection of cortisol has been in the range 0.01–0.02 μg. in the author's laboratory, using the above conditions for carrying out the treatment with NaOH (spots ≤ 1 cm. diameter).

The incorporation of minimal amounts of "red" or blue" tetrazolium (BT) in the reagent enables a check to be made on the presence or absence of a reducing group in the compound to be estimated (4,16). With quantities less than 1.0 μg., however, the steroid will not be detected unless the concentration of BT is high enough to reduce the intensity of the fluorescence obtained with the NaOH. The "double-reagent" has therefore not been recommended above. The specificity of the reaction has been discussed fully before (18). The method given above is based on the work of Bush (15,18), Ayres et al. (4), Bush and Mahesh (22), Gowenlock (31), and of Tait and Tait (61).

5. Dinitrophenyl Derivatives

Reagents. While it is possible to intensify the colors of such derivatives with alkali, it has been found better to scan the chromatograms in the ultraviolet without prior treatment with reagents.

Procedure. (Blood ketoacids as their dinitrophenylhydrazones.)

Blood (0.1–0.5 ml.) is added to metaphosphoric acid (5% w/v) and the precipitate removed by centrifugation. The supernatant (or a convenient fraction thereof) is transferred by pipette to a glass-stoppered tube and one tenth of its volume of 2,4-dinitrophenylhydrazine (0.1% w/v) in 2N HCl is added. After mixing, the tube is left at 16–20°C. for 30 minutes.

After dilution with water (approx. 2 vol.), the final solution is extracted once with twice its volume, and once with an equal volume of peroxide-free ether.

The ether extracts are combined and washed once with ¹/₂₀ vol. 0.01N HCl. The acid dinitrophenylhydrazones are extracted with

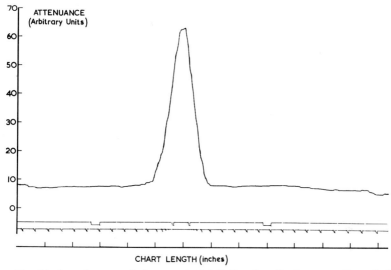

Fig. 14. Scanning record of pyruvate 2,4-dinitrophenylhydrazone.   Record of
a typical single-length run of pyruvate 2,4-dinitrophenylhydrazone in the system
light petroleum–toluene–acetic acid–water (50:50:85:15) at 18°C. on Whatman
3MM paper (see text, Section IV.5).   Direct and integral records as in Fig. 10.
Scanned at approximately 3900 A.

0.1 vol. NaHCO₃ (10% w/v).   The bicarbonate extract is now added
to a stoppered tube or separating funnel containing 5 vol. ether and a
previously determined volume of 2.5N HCl is added to bring the pH
of the aqueous phase to 2–3.   When the effervescence has subsided,
the mixture is shaken to re-extract the hydrazones into ether.   The
aqueous layer is extracted once more with 1 vol. ether.   The combined
ether extracts are washed once with 0.1 vol. saturated aqueous NaCl.
The final ether extract is cleared by filtering through Whatman No. 2
paper and evaporated at approximately 25°C. by a stream of filtered
air.

This extract is then deposited on Whatman No. 3MM paper (5 cm.
wide) for chromatography in the system light petroleum–toluene–
acetic acid–water (100:100:80:20 v/v) at 16–25°C.; or in a similar
system (20).

For pyruvate and α-ketoglutarate determinations, a single-length
run is sufficient.   The chromatograms can either be run in the
orthodox fashion taking ≥ 3 hours for equilibration and 1.8–2.0 hours

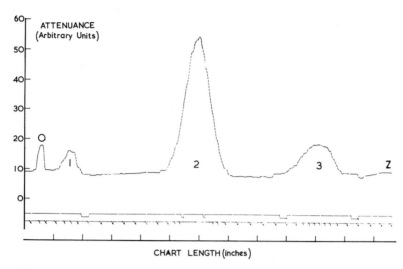

Fig. 15. Ketoacid 2,4-dinitrophenylhydrazones. Typical record of a chromatogram of the 2,4-dinitrophenylhydrazones of ketoacids in mammalian blood (human). (*0*) Origin (mainly oxaloacetate and impurities). (*1*) α-Ketoglutarate. (*2*) Pyruvate. (*3*) Nonpolar material (mainly impurities and acetone-2,4-dinitrophenylhydrazone from decomposition of acetoacetate-2,4-dinitrophenylhydrazone).

for the run, or by the modified impregnation technique described by Bush (18) in which no equilibration is required.

When the run is completed the strips are partially dried in the fume cupboard for 0.5–16 hours and then suspended for 1–2 hours in a large oven at 80°C. over a large dish of water. Drying is completed in the fume cupboard at room temperature (10–30 minutes) and the strips are then scanned using a wavelength of 3900 A. Alternatively, they can be hung in a fume cupboard overnight.

Sensitivity. A convenient working range for scanners without background compensators is 0.2–2.0 μg. (0.0018–0.018 μmole) pyruvate per centimeter width of paper. With full sensitivity a range of 0.04–2.0 μg. (0.00036–0.018 μmole)/cm. can be used successfully with a slightly larger error due to background variation. Calibration curves are linear up to amounts of 8.0–10.0 μg./cm. pyruvate (Figs. 14, 15, and 16).

Error. The error (95% fiducial limits) of the scanning procedure over these ranges is approximately ±2%, and of the whole proce-

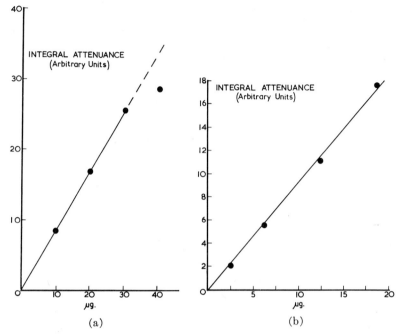

Fig. 16. Calibration curves for 2,4-dinitrophenyl derivatives. (a) Typical calibration curve for pyruvate-2,4-dinitrophenylhydrazone over the usual working range. (1.00 μg. sodium pyruvate-2,4-dinitrophenylhydrazone ≡ 0.410 μg. sodium pyruvate). (b) Typical calibration curve for 2,4-dinitrophenylalanine over a useful working range. Chromatogram run on Whatman 3MM paper for 15 hours in solvent system light petroleum–toluene–acetic acid–water (67:33:85:15 v/v) at 25.5°C. (1.00 μg. alanine ≡ 2.09 μg. N-2,4-dinitrophenyl-alanine).

dure approximately ±4%. Most of the error of the scanning procedure is of instrumental origin.

Notes. The procedure for the formation and extraction of keto-acid dinitrophenylhydrazones is based on the methods of Friedemann and Haugen (30) and of Abdel-Tawab et al. (1) [see Hockaday (38)]. The chromatography is based on Bush and Hockaday (17,20), Hockaday (38), and further work by Bush and Wall (unpublished). The conditions have been worked out for optimal estimation of pyruvate. Other solvent systems [Bush and Hockaday (20)] could be used to obtain optimal conditions for the estimation of less polar keto acids such as phenylpyruvate, or more polar ones such as oxaloacetate.

The same family of solvent systems can be used for estimating dinitrophenyl amino acids [Bush and Hood, unpublished] and for 1-dimethylaminonaphthalene-5-sulfonyl amino acids (65; Bush, unpublished) by fluorometric scanning.

The methods described above demonstrate that, with appropriately designed scanners, the estimation of substances possessing chromophores or fluorescent groups is limited only by the instrumental errors of the recording and integrating system. In general, such methods will have a smaller error than those in which a color or fluorescence reaction has to be carried out on the paper. It is reasonable to suggest that this type of procedure could be used to obtain a reliable method of determination of any substance which can be converted stoichiometrically to a fluorescent or light-absorbing derivative by the suitable treatment of biological material. The following examples of such substances and derivatives would seem to be promising candidates: phenols as diazo derivatives (36,37); amines as 2,4-dinitrophenyl derivatives or 1-dimethylamino-naphthalene-5-sulfonyl derivatives; hydroxy compounds as their dinitrobenzoates (48,49); nucleotides by ultraviolet absorption (46). In some cases, the most convenient derivative has unfavorable solubility properties and a search must be made for more suitable variants. Thus, the 2,4-dinitrophenylhydrazones and p-nitrophenylhydrazones of 17-ketosteroids run well on paper chromatograms (18) but the derivatives of C_{21}-steroids (mono-, at 3-carbonyl) streak badly in the usual solvent systems.

6. Amino Acids by the Ninhydrin Method

The ninhydrin method has been found to work extremely well with the automatic machine described above. As a manual method, however, the ninhydrin–cadmium reagent (5,6) has been found more suitable since the reaction proceeds conveniently rapidly at room temperature and is more sensitive ($\epsilon = 18,000$–$35,000$) as well as giving a more regular background.

Reagents. *Ninhydrin.*
Cadmium acetate.

Dissolve the cadmium acetate (1.2 g.) and ninhydrin (12 g.) in 30 ml. water and 15 ml. glacial acetic acid. Make up to 800 ml. with redistilled *n*-propanol and store in the refrigerator in a tightly stoppered brown bottle. This reagent will keep for at least 2 months if care is taken to avoid contamination with dust, ammonia, amines, finger grease, or perspiration. Note the large concentrations of ninhydrin and cadmium acetate which are four times those used by Barrollier (see Section II.5, above). For large surface concentrations of amino acids (e.g., in the very sharp bands of high-voltage electrophoretograms), we have, on occasion, used a reagent containing six times the original concentrations of the two major components.

Procedure. The chromatograms (preferably on Whatman No. 3MM) are dried in a fume cupboard when volatile and acid solvent systems have been employed. If systems containing ammonia or amines have been used, the strips are hung for 1–2 hours in an oven at 75°C. over a large dish of water.

The best method for avoiding serious background color on strips which have been run in phenol–ammonia systems is to hang them in a fume cupboard for 6–7 days before treating with the ninhydrin–cadmium reagent. A far quicker method which is almost equally good is to hang the strips in the fume cupboard and then overrun them (approximately 1.3 times) with water-saturated diisopropyl ether (see Section II.4). The conventional rinse with diethyl ether is only moderately successful in avoiding background color.

The dried chromatograms are dipped over the ninhydrin–cadmium reagent once at a speed of 2–3 cm./sec. and then left in a closed chamber for 2–2.5 hours. Serious defects are not caused by hanging the strips vertically, but a horizontal position is preferred. The strips are then hung in a fume cupboard for a further 0.3–0.5 hours until dry. The intensity of the red color that is produced increases slowly over the third hour ($\leq$ 6.5%/hr. at 18°C.); this should be allowed for by scanning the chromatograms in the order in which they were treated with the reagent, or by including a foreign amino acid on each chromatogram as an internal control. It is usually not difficult to arrange things so that the time interval between treatment of the strips with reagent and scanning them is the same for each strip to within one or two minutes, which reduces this source of error to negligible proportions.

The strips are scanned at 500 mμ (Fig. 17).

Sensitivity. In order to minimize errors due to background variation, it is best to work in the range 0.0025–0.025 μmole per

I. E. BUSH

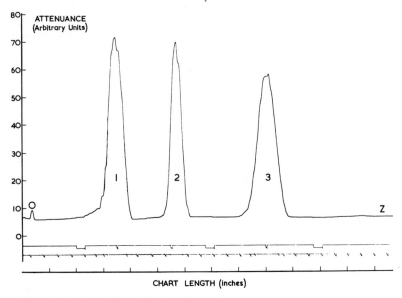

Fig. 17. Amino acids with Barrollier's reagent. Typical record of chromatogram of amino acids treated with the ninhydrin–cadmium reagent (modified: see text, Section IV.6) at room temperature (approx. 18°C.) for 2.5 hours. Solvent system propanol–$2N$ ammonium hydroxide (100:26 v/v) at 25.5°C.: run 16 hours on unwashed Whatman 3MM paper. The slight "tailing" is probably due to impurities in the unwashed paper (see Hanes, reference 33). (*0*) Origin. (*1*) Lysine. (*2*) Alanine. (*3*) Valine.

centimeter width of paper. This, however, is well below the maximum sensitivity of a good scanner, and, with close attention to the factors affecting the quality of the background, it is possible to obtain equally good results in the range 0.0006–0.006 μmole/cm.

Error. This method has only been in use for a relatively short time and a reliable measure of its error cannot be given yet. Using unwashed Whatman 3MM paper, it has been possible to achieve linear four-point regressions up to 0.025 μmole per centimeter width of paper in which the range of deviation from linearity was $\pm5\%$ (Figs. 18 and 19). It is reasonable to anticipate that with the use of washed paper and the introduction of air conditioning (the laboratory was seriously affected by smog and builders' dust during this work) it should be possible to achieve an error (95% fiducial limits) of ±2–3% in future work.

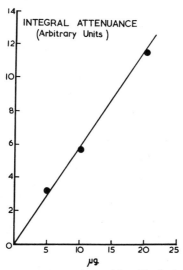

Fig. 18. Calibration curve for amino acids. Typical calibration curve for valine using fourfold-concentrated ninhydrin–cadmium acetate reagent (see text, Section IV.6) and the *lowest* convenient sensitivity of the author's scanner. Conditions as given in Figure 16.

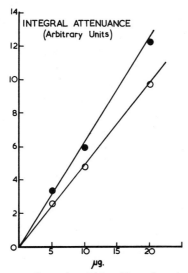

Fig. 19. Calibration curves for amino acids. Records as in Figures 16 and 17 for lysine (●) and alanine (O).

Notes. The reaction can easily be hastened by using heat, but this is best done with the automatic machine, described above, because of the need to minimize variations of the background (cf. Zimmermann reaction, Section IV.3).

When solvent systems based on pyrophosphate buffers are used (33,34), it may be found necessary to increase still further the concentration of cadmium acetate. With the original Barrollier reagent the cadmium is entirely taken up as the pyrophosphate salt and ordinary (purplish) ninhydrin colors are obtained.

The method is still rather unreliable with strips which have been run in phenolic solvent systems. The complete removal of phenol, or impurities therein, is difficult and some destruction of the amino acids takes place, which is difficult to control.

This method is based on the methods of Hanes and his colleagues (34), Barrollier (5,6), and on unpublished work by Bush and Hood (under preparation).

V. CONCLUSIONS

Experience with the methods described in Section IV suggests that it is not difficult to find conditions in which the method of direct scanning of paper chromatograms will give quantitative results with an error that is no greater than the best published methods using effluents from columns. Furthermore, this can be achieved by scanning dry strips of paper at high speed without "oiling" them before densitometry or fluorometry. This type of procedure lends itself well to the automation both of the process of treating strips with reagents, and of their densitometry or fluorometry. When light-absorbing or fluorescent substances are run on paper chromatograms, it is relatively easy to achieve quantitative determinations with an error of the order of $\pm 2\%$ (95% fiducial limits). This error is likely to be reduced by at least one half by improvements in instrumentation, mainly on the electronic side.

When the light-absorbing or fluorescent substances are produced by treating the chromatograms with reagents, after the substances have been separated, the original substances can usually be determined with an error of ± 3–5% (95% fiducial limits) without much difficulty. With automation of this step, the lower figure for the error is not hard to achieve, even when treatment with heat is necessary.

The apparatus required for such methods is not yet available commercially, but a number of slower scanners are available which can easily be modified so as to improve their optical systems. A great advantage of the automatic apparatus is that a wide range of methods of determination can be handled by appropriate programming. One apparatus can therefore serve the needs of several research groups, and the present machine could provide (integrated) records of 300 chromatograms (60 cm.) of six different classes of substances every day in 7 working hours.

Such methods are therefore extremely productive and are no longer to be considered inferior to effluent methods on the previously justifiable grounds of greater errors in the determinations.

Acknowledgments

The author is grateful for the support of the Medical Research Council (U.K.), the Rockefeller Foundation (U.S.A.), the National Research Development Corporation (U.K.), and the Nuffield Foundation (U.K.), and for the encouragement and interest of Professor Sir George Pickering, F.R.S. during the course of his own work in this field. He would also like to acknowledge the help of many collaborators, especially Dr. M. L. N. Willoughby, Dr. T. D. R. Hockaday, Miss Muriel Gale, Miss Sheila Hunter, Miss Bridget Hood, Mr. E. Reeves (electronics), Mr. D. Groves (electronics), Mr. A. White (electronics), Mr. A. J. Honour and Mr. W. C. Brown (engineering), and Mr. J. Bowring (engineering). The present scanner was made to the author's design by Mr. Edgar Schuster without whose generosity most of the author's work could not have been carried out.

I am also grateful to Dr. S. Burstein for valuable comments and an advance copy of the paper by Burstein and Kimball (reference 14).

References

1. Abdel-Tawab, G. A., E. Broda, and G. Kellner, *J. Chromatog.*, *2*, 99 (1959).
2. Abelson, D., *Mem. Soc. Endocrinol.*, *8*, 63 (1960).
3. Axelrod, L., *Recent Progr. in Hormone Research*, *9*, 69 (1954).
4. Ayres, P. J., S. A. Simpson, and J. F. Tait, *Biochem. J.*, *65*, 647 (1957).
4a. Balfour, W. E., Cambridge, personal communication.
5. Barrollier, J., *Naturwissenschaften*, *42*, 416 (1955).
6. Barrollier, J., *Z. physik. Chem.*, *309*, 219 (1957).
7. Bate-Smith, E. C., and R. G. Westall, *Biochim. et Biophys. Acta*, *4*, 427 (1950).

8. Block, R. J., *Science, 108*, 608 (1948).
9. Block, R. J., E. L. Durrum, and G. Zweig, *Manual of Paper Chromatography and Paper Electrophoresis*, 2nd Ed., Academic Press, New York, 1958.
10. Brooks, R. V., *Biochem. J., 68*, 50 (1958).
11. Brooks, R. V., *Mem. Soc. Endocrinol., 8*, 9 (1960).
12. Brown, J. A., and M. M. Marsh, *Anal. Chem., 25*, 1865 (1953).
13. Bull, H. B., J. W. Hahn, and V. H. Baptist, *J. Am. Chem. Soc., 71*, 550 (1949).
14. Burstein, S., and H. L. Kimball, *Anal. Biochem., 4*, 132 (1962).
15. Bush, I. E., *Biochem. J., 50*, 370 (1952).
16. Bush, I. E., in G. W. Wolstenholme, and E. Millar, eds., *Ciba Foundation Colloq. on Endocrinology*, Vol. 5, Churchill, London, 1953, p. 203.
17. Bush, I. E., *Mem. Soc. Endocrinol., 8*, 24 (1960).
18. Bush, I. E., *The Chromatography of Steroids*, Pergamon Press, Oxford, 1961.
19. Bush, I. E., and M. Gale, *Analyst, 83*, 532 (1958).
20. Bush, I. E., and T. D. R. Hockaday, *J. Chromatog., 8*, 433 (1962).
21. Bush, I. E., and S. Hunter, unpublished.
22. Bush, I. E., and V. B. Mahesh, *J. Endocrinol., 18*, 1 (1959).
23. Bush, I. E., and M. L. N. Willoughby, *Biochem. J., 67*, 689 (1957).
24. Connell, G. E., G. H. Dixon, and C. S. Hanes, *Can. J. Biochem. and Physiol., 39*, 416 (1961).
25. Crook, E. R., M. Harris, F. Hassan, and F. L. Warren, *Biochem. J., 56*, 434 (1954).
26. Crook, E. R., M. Harris, and F. L. Warren, *Biochem. J., 51*, xxvi (1952).
27. Durrum, E. L., see ref. 9, p. 554.
28. Durrum, E. L., and S. R. Gilford, *Rev. Sci. Instr., 26*, 51 (1955).
29. Edwards, R. H., in I. Smith, ed., *Chromatographic Techniques*, Heinemann, London, 1958.
30. Friedemann, T. E., and G. E. Haugen, *J. Biol. Chem., 147*, 415 (1943).
31. Gowenlock, A., *Mem. Soc. Endocrinol., 8*, 77 (1960).
32. Grassmann, W., and K. Hannig, *Naturwissenschaften, 37*, 397 (1950).
33. Hanes, C. S., *Can. J. Biochem. and Physiol., 39*, 119 (1961).
34. Hanes, C. S., C. K. Harris, M. A. Moscarello, and E. Tigane, *Can. J. Biochem. and Physiol., 39*, 163 (1961).
35. Hanes, C. S., and F. A. Isherwood, *Nature, 164*, 1107 (1949).
36. Heftmann, E., *Science, 111*, 571 (1950).
37. Hoftmann, E., *J. Am. Chem. Soc., 73*, 851 (1951).
38. Hockaday, T. D. R., *Biochem. J., 80*, 31P (1961).
39. Hrubant, H. E., *J. Chromatog., 6*, 94 (1961).
40. Isherwood, F. A., *Brit. Med. Bull., 10*, 207 (1954).
41. Isherwood, F. A., and C. S. Hanes, *Biochem. J., 55*, 824 (1953).
42. Keilin, D., and E. F. Hartree, *Nature, 164*, 254 (1949).
43. Keilin, D., and E. F. Hartree, *Nature, 165*, 504 (1950).
44. Laurence, D. J. R., *J. Sci. Instr., 31*, 137 (1954).
45. McFarren, E. F., K. Brand, and H. R. Rutkowski, *Anal. Chem., 23*, 1146 (1951).
46. Markham, R., and J. D. Smith, *Biochem. J., 45*, 294 (1949).

47. Matheson, A. T., E. Tigane, and C. S. Hanes, *Can. J. Biochem. and Physiol.*, *39*, 417 (1961).
48. Meigh, D. F., *Nature, 169*, 706 (1952).
49. Meigh, D. F., *Nature, 170*, 579 (1952).
50. Neher, R., *Chromatog. Rev.*, *1*, 99 (1959).
51. Ough, L. D., A. Jeanes, and J. E. Pittsley, *J. Chromatog.*, *6*, 80 (1961).
52. Price, T. D., P. B. Hudson, and D. F. Ashman, *175*, 45 (1955).
53. Rees, V. H., J. E. Fildes, and D. J. R. Laurence, *J. Clin. Pathol.*, *7*, 336 (1955).
54. Rockland, L. B., J. L. Blatt, and M. S. Dunn, *Anal. Chem.*, *23*, 1142 (1951).
55. Roland, J. F., and A. M. Gross, *Anal. Chem.*, *26*, 502 (1954).
56. Schwarz, V., *Biochem. J.*, *53*, 148 (1953).
57. Shibata, K., in D. Glick, ed., *Methods of Biochemical Analysis*, Vol. 7, Interscience, New York, 1959, p. 77.
58. Spackman, D. H., W. H. Stein, and S. Moore, *Anal. Chem.*, *30*, 1190 (1958).
59. Strohecker, R., W. Heimann, and F. Matt, *Z. anal. Chem.*, *145*, 401 (1955).
60. Sweet, M. H., *Electronics, 1946*, 105.
60a. Tait, J. F., personal communication.
61. Tait, J. F., and S. A. Tait, *Mem. Soc. Endocrinol.*, *8*, 40 (1960).
62. Takemoto, Y., *Nature, 190*, 1094 (1961).
63. Tigane, E., E. H. M. Wade, Tze-Fei Wong, and C. S. Hanes, *Can. J. Biochem. and Physiol.*, *39*, 427 (1961).
64. Wade, E. H. M., A. T. Matheson, and C. S. Hanes, *Can. J. Biochem. and Physiol.*, *39*, 141 (1961).
65. Weber, G., *Biochem. J.*, *51*, 155 (1952).
66. Wieme, R. J., *J. Chromatog.*, *1*, 166 (1958).
67. Winslow, E. H., and H. A. Liebhafsky, *Anal. Chem.*, *21*, 1338 (1949).

Automated Methods for Determination of
Enzyme Activity*

Morton K. Schwartz and Oscar Bodansky, *Sloan-Kettering Institute for Cancer Research*

* This work has been supported in part by the following grants: American Cancer Society Grants No. P-163 and P-164: Research Grant C-4251 (C3) from the National Cancer Institute, National Institutes of Health, United States Public Health Service; Grant No. DRG 332E from the Damon Runyon Memorial Fund for Cancer Research.

I. INTRODUCTION

The term "automation" has been applied to a wide variety of processes. These range from discrete replacements of man's muscular actions by simple machines to highly intricate instrumental assemblies which greatly accelerate the speed of performance, incorporate devices for controlling and correcting the action of the component parts, and through rapid computation from primary data elicit meanings at several levels of complexity. The present review will be concerned with this spectrum of automation as it has been employed in the determination of enzyme activities under various conditions.

Although the advantages of automation have been frequently noted, it is well to recognize that automation also bears certain inherent hazards. The serious economic, social, psychological, and even moral consequences of automation have been commented on by many writers (13,21,57,69). Here, we shall confine ourselves to those aspects which concern the laboratory research worker and the technicians who aid him. The simpler instances of automation are exemplified by machines that have few if any feedback mechanisms for controlling and correcting their action. They are impressive because of the rapidity and precision of their action, but they tend occasionally to entrance the laboratory worker and to lull him into a false sense of security. Many a technician, and occasionally even a professional investigator, feels that once a material is introduced into a machine the precision and correctness of the final analysis is assured. In such instances, certain safeguards must be taken lest automatism on the part of the research worker replace automation by the machine.

In the case of sophisticated instrumental assemblies with feedback control, a more serious scientific–philosophical problem may ensue. Wiener (70) has pointed out that such machines may collect and formulate data so rapidly that "an intelligent understanding of their mode of performance may be delayed until long after the task which they have set has been completed." Because of the relative slowness of human actions, criticism of the machine's performance or products could become effective only long after such criticism is relevant, and effective control of machines would thus be nullified.

As has already been indicated, all instrumentation represents some degree of automation. In this sense the introduction of various devices of general use in biochemistry during the past 20 years has proven of aid in accelerating the determination of enzyme activity. Such devices include general glassware washers; syringe and other types of automatic pipets; motor-driven instruments for mixing, agitating, shaking, and homogenizing; adsorbing columns and fraction collectors; photoelectric colorimeters and spectrophotometers. These aspects will receive only incidental mention in this review.

The optimal degree of automation for a particular assay has been considered by Patient (48). In some cases, the complexity of the procedure and of the equipment necessary for complete automation may result in a method that is not economically feasible. Another danger is "over-automation" in the sense that automation of relatively simple manual method will yield a much more complicated procedure and perhaps take more time for performance than the manual method. It therefore is the responsibility of both the investigator and the manufacturer to decide where automation is needed and the optimal extent of automation.

For the purposes of the present review, three degrees or stages of automation may be considered to exist. The first stage covers those instances in which the reaction mixtures are prepared manually but in which the measurement of enzyme activity is instrumentally recorded. The second stage involves this type of measurement as well as the automated preparation of the reaction mixture. The third stage of automation has not yet been achieved, but, in addition to the previous sets of procedures, would incorporate feedback devices for controlling and correcting the action of the instrumental components and transformation of the enzyme activities into numerical values. The present review will be concerned with the first two stages.

II. FIRST-STAGE AUTOMATION

1. General

The assay of many enzyme activities utilizes the measurement at 340 mμ of the oxidation or reduction of pyridine nucleotides (65,78).

For those initial stages of the enzyme reactions that are of zero order, the change in absorbancy per minute is a measure of the reaction velocity. These measurements require the use of a Beckman DU or some similar spectrophotometer, exact observance of timing, and the drawing of the best straight line through the observed points. Automation of this aspect of enzyme activity measurement has been accomplished by the use of recording spectrophotometers (24,47) and of special equipment designed to convert the Beckman DU or similar spectrophotometer into a linear recording instrument (6,42,74,75). Auxiliary equipment has also been developed to position automatically and periodically the cuvet into the light path of the spectrophotometer so that a number of reaction mixtures can be analyzed simultaneously (75).

2. Recording Spectrophotometers

Recording spectrophotometers such as the Beckman DK, the Cary recording quartz spectrophotometer, and the Bausch & Lomb Spectronic 505 have been designed for the automatic recording of absorption spectra. A wavelength drive automatically and continuously changes the absorbing frequency and allows the measurement and recording of absorption spectra. However, these instruments have been employed for the measurement of absorbancy changes at a single wavelength (24,47). In general, these instruments utilize a source of radiation optically directed to fall on a prism or a system of reflectance gratings in a monochromator. The prism or gratings may be rotated, and the setting determines the wavelength of the reflected energy. Upon emergence from the monochromator, the narrow band of reflected light is either divided into two beams or, as in the Beckman DK, is oscillated so as to be directed alternately through a sample cuvet and a reference cuvet. The principle of measurement may be illustrated by the Cary spectrophotometer. Where there is no absorbing material in the sample cuvet, the outputs of the two phototubes are equal and cancel each other. Hence, no voltage actuates the servo balancing motor connected to the pen of the recorder, and the pen remains in its preset position at zero absorbancy. When the sample contains absorbing material, the voltage output of the corresponding phototube is less than that of the reference phototube. The motor is activated and moves the pen away from the reference point in direct proportion to the imbalance. The greater the amount of absorbing material, the greater the imbalance, and hence the larger the pen deflection.   In the measurement of enzyme activities with these spectrophotometers, one cuvet contains a "blank" solution, and the other contains the enzyme reaction mixture.   The change in absorbancy is recorded on a chart moving at a predetermined speed.   The change in absorbancy per minute, or reaction velocity, may easily be calculated.

3. Linear Recording Instruments

The Beckman DU spectrophotometer which is a single-beam, potentiometric, null balance instrument, has been adapted for recording absorbancy changes at a fixed wavelength (6,42,74,75).   This has been accomplished by attaching an external direct current amplifier to the optical phototube system of the instrument; the built-in d.c. amplifier of the Beckman DU spectrophotometer is not sufficiently stable or linear for direct recording.   The transmittancy output of the phototubes is converted to absorbancy by an electronic circuit fed from the amplifier.

In the routine operation of the instrument described by Marr and Marcus (42) the dark current knob of the spectrophotometer is adjusted, with the shutter closed, until a full scale reading on the recorder is obtained.   The reference absorption cell is then placed in the optical path; the shutter is opened, and the slit-width knob is adjusted until the recorder pen returns to zero.   The appropriate absorbancy scale on the electronic circuit (1, 2, or 4 $\times$) is selected.   The cuvet containing the enzyme reaction mixture is placed in the optical path; the shutter is turned on and the absorbancy change recorded. According to Marr and Marcus (42), their instrument exhibited no drift in dark current during a 12-min. period and less than 1% change in the zero absorbancy setting in this period.   There was excellent agreement between absorbancy readings made on the recorder and by the usual manual technique.   The response time to change in absorbancy was less than 1 sec. and was a function of the balancing time of the recorder motor.   Assays of mannitol dehydrogenase activity with this recording system were replicated within $\pm 1\%$.

4. The Multiple-Sample Absorbance Recorder

Wood and Gilford (75) have described a special photometer which can be attached to the monochromator of a Beckman DU or any

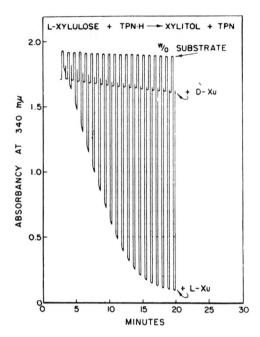

Fig. 1. Reduction of L-xylulose (L-Xu) and of D-xylulose (D-Xu) by xylitol dehydrogenase as recorded by the multiple-sample absorbance recorder.   Data of Wood and Gilford (76).

other similar spectrophotometer and makes possible the direct recording of absorbancy.   This instrument, which is now available commercially (Model 200, Optical Density Converter, Gilford Instrument Laboratories, Inc., Oberlin, Ohio), is reported to have a random fluctuation of 0.002 absorbancy units at 1.50 absorbancy units and a long term drift of 0.010 absorbancy units per hour.

This instrument and that previously described allow the recording of absorbancy changes of only one reaction mixture at a time.   Wood and Gilford (76) have developed an automatic cuvet positioner which allows the simultaneous recording of absorbancy changes in reaction mixtures contained in 2 to 4 cuvets.   The recording yields a series of interrupted lines equivalent to segments of a continuous tracing.

The instrument is controlled by a programmer which by a system of cams, microswitches, and relays, positions the cuvets in front of the optical path and times the period of observation.   The programmer also disconnects the recorder motor during cuvet positioning and indicates which cuvet is being observed. The velocity of reaction in each cuvet is accurately recorded even though each cuvet is observed for only 15 sec. of the total cycle. The absorbancy indicated by the height of each peak must then be read from the recorder chart, and the enzyme reaction velocities are calculated in the same manner as in manual determinations. This positioning instrument, in association with a spectrophotometer, a recorder, and the linear absorbancy amplifier which has already been described, allows the automated simultaneous determination of up to 4 enzyme reactions. Reaction mixtures must be prepared manually before the automated recording is begun. Figure 1 illustrates the reduction of L-xylulose and D-xylulose by xylitol dehydrogenase in the presence of TPNH.

5. Recording Titrimeters

The partial automation of the determination of cholinesterase activity has been described by Jørgensen (27) using the system of "continuous titration" (60). The measure of enzyme activity is the amount of alkali that must be added to maintain a constant pH during the reaction. In the automated system the rate of addition of a standard solution of NaOH is regulated and recorded automatically. The equipment (Radiometer, 72, Emdrupvej, Copenhagen, Denmark) consists of a thermostatically maintained reaction vessel, a syringe buret, and an automatic device to control the addition of NaOH and maintain the pH at a preselected value of 7.40 ± 0.01. The recording instrument (Titragraph, type SBR2) is preset to record a maximum titration rate of 0.06 μmoles per minute.

In the determination of cholinesterase activity in serum, 0.5 ml. of serum is added to 10 ml. of prewarmed saline in the reaction vessel. At zero time 550 μmoles of acetylcholine in 2 ml. of H_2O is added, and the titration is started and recorded for 2 to 3 min. A straight line is obtained, and the slope yields the reaction rate. Later in this report a method for the second-stage automation of cholinesterase determinations will be described. A similar instrument and technique have been used for the assay of DNAse (63).

Neilands and Cannon (45) have devised an automatic titrator and recording pH meter. The titration cell is made of fused borosilicate glass cylinders, one of which is smaller than the other. The outer chamber permits the circulation of thermostatically heated water. The titration cell requires a 5.0-ml. sample to cover the tips of the microelectrodes (Beckman electrodes Nos. 4990–29 and 4970–29). The detecting device is the Beckman model R pH meter and a Minneapolis-Honeywell recorder. Titration is accomplished by using a motor-driven micrometer syringe. A milliammeter equipped with contracts and attached to the pH meter controls the activation of the motor and the delivery of titration fluid from the buret. As the micrometer on the syringe turns and delivers the standardized titrating solution, its movement electronically operates a pen which records the volume of titrating fluid added to maintain constant pH.

In the assay of acetylesterase activity (45), the titration cell contains 2.5 ml. of 10% triacetin, 0.5 ml. of $2.5M$ NaCl, sufficient $0.02N$ NaOH to bring the pH to 7.05, and a sufficient volume of H_2O so that the final volume will be 5.0 ml. when enzyme is added. Immediately upon the addition of the enzyme sample, the syringe containing $0.02N$ NaOH is activated by turning on an appropriate switch. The reaction is carried out at 25°C. The volume of alkali added to maintain the pH at 7.00 is registered on the recorder. To minimize the absorption of atmospheric CO_2, a stream of nitrogen is passed over the surface of the reacting fluid which is mixed continuously with a magnetic stirrer.

Although, as Neilands and Cannon (45) state, lactic dehydrogenase determinations may be carried out more expeditiously by spectrophotometric methods, the titrimetric assay of this enzyme has been described to illustrate the general applicability of this instrument. The interaction of sodium lactate with DPN at pH 9.50 liberates protons since the strongly basic quaternary N atom of the coenzyme is converted to a weakly basic tertiary N atom. The volume of $0.02N$ NaOH added is a measure of the rate of liberation of protons and therefore of the enzyme activity. Neilands and Cannon's instrumentation has also been used by Schumaker and his associates (53) to assay DNAse activity.

6. Quantitation of Radioactive Material

First-stage automation has been used in enzyme studies in which the method of assay utilizes the separation and quantitation of radioactive material on paper chromatograms. De Verdier and Potter (19) have conducted studies of the enzymatic exchange reactions between thymine-2-C^{14} or uracil-2-C^{14} and ribose or deoxyribose nucleosides by the automatic localization and direct recording of the amount of radioactivity on each spot of a paper chromatogram.

The equipment (35) utilizes the commercially available Nuclear Chicago Actigraph II (strip feeding and scanner) and the Beckman-Berkeley model 1452 printout digital recorder (printer). Minor modifications in this equipment have made available an instrument which localizes the spot, scans the strip for radioactivity, and records the rate of scanning on a moving chart and the total number of counts in each peak. Up to a total of 50 feet of paper strips can be taped together, and the machine will function without attention for two days.

7. Automation of Techniques for Studying Cell Metabolism

Chance (14) and Lundegårdh (36,37) have been prominent in developing automated techniques for the measurement of respiratory enzymes in living material. The principles underlying these measurements are the changes that occur in the absorption bands when flavoprotein, pyridine nucleotides, and the cytochromes are oxidized or reduced. For example, in the completely reduced state, cytochrome a has an α band at 604 mμ, no β band, and a γ band at 452 mμ. In the completely oxidized state this compound has neither an α nor a β band. The molar extinction coefficient of reduced cytochrome a at 604 mμ is 1.7×10^4. In a mixture of several or n respiratory pigments, the concentration of each is determined by measurements of absorption at n wavelengths and solution of the n simultaneous equations that can be set up from these measurements. If molar extinction coefficients are defined in terms of the difference between absorbancies at the maximum for one component and at a nearby wavelength (36,37), this difference tends to be negligible for the other components. The relative concentrations of the several components can therefore be determined much more readily.

The instruments devised in connection with the preceding types of measurements are automated at the spectrophotometric recording stage. The chief problem in connection with the measurements in living material are the effects of the opacity or turbidity of the cell suspension. Much light is lost by scattering, and gross errors may result. Lundegårdh (37) has attempted to correct for this by using a layer of filter paper or cotton wool in the reference cell. For example, he considers that 4–6 layers of Munktell No. 3 filter paper are comparable to a 17-mm. thick layer of a 15% yeast suspension. Chance

(14) has used a double-beam spectrophotometer which is capable of measuring small specific absorbancy changes in the presence of the nonspecific light-scattering absorbancy inherent in turbid solutions. This instrument eliminates the light-scattering interference by repetitively and continuously measuring the difference in absorbancy at two adjacent wavelengths and assuming that there is relatively little change in the absorbancy due to light scattering at these two nearby frequencies.

The very high sensitivity, characteristic of fluorescence spectrophotometry, has made it particularly applicable to the study of enzyme systems in intact cells (17,20,64). In the instrument described by Duysens and Amesz (20), an excitation frequency of 366 mμ from a mercury arc passes through a series of filters which remove all existing energy below this wavelength. With this excitation energy, DPN has no fluorescence but DPNH exhibits a maximum at 462 mμ. In yeast cells, the point of maximum fluorescence shifts slightly, presumably because of the combination of DPNH with cell constituents. The spectra are similar to that of DPNH and may be utilized in following metabolic reactions in the cell involving DPN $\rightleftharpoons$ DPNH conversion. Current automation in fluorescence spectrophotometry involving enzyme activity is concerned largely with the recording of the extent of DPN $\rightleftharpoons$ DPNH conversion. In the instrument used by Duysens and Amesz (20) to study the metabolism of yeast cells, the recording was automated with an RCA IP 21 multiplier and a 1-sec. Philips recorder.

III. SECOND-STAGE AUTOMATION

1. General

As noted earlier in this review, instruments utilized chiefly in recording the enzyme activity represent partial or first-stage automation. The reaction mixture is prepared manually and placed in the automatic recording unit. A number of commercially available instruments have been used for automating the preparation of the reaction mixture in various enzyme activity assays, and these will now be described.

2. Robot Chemist

This instrument (Research Specialties Co., Richmond, California), depicted semirepresentationally in Figure 2, utilizes a system of turn-

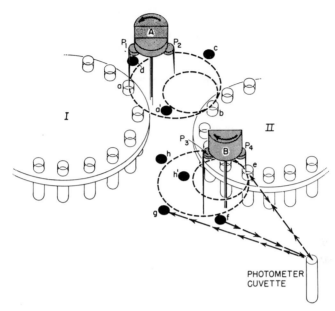

Fig. 2. Diagrammatic representation of the robot chemist, developed by the Research Specialties Co., Richmond, California, in conjunction with Dr. Nathan O. Kaplan under a grant of the American Cancer Society. See the text for details. (The authors are indebted to Dr Kaplan for the courtesy of observing this instrument in operation in his laboratory.)

tables and of aliquot transfer units each having two automatic piston-type syringe pumps. The Sample Turntable (I) contains places for 100 test tubes and rotates at a predetermined speed to present each sample tube to the Aliquot Transfer Unit A. This unit aspirates through one of its pumps, P_1, an aliquot of the sample at position a, then rises and swings around through an arc of 90°, and lowers to deliver the aliquot into a test tube at position b in a second or Process Turntable (II). While this delivery is taking place, the other pump, P_2, of the Aliquot Transfer Unit A, following an eccentric inner circle, aspirates reagent from a storage bottle at a'. At the end of the delivery, the transfer unit A rises, withdrawing the pumps from the tube and the bottle, respectively, and rotates again through an arc of 90°. Then the transfer unit A lowers so that the first pump, P_1, reaches into a bottle of distilled water at c and the second, P_2, into the test tube at position b which already received the aliquot of sample. As the reagent, picked up at a', is now discharged through the second pump, P_2, into the test tube at b, the first pump, P_1, aspirates water at c. At the end of this tandem process, the transfer unit A rises, swings once more through an arc of 90°, discharges the wash water through the first pump, P_1, into a drain at d, while the second pump, P_2, following the inner circle merely draws air. Another swing of 90° and the first pump, P_1, is ready for another aliquot in a test tube at position a on the sample turntable (I), which has meanwhile rotated to present this sample.

While this is taking place, the process turntable (II) advances the test tube containing the reaction mixture to a position e under a second transfer unit B which discharges a second reagent, previously obtained from h', through a pump, P_4, into this test tube. If this addition completes the reaction mixture, the transfer unit B rises and swings through an arc of 90° so as to bring pump P_3 to the test tube where it lowers and aspirates the reaction mixture into the cuvet of the spectrophotometer or other measuring instrument. Pump P_4 has meanwhile moved on the inside track. The reaction mixture remains in the cuvet for a precisely predetermined interval of 1 to 2 min. Then the transfer unit B aspirates the contents of the cuvet through pump P_3, back into the test tube. The transfer unit B now turns through an arc of 90°, bringing pump P_3 to position f. Here, pump P_3 siphons water from a reservoir and relays it into the cuvet. Another arc of 90° and pump P_3 is brought to a drain at g where it aspirates the water from the cuvet into this drain. Meanwhile, the inside pump, P_4, has been brought to a position over h' from which it can descend to obtain another sample of reagent in preparation for the next tube in the process turntable (II). Again a turn of 90°, and the outside pump, P_3, is at position h and the inside pump, P_4, is brought into position at e, in preparation for delivery of reagent to the next tube brought to it by the rotation of the process turntable (II).

Certain general features concerning this system may be emphasized. The transfer units can rise or descend at each position, so that the pumps can discharge or aspirate. The two pumps on each transfer unit work in tandem: while one is discharging, the second is aspirating. One of the pair of pumps, P_1 or P_3, in each unit travels on an outside circle, while the other member of the pair, P_2 or P_4, traverses an inside circle. Figure 2 indicates a system with two transfer units.

However, if more reagents are needed, additional transfer units can be integrated into the system. The positioning and operation of the pumps and the movements of the turntables are accomplished by a programmer, which consists of synchronous motors, cams, and microswitches. By substituting the removable cams, different sequences of operation can be obtained.

The use of this instrument may be illustrated by the automated assay of lactic dehydrogenase activity, as developed by Kaplan (29). The undiluted sample or, in the case of samples with high activities, appropriate dilutions are poured into test tubes and placed in the sample turntable (I, Fig. 2). This turntable then moves to bring a tube with sample into position a. The first of two syringe pumps, P_1, on transfer unit A picks up 0.4 ml. of sample, transfers it to the tube at position b on the process turntable (II, Fig. 2). This turntable is located in a well which contains thermostatically heated water and maintains the tubes at 27°C. While the sample is being discharged, the other pump, P_2, aspirates 16 mg. DPNH dissolved in 1.6 ml. of 0.1M phosphate buffer, pH 7.5, from a storage bottle at a'. The transfer unit A moves 90° to bring the pump, P_2, over the test tube at position b where it discharges the buffered DPNH solution.

The process turntable (II) containing the tube with the mixture of enzyme sample and buffered DPNH is then advanced to position e under transfer unit B. The enzyme reaction is started by the addition from P_4 of 2.0 ml. of 0.1M sodium pyruvate in 0.1M phosphate buffer pH 7.5. After this addition, the transfer unit rotates 90°, bringing pump P_3 over the tube. The contents are aspirated by P_3 into a flow cuvet in a Zeiss PMQ II spectrophotometer equipped with thermospacers. The reaction mixture is maintained in the cuvet for a predetermined period of time, usually 2 min. During this period, the change in absorbancy, representing the enzyme activity, is transcribed on a Brown recorder. The subsequent procedures are similar to those described in our general consideration of this system of analyses.

3. The Astra Enzyme Assayer

The Astra enzyme analyzer, devised by Weinberg (67) and manufactured by Astra, Inc., Raleigh, North Carolina, was originally designed to measure the adenosine triphosphatase activity of avian

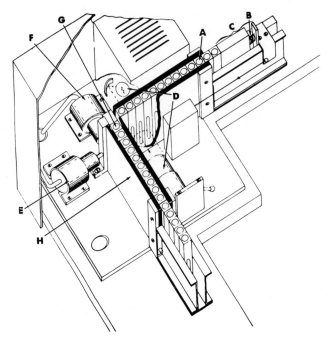

Fig. 3. The Astra enzyme assayer (67).   See the text for details.

erythromyeloblastic leukosis virus.   The preparation of the reaction mixture is automated.   The final measure of activity is expressed as the time required to achieve a stated change of absorbancy.   In general, the reciprocal of the time necessary to effect a given change may validly be used as a measure of reaction velocity, when the form of the time–change curve does not change with variation of a given condition (11).   In the present system, the reciprocal of the time necessary to effect a stated change in absorbancy at some interval during the linear portion of the reaction is employed.

The principle of this instrument is illustrated by the automation of an adenosinetriphosphatase assay (5) based on the manual method of Beaudreau and Becker (4).   Fifty-μl. samples of the enzyme specimens are pipetted manually into cuvets in the samples holders held in the chute, A (Fig. 3).   A constant-force spring, B, acts on a follower block, C, to feed the sample cuvets toward the colorimeter, D.   However, before reaching the light path, 1 ml. of ATP solution containing phenol red is automatically introduced from a reagent reservoir into the cuvet through a syringe activated by a pneumatic cylinder. The movement of the cuvet is also controlled by two electrically operated pneumatic pistons, E and F. E, the antishock piston, impinges through a block upon the cuvet, G, that has just passed through the light path of the colorimeter. As this piston, E, is gently withdrawn, the transfer piston, F, applies gentle pressure to the cuvet, G, resulting in movement down the other arm of the chute, H. Electrical impulses for the pistons originate from the timer mechanisms built into the colorimeter. These mechanisms are actuated when, as a result of the cleavage of ATP and the release of protons, the absorbancy of the phenol red falls to a value of 0.350. As the reaction proceeds and the absorbancy reaches 0.300, the timer stops. The sample number and time required for the change in absorbancy are recorded on a paper tape. The timer is then automatically reset. As has been previously described, the cuvet containing the sample that has been read leaves the path of the colorimeter, and the next sample is pushed into place for the next period of timing.

The absorbancy change from 0.350 to 0.300 was chosen for measurement because manual experiments indicated this area to be a part of the initial linear portion of the time–enzyme reaction curve. The absorbancy of the unreacted reagent is sufficiently above 0.350 to allow adequate time for mixing and transfer before the timing mechanism is activated. If enzyme activity is very high and the absorbancy of the reaction mixture is less than 0.350 by the time it enters the colorimeter, the sample number and a symbol $(-)$ are printed on the tape.

If the enzyme activity is low and the absorbancy does not drop to 0.350 in one hour from the time the sample enters the colorimeter, or the absorbancy does not drop from 0.350 to 0.300 within 1000 sec., the sample number and a symbol $(+)$ are printed on the tape. Standard enzyme solutions are periodically assayed to serve as a check on the calibration of the instrument and the indexing of samples. The standards are placed in specially grooved sample holders which activate a signal to the printout device and the symbol $(*)$ is printed along with the sample number and the value of the standard.

A modification of the instrument used for the assay of adenosine triphosphatase activity has been proposed for the determination of xanthine oxidase activity (68). In this instance a 1.0-ml. aliquot of sample is automatically withdrawn from a vial in the sample-transfer chute and introduced into a stationary cuvet in a fluorimeter. Reagents are automatically added from syringe pumps, and the time required for a predetermined change in fluorescence during the enzyme reaction is measured. At the end of the reaction, the mixture is removed from the cuvet by suction and the cuvet automatically washed with water and dried with compressed air before the next cycle.

4. The AutoAnalyzer

A. GENERAL

The AutoAnalyzer (Technicon Instruments Co., Chauncey, New York) is an instrument developed by Skeggs (58) for the rapid colorimetric determination of various biochemical constituents. Samples are placed in a constant-speed turntable and are aspirated by a constant-flow pump at intervals of 40, 60, or 120 sec., depending upon the particular determination, into a glass–plastic tubing system. The samples are diluted if necessary; reagents are added, and the flow stream is segmented with air to help regulate the flow and clean the system between the samples. When necessary, the reaction mixture can be passed through a combination of modules for dialysis, incubation, heating, or other function and finally into a constant-flow cuvet in a colorimeter where the absorbancy of the solution is read and registered on a recorder. The automated assay of the activity of a number of enzymes has been accomplished with this instrument (43,55,56,72). Several analyses in which enzymes are used as reagents (25,52,71,73) have also been adapted for the AutoAnalyzer.

B. ALKALINE PHOSPHATASE (43)

Up to 40 enzyme samples, previously poured into plastic cups, are placed in the sample plate (Fig. 4). The time of sampling is adjusted so that the 40 samples are assayed in one hour. At this rate, the sampling tube A (Fig. 4) aspirates sample for 60 sec., then retracts and aspirates air for 30 sec. while the sample plate is positioning the next sample. The reaction mixture is prepared by the addition through plastic tube C of disodium phenylphosphate (2.00 g./l.) dissolved in Na_2CO_3–$NaHCO_3$ buffer, pH 10.0. For the deter-

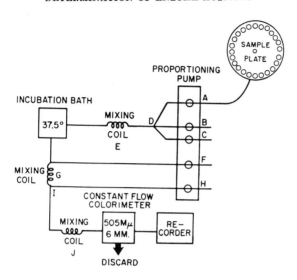

Fig. 4. Schematic outline for the automated determination of alkaline phosphatase activity (12). See the text for details.

mination of the blank values, buffer alone is substituted for buffered substrate. The reaction mixture is segmented by air aspirated through tube B (Fig. 4), passed through a mixing coil, E, and then through a 37.5°C. incubation bath. The precise incubation time is established before the run by aspirating 4% $K_4Fe_3(CN)_6$ through the sample line and noting with a stop watch the time of transit of the colored solution between D and I.

When the reaction mixture emerges from the incubation bath, the enzyme reaction is stopped at I by the addition of aminoantipyrine (1.0 g./l.) coming from line F and potassium ferricyanide (5 g./l.) coming from line H. These are also the reagents needed for the colorimetric determination of the phenol liberated during the enzyme reaction. The colored solution passes to coil J, where it is thoroughly mixed, and enters the 6-mm. constant-flow cuvet in the colorimeter equipped with a 505-mμ filter. The absorbancy of the solution is entered as a deflection on the recorder. Phenol standards are placed on the sample plate and run in a similar manner.

Activity is expressed in King-Armstrong units, i.e., as milligrams of phenol liberated in 15 min. at 37.5°C. under the conditions used. As the mixture is incubated for 6–7 min. the following formula is applied:

K.A. units = μg. phenol liberated/ml. serum $\times$ 15/t $\times$ $^{1}/_{10}$ where t is the time of the enzyme reaction, 15 represents the time in minutes used in the method of Kind and King (33), and $^{1}/_{10}$ is the factor required to convert micrograms of phenol liberated per 100 ml. We found that the King-Armstrong values may be converted to Bodansky units (7,54) by using a factor, 0.30, for the conversion: K.A. units $\times$ 0.30 = Bodansky units.

C. ACID PHOSPHATASE

The use of the AutoAnalyzer in the automated assay of serum acid phosphatase activity has been proposed by Kessler (31). The method is based on the enzymic hydrolysis of phenylphosphate and is adapted from the manual methods described by Powell and Smith (49) and Kind and King (33). The normal values obtained with the automated method for acid phosphatase are higher than those reported with the manual procedures (33,49) since the concentration of substrate is higher in the automated than in the manual procedures. Serum acid phosphatase determinations are primarily used as aids in the diagnosis of prostatic carcinoma. Determinations with phenylphosphate as the substrate, whether by manual or automated means, may give elevations in diseases other than cancer of the prostate such as hyperparathyroidism, heptatitis, Paget's disease, pneumonia, mammary carcinoma in females, and Gaucher's disease (12). Sodium β-glycerophosphate has greater specificity, and serum elevations are not usually observed in diseases other than prostatic carcinoma (77). Because of these considerations, the automated method using phenylphosphate as substrate will not be described.

D. PHOSPHOHEXOSE ISOMERASE (55)

The automated determination of phosphohexose isomerase activity was accomplished by adapting the manual method of Bodansky (10) to the AutoAnalyzer. The flow diagram for this assay is shown in Figure 5. The samples are aspirated through tube A from specimens in the plastic cups on the plate at a rate of 40 per hour. The sample is segmented by air brought into the system through tube B and is diluted with buffered substrate, 0.0025M glucose-6-phosphate dissolved in 0.1M tris(hydroxymethylaminomethane) buffer, pH 7.4, aspirated through tube c. When blanks are run, buffer alone is substituted for the buffered substrate. The complete reaction solution which contains $0.00197M$ glucose-6-phosphate, $0.08M$ buffer, and 0.21 ml. of enzyme sample per milliliter of reaction mixture is mixed in coil E and is introduced into the 37.5°C. incubation bath. The incubation period is about 11 min. and is determined exactly each day by timing the transit of a colored solution from point D where substrate and sample join to point F where reagent is added to stop the enzyme reaction.

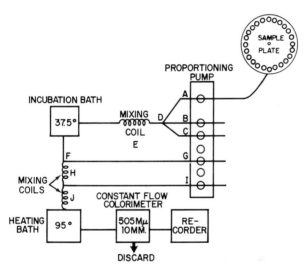

Fig. 5. Schematic outline for the automated determination of phosphohexose isomerase (55). See the text for details.

At point F 50% sulfuric acid is added to the reaction mixture through tube G, and the solution is mixed in coil H. The sulfuric acid stops the enzyme reaction without precipitating protein and also dehydrates the fructose formed during the enzyme reaction to hydroxymethylfurfural. A 0.1% solution of resorcinol in 50% ethylene glycol is aspirated through tube I and is mixed with the reaction mixture in coil J. The completed mixture is then passed into a heating bath at 95°C. where it remains for approximately 100 secs. Heating for this period results in the interaction of resorcinol with hydroxymethylfurfural to form a cherry red colored compound. The solution is then passed into a 10-mm. flow cell in the colorimeter equipped with 505-mμ filter, and the absorbancy is registered as a deflection on the recorder.

The units of phosphohexose isomerase activity are derived from an equation that permits the expression of enzyme activity in terms of the amount of substrate changed in any stage within or beyond the zero-order portion of the reaction (8).   In the case of the phospho-hexose isomerase reaction, the activity is expressed as the reciprocal of the concentration of enzyme sample, expressed as milliliters or grams per cubic milliliter of reaction mixture, that would cause the formation of 25 μg. of fructose as fructose-6-phosphate in 30 min. per milliliter of reaction mixture from 0.002M glucose-6-phosphate at pH 7.4 and 37°C. (10).   The manual method is based on an incuba-tion period of 30 min. and an enzyme sample of 0.04 ml. of serum or 0.200 mg. of tissue per milliliter of reaction mixture.   For any devia-tion from these conditions, as in the automated method where the incubation period is about 11 min. and the enzyme sample is about 0.042 ml. of serum or 0.210 mg. of tissue, corrections are necessary. The correction for the concentration of enzyme is made only when the change is beyond the zero order reaction of 49 μg. or less of fructose as fructose-6-phosphate.   Beyond the zero-order portion, the equation

$$F = 0.65 + 8.60C$$

is employed, where C is the concentration of enzyme in the reaction mixture.   The factor, F, is multiplied by the micrograms of fructose-6-phosphate actually formed to obtain the amount that would have been formed if 0.040 ml. or 0.200 mg. of enzyme had been used. This amount of fructose as fructose-6-phosphate is converted by an equation previously reported (10) or by tables based on the equation (10).   These units are now corrected for a 30-min. incubation period by multiplying by 30/t, where t is the exactly measured incubation period in the automated method.

E. ENZYME ASSAYS BASED ON THE DPN $\rightleftharpoons$ DPNH REACTION (56)

The automation of enzymes which use the DPN $\rightleftharpoons$ DPNH reac-tion at 340 mμ has been accomplished with the AutoAnalyzer equipped with a special colorimeter (56).   To illustrate the method of application, methods for the assay of glutamic oxaloacetic acid trans-aminase, alcohol dehydrogenase, and lactic dehydrogenase have been described and will be outlined in this review. The special Auto-Analyzer colorimeter was equipped with blue-sensitive phototubes and an interference filter that permitted the passage of light primarily at 680 mμ and to a lesser extent at 340 mμ. The primary 680 mμ band was cut off by a Corning 5840 blocking filter. The absorbancy of DPNH read in the automation colorimeter was 75.3 $\pm$ 2.8% of that of the same solutions read in the Beckman DU spectrophotometer. The molar absorbancy index of DPNH in this instrument was, therefore, 4.68 $\pm$ 0.13 $\times$ 10^3 cm.^{2} mole^{-1}. This factor is used in the calculation of data obtained with the automation colorimeter.

Glutamic Oxaloacetic Transaminase. The flow diagram for this assay, which is based on the manual method described by Karmen (30) is shown in Figure 6. The enzyme sample, diluted when necessary with 0.15% human serum albumin in 0.067M phosphate buffer, pH 7.5, is aspirated through tube A from the plastic cups in the sample plate. The sample is segmented with air introduced through tube B and is diluted with 0.057M sodium DL-aspartate containing 140 mg. of DPNH per liter coming through tube C. The partially prepared reaction solution is mixed in coil E, and 370 Sigma units per milliliter of malic dehydrogenase is added through tube F. After being mixed in coil G, the solution is passed through a 37.5°C. incubation bath where it is maintained for about 2 min. When it emerges, the reaction mixture is completed at point I by the addition of 0.056M sodium α-ketoglutarate, is mixed in coil J, and passes through coils in two incubation baths, joined in series, where the reaction continues for about 15 min. The exact period is determined by measuring the time of passage of a colored solution between point I and the cuvet in the colorimeter. In the special colorimeter the extent of oxidation of DPNH is registered on the recorder as a deflection toward zero absorbancy. These readings must be corrected for any absorbancy unrelated to DPNH oxidation. The "blank" values are determined by rerunning the sample, but allowing tube H to aspirate buffer in place of α-ketoglutarate.

The transaminase activity obtained by the automated method may be expressed in terms of micromoles of DPNH converted per minute per milliliter of reaction mixture by using the following equation:

$$\left(\frac{0.167}{F}\right) \times \left(\frac{\Delta A}{t}\right) \times \left(\frac{1}{4.68}\right)$$

where ΔA is the total change in absorbancy, t is the reaction time in minutes, and F is the sample dilution factor made necessary by slight deviations from manufacturer's specification in the flow rates of the various tubes. This factor is obtained by measuring the flow rate of the individual tubes by aspirating water from individual, graduated cylinders for a 10-min. period through tubes A, C, G, I, and K. F is then a ratio of the flow rates in milliliters per minute:

$$ F = \frac{[A_d/(A_d + C_d)]\, G_d}{G_d + I_d + K_d} $$

where the subscript d represents the flow in milliliters per minute. The number 0.167 is the sample concentration in milliliters per milliliter of reaction mixture.

Lactic Dehydrogenase. The glass–plastic tubing manifold for the automated determination of lactic dehydrogenase activity is shown in Figure 7. The sample is aspirated through A, is segmented with air from tube B, and is diluted with $0.067M$ phosphate buffer, pH 7.4, introduced through tube C. These solutions are mixed in coil E, and the diluted, segmented sample is passed to a glass reservoir, F, where an aliquot of the total solution is drawn off through tube G. The aliquot is mixed in coil J with a solution of 160 mg. DPNH in 1 liter of $0.067M$ sodium phosphate buffer, pH 7.4, entering through tube I, and is segmented with air from tube H. The enzyme reaction is started at point L by the addition through tube K of $0.0024M$ sodium pyruvate in $0.067M$ sodium phosphate buffer, pH 7.4. The complete reaction solution is mixed in coil M and is passed into the 37.5°C. incubation bath where it is maintained for about 5 min. The exact incubation time is determined as described in the glutamic oxaloacetic transaminase method. After incubation, the reaction mixture enters the cuvet in the colorimeter, and the decrease in absorbancy of DPNH is registered as a deflection on the recorder. Blank determinations are run in a similar fashion with buffer substituted for the sodium pyruvate and entering through tube K. The concentrations of the stock reagents are prepared so that the final concentration of all reactants, except the enzyme sample, are the same as those employed in the manual method (46). The factor, F, needed to correct the enzyme volume to that employed in the manual method is obtained as described in the transaminase section. The units of lactic dehydrogenase activity in terms of micromoles of

DPNH converted per milliliter of reaction mixture per minute in the automated method are expressed by the following equation:

$$\left(\frac{0.0167}{F}\right) \times \left(\frac{\Delta A}{t}\right) \times \left(\frac{1}{4.68}\right)$$

where ΔA is the sum of the decrease of absorbancy during the enzyme reaction and of the increase of absorbancy is the "blank" determination; t is the exact incubation time in minutes measured as previously described; F is the dilution factor; and 0.0167 is the enzyme concentration in milliliters per milliliter of reaction mixture that is employed in the manual method.

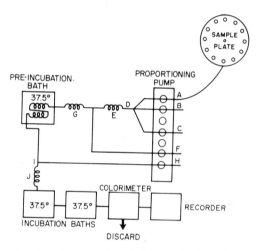

Fig. 6. Schematic outline for the automated determination of glutamic oxaloacetic transaminase (56). See the text for details.

Other Enzymes. The principles of the methods described in the preceding sections are applicable to the automated assay of other enzymes utilizing DPN $\rightleftharpoons$ DPNH. For example, the automated assay of the activity of alcohol dehydrogenase (56) has been based on the increase in absorbancy of DPN at 340 mμ, following the manual method devised by Racker (50). A flow system was devised that was similar to those shown in Figures 6 and 7. The following reactants were aspirated per minute: 0.32 ml. of enzyme solution in 0.067M phosphate buffer, pH 7.4, and 0.15% human serum albumin; 0.80 ml.

of air; 2.50 ml. of 0.0246M sodium pyrophosphate buffer, pH 8.5. These solutions were joined and mixed with additional air at the rate of 0.80 ml./min. and with 0.341M ethanol at the rate of 2.0 ml./min. The reactants were brought to 37.5°C. by passage through an incubation bath for approximately 30 sec. and mixed with an aqueous solution of 113 mg. DPN per liter, introduced at the rate of 2.0 ml./min. The complete reaction mixture was then incubated at 37.5°C. for a precisely determined interval of about 2 min. The extent of the reduction of DPN was recorded, and the velocity per minute was calculated.

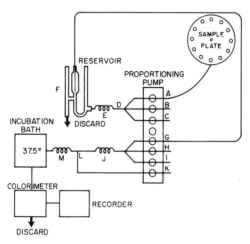

Fig. 7. Schematic outline for the automated determination of lactic dehydrogenase (56). See the text for details.

Similar methods are applicable to the automated assay of enzymes involving TPN $\rightleftharpoons$ TPNH reaction. Wu and Racker (78) have described a scheme for the analysis of various glycolytic enzymes such as hexokinase, glucose-6-phosphate isomerase, aldolase, phosphofructokinase, α-glycerophosphate dehydrogenase, and D-glyceraldehyde-3-phosphate dehydrogenase in which the final step of the assay depends on the reactions DPN $\rightleftharpoons$ DPNH or TPN $\rightleftharpoons$ TPNH. It would appear quite feasible to automate the assays of these enzymes according to the principles which have been described in this section.

F. CHOLINESTERASE

Winter (72) has described a method for the automated assay of cholinesterase activity by means of the AutoAnalyzer. The method is based on the change in pH of a buffered solution containing phenol red produced by the acetic acid enzymatically liberated from the substrate, acetylcholine (3). The flow diagram for this assay is shown in

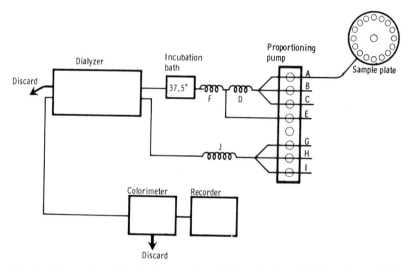

Fig. 8. Schematic outline for the automated determination of cholinesterase (72). See the text for details.

Figure 8. The sample is aspirated through tube A and segmented with air drawn through tube B. Barbital phosphate buffer containing NaCl and saponin and having a pH of 8.10 is aspirated through tube C. The components are mixed in coil D. An aqueous solution of 20 g. acetylcholine iodide per liter is added through tube E; the completed reaction solution is mixed in coil F and is then introduced into a 37.5°C. incubation bath. After emerging from the incubation bath the reaction mixture passes to the upper portion of a dialyzer module. A phenol red solution, prepared by aspirating 0.0225% aqueous phenol red through tube G, air through tube H, and 10% NaCl through tube I, is mixed in coil J, and passes into the lower portion of the dialyzer. The protons of the acetic acid liberated from acetylcholine by cholinesterase pass through the dialysis membrane into the phenol red solution. The extent of decolorization is measured when this solution enters the constant flow 6 mm. cuvet of the colorimeter equipped with a 555 mμ filter. The units of cholinesterase activity are determined from a standard curve based on the activities of various dilutions of purified acetylcholinesterase preparation (Winthrop Laboratories, New York, New York.) The working solutions are prepared to contain from 10 to 100 units of cholesterase activity per milliliter (3).

IV. COMPUTER TECHNIQUES

Most of the automated methods for enzyme assay that have been described in the preceding sections yield recorded deflections that represent transmittancies or absorbancies. Calculations, which are largely manual in nature, are then required to transform these deflections into units of enzyme activity or various kinetic or other formulations based on such activity. These calculations are very often laborious and time-consuming.

Computer technology, or the science of speeding up calculation and storing information necessary for such calculation, has a history of over 300 years (61). The development of high-speed computers began largely during World War II. One class of computers, the digital, is based on the performance of computations in terms of discrete numbers, as contrasted with a second class of analog computers which are devised to deal with continuous quantities. Computer techniques have so far not been applied to the output of instruments used in the automated enzyme methods that have been described earlier in this paper, but have been utilized in several kinetic and other enzyme studies (1,14–16,26,44).

Computer techniques have, of course, been used widely in biological problems (18,66). Of particular relevance to the subject of this review is the study of Mason et al. (44). The effect of five treatments each of 25 days on the daily volume of urine and the activity of glutamic oxaloacetic transaminase was studied in each of six dogs. The data were subjected to analysis of variance by means of a digital computer. It was found that the total excretion of enzyme was significantly increased when the animals were drinking saline or water. According to the investigators, the manual calculations would have taken weeks of labor with paper, pencil, and desk calculator, whereas the whole procedure was accomplished by the computer in less than one minute.

Chance and his associates (14–16,18) have been most prominent in the application of computer techniques to the kinetics of enzyme reactions and of cellular intermediary metabolism (16,18). For example, oxidative phosphorylation was studied by means of both analog and digital computers. Within the past few years, Chance and his associates have developed a digital computer which can accept up to 49 chemical components, each of which may be variable throughout the course of the reaction. These components may participate in one or more first-, second- or third-order, reversible or irreversible reactions. The computer is able to produce graphic data showing the concentrations of initial reactants and of metabolic intermediates at various stages of the reaction. For studying an ascites tumor system involving 32 compounds, the time for the solution of this problem by the computer was 45 min. The programming required about 6 man-years and 500 hours of computer time (18). The kinetics of the reaction of a single enzyme has been studied by the differential mechanical analyzer, by the analog computer, and, most recently, by the digital computer (16). The last procedure yields values for the concentrations of substrate, enzyme substrate intermediate, free enzyme, and reaction product at any time during the course of the reaction. The accuracy of these computers has been discussed by Chance (16,18).

The use of computer techniques in the determination of reaction rates and Michaelis constants or other parameters of the actions of various enzymes will undoubtedly find increasing application. Hommes (26) has recently utilized the analog computer in studying these aspects in the carboxypeptidase A-catalyzed hydrolysis of chloracetyl phenylalanine at three different substrate concentrations, three different enzyme concentrations, and five pH levels between 6.5 and 9.0.

V. USE OF ENZYMES IN AUTOMATED ANALYTICAL PROCEDURES

1. General

For many years, enzymes have been employed as reagents to increase the specificity of manual methods for the quantitative biochemical determination of components in the blood and urine. These have included the use of urease for urea (23), a bacterial enzyme preparation for creatinine (2), uricase for uric acid (28), glucose oxidase for glucose (32,51,62), and alcohol dehydrogenase for alcohol (34). Several automated biochemical analyses have been based on the use of such enzyme methods. These include the determination of glucose (25,38–40,71), L-lysine (52), organic phosphate pesticides (73), and alcohol (41).

2. Glucose

The determination by means of glucose oxidase involves a coupled reaction (25,38–40,71). In the presence of the oxidase, glucose interacts with water and oxygen to form gluconic acid and H_2O_2. Under the influence of peroxidase, H_2O_2 oxidizes the leuco form of an appropriate dye to the colored form, the absorbancy of which is determined colorimetrically or spectrophotometrically. Malmstadt and Pardue (39) couple the production of H_2O_2 in the first reaction with a second reaction in which, under the catalytic influence of molybdenum, H_2O_2 interacts with iodide in acid solution to form free iodine. As will be noted later, the resultant change in electromotive force (e.m.f.) measures the rate of reaction.

Two automated procedures employing the AutoAnalyzer have been proposed for this assay. In the method described by Wincey and Marks (71) the sample of blood, spinal fluid, or urine flows at a rate of 0.6 ml./min. into a dialyzing module. The glucose is partially dialyzed into a stream of distilled water flowing at the rate of 1.2 ml./min. and containing two drops of Tween 20 per liter. When the dialysate emerges, it is mixed with 2.9 ml./min. of $0.465M$ sodium acetate buffer, pH 5.0, containing in each milliliter 0.01 mg. of hydrogen peroxidase (C. F. Boehringer U. Soehne, Mannheim-Waldhof, Germany); 0.01 mg. tolidine and 0.01 ml. of a solution of glucose oxidase (Fermcozyme, Hughes & Hughes, London). The solution is successively passed through a coil maintained at 25°C. and a colorimeter equipped with a 6-mm. flow cell and 660-mμ filters. The absorbancy of the solution is registered on a recorder and compared with that obtained with glucose standards processed in a similar fashion.

In the method of Hill and Kessler (25), the sample containing glucose is aspirated at the rate of 0.42 ml./min., segmented with air, diluted with 2.90 ml. of 1.61% Na$_2$SO$_4$ per minute, and then introduced into the dialyzer. The glucose is dialyzed into a solution of 1.61% Na$_2$SO$_4$ and 0.25% Triton X-100, flowing at the rate of 5.00 ml./min. The dialysate is mixed with 2.5 ml./min. of 0.1M phosphate buffer, pH 7.0, containing per milliliter 25 mg. of a glucose oxidase preparation (Miles Chemical Co.) and 0.2 mg. of a horseradish peroxidase (Worthington Chemical Co.). The resulting mixture, flowing at a rate of 7.5 ml./min., then mixes with a solution of o-dianisidine (0.5 mg./ml.), glycerol (0.25 g./ml.), and ethanol (0.10 g./ml.), flowing at a rate of 2.50 ml./min. The complete reaction mixture is passed into the 37°C. incubation bath and then into a colorimeter with a 10-mm. flow cell and a 460-mμ filter. The recorded absorbancy is compared with those obtained from known standards, and the appropriate calculations are made.

Malmstadt and his associates (38–40) have described three procedures for first-stage automated determination of glucose by the glucose oxidase reaction. In these procedures a protein-free filtrate is prepared manually when the sample contains protein, and sample aliquots as well as reagents are pipetted into a reaction vessel before the automated procedure is instituted. In the first method (38), 2.00 ml. of sample or protein-free filtrate and 10 ml. of 0.01M phosphate buffer, pH 7.0, containing 0.025 mg. of horseradish peroxidase and 0.25 mg. of o-dianisidine per milliliter, are pipetted into a 30-ml. beaker. The beaker is placed in the spectrophotometric section of a spectrophotometric–electrometric titrator (E. H. Sargent and Co., Chicago, Ill.). This is equipped with interference and glass cutoff filters to provide a single narrow transmittance band near 400 mμ. The pressing of a button on a control unit activates an injector unit to add 1.0 ml. of a solution containing 20 mg. glucose oxidase preparation. The completed reaction mixture is continuously mixed by a microstirrer (E. H. Sargent & Co.). After a 20–30 sec. lag period to allow for initial mixing, the time interval between two arbitrarily predetermined voltage outputs of the photoconductive detector circuit of the spectrophotometric unit is registered as the enzyme reaction proceeds and as o-dianisidine is oxidized to the colored form. A standard of 50 mg./100 ml. requires about 100 sec. to achieve the prescribed voltage difference. The time to reach the voltage difference for other standards is inversely proportional to the concentration.   However, these times must be precisely determined with each run.

In a second procedure Malmstadt and Pardue (39) describe the measurement of glucose by an automatic potentiometric reaction rate method.   As noted previously, the H_2O_2 formed during the action of glucose oxidase reacts in a sample cell with iodide in the presence of molybdenum to form iodine.   The sample cell is connected electrically through its sealed end with a reference cell containing iodine and iodide.   The formation of iodine in the sample cell results in a change in e.m.f. which is recorded in terms of glucose concentration.   According to the authors, the sensitivity of the method permits measurements of glucose concentrations as low as 5 μg./ml.   In this method, just as in the one previously described, reagents and prepared sample are added manually to the reaction vessel before the automated measurement of the time between two predetermined voltage outputs.   Malmstadt and S. I. Hadjiioannou have recently reported another modification (40).

3. L-Lysine

In 1960 Schwaiberger and Ferrari (52) described the application of the AutoAnalyzer to the assay of L-lysine in fermentation broth obtained during the microbiological manufacture of amino acids. The method is based on the continuous colorimetric determination of the carbon dioxide formed during the enzymatic decarboxylation of L-lysine by L-lysine decarboxylase.

A glass–plastic tubing manifold similar to those described for other AutoAnalyzer methods is prepared.   The sample of broth, flowing at 0.32 ml./min., is segmented with air and is diluted with 2.8 ml./min. of distilled water containing a few drops of Tween 20.   Further dilution of the sample is achieved by passage into an overflow sampler. An aliquot of 0.8 ml./min. is withdrawn, segmented with air, and mixed with 1.6 ml./min. of 0.2M phosphate buffer, pH 6.0, containing 5 mg. of L-lysine decarboxylase (Nutritional Biochemical Co.) per milliliter and a small amount of an antifoam reagent (Dow Corning Antifoam B).   The complete reaction mixture is introduced into a coil in a 37°C. incubator.   When the stream emerges from the coil, it passes into a liquid–gas separator.   The enzymatically produced CO_2 is aspirated off and is introduced into a sodium bicarbonate–carbonate buffer containing phenolphthalein.   The extent of phenolphthalein decolorization is a measure of the amount of CO_2 and is indicated by a recorder deflection toward zero absorbancy. The colorimeter is equipped with a 6-mm. flow cell and 555-mμ filters. The CO_2 assay is essentially that described by Skeggs (59) for measurement of this substance in blood serum. The method used for the assay of L-lysine may be adapted to the assay of any amino acid where a specific decarboxylase is available. In addition, the assay of any decarboxylase could also be performed in this manner.

4. Organic Phosphate Pesticide Residue

The automated procedure described previously for the determination of cholinesterase activity (72) has been utilized for the estimation of organic phosphate pesticide residues. This consists in determining the degree of inhibition of cholinesterase activity by the oxidized forms of these compounds (73). Many of these substances are thionophosphate or dithiophosphate esters and themselves do not inhibit or inhibit weakly cholinesterase *in vitro*. Oxidation, preferably by bromine water, convert them to effective inhibitors (22).

The manifold for the assay utilizes two AutoAnalyzers: one for the preparation of pesticide-inhibited cholinesterase and the other for the cholinesterase assay as previously described. A specially machined sample plate which has two opposite rows of holes to contain plastic cups is used. In the outer row are placed the samples of pesticide, and in the inner row are placed standard aqueous solutions (100 units/ml.) of bovine erythrocyte acetyl cholinesterase B (Winthrop Laboratories). The standard solution of cholinesterase is aspirated at a rate of 0.42 ml./min., is segmented with air, and is diluted with 0.6 ml./min. of a buffer solution containing 0.400 g. sodium barbital, 0.400 g. KH_2PO_4, and 12.00 g. NaCl per liter. The aqueous or alcohol solution of the insecticide sample is aspirated simultaneously from the outer row of cups at a rate of 0.6 ml./min., is segmented with air, and is diluted with 0.42 ml./min. of a solution containing 0.05 ml. saturated bromine water per milliliter H_2O. The streams of diluted enzyme and inhibitor are joined, mixed, and then introduced into a coil maintained at 37°C. Upon emerging from the incubator, the inhibited enzyme passes into an overflow sampler, and an aliquot is aspirated at a rate of 1.20 ml./min. The inhibited cholinesterase is then assayed for activity, as described earlier in this review (72). Standard solutions of the pesticide are assayed in a similar fashion, and the concentration of the pesticide is thus determined. If the chemical nature of the pesticide is unknown, its concentration can nonetheless be expressed in terms of a known cholinesterase-inhibiting pesticide, such as Parathion.

5. Ethanol

Malmstadt and T. P. Hadjiioannou (41) have recently described a first-stage automation procedure for the determination of ethanol. This is based on the oxidation of ethanol in the presence of alcohol dehydrogenase and DPN. The time required for the formation of sufficient DPNH during the initial stage of the reaction to correspond to a change of 0.06 in absorbancy is measured and recorded. The principles and instrument are similar to those employed by Malmstadt and his associates for the determination of glucose (38–40).

VI. CONCLUDING REMARKS

The present article has reviewed available methods for the automated determinations of the activities of various enzymes, and the analysis of biochemical components based on the use of enzymes as reagents. In these connections, it has been convenient to conceive of three stages of automation. The first stage includes those procedures in which the reaction mixtures are prepared manually, but in which the measurement of the enzyme activity is recorded instrumentally. Second-stage automation is characterized by automated preparation of the reaction mixtures as well as the instrumental recording of the activity. The future will see the achievement of the third stage of automation. In addition to the previous procedures, this stage will incorporate feedback devices for controlling and correcting the action of the instrumental components, the transformation of the enzyme activities into numerical values, and through built-in computers, yield values for such enzyme characteristics as Michaelis constants, inhibitor constants, or energy of activation. This stage of automation would therefore speed the performance and increase the efficiency of many research projects.

Many hospital laboratories today perform determinations of alkaline and acid phosphatase, glutamic oxaloacetic transaminase, amylase, and lipase. There are also increasing demands for determinations of other serum enzymes, such as lactic dehydrogenase, nucleotidase, leucine aminopeptidase, and cholinesterase. Several present research activities and trends create prospects for an expanding role of enzymology in diagnostic biochemistry.

Within recent years it has been recognized that what was formerly considered a single enzyme protein now may have several variants, that these variants may have different constellations in different tissues, and that these differences may be exploited diagnostically (9). In several inherited metabolic diseases such as galactosemia, hypophosphatasia, and acatalasia, the basic enzymatic defect is reflected in the peripheral blood and is thus susceptible of ready detection. The possibility exists that other members of this group of diseases or even other diseases may be found to have enzymatic alterations that can be analyzed for either in the blood or in very small pieces of tissues. Second-stage automation is being used today in the determination of some of the presently accepted enzyme determinations but will be inadequate for all the aspects that have been outlined above.

Non-enzymatic procedures are also within the province of the present diagnostic biochemistry laboratory, and several of these have now been successfully automated at a second-stage level. The role of diagnostic biochemistry in clinical medicine, greatly as it has increased in the past decade, will undoubtedly show still further expansion during the next ten years.

The economics of handling the increased demands by the clinician for enzyme determinations and, more generally, for all diagnostic biochemical determinations, will be burdensome unless automation in its final or third stage is realized. The diagnostic biochemistry laboratory of the future may therefore contain a dozen or more of presently automated instruments, such as the Robot Chemist, the Astra Assayer, the AutoAnalyzer, or other types still under development, and even large consoles combining several of these instruments. One may envision that feedback devices would ensure precision and accuracy of the determinations, and that suitable instrumentation would classify the results of these determinations according to the patients' floors or wards and continuously and electronically relay and enter them in the patients' records, ready for the physician's perusal.

It might also be economically advantageous to maintain central city, county, or state laboratories for the automation of those determinations which the staff of any single hospital requests infrequently, such as serum bromide, gastric and urinary barbiturates, urinary porphobilinogen, steroid metabolites, or any others that future clinical investigation might reveal to be of value in the difficult or unusual case. Adequate instrumentation for the dispatch of the specimen and the electronic relaying of the result to the physician would overcome the disadvantages of distance.

Considerable data are already available on the correlation of biochemical and, more broadly, on other laboratory parameters with clinical findings in various diseases, and with the various stages of these diseases. This body of information could be expanded and incorporated into memory units in computers which would facilitate the rapid diagnosis of disease and the management of the patient.

References

1. Abrush, H. I., A. N. Kurtz, and C. Niemann, *Biochem. et Biophys. Acta, 45*, 378 (1960).
2. Allinson, M. J. C., *J. Biol. Chem., 157*, 169 (1945).
3. Ammon, R., *Pflüger's Arch. ges. Physiol., 233*, 486 (1933).
4. Beaudreau, G. S., and C. Becker, *J. Natl. Cancer Inst., 20*, 339 (1958).
5. Becker, C., G. S. Beaudreau, D. I. Weinberg, and J. W. Beard, *J. Natl. Cancer Inst.* (in press).
6. Bock, R. M., and R. A. Alberty, *J. Am. Chem. Soc., 75*, 1921 (1953).
7. Bodansky, A., *J. Biol. Chem., 101*, 93 (1933).
8. Bodansky, O., *J. Biol. Chem., 205*, 731 (1953).
9. Bodansky, O., in A. Haddow and S. Weinhouse, eds., *Advances in Cancer Research, Vol. 6*, Academic Press, New York, 1961, p. 1.
10. Bodansky, O., *Cancer, 7*, 1191 (1954).
11. Bodansky, O., *Am. J. Med., 27*, 861 (1959).
12. Bodansky, O., and M. K. Schwartz, in J. A. Quastel, ed., *Methods in Medical Research, Vol. 9*, Year Book Medical Publishers, Inc., Chicago, 1960, p. 92.
13. Bright, J. R., *Harvard Business Review, 36*, 85 (1958).
14. Chance, B., *Proceedings of the IRE, 47*, 1821 (1959).
15. Chance, B., D. Garfinkel, J. Higgins, and B. Hess, *J. Biol. Chem., 235*, 2426 (1960).
16. Chance, B., *J. Biol. Chem., 235*, 2440 (1960).
17. Chance, B., and H. Baltscheffsky, *J. Biol. Chem., 233*, 736 (1958).
18. Chance, B., J. J. Higgins, and D. Garfinkel, *Federation Proc., 21*, 75 (1962).
19. De Verdier, C., and V. R. Potter, *J. Natl. Cancer Inst., 24*, 13 (1960).
20. Duysens, L. N. M., and J. Amesz, *Biochem. et Biophys. Acta, 24*, 19 (1957).
21. Einzig, P., *The Economic Consequences of Automation*, W. W. Norton & Co., Inc., New York, 1957.
22. Fallscheer, H. O., and J. W. Cook, *J. Assoc. Offic. Agr. Chemists, 39*, 691 (1956).
23. Folin, O., and A. Svedberg, *J. Biol. Chem., 88*, 77 (1930).

24. Garcia-Hernandez, M., and E. Kuh, *Biochem. et Biophys. Acta*, *24*, 78 (1957).
25. Hill, J. B., and G. Kessler, *J. Lab. Clin. Med.*, *57*, 970, (1961).
26. Hommes, F. A., *Arch. Biochem. Biophys.*, *96*, 28; 32; 37 (1962).
27. Jørgensen, K., *Scand. J. Clin. Lab. Invest.*, *11*, 282 (1959).
28. Kalckar, H. M., *J. Biol. Chem.*, *167*, 429 (1947).
29. Kaplan, N. O., personal communication.
30. Karmen, A., *J. Clin. Invest.*, *34*, 131 (1957).
31. Kessler, G., personal communication.
32. Keston, A. S., *Abstracts 129th Meeting Am. Chem. Soc.*, 31C (1956).
33. Kind, P. R. N., and E. J. King, *J. Clin. Pathol.*, *7*, 322 (1954).
34. Kirk, P. L., A. Gibor, and K. P. Parker, *Anal. Chem.*, *30*, 1418 (1958).
35. Ludwig, H., V. R. Potter, C. Heidelberger, and C. H. De Verdier, *Biochem. et Biophys. Acta*, *37*, 525 (1960).
36. Lundegårdh, H., *Endeavour*, *18*, 191, (1959).
37. Lundegårdh, H., *Biochem. et Biophys. Acta*, *20*, 469 (1956).
38. Malmstadt, H. V., and G. P. Hicks, *Anal. Chem.*, *32*, 394 (1960).
39. Malmstadt, H. V., and H. L. Pardue, *Anal. Chem.*, *33*, 1040 (1961).
40. Malmstadt, H. V., and S. I. Hadjiioannou, *Anal. Chem.*, *34*, 452 (1962).
41. Malmstadt, H. V., and T. P. Hadjiioannou, *Anal. Chem.*, *34*, 455 (1962).
42. Marr, A. G., and L. Marcus, *Anal. Biochem.*, *2*, 576 (1961).
43. Marsh, W., B. Fingerhut, and E. Kirsch, *Clin. Chem.*, *5*, 119 (1959).
44. Mason, E. E., F. Chernigoy, and B. Cusminsky, *J. Am. Med. Assoc.*, *178*, 110 (1961).
45. Neilands, J. B., and M. D. Cannon, *Anal. Chem.*, *27*, 29 (1955).
46. Nisselbaum, J. S., and O. Bodansky, *J. Biol. Chem.*, *234*, 3276 (1959).
47. Noltmann, E. A., C. J. Bubler, and S. A. Kuby, *J. Biol. Chem.*, *236*, 1225 (1961).
48. Patient, D. A., *Ann. N.Y. Acad. Sci.*, *87*, 830 (1960).
49. Powell, M. E. A., and M. J. H. Smith, *J. Clin. Pathol.*, *1*, 245 (1954).
50. Racker, E., *J. Biol. Chem.*, *184*, 313 (1950).
51. Saifer, A., and S. Gerstenfeld, *J. Lab. Clin. Med.*, *51*, 448 (1958).
52. Schwaiberger, G. E., and A. Ferrari, *Ann. N.Y. Acad. Sci.*, *87*, 890 (1960).
53. Schumaker, V. N., E. G. Richards, and H. K. Schachman, *J. Am. Chem. Soc.*, *78*, 4230 (1956).
54. Schwartz, M. K., G. Kessler, and O. Bodansky, *Am. J. Clin. Pathol.*, *33*, 275 (1960).
55. Schwartz, M. K., G. Kessler, and O. Bodansky, *Ann. N.Y. Acad. Sci.*, *87*, 616 (1960).
56. Schwartz, M. K., G. Kessler, and O. Bodansky, *J. Biol. Chem.*, *236*, 1207 (1961).
57. Schultz, G. P., and G. B. Baldwin, *Automation, A New Dimension to Old Problems*, Public Affairs Press, Washington, D.C., 1955.
58. Skeggs, L. T., Jr., *Am. J. Clin. Pathol.*, *28*, 311 (1957).
59. Skeggs, L. T., *Am. J. Clin. Pathol.*, *33*, 181 (1960).
60. Stedman, E., E. Stedman, and L. H. Easson, *Biochem. J.*, *26*, 2056 (1932).
61. Stibitz, G. R., and J. A. Larrivee, *Mathematics and Computers*, McGraw-Hill, New York, 1957.

62. Teller, J. D., *Abstracts 130th Meeting, Am. Chem. Soc.*, 69C (1956).
63. Thomas, C. A., Jr., *J. Am. Chem. Soc.*, *78*, 1861 (1956).
64. Udenfriend, S., *Fluorescence Assay in Biology and Medicine*, Academic Press, New York, 1962, p. 338.
65. Warburg, O., and W. Christian, *Biochem. Z.*, *314*, 149 (1942).
66. Warner, H. R., *Federation Proc.*, *21*, 87 (1962).
67. Weinberg, D. I., *IRE International Convention Record*, Part 9, 88 (1960).
68. Weinberg, D. L., personal communication.
69. Wiener, N., *Cybernetics*, Wiley, New York, 1948.
70. Wiener, N., *Science*, *131*, 1355 (1960).
71. Wincey, C., and V. Marks, *J. Clin. Pathol.*, *14*, 558 (1961).
72. Winter, G. D., *Ann. N.Y. Acad. Sci.*, *87*, 629 (1960).
73. Winter, G. D., *Ann. N.Y. Acad. Sci.*, *8?*, 875 (1960).
74. Wolfe, R. G., and J. B. Neilands, *J. Biol. Chem.*, *221*, 61 (1956).
75. Wood, W. A., and S. R. Gilford, *Anal. Biochem.*, *2*, 589 (1961).
76. Wood, W. A., and S. R. Gilford, *Anal. Biochem.*, *2*, 601 (1961).
77. Woodard, H. Q., *Cancer*, *5*, 236 (1952).
78. Wu, R., and E. Racker, *J. Biol. Chem.*, *234*, 1029 (1959).

Estimation of Magnitudes of Alternative Metabolic Pathways

Irwin J. Kopin, *National Institutes of Health, Bethesda*

I. INTRODUCTION

Many biochemical processes have been elucidated in which there has been conversion of one compound to another by more than one pathway. Once the existence of alternative metabolic pathways has been established, the relative magnitudes of each must be assessed. The degree of difficulty encountered in evaluating the magnitudes of the pathways varies with the particular metabolic scheme and the system in which it is studied. It is often difficult to determine the relative rates of reactions in simple systems, and the difficulty increases when the complex systems in an organ or in the intact animal are studied. An isotopic tracer is often required in such studies, and occasionally use of more than one isotope is expedient.

When the compound being investigated is totally metabolized to carbon dioxide and water, e.g., glucose, the problem has been approached by study of the differential rates of appearance of $C^{14}O_2$ (or the appearance of C^{14} in a key product, e.g., lipids) from the precursor labeled on specific carbon atoms. A critique of the methods employed in the study of alternate pathways of glucose metabolism may be found in the reviews of Korkes (22) and Wood (37). More recent assessments in isolated tissues (16) and in the intact organism (32) should be consulted regarding further application of this method.

Many substances are converted to products which are ultimately excreted in the urine or bile. Several metabolites may arise from a single precursor. Examination of these products can provide information about the magnitudes of the pathways through which they are formed.

The major pathways of catecholamine metabolism have recently been established (1,4,5,7). The products of isotopically labeled epinephrine have been studied (17,18,23,30) and the relative magnitudes of the alternative pathways estimated (18,24) in man. These investigations provide an example of some of the methods by which alternative pathways may be studied in the intact animal. A consideration of the principles, assumptions, and limitations of such studies will be the main subject of this chapter.

II. DEFINITIONS AND PRINCIPLES

1. Types of Alternative Pathways

More than one product may be formed from a single compound when alternative portions of the molecule serve as a substrate for a single enzyme (e.g., catechol O-methyl-transferase as discussed below) or when the substance is a substrate for several enzymes. The proportional activities of competing enzymes may vary in different tissues. A discussion of the mechanisms of formation of different products

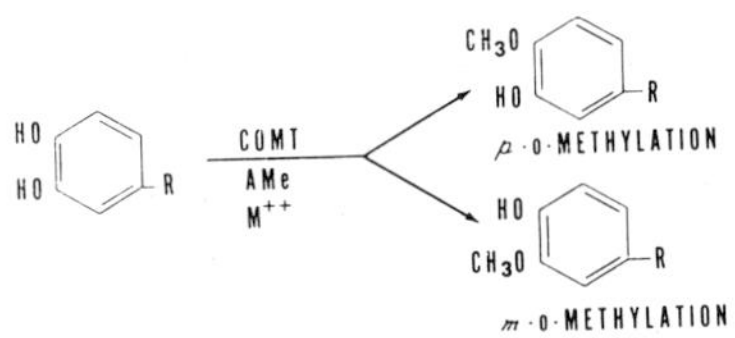

Fig. 1. O-Methylation of catechol derivatives. Catechol derivatives are O-methylated enzymatically by transfer of the methyl group of S-adenosyl-methionine (AMe) to one of the phenolic hydroxy groups. Divalent cations (M^{2+}) are capable of either positive or negative catalysis.

from a single precursor, *in vivo*, is desirable for an understanding of the assumptions and limitations of the methods for quantitative assessment of alternative metabolic pathways.

A. MULTIPLE PRODUCTS OF A SINGLE ENZYME–SUBSTRATE COMPLEX

The action of an enzyme on a substrate usually results in the formation of a single product. When the compound has two functional groups which may alternatively serve as a substrate for the enzyme, more than one product may be formed. Catechol-O-methyltransferase (8) is an enzyme which can transfer the methyl group from S-adenosylmethionine to one of the two phenolic hydroxyl groups of catechol and its derivatives (Fig. 1). Catecholamines are metabolized by m-O-methylation (the hydroxy group in the 3 position is methylated). Studies, *in vitro*, have shown that methylation may, with some substrates, occur on the para hydroxyl group (33). Using a partially purified enzyme, it has been reported that the nature of the side chain of the substrate, the pH of the reaction mixture, and the bivalent metallic ion present (34) influence the proportion of p-O-methylated products. Extension of these studies to intact animals (12) indicates that although m-O-methylation is usually predominant, some catechol derivatives may undergo significant p-O-methylation as well. This, then, is an example of the unusual phenomenon of a single enzyme which can form two products from a single substrate.

B.   COMPETING ENZYMES IN A SINGLE COMPARTMENT

Substances which are substrates for more than one enzyme are often precursors for several products.   The variation in the proportion of the products depends on the relative availability and activity of the competing enzymes, but even in a system in which there is a homogeneous distribution of the enzymes, the substrate concentration may influence the relative rates of the reactions.   At low substrate concentrations the rate of an enzymatic reaction is approximately proportional to this concentration;   however, when large amounts of substrate are present the rate becomes almost constant.   The gradual transition from first-order to zero-order kinetics is defined by the Michaelis-Menten equation,

$$v = V_M[S]/(K_M + [S])$$

where v is the rate of the reaction at substrate concentration $[S]$, V_M is the maximum rate of the reaction, and K_M is a constant characteristic of the particular enzyme–substrate system.

Consider a homogeneous system in which two enzymes compete for the removal of a single substrate which is formed at a constant rate:

$$S + E_1 \rightleftharpoons E_1S \rightarrow E_1 + P_1$$

$$S + E_2 \rightleftharpoons E_2S \rightarrow E_2 + P_2$$

The rate of formation of P_1 is given by

$$v_1 = V_{M_1}[S]/(K_{M_1} + [S])$$

and the rate of formation of P_2 is

$$v_2 = V_{M_2}[S]/(K_{M_2} + [S])$$

The ratio of the products, P_1/P_2, formed during any interval, T, is

$$P_1/P_2 = V_1T/V_2T = V_1/V_2 \tag{1}$$

$$\frac{V_1}{V_2} = \frac{V_{M_1}[S]/(K_{M_1} + [S])}{V_{M_2}[S]/(K_{M_2} + [S])} = \frac{V_{M_1}(K_{M_2} + [S])}{V_{M_2}(K_{M_1} + [S])} \tag{2}$$

$$P_1/P_2 = a(K_{M_2} + [S])/(bK_{M_2} + [S]) \tag{3}$$

where $a = V_{M_1}/V_{M_2}$ and $b = K_{M_1}/K_{M_2}$.   If $K_{M_1} = K_{M_2}$, then $b = 1$, and $P_1/P_2 = a = V_{M_1}/V_{M_2}$;   the relative amounts of P_1 and P_2

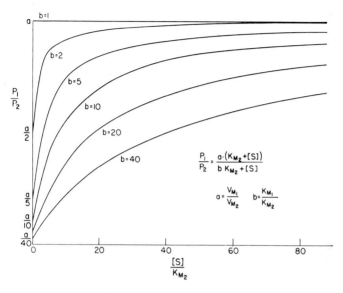

Fig. 2. Variation in the ratio of products with substrate concentration.   The
ratio of the products of the reaction of a substrate $[S]$ with two enzymes having
different K_M values ($K_{M_1} > K_{M_2}$) varies with the substrate concentration.   When
$K_{M_1} = K_{M_2}$ or when $[S]/K_{M2}$ becomes very large, the ratio of the products is
independent of substrate concentration, becoming equal to the relative maximum
rates of the reactions, V_{M_1}/V_{M_2}.

formed would be proportional to the relative magnitudes of V_{M_1} and
V_{M_2} and independent of substrate concentration.

It is unusual for competing enzyme systems to have identical values
for K_M.   One of the enzyme–substrate systems will have a smaller
value for K_M and will approach zero-order kinetics more rapidly with
increasing concentrations of substrate.   The ratio of the products
varies with the substrate concentrations (Fig. 2).   The greater the
difference in the values of K_M for the enzymes, the more marked are
the changes in the ratios of the products.   At sufficiently high concentrations of substrate, both enzymes follow zero-order kinetics and the
ratio of the products approaches the ratio of the maximum velocities
of the reactions; $P_1/P_2 = a$.   In a steady state, the rate of production of the substrate equals the rate of removal.   An increase in the
rate of production of the precursor results in an increase in substrate
concentration and subsequently more rapid removal, but the propor-

tions removed by each of the pathways may be changed. Similarly, an increase in concentration, due to administration of the substrate, may alter the relative magnitudes of the pathways of removal. Thus, in studies designed to assess the quantitative fate of a substance, conditions which alter the concentration of the compound must be avoided.

C.   COMPETING ENZYMES AT DIFFERENT SITES

In the intact cell there is a non-uniform distribution of enzymes and their substrates. The intracellular compartmentalization introduces further considerations which begin to defy analysis. When further complicated by the many compartments in tissues and organs of varying structure, varying substrate and enzyme concentrations, permeability differences, and blood flow alterations, the problem of analysis becomes insuperable.

Although analysis of the components of the systems involved in the determination of the relative magnitudes of alternative pathways in the intact animal is not possible, the resultant magnitudes in the whole animal can be determined. Since one pathway may predominate in one tissue, while another predominates in another tissue, the distribution of the substrate may be a major factor in determining which is the major pathway in the whole animal. The assumptions regarding the mixing of an intravenously administered, isotopically labeled compound with the endogenous substance will be discussed below.

2. Isotopic Tracers

Isotopes provide a unique method for labeling of organic molecules so that they may be traced in their distribution, metabolism, and excretion in the intact animal. When an isotopically labeled compound is to be used in the study of intermediary metabolism, the site on the molecule to carry the label and the isotope to be used must be carefully selected. Equally important is an examination of the assumption that the tracer molecules will mix with the endogenous compound and undergo the same physical transfers and metabolic reaction sequences, quantitatively as well as qualitatively

A. CHOICE OF THE SITE OF LABELING

The portion of the molecule which is selected for labeling depends on the substance to be studied and the purpose of the experiment. Consideration must be given to (a) the methods of synthesis of the labeled molecules, (b) the chemical stability of the isotope in the substance and its products, and (c) the effect of the isotope on the rates of the reactions of the molecule.

In general, methods are available for the labeling of almost any portion of a molecule using organic chemical or enzymatic techniques (26). The label, however, must be firmly attached to the part of the molecule of interest. Thus, hydrogen isotopes on positions of the molecule that readily exchange with the hydrogen ion of water are useless in biological experiments. Similarly, portions of the molecule which will be lost during metabolism cannot be used to label the products containing the unlabeled portion of the administered compound.

Isotopes differ in mass so that the chemical bonds formed by them vary in both zero-point energy and vibrational frequency of the activated complex. These factors control the rate of the reaction, and it can be theoretically predicted that molecules bearing the heavier isotope will generally react more slowly (11). The alterations in the rate of chemical reactions resulting from the difference in mass of the isotopes is called the *isotope effect*. These effects may be used to advantage (e.g., 10), but in quantitative studies of metabolic pathways they must be minimized. Because of the large proportional increments in mass, the nuclides of hydrogen, deuterium and tritium, have the largest isotope effects. When these isotopes are used, effects on the rate of the reactions may be minimized by placing the label at a position remote from the site of chemical change.

B. CHOICE OF THE ISOTOPE

Both stable and radioactive isotopes have been widely used to study the processes of intermediary metabolism. Stable forms of oxygen and nitrogen are used in biological investigations; the radioactive isotopes of these elements are too short-lived to be of use in biology. Carbon, hydrogen, and sulfur are available as both stable and radioactive isotopes. Although the stable forms have the advantage of raising no question of radiation damage, radioactivity is more widely used because of the greater sensitivity and accuracy of the methods, the greater ease of preparation of the samples, and the greater availability and lower cost of the equipment required for radioactive determinations. There are many excellent monographs and reviews concerning the properties and methods of determination of isotopes, and the hazards and precautions required in handling radioactivity (e.g., 2,3,14,15). These subjects are beyond the scope of this review.

C. ASSUMPTIONS REGARDING MIXING

An extremely small amount of radioactive isotopically labeled material injected into the body of an animal is assumed to mix with the endogenous compound and thus provide a means for tracing the metabolism of that substance. Obviously, the administered labeled compound does not instantaneously and uniformly mix with the substance present in the tissues. Once mixing has occurred, the changes in specific activity of the substance and its products have been used to provide information about the size and turnover rates of the metabolic pools which have become labeled. The assumption that an intravenously administered tracer has the same fate as the naturally occurring substance is valid only when all of the endogenously formed compound is normally discharged into the peripheral venous circulation prior to its metabolism. Only under these circumstances can the distribution of the administered material be identical to that of the

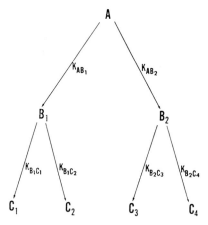

Fig. 3. A divergent metabolic pattern in which all of the products are derived from a single precursor.

endogenously formed compound.   Occasionally it is possible to make a correction for excessive urinary losses (see below), but the distribution factor limits the applicability of isotopic tracers in the quantification of metabolic pathways *in vivo*.

3. Divergent and Convergent Alternative Pathways

The further metabolism of the products of a single compound may result in the formation of totally different compounds, or in the production of one or more identical substances.   When each of the final products is formed through only one of the intermediate compounds, the pathways will be called "divergent" (Figs. 3 and 4).   If one or

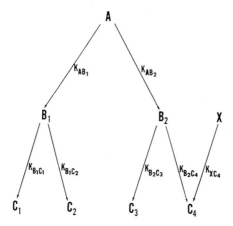

Fig. 4. A divergent metabolic pattern in which one of the products, C_4, is derived from a source, X, other than the precursor, A.

more of the final products can be formed from the precursor through more than one pathway, the metabolic pattern will be termed "convergent" (Figs. 5 and 6).   In either divergent or convergent alternative metabolic pathways, each of the excreted metabolites may be uniquely derived from the precursor (Figs. 3 and 5) or one (or more) of the products may have an additional origin (Figs. 4 and 6).   When estimating the magnitudes of pathways of metabolism it is necessary to consider both the sources and the modes of production of each of the excretion products of the precursor studied.

256 IRWIN J. KOPIN

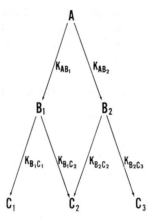

Fig. 5. A convergent metabolic pathway where all of the products are derived from a single precursor. One of the products, C_2, is common to both intermediates B_1 and B_2.

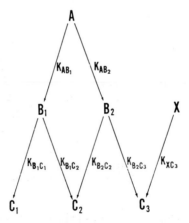

Fig. 6. A convergent metabolic pathway where one of the products, C_3, is derived from a source, X, other than the precursor, A.

4. Assessment of Magnitudes of Alternative Pathways

An estimate of the relative magnitudes of alternative metabolic pathways can be made by determination of the absolute amounts of precursor metabolized through each pathway or by isotopic methods which yield information regarding only the relative magnitudes of the pathways. Accurate determination of the excreted metabolites is necessary for estimation of the absolute magnitudes of the pathways. Requirements for the use of isotopic tracers vary with the metabolic pattern and the availability of methods for the estimation of the metabolites. Methods of assessment of the absolute and relative magnitudes of divergent and convergent pathways with products of unique or multiple origin, therefore, will be considered separately.

A. DIVERGENT PATHWAYS

(1) **With Products of Unique Origin which Can be Assayed.** If all the excreted products are derived solely from the precursor studied, and all of the precursor is excreted in the urine as these products, then the rates and relative magnitudes of divergent metabolic pathways may be determined without the use of isotopic tracers. Thus, in Figure 3, if the rates of excretion of C_1, C_2, C_3, and C_4 can be determined, then the rates of all the reactions can be calculated.

In the steady state, the rate of removal of a compound, by excretion or conversion to another substance, is equal to its rate of formation. The rate of a reaction is assumed to be proportional to a rate constant, K_{XY}, where the subscripts refer to the precursor X and the product Y. The rate of conversion of A and B_1, in Figure 3, is $[A]K_{AB_1}$. The fraction of a metabolite entering any given reaction is equal to the rate constant of that reaction divided by the sum of the rate constants of all the reactions (or transfers) through which the substance leaves its metabolic pool. The precursor, A, in Figure 3, is converted to B_1 at a rate $[A]K_{AB_1}$ and to B_2 at a rate $[A]K_{AB_2}$. The amount of B_1 formed during any interval T, is $[A]K_{AB_1}T$. Similarly, the amount of B_2 formed during the same interval, T, is $[A]K_{AB_2}T$. The amount of A present at any time is assumed to remain constant, so that the rate of formation of A must equal the rate of its removal. The rate of removal of A is the sum of the rates of formation of its products, B_1 and B_2,

$$\text{Rate of removal of } A = [A]K_{AB_1} + [A]K_{AB_2} \qquad (4)$$

The amount of A destroyed during the interval, T, is

$$A = [A](K_{AB_1} + K_{AB_2})T \qquad (5)$$

The proportion of A which has been converted to B_1 during this interval is, therefore,

$$f_{AB_1} = \frac{[A]K_{AB_1}T}{[A](K_{AB_1} + K_{AB_2})T} = \frac{K_{AB_1}}{K_{AB_1} + K_{AB_2}} \tag{6}$$

The total rate of urinary excretion of C_1 and C_2, $(C_1{}^U + C_2{}^U)$, is equal to their rates of formation, $[B_1] (K_{B_1C_1} + K_{B_1C_2})$; the rate of excretion of C_3 and C_4, $(C_3{}^U + C_4{}^U)$, is $[B_2] (K_{B_2C_3} + KB_{2C_4})$. The proportion of A converted to B_1 can thus be determined from the rates of excretion of the final products.

$$f_{AB_1} = \frac{K_{AB_1}[A]}{(K_{AB_1} + K_{AB_2})\,[A]}$$

$$= \frac{[B_1](K_{B_1C_1} + K_{B_1C_2})}{[B_1]\,(K_{B_1C_1} + K_{B_1C_2}) + [B_2]\,(K_{B_2C_3} + K_{B_2C_4})} \tag{7}$$

$$f_{AB_1} = \frac{C_1{}^U + C_2{}^U}{C_1{}^U + C_2{}^U + C_3{}^U + C_4{}^U} \tag{8}$$

Both the rate of formation of A, $[A](K_{AB_1} + K_{AB_2})$, and the proportion of A converted to B_1 can be calculated from the rate of urinary excretion of the final products of a divergent metabolic pattern.

(2) **With Products of Unique Origin which Cannot be Assayed.** When it is not possible to determine accurately the total amounts of all the excreted products, use of an isotopic tracer is desirable. If it can be assumed that the administered labeled precursor will be distributed and metabolized in the same manner as the unlabeled endogenous compound, the distribution of isotope in the metabolites may be used to determine the relative rates of the reactions of the divergent pathways. The fraction of precursor, A, converted to the intermediate B_1, f_{AB_1}, is the same for the isotopically labeled A as for endogenous A. After all of the administered isotope has been excreted, the proportion of the label in each of the products should be the same as the proportion of the endogenous precursor converted to these products. Thus, the fraction of A converted to B_1, f_{AB_1}, can be calculated from the isotopically labeled urinary metabolites, $(C_j{}^{U*}$, etc.) as in equation 8.

$$f_{AB_1} = \frac{K_{AB_1}}{K_{AB_1} + K_{AB_2}} = \frac{C_1{}^{U*} + C_2{}^{U*}}{C_1{}^{U*} + C_2{}^{U*} + C_3{}^{U*} + C_4{}^{U*}} \tag{9}$$

Because the rates of excretion of the labeled metabolites may vary, this fraction must be determined after all of the administered isotope has been excreted—the total of the urinary isotope excreted should be equal to the amount of isotope administered. Since all of the products are derived from only one precursor, if the assumption that the endogenous compound and the administered tracer molecules are distributed and metabolized identically is valid, then all portions of the precursor or the intermediates found in the urine should have the same specific activity as the final products. The assumption regarding identical distribution and metabolism can be tested by comparing the specific activity of any excreted precursor with that of a product uniquely derived from the precursor. If the specific activities are identical, then the specific activities of other products derived from the precursor should be the same. The production rate of the precursor can then be estimated from the specific activity of its product and the dose of the administered isotope. This method has been used for the estimation of secretion rates of some steroid hormones (9,29,35).

When the specific activity of the excreted precursor is higher than that of a product derived solely from that precursor, complete mixing cannot be assumed. The specific activity of the excreted precursor, S_A, would be expected to be the same as that of its product, S_{C_1}. The amount of precursor-carried isotope (A^v*) that would be expected to be found in the urine would be $S_{C_1} \cdot A^v$. The amount of isotope actually excreted, however, is greater than this due to the excess isotopic A excreted, R_x; thus the specific activity is

$$S_A = (S_{C_1}A^v + R_x)/A^v \tag{10}$$

The excess, R_x, can be calculated as follows:

$$R_x = A^v(S_A - S_{C_1}) \tag{11}$$

This amount of administered isotopic A, if significant, should be deducted from the amount of isotope injected to correct for any rapid initial excretion, and the corrected value used in calculations of relative rates and magnitudes of alternative convergent pathways (see below).

(3) **With Products of Multiple Origin.** Although the pathways of metabolism may diverge from a single precursor, one or more of the excretion products may have a multiple origin (C_4 in Fig. 4). If the magnitudes of alternative pathways of metabolism of the pre-

cursor (A) are to be assessed, it is necessary to estimate the amount of products (C_4) derived from the precursor (A). This requires the administration of isotopically labeled precursor. After excretion of all of the administered isotope, the specific activity of excretion products derived only from the labeled precursor $(C_1, C_2,$ and $C_3)$ will be identical. If there is another source of one of the excreted products (C_4), the specific activity of this metabolite will be lowered by the product from the unlabeled source (X). The extent of dilution of the labeled metabolite by unlabeled product may be used to estimate the proportion of the product derived from the tracer compound,

$$f_{C_4 \leftarrow A} = S_{C_4}/S_{C_3} \tag{12}$$

where $f_{C_4 \leftarrow A}$ is the fraction of C_4 derived from A and S_{C_3} and S_{C_4} are the specific activities of C_3 and C_4. When calculating the rates of the formation of B_2 from A, using equation 8, only this portion of C_4 should be used:

$$f_{AB_1} = \frac{(S_{C_4}/S_{C_3})C_4{}^U + C_3{}^U}{(S_{C_4}/S_{C_3})C_4{}^U + C_2{}^U + C_3{}^U + C_1{}^U} \tag{13}$$

If methods for determination of C_4 are unavailable, but the total isotope excreted as C_4, $C_4{}^{U*}$, can be assayed, then an attempt may be made to approximate the amount of C_4 formed from A ($f_{C_4 \leftarrow A}$) from the specific activity of C_3 (S_{C_3}).

$$f_{C_4 \leftarrow A} = C_4{}^{U*}/S_{C_3} \tag{14}$$

and this used in place of $(S_{C_4}/S_{C_3})C_4{}^U$ in equation 13.

B. CONVERGENT PATHWAYS

(1) **With Products of Unique Origin which Can be Assayed.** Estimation of the magnitude of alternative convergent pathways (Fig. 5) requires isotopic labeling of one of the intermediates (B_1 or B_2) forming the product(s) (C_2) common to the alternative pathway. The metabolic pattern, with respect to the intermediate, is a divergent metabolic pathway. The specific activity of all the products formed from the intermediate (B_2) should be identical, but since there is an unlabeled source of the product(s) (C_2) (from the other intermediate, B_1), the specific activity of this product will be lower than that of a product (C_3) derived only from the labeled intermediate

(B_2). Thus, in Figure 5, after the excretion of the isotope administered as labeled B_2, the specific activity of C_2 will be lower than that of C_3 because of the unlabeled C_2 formed from B_1. The proportion of C_2 formed from B_2 can be estimated from the ratios of the specific activities of C_3 and C_2 as shown above for divergent pathways with a product having a multiple origin:

$$f_{C_2 \leftarrow B_2} = S_{C_2}/S_{C_3} \tag{15}$$

If the excretion products (C_1, C_2, and C_3) are derived only from the precursor, A, then the magnitudes of the pathways can be estimated from this ratio and the rates of C_1, C_2, and C_3 excretion. The rate of removal of B_2, equal to its rate of formation, can be calculated

$$[B](K_{B_2C_2} + K_{B_2C_3}) = (S_{C_2}/S_{C_3})C_2{}^U + C_3{}^U \tag{16}$$

The rate of formation of A is equal to the sum of the rates of excretion of its metabolites, $C_1{}^U + C_2{}^U + C_3{}^U$. The proportion of the precursor, A, converted to the intermediate which has been labeled, B_2, is calculated as follows:

$$\frac{[A]K_{AB_2}}{[A](K_{AB_1} + K_{AB_2})} = \frac{(S_{C_2}/S_{C_3})C_2{}^U + C_3{}^U}{C_1{}^U + C_2{}^U + C_3{}^U} \tag{17}$$

(2) **With Products of Unique Origin which Cannot be Assayed.** If accurate methods of estimation of the metabolites are unavailable, only the relative magnitudes of the alternative pathways may be determined. Both the precursor and its intermediate must be labeled. This may be done in separate experiments, but simultaneous labeling of the two substances with different isotopes is preferable. Following administration of the labeled precursor, the proportional distribution of the precursor among its final products can be determined, as for divergent pathways (eq. 5). The labeled intermediate serves the same function as described above, but the ratio of the isotopes in the products, rather than the specific activities, may be used. In Figure 5, the fractions of A converted to B_1 and B_2 are

$$f_{AB_1} = \frac{K_{AB_1}}{K_{AB_1} + K_{AB_2}} \qquad f_{AB_2} = \frac{K_{AB_2}}{K_{AB_1} + K_{AB_2}} \tag{18}$$

the fractions of B_1 converted to C_1 and C_2 and the fractions of B_2 converted to C_2 and C_3 may be expressed similarly

$$f_{B_1C_1} = \frac{K_{B_1C_1}}{K_{B_1C_1} + K_{B_1C_2}} \qquad f_{B_1C_2} = \frac{K_{B_1C_2}}{K_{B_1C_1} + K_{B_1C_2}} \tag{19}$$

and

$$f_{B_2C_2} = \frac{K_{B_2C_2}}{K_{B_2C_2} + K_{B_2C_3}} \qquad f_{B_2C_3} = \frac{K_{B_2C_3}}{K_{B_2C_2} + K_{B_2C_3}} \tag{20}$$

If the amount of isotope, R, administered as A is R_0, then the amounts of R excreted in the metabolites C_1, C_2, and C_3 are

$$C_1^R = f_{AB_1}f_{B_1C_1}R_0 \tag{21}$$

$$C_2^R = (f_{AB_1}f_{B_1C_2} + f_{AB_2}f_{B_2C_2})R_0 \tag{22}$$

$$C_3^R = f_{AB_2}f_{B_2C_3}R_0 \tag{23}$$

The amounts of isotope, S, excreted in C_2 and C_3 following administration of S labeled B_2 are

$$C_2^S = f_{B_2C_2}S_0 \tag{24}$$

$$C_3^S = f_{B_2C_3}S_0 \tag{25}$$

The ratio of isotope R to isotope S in C_3 is

$$\left[\frac{R}{S}\right]_{C_3} = \frac{C_3^R}{C_3^S} = \frac{f_{AB_2}f_{B_2C_3}R_0}{f_{B_2C_3}S_0} = f_{AB_2}(R_0/S_0) \tag{26}$$

Since R_0 and S_0 are known, the fraction of A converted to B_2 can be calculated

$$f_{AB_2} = \left[\frac{R}{S}\right]_{C_3} \bigg/ \frac{R_0}{S_0} \text{ or } \frac{C_3^R/R_0}{C_3^S/S_0} \tag{27}$$

The portion of a product common to both routes formed through the pathway of the labeled intermediate may be estimated from the ratio of the isotopes in this product and one uniquely derived from the intermediate.

The ratios of R/S in C_2 and C_3 are

$$\left[\frac{R}{S}\right]_{C_2} = \frac{(f_{AB_2}f_{B_2C_2} + f_{AB_1}f_{B_1C_2})R_0}{f_{B_2C_2}S_0} \tag{28}$$

$$\left[\frac{R}{S}\right]_{C_3} = f_{AB_2} \frac{R_0}{S_0} \tag{29}$$

The proportion of C_2 derived from B_2 is

$$C_2 = \frac{f_{AB_2} f_{B_2 C_2}}{f_{AB_1} \cdot f_{B_1 C_2} + f_{AB_2} f_{B_2 C_2}} \tag{30}$$

This fraction may be calculated by dividing the ratio of R/S in C_3 (eq. 29) by the ratio of R/S in C_2 (eq. 28).

$$C_2 = \left[\frac{R}{S}\right]_{C_3} \Big/ \left[\frac{R}{S}\right]_{C_2} \tag{31}$$

The intermediate, B_2, is normally formed from the precursor, A, in the tissues. Further metabolism of the intermediate may occur in the tissues, prior to entry into the circulation. The administered tracer may not then behave exactly as the endogenous intermediate. When excessive amounts of intravenously administered labeled substance appear in the urine because the rapid injection produced unusually high circulating levels, the amount of tracer which has been excreted prior to mixing with the endogenous pool (S_x) may be estimated from the specific activities (or the ratios of the isotopes) as described in equation 11.

$$S_x = B_2{}^U(S_{B_2} - S_{C_3}) \tag{32}$$

or

$$R_x = B_2{}^S \left(\left[\frac{R}{S}\right]_{B_2} - \left[\frac{R}{S}\right]_{C_3}\right) \tag{33}$$

The calculated excess isotope excreted, if significant, may be subtracted from the amount of isotope administered.

(3) **With Products Having Multiple Origins.** The convergent pathway with products having multiple origins (Fig. 6) requires the labeling of the precursor and an intermediate even when the products can be accurately determined. The labeled precursor and intermediate behave as described above, and equations 27 and 31 may be used to estimate the relative magnitudes of the pathways. Since some of the products are derived from other sources, the absolute magnitudes of the pathways can be estimated only if a product uniquely derived from the precursor can be assayed. For a metabolite

having several origins, the proportion derived from the precursor may be determined if both the metabolite and a product uniquely derived from the labeled precursor can be assayed (eq. 15), i.e., $f_{C_3} \leftarrow_A = S_{C_3}/S_{C_1}$. The fraction of this portion formed through each of the pathways may then be used to estimate the absolute magnitudes of the pathways.

C. LIMITATIONS

The assumptions and requirements outlined in the above discussions necessarily impose restrictions on the applicability of the method.

1. The labeled precursor must be distributed in a manner similar to the endogenous compound; in general this limits the method to substances normally entering the circulation prior to metabolism, or products of such substances which have similar distributions to the tissues.

2. A significant portion of the products of metabolism of the precursor must be excreted.

3. Since all the administered isotope must be excreted and collected, the length of time and completeness of the urine collections may constitute a real problem.

4. The length of time required strains the assumption regarding a steady state and makes assessment of rapid changes in the magnitudes of the pathways difficult.

5. The use of isotopes makes necessary the availability of special equipment and introduces the hazard of radioactive exposure to the workers and the subject. In selected metabolic patterns, however, the magnitudes of the pathways can be assessed in one individual in a single experiment.

III. APPLICATION TO NOREPINEPHRINE AND EPINEPHRINE METABOLISM

The metabolic fate of the catecholamines has recently been elucidated and methods for the separation and estimation of the major excretion products have been developed. The major metabolic pathways of norepinephrine and epinephrine are illustrated in Figure 7.

Several divergent and convergent alternative routes are evident in this scheme.

Estimation of the magnitudes of several of these pathways will be used to illustrate the principles of assessment of alternative metabolic pathways.

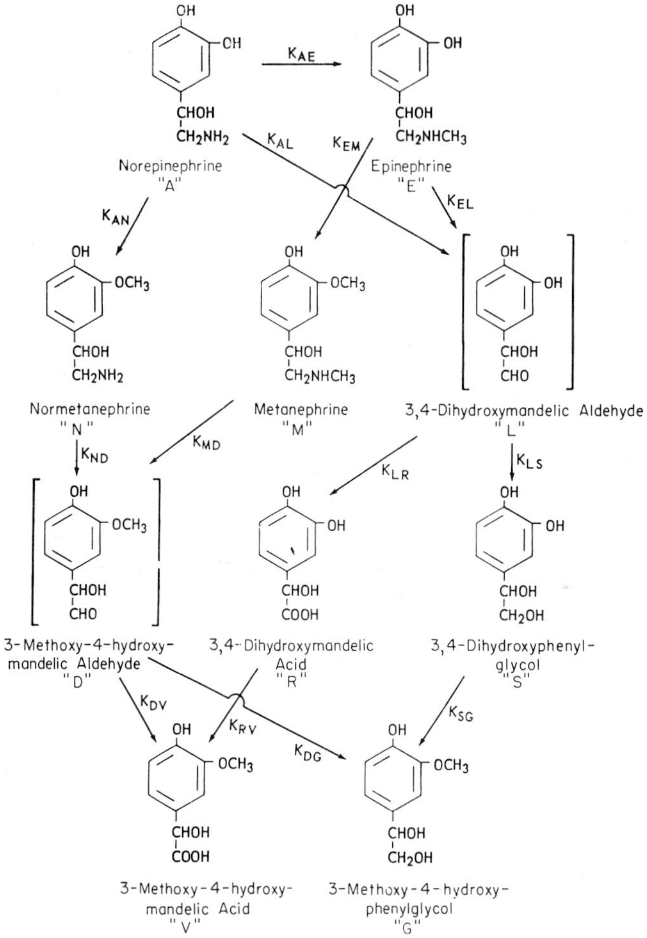

Fig. 7. The major metabolic pathways of epinephrine and norepinephrine. All compounds, except those in brackets, have been demonstrated in the urine in free or conjugated form and are metabolites of isotopically labeled norepinephrine or epinephrine.

1. Norepinephrine and Epinephrine Metabolism

A. EXCRETION PRODUCTS

Although norepinephrine, epinephrine, and their conjugates have been demonstrated in urine, it has long been known that these represent only a small fraction of administered, and presumably endogenous, catecholamines (5). Schayer (31) demonstrated that there were at least five urinary metabolites of C^{14}-labeled epinephrine, but these could not be identified. There was speculation regarding the role of oxidation of the catechol or oxidative deamination until Armstrong et al. (1) demonstrated that 3-methoxy-4-hydroxymandelic acid (VMA) was a major metabolite of the catecholamines. Shortly thereafter, Axelrod (4) showed that 3-O-methylation could precede oxidative deamination and demonstrated that the O-methylated derivatives of the catecholamines, metanephrine and nor-metanephrine, were also major urinary excretion products. The compounds are found in urine from normal individuals in both free and conjugated forms and are markedly increased in the urine of patients having pheochromocytoma. The major deaminated O-methylated metabolite excreted by the rat is conjugated 3-methoxy-4-hydroxyphenylglycol (MHPG). This compound is also a normal excretion product of the catecholamines in man (7). Deaminated catechols are present in small amounts in urine from normal individuals.

The administration of labeled normetanephrine and metanephrine is followed by excretion of labeled VMA and MHPG sulfate, indicating that the O-methylated catecholamines may be intermediates in the formation of the O-methylated deaminated products of the catecholamines.

B. METABOLIC PATHWAYS

Our current concept of the metabolic pathways for the catecholamines is illustrated in Figure 7. The conversion of labeled norepinephrine to epinephrine has been demonstrated *in vivo* (25). It is generally believed that this is the major biosynthetic pathway for epinephrine. O-Methylation and deamination are the two major pathways of metabolic inactivation of these catecholamines. Conjugation with sulfate or glucosiduronic acid and excretion of the free compounds are minor pathways of removal.

Deamination of either of the catecholamines (or their O-methylated derivatives) results in the formation of a mandelic aldehyde derivative (3,4-dihydroxymandelic aldehyde or 3-methoxy-4-hydroxymandelic

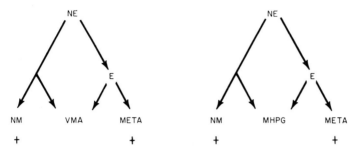

Fig. 8. Simplified pathways for conversion of norepinephrine to the deaminated-O-methylated catechols (VMA and MHPG), considering epinephrine as an intermediate in one of the pathways.

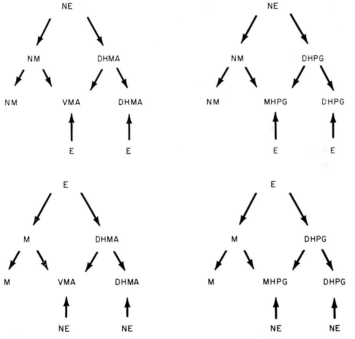

Fig. 9. Pathways for conversion of the catecholamines to VMA and MHPG by primary O-methylation or deamination.

aldehyde). This aldehyde intermediate may then undergo oxidation to the corresponding mandelic acid derivative, or be reduced to a phenylglycol derivative. Thus the formation of VMA and MHPG may proceed by O-methylation and subsequent deamination or by deamination and subsequent O-methylation.

Three pairs of overlapping alternative convergent metabolic pathways may be traced through this metabolic pattern. Conversion of norepinephrine to VMA or MHPG may occur with or without prior formation of epinephrine. Ignoring the sequence of deamination and O-methylation of the catecholamines and considering epinephrine in the role of an intermediate, the formation of VMA and MHPG from norepinephrine occurs through a pair of overlapping convergent alternative pathways (Fig. 8). Similarly, alternative convergent metabolic sequences may be traced for the conversion of either of the catecholamines to the O-methylated deaminated derivative (Fig. 9). In the formation of VMA and MHPG from norepinephrine or epinephrine, deamination may be the primary reaction, or O-methylation may precede deamination. These simplified tracings are useful in clarifying the more elaborate scheme (Fig. 7) when assaying the magnitude of the pathways.

C. SEPARATION AND ASSAY OF RADIOACTIVE METABOLITES

The estimation of the relative magnitudes of alternative pathways requires that the various metabolites of the isotopically labeled compound be separated in radio-chemically pure form. The procedures for such separations are based on the presence of an intact or O-methylated catechol group and the acidic, neutral, or basic nature of the side chain. Hydrolysis of the sulfate or glucuronosidic acid conjugates is effected by heating at acid pH or treatment with specific enzymes. There are several adequate methods for the separation of the radioactive metabolites (6,17,24). The methods used by the author are illustrated in a flow chart (Fig. 10). These have been described in detail elsewhere (6,24), and since they are unimportant to an understanding of the technique for alternative pathway estimation they will not be discussed here. The radiochemical purity of the isolated compounds has been demonstrated by co-chromatography with the authentic compounds.

Radioactivity is conveniently assayed by liquid scintillation spectrophotometry. The sample is evaporated in a counting vial, the dry residue dissolved in 0.2 ml. water, 4 ml. ethanol, and 10 ml. quantities of 0.4% 2,5-diphenyloxazole and 0.005% 1,4-di(2-5-phenyloxazole) benzene in toluene (28). H^3 and C^{14} may be determined simultaneously (27). Internal standards of H^3 and C^{14} are used to correct for quenching and efficiency of counting.

D.   ESTIMATION OF EXCRETED METABOLITES

Although radiochemically pure compounds may be obtained by the described procedures, other phenolic compounds present interfere with assay of the O-methylated metabolites. Only after separation from these interfering substances can the specific activities of the metabolites be determined. Chromatographically pure VMA is isolated by column chromatography (36), while metanephrine, normetanephrine, and MHPG may be isolated by paper chromatography. All of these O-methylated phenolic metabolites can be determined colorimetrically. The dye solution formed for colorimetric assay may also be assayed for radioactivity as described above, and the specific activity calculated. The total unlabeled metabolite may be calculated from the total radioactivity and the specific activity of the metabolite (21).

2. Choice of the Isotope and Site of Labeling

Epinephrine may be totally synthesized from catechol so that any atom in the molecule may be selectively labeled (26). The N-methyl group, the nitrogen, and the hydrogen atoms on the carbon adjacent to the nitrogen cannot be used to label VMA and MHPG. Only the hydrogens directly on the benzene ring and the adjacent carbon atom are both non-exchangeable and remote from the site of monoamine oxidase activity. Metabolic studies have been done utilizing αC^{14}-, βC^{14}-, and βH^3-labeled epinephrine. Tritium-labeled epinephrine can be synthesized with an extremely high specific activity by use of H_2^3 for the reduction of adrenalone (23) and has been used in our laboratory for tracer studies in small animals and isolated tissue as well as metabolic studies in man. About 97% of the administered-H^3 is recovered in the excreted metabolites (24) so that there is negligible loss of the tracer isotope.

Metanephrine may be labeled on the same positions as epinephrine and on the methoxy group as well. Loss of the O-methyl group does

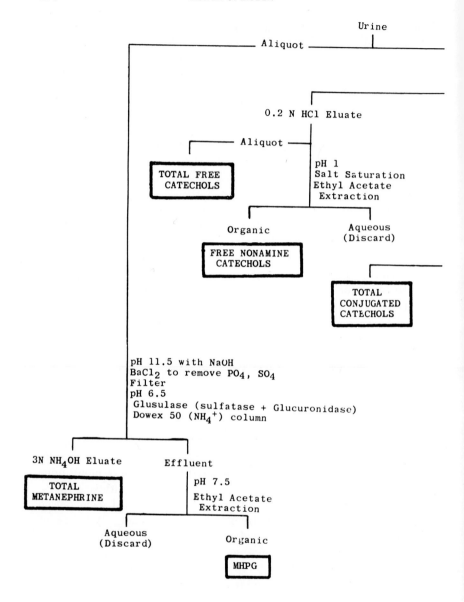

Fig. 10. Flow chart of the procedure for radiochemical

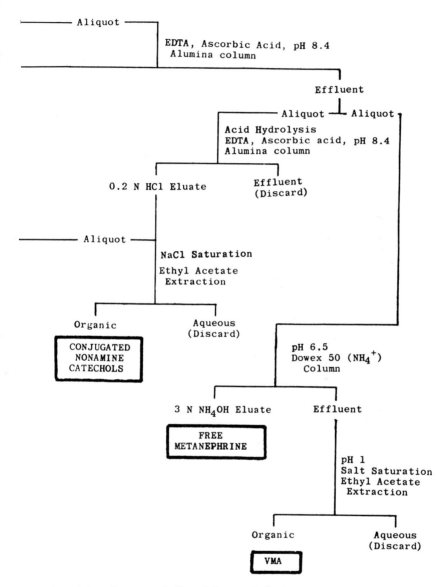

separation of the urinary metabolites of the catecholamines.

not occur in man (4), and enzymatically prepared metanephrine-methoxy-C^{14} has been used to study the alternative routes of epinephrine metabolism (18).

3. Assessment of Magnitudes of Alternative Pathways

The availability of isotopically labeled epinephrine and metanephrine and the development of methods for the determination of the specific activity of the metabolites makes possible assessment of the pathways of metabolism. The validity of the assumptions implicit in the use of isotopic tracers will first be examined, then the magnitudes of some of the metabolic routes shown in Figure 7 will be estimated using the typical data (Table I) from one normal young male.

TABLE I

Typical Data from Normal Human Male Urinary Excretion of Catecholamines and their Metabolites following Intravenous Infusion of Epinephrine-H^3 and Metanephrine-C^{14}

	Percent of administered			Excretion rate		Relative S.A. ($\%H^3/$ mμM)
	H^3	C^{14}	H^3/C^{14}	μg./ day	mμM./ day	$\times$ 100
Epinephrine	3.2			6.0	30.0	10.68
Deaminated catechols	1.5					
Metanephrine						
Free	5.4	8.6	0.63	35.0	160	3.38
Conjugated	35.2	52 4	0.67	210	986	3.57
VMA	45.1	31.7	1.42	2,710	13,700	0.329
MHPG	7.0	4.9	1.43	690	3,750	0.187
Normetanephrine				430	2,130	
Norepinephrine				32	174	
Total	97.4	97.6			20,930	

A. EXAMINATION OF THE ASSUMPTIONS

Chemical stability of the isotopic label in epinephrine-H^3 and metanephrine-methoxy-C^{14} and their metabolites has already been discussed. The position of the heavier atom is remote from the site of chemical changes so that isotope effects are minimized.

In the study of catecholamine excretion, it has been found that following adrenalectomy there is a marked decrease in epinephrine, but not norepinephrine, excretion (13). Most epinephrine seems to originate in the adrenal medulla and is probably not metabolized to a significant extent prior to discharge into the blood stream. Thus, the metabolism of intravenously administered H^3-epinephrine probably approximates the fate of endogenously formed epinephrine. This may not be true for administered H^3-norepinephrine, because norepinephrine is present throughout the adrenergic system, as well as in the central nervous system, and a major portion of the endogenously formed norepinephrine can be metabolized prior to reaching the circulation (20).

The distribution of metanephrine-methoxy-C^{14} parallels that of epinephrine-H^3 following injection into the rat (19). It is assumed that the metabolism of the administered metanephrine will be similar to that of metanephrine formed from the injected epinephrine in each tissue and therefore in the whole animal.

With rapid intravenous injection, excessive urinary excretion might be expected. Estimation of this rapid initial excretion may be attempted by use of equations 32 and 33, and data in Table 1. For epinephrine-H^3, equation 32 becomes

$$\text{Excess } H^3 = (S_E - S_M)E_0^U = \frac{10.68 - 3.57}{100} \times 30 = 2.13\%$$

For metanephrine-C^{14}, equation 33 is used, utilizing conjugated metanephrine as a product uniquely derived from metanephrine.

$$\text{Excess } C^{14} = \left(\left[\frac{C^{14}}{H^3} \right]_{\text{free meta}} - \left[\frac{C^{14}}{H^3} \right]_{\text{conj meta}} \right) H^3_{\text{free meta}} = 0.95\%$$

These small amounts of excessive excretion do not greatly alter the amount of isotope that may be considered to have mixed with the endogenous substances.

B. RATE OF FORMATION OF DEAMINATED O-METHYLATED CATECHOLS FROM EPINEPHRINE

Using the simplified pathways illustrated in Figure 8, the proportion of VMA or MHPG formed from norepinephrine through the epinephrine pathway may be estimated from the relative specific activities of these products and a product uniquely derived from epinephrine (e.g., conjugated metanephrine). Using equation 15 and the data of Table I, the proportions of VMA and MHPG derived from epinephrine are

$$f_{V \leftarrow E} = \frac{S_{\text{VMA}}}{S_{\text{meta}}} = \frac{0.329}{3.57} = 9.22\%$$

Proportion of MHPG from epinephrine $= \dfrac{S_{\text{MHPG}}}{S_{\text{meta}}} = \dfrac{0.187}{3.57} = 5.24\%$

The rate of VMA excretion (Table I) was found to be 13,700 mμ moles/day; about 9.22% of this, or 1263 mμ moles is formed from epinephrine. Similarly, it may be calculated that 197 of the 3,750 mμ-moles MHPG excreted daily is derived from epinephrine.

C. APPROXIMATION OF DEAMINATED CATECHOL EXCRETION RATE

The specific activity of the combined deaminated-O-methylated catechols may be used as a rough approximation of the specific activity of the deaminated catechols. The total H^3 excreted as deaminated catechols is 1.5%, the relative specific activity of the combined VMA and MHPG is 52.1% H_0^3/17,450 mμ moles/day. If the deaminated catechols are assumed to have a similar specific activity, the excretion rate of deaminated catechols may be approximated using equation 14.

$$\text{Deaminated catechols} = \frac{17,450}{52.1} \times 1.5 = 503 \text{ m}\mu \text{ moles/day}$$

About 8% of this, or 42 mμ moles/day, may be considered to be formed from epinephrine.

D. ESTIMATION OF THE PROPORTION OF NOREPINEPHRINE CONVERTED
    TO EPINEPHRINE

The total rate of excretion of epinephrine metabolites divided by the total rate of excretion of norepinephrine metabolites (eq. 17) is an estimate of the proportion of norepinephrine converted to epinephrine. The total rate of excretion of norepinephrine and its metabolites is 20,930 mμ moles/day. The rate of excretion of epinephrine metabolites is calculated as the sum of the rates of excretion of epinephrine (30 mμmoles/day), metanephrine (1146 mμmoles/day), and the portion of the deaminated products derived from epinephrine (42 mμmoles deaminated catechol/day, 197 mμmoles MHPG/day, and 1263 mμmoles VMA/day). Thus, 2678 mμmoles of epinephrine (532 μg.) are formed daily. This represents 12.8% of the norepinephrine produced.

E. ASSESSMENT OF THE MAGNITUDES OF O-METHYLATION AND DE-
   AMINATION OF EPINEPHRINE

The relative magnitude of O-methylation in the metabolic disposition of epinephrine may be calculated from the H^3/C^{14} ratios in the metanephrine (Table I and eq. 27).

$$f_{EM} = \frac{[H^3]_{conj\ meta}/[H_0^3]}{[C^{14}]_{conj\ meta}/[C_0^{14}]} = \frac{0.352}{0.524} = 0.67$$

Thus, 67% of administered epinephrine-H^3 is O-methylated.

The proportions of VMA-H^3 and MHPG-H^3 derived from metanephrine can be calculated using equation 31.

$$VMA = \left[\frac{H^3}{C^{14}}\right]_{meta} \bigg/ \left[\frac{H^3}{C^{14}}\right]_{VMA} = \frac{0.67}{1.42} = 0.46$$

$$MHPG = \left[\frac{H^3}{C^{14}}\right]_{meta} \bigg/ \left[\frac{H^3}{C^{14}}\right]_{MHPG} = \frac{0.67}{1.43} = 0.46$$

About 46% of VMA and MHPG derived from epinephrine is formed by O-methylation followed by deamination, the remainder being formed by the other pathway. As calculated above, 1263 mμmoles VMA and 197 mμmoles MHPG are formed from epinephrine daily. The pathway to metanephrine therefore accounts for 1146 mμmoles (as metanephrine) and 672 mμmoles (46% of VMA and MHPG) daily. Thus, 1818 mμmoles of the calculated 2678 mμmoles epinephrine produced daily (67.8%) is converted to metanephrine. This method of calculation is only partially dependent on the H^3/C^{14} ratio of metanephrine, but agrees well with it as an indicator of the relative magnitude of the O-methylation pathway.

Using the techniques described, it is possible, in a single experiment, to estimate the magnitudes of many of the metabolic pathways of norepinephrine transformation. Tables II and III list the estimates of the absolute and relative magnitudes of the pathways determined from the data presented in Table I.

TABLE II
Pathways of Catecholamine Metabolism

	%	mμ M./day
Norepinephrine		
Formed	100	20,930
Excreted unchanged	0.8	174
Converted to Epinephrine	12.8	2678
Converted to VMA	59.4	12,437
Converted to MHPG	15.6	3163
Excreted as normetanephrine	10.2	2130
Epinephrine		
Formed	100	2678
Excreted unchanged	1.1	30
Converted to metanephrine	67.8	1818
Excreted as metanephrine	42.8	1146
Excreted as VMA	47.2	1283
Excreted as MHPG	7.9	197
Metanephrine		
Formed	100	1818
Excreted unchanged	8.8	160
Conjugated	54.2	986
Converted to VMA	31.9	581
Converted to MHPG	5.1	91

TABLE III
Metabolic Origins of VMA and MHPG

	VMA		MHPG	
	%	mμ M./day	%	mμ M./day
Total	100	13,700	100	3750
Derived from norepinephrine (without epinephrine formation)	90.8	12,437	94.8	3553
Derived from epinephrine Total	9.2	1263	5.2	197
Via metanephrine (46%)		581		91

IV. SUMMARY

A technique for the estimation of metabolic pathways, *in vivo*, by examination of the urinary metabolites of endogenous and administered labeled precursor has been described. The requirements for the assessment of the magnitude of alternative pathways of metabolism varies with the particular metabolic pattern. Estimation of magnitudes of divergent alternative reaction sequences require administration of labeled precursor only when one or more of the final excretion products can be formed from several precursors. The relative magnitudes of divergent pathways may be determined by labeling the precursor and assaying only the isotope excreted in each of the products. When a product may be formed by more than one reaction sequence, it is necessary to label isotopically one of the intermediates of one of the pathways. The absolute magnitudes of the convergent pathways can be assessed only if there are methods available for the accurate determinations of at least one of the products uniquely derived from the precursor studied. When satisfactory methods for estimation of the unlabeled metabolites are unavailable, only the relative magnitudes of the pathways may be estimated. This requires radiochemical isolation of the products. The simultaneous administration of isotopically labeled precursor and intermediate is expedient in the determination of the relative magnitude of convergent alternative pathways when the products cannot be chemically assayed or when there are multiple origins of the products.

References

1. Armstrong, M. D., A. McMillan, and K. N. F. Shaw, *Biochim. Biophys. Acta*, *25*, 442 (1957).
2. Arnstein, H. R. U., and P. T. Grant, *Progr. Biophys.*, *7*, 165 (1957).
3. Aronoff, S., *Techniques of Radiobiochemistry*, Iowa State College Press, Ames, Iowa, 1956.
4. Axelrod, J., *Science*, *126*, 400 (1957).
5. Axelrod, J., *Physiol. Rev.*, *39*, 751 (1959).
6. Axelrod, J., and I. J. Kopin, *Methods in Med. Research*, *9*, 153 (1961).
7. Axelrod, J., I. J. Kopin, and J. D. Mann, *Biochim. Biophys. Acta*, *36*, 576 (1959).
8. Axelrod, J., and R. Tomchick, *J. Biol. Chem.*, *233*, 702 (1958).
9. Ayres, P. J., O. Garrod, S. A. S. Tait, J. F. Tait, G. Walker, and W. H. Pearlman, *Ciba Foundation Colloq. on Endocrinology*, *11*, 309 (1957).
10. Belleau, B., J. Burba, M. Pindell, and J. Reiffenstein, *Science*, *133*, 102 (1961).
11. Bigeleisen, J., *J. Chem. Phys.*, *17*, 675 (1949).
12. Daly, J. W., J. Axelrod, and B. Witkop, *J. Biol. Chem.*, *235*, 1155 (1960).
13. Euler, U. S. von, E. Franksson, and J. Hellstrom, *Acta Physiol. Scand.*, *31*, 1 (1954).

14. Francis, G. E., W. Mulligan, and W. Wormall, *Isotopic Tracers*, The Athlone Press, London, 1954.
15. Hevesy, G., *Radioactive Isotopes*, Interscience, New York, 1948.
16. Katz, J., and H. G. Wood, *J. Biol. Chem., 235*, 2165 (1960).
17. Kirshner, N., McC. Goodall, and L. Rosen, *Proc. Soc. Exptl. Biol. Med., 98*, 627 (1958).
18. Kopin, I. J., *Science, 131*, 1372 (1960).
19. Kopin, I. J., J. Axelrod, and E. Gordon, *J. Biol. Chem., 236*, 2109 (1961).
20. Kopin, I. J., and E. Gordon, *Federation Proc., 21*, 332 (1962).
21. Kopin, I. J., E. H. LaBrosse, and E. Gordon, to be published.
22. Korkes, S., *Ann. Rev. Biochem., 25*, 685 (1956).
23. LaBrosse, E. H., J. Axelrod, and S. S. Kety, *Science, 128*, 210 (1958).
24. LaBrosse, E. H., J. Axelrod, I. J. Kopin, and S. S. Kety, *J. Clin. Invest., 40*, 253 (1961).
25. Masuoka, D. T., H. F. Schott, R. I. Ahawie, and W. G. Clark, *Proc. Soc. Exptl. Biol. Med., 93*, 5 (1956).
26. Murray, A., III, and D. L. Williams, *Organic Syntheses With Isotopes*, Interscience, New York, 1958, pp. 722, 723, 1351.
27. Okita, G. T., J. J. Kabara, F. Richardson, and S. S. Kety, *Nucleonics, 15*, 111 (1957).
28. Okita, G. T., J. Sprott, and G. V. LeRoy, *Nucleonics, 14*, 76 (1956).
29. Pearlman, W. H., *Biochem. J., 67*, 1 (1957).
30. Resnick, O., and F. Elmajian, *J. Clin. Endocrinol., 18*, 28 (1958).
31. Schayer, R. W., *J. Biol. Chem., 189*, 301 (1951).
32. Segal, S., M. Berman, and A. Blair, *J. Clin. Invest., 40*, 1263 (1961).
33. Senoh, S., J. Daly, J. Axelrod, and B. Witkop, *J. Am. Chem. Soc., 81*, 6240 (1959).
34. Senoh, S., Y. Tokuyama, and B. Witkop, *J. Am. Chem. Soc.*, (1962) in press.
35. Ulick, S., J. Laragh, and S. Lieberman, *Trans. Assoc. Am. Physicians, 71*, 225 (1958).
36. Weiss, V. K., R. K. McDonald, and E. H. LaBrosse, *Clin. Chim. Acta, 6*, 79 (1961).
37. Wood, H. G., *Physiol. Rev., 35*, 841 (1955).

Determination of Coenzyme Q (Ubiquinone)

F. L. Crane and R. A. Dilley, *Purdue University, Lafayette, Indiana*

I. INTRODUCTION

Coenzyme Q is a generic name for a group of homologous quinones which are widely distributed in animals, plants, and microorganisms. All of the compounds in this group contain a 2,3-dimethoxy-5-methyl benzoquinone nucleus with an isoprenoid side chain in the 6 position. They differ from one another in the length of the isoprenoid side chain. The nomenclature of the compounds is based on the number of unsaturated isoprene units (2-methyl butene) in the side chain as indicated by a subscript following the Q. Thus coenzyme Q_{10} indicates the quinone with a side chain containing 10 isoprenoid units or 50 carbon atoms in the side chain. The members of the series which have been found in nature are coenzymes Q_{10}, Q_9, Q_8, Q_7, and Q_6 (26).

An alternative nomenclature of these compounds has been proposed by Morton in which the generic term ubiquinone is followed by a number to indicate the number of carbon atoms in the isoprenoid chain (33). Thus ubiquinone (50) is identical with coenzyme Q_{10} and ubiquinone (30) is identical with coenzyme Q_6.

The only other quinones which are widely distributed in nature and which have properties which may cause interference in coenzyme Q estimation are members of vitamin K series and the plastoquinones. It is also probable that tocopherol quinones occur at times in natural products or may be formed therein by oxidation of tocopherols.

II. CHEMICAL STRUCTURES OF SOME QUINONES

The structures of some quinones are indicated at the top of page 281.

Compounds of the coenzyme Q type were first recognized on the basis of their characteristic absorption spectra and purified by Morton and co-workers (33) at the University of Liverpool. The first member of the group to be isolated and clearly defined was coenzyme Q_{10} which was found in lipid extracts from beef heart mitochondria at the laboratory of D. E. Green at Wisconsin. In 1957, Crane et al. (8) reported the isolation of the compound as a quinone and presented evidence for its function as a coenzyme in the succinoxidase system of beef heart mitochondria. Subsequently, the other members of the coenzyme Q group were isolated by Lester et al. (28) and shown to have similar coenzymatic activity.

Plastoquinone was originally isolated by Kofler in 1946 during his investigation of vitamin K in alfalfa as determined by the Dam-

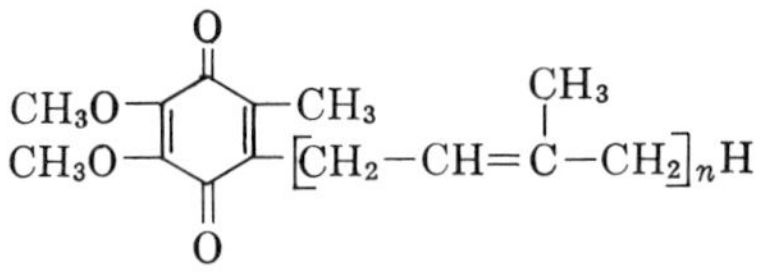

Coenzyme Q_n 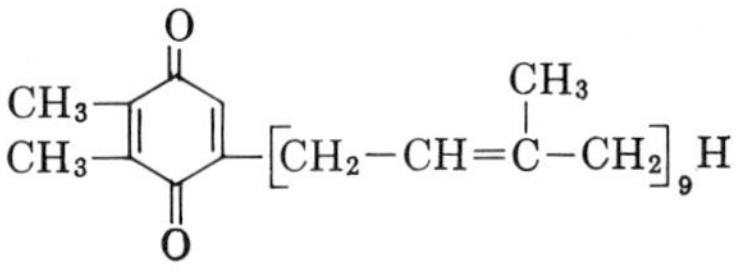   Plastoquinone

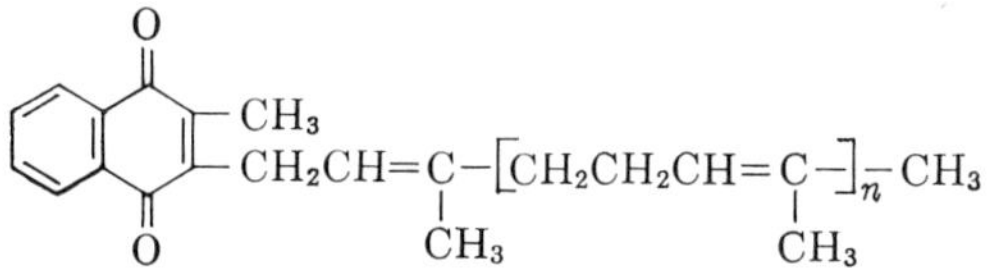

$$CH_3O\text{—}\!\!\!\overset{\displaystyle O}{\underset{\displaystyle O}{\bigcirc}}\!\!\!\text{—}CH_3 \quad [CH_2\text{—}CH\!=\!\overset{CH_3}{\underset{}{C}}\text{—}CH_2]_n H$$

Vitamin K$_2$

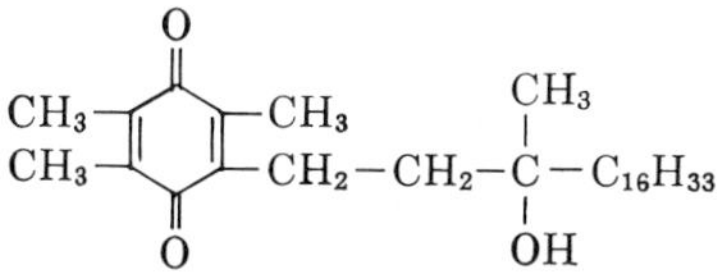

α-Tocopherol quinone

Karrer reaction (23). The compound was rediscovered in 1957 in our laboratory (6) while we were investigating the coenzyme Q content of spinach leaves. The only well-documented form of this compound contains a 45-carbon side chain (solanosyl), but we have observed two other forms which are chromatographically different. This situation is not unusual in view of the variety of side chains among these terpenoid quinones.

III. CHROMANOLS AND CHROMENOLS

Several compounds have been isolated from natural materials which can be considered as derivatives of the terpenoid quinones. Ubichromenol has been found in animal tissue by Morton (32) and may be considered to derive by cyclization of coenzyme Q. Solanochromene, which is the chromenol derived from plastoquinone, has been isolated by Rowland (39) from flue-cured tobacco. The corresponding chromanols of coenzyme Q and plastoquinone have not been isolated from natural sources. The chromanol of vitamin K$_1$ has, however, been isolated by Brodie (3) from a mycobacterium. Also, the tocopherols represent a widely distributed group of natural chromanols. It should be considered likely that chromenols and chromanols will form from the quinones and hydroquinones, respectively, of these terpenoid quinones with β unsaturation in the side chain, especially under strongly acidic conditions. The type of structure involved is shown below.

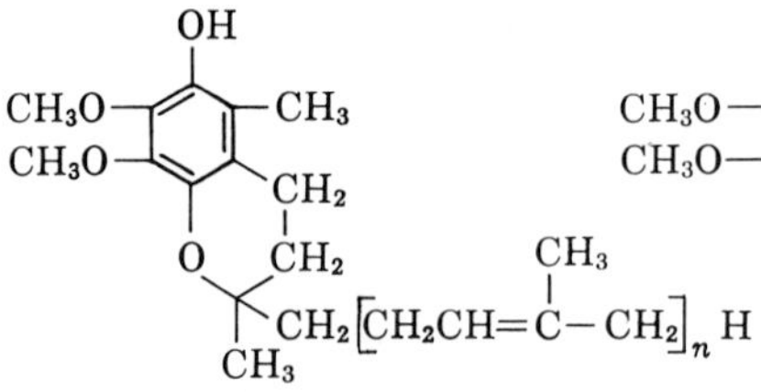

Chromanol 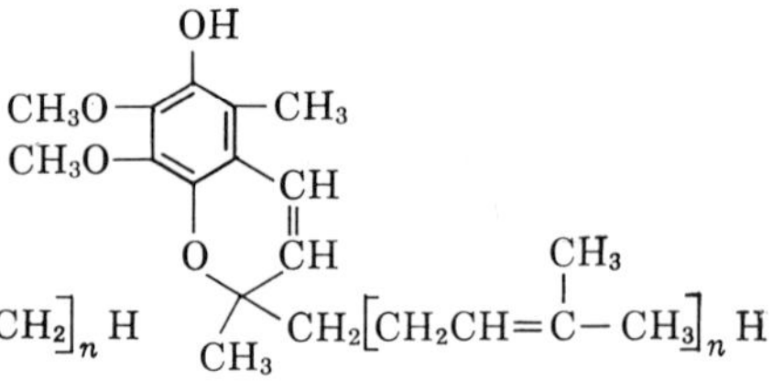   Chromenol

Further difficulties arise when the compounds with polyunsaturated side chains are exposed to drastic conditions, since continued cyclization of the side chain will occur. Thus it has been shown by Folkers et al. (17) that exposure of coenzyme Q to strong acid under reducing conditions will cause the formation of a chromanol with a cyclic paraffin side chain as shown below.

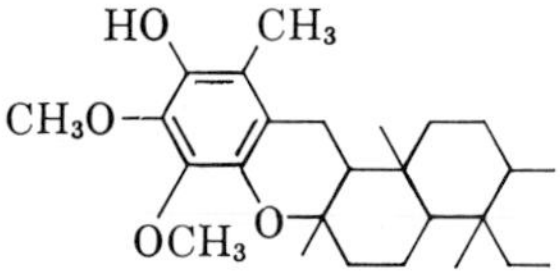

,etc.

In fact, they have found it impossible to produce ubichromanol from coenzyme Q under these conditions, which are the same conditions used to form tocopherol from tocopherol quinone. Of course, in the latter compounds only a single double bond is present in the phytyl side chain.

IV. ETHOXY DERIVATIVES

Another series of compounds related to coenzyme Q has been found in lipid extracts obtained after saponification of natural products. These compounds are artifacts produced by substitution of ethoxy groups for the methoxy groups of coenzyme Q during saponification of tissues in ethanolic alkali. They were first identified by Linn et al. (31) as compounds found in preparations of coenzyme Q obtained after saponification which were identical with coenzyme Q in spectral absorbance, but which had lower melting points and showed different chromatographic properties.   Both the monoethoxy and diethoxy derivatives, shown below, have been identified in the nonsaponifiable fraction from tissue lipids.

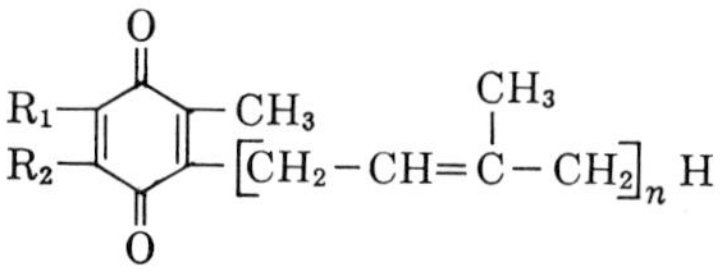

Derivative	R_1	R_2
Monoethoxy coenzyme Q_n	OCH_2CH_3	OCH_3
Monoethoxy coenzyme Q_n	OCH_3	OCH_2CH_3
Diethoxy coenzyme Q_n	OCH_2CH_3	OCH_2CH_3
Coenzyme Q_n	OCH_3	OCH_3

Folkers et al. (17) report the formation of other alkoxy-substituted derivatives of coenzyme Q such as the diisoamyloxy coenzyme Q_{10} by treatment of coenzyme Q_{10} with isoamyl alcohol under alkaline conditions.   Linn et al. (31) have shown that the use of methanol during saponification will prevent formation of the alkoxy-substituted derivatives.   It is important that the formation of these derivatives be minimized during assay procedures, especially if chromatographic identification of the coenzyme Q homologs is necessary.

V. SOME OTHER NATURALLY OCCURRING QUINONES

1. Aurantiogliocladin

The first quinone to be isolated from natural products that is related to coenzyme Q was aurantiogliocladin or 2,3-dimethoxy-5,6-dimethyl benzoquinone.   This quinone has been isolated as an

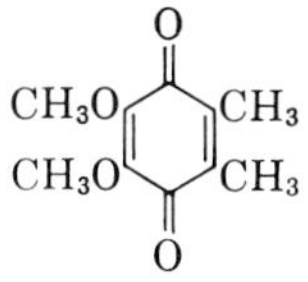

Aurantiogliocladin 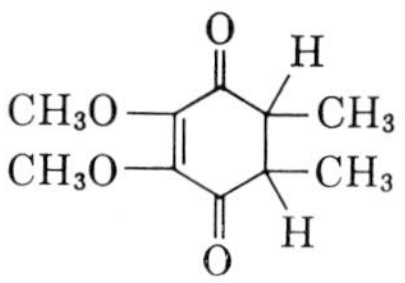   Gliorosein

antibiotic from the culture broth of a fungus gliocladium (43).

2. Gliorosein

Another material, gliorosein, was also found along with the auran-tioglioeladin and is isomeric with the hydroquinone. The formula shown has been proposed as most likely for this nonquinoid isomer (42). Aurantioglioeladin does not have coenzyme Q activity in enzyme systems where it has been tested, so it should not be considered as a true coenzyme Q. It does have spectral properties close to those of coenzyme Q, however, and should be considered for possible interference in fungal extracts. The conversion into gliorosein should also be considered as a model reaction which could cause potential interference in coenzyme Q determinations by hiding coenzyme Q in an unrecognizable form or in a form capable of unknown reactions. We have not encountered this problem as yet, but, as will be discussed below, there are many organisms which might be expected to contain coenzyme Q in which the coenzyme has not been found.

VI. DISTRIBUTION OF COENZYME Q

The quinones of the coenzyme Q group are the most widely distributed quinones in nature. They are found in animals, plants, and many microorganisms. The distribution of these compounds is closely correlated with the aerobic metabolism of a tissue or organism, a pattern which is consistent with the evidence that these quinones are coenzymes in the cytochrome-containing terminal respiratory system in most organisms. As a general rule, coenzyme Q has not been found in strict anaerobes (e.g., *Clostridium*) or in facultative anaerobes with other than the usual cytochrome system (e.g., *Lactobacillus*). There are also some other microorganisms which contain terminal cytochrome systems without any coenzyme Q (e.g., *Mycobacteria* and *Bacilli*). These latter forms contain large amounts of vitamin K and there is evidence that the vitamin K in these organisms performs a catalytic function similar to coenzyme Q. We may also suspect that certain lower plants such as blue-green algae and actinomycetes, where preliminary investigation reveals vitamin K without coenzyme Q, have a vitamin K-dependent system. The studies of coenzyme Q distribution are still far from complete, and there are several lower animals with typical cytochrome systems in which coenzyme Q has not been found, but where it would be expected to occur (25). Careful assay of these and many other organisms will be helpful in a final interpretation of coenzyme Q function. There are several papers which give a summary of distribution studies to date. Lester and Crane (25) have reported an analysis of a wide variety of organisms. Erickson et al. (16) have reported on coenzyme Q in basidiomycetes. Pandya et al. (37) and Page et al. (36) have examined many microorganisms. Page et al. (35) have also examined the coenzyme Q content of certain experimental diets and Folkers et al. have reported on the distribution in human tissues (17).

Coenzyme Q is also found in large amounts in the photosynthetic bacteria *Rhodospirillum* and *Chromatium* (18,25). Since the latter of these is an obligate anaerobe, it would appear that the quinone is involved in electron transport associated with photosynthesis in this organism.

VII. FUNCTION OF COENZYME Q

Coenzyme Q has been found in all mitochondria which have been examined, including those from beef heart (8), rat liver (40), pig heart (38), horse heart (2), *Arum* spadix (38), and cauliflower (4). It is also concentrated in particles containing the terminal electron transport system from *Azotobacter* (25) and *Escherichia coli* (4). In many of these systems it has been shown that the quinone undergoes oxidation–reduction changes during electron transport. It has also been shown that extraction of coenzyme Q by organic solvents stops electron transport and that activity can be restored when the quinone is added back to the extracted systems. The restoration of activity in a solvent-extracted enzyme system is the only biological assay system for coenzyme Q. Studies with selective inhibitors such as antimycin A, thenoyltrifluoroacetone and amytal, as well as studies using purified succinic dehydrogenase, indicate that coenzyme Q is a coenzyme of the succinic dehydrogenase system catalyzing transfer of electrons from the non-heme iron on succinic dehydrogenase to cytochrome c_1. From extraction data it would appear that the quinones are not covalently bonded to the enzyme, but maintain close association by immersion in the lipid matrix of the mitochondrial structure. It is not clear yet that the quinones function in a similar fashion with dihydrodiphosphopyridine nucleotide dehydrogenase, which is the other major source of electrons for the terminal oxidase and phosphorylation system.

VIII. EXTRACTION OF COENZYME Q

There are three basic methods which have been employed for extraction of coenzyme Q from tissues. The first involves saponification of the tissue lipids with alcoholic alkali in the presence of pyrogallol, followed by extraction of the nonsaponifiable lipid fraction. The second is based on the usual methods for direct extraction of tissue lipids using solvents such as acetone or mixtures such as ethanol–ether or chloroform–methanol. Finally, dried or lyophylized tissue may be extracted with many solvents, including hydrocarbons. Each of these methods has certain advantages and disadvantages so that their application depends upon the type of material under study.

The saponification procedure has been used most extensively and has been most successful as a general method applicable to a great variety of materials. It has a primary advantage in that many interfering substances are removed either in the saponifiable fraction or by alkali-induced destruction of interfering compounds like vitamin K. This procedure also insures complete extraction of coenzyme Q. The main disadvantage lies in possible destruction of coenzyme Q or in conversion of coenzyme Q to the ethoxy analogs. These problems can be avoided by the use of pyrogallol in the saponification and by limiting the length of exposure to alkali. Further protection is afforded by carrying out the treatment under a nitrogen atmosphere. Under no circumstances should the exposure to hot alkali last more than 30 min. if formation of the ethoxy derivatives is to be kept to a minimum. These ethoxy compounds will, of course, give equivalent values to coenzyme Q in the spectrophotometric assays but will not show activity in the enzymatic assay. The ethoxy derivatives also show a lower R_f than the corresponding coenzyme Q homolog on reversed-phase paper chromatography, so that if they are present in significant amounts they will cause trailing, or if they predominate they will appear as a spot close to the next higher homolog of the coenzyme present in the tissue. Thus, rat liver which contains coenzyme Q_9 could give the diethoxy coenzyme Q_9 after extensive saponification, which would show chromatographic behavior similar to coenzyme Q_{10}. If the nature of the coenzyme Q homologs present in a tissue is important, it would be well to check their identity by chromatography after both saponification and a direct solvent extraction. As a second alternative, the saponification should be carried out in methanolic alkali. Although methanol has not been substituted for ethanol in most previous assay work, we find that the recovery of coenzyme Q is not satisfactory under methanolic potassium hydroxide, which would indicate that this method should be developed further before it becomes the method of choice whenever the nature of the coenzyme Q homologs is to be determined.

After saponification it is important for the alkaline samples to be cooled rapidly and extracted two or three times with a hydrocarbon solvent such as heptane. The heptane extract should then be washed by repeated extraction with water to remove traces of alkali and decomposition products of pyrogallol. Finally, the samples should be dried by adding a small amount of anhydrous sodium sulfate.

Extraction of fresh or frozen tissue with ethanol–ether, chloroform–methanol, or acetone has the advantage that the coenzyme Q is not exposed to strong alkali. Precautions must be taken, however, to insure maximum extraction of coenzyme Q. In many tissues the direct solvent extraction removes, along with the coenzyme Q, many impurities which can interfere with both the quantitative assays and chromatography. It should also be borne in mind that direct extraction cannot be expected to release certain chemically bound forms of coenzyme Q that saponification would release. We do not know if such bound forms of coenzyme Q exist, but we do know that in many tissues direct solvent extraction leads to lower values for coenzyme Q than the saponification method. Again, a preliminary check by both methods, especially in tissues where coenzyme Q has not been investigated previously, would seem to be desirable.

We have found that direct solvent extraction should be carried out over a long period of time with repeated extractions in order to insure maximum release. Thus for ethanol–ethyl ether (3:1) extraction, the tissue should be finely ground or homogenized (e.g., with a Waring Blendor) and then suspended in three to four volumes of ethanol–ether overnight. The residue obtained after removing the solvent by filtration is then re-extracted with ethanol–ether for two or three times or until an assay of the extract shows no more coenzyme Q.

The chloroform–methanol (1:3) solvent system may also be used as with ethanol–ether. It is better used with dry material or material with low water content. With this type of material, refluxing for several hours with chloroform–methanol will extract most of the coenzyme Q.

Acetone is also a good solvent for extraction when used in a fashion similar to ethanol–ether as described above.

In some special cases (e.g., mitochondria), direct extraction with hydrocarbon solvents has been employed for determination of coenzyme Q (10). In our use of this type of system we have found that the material must be acidified for effective extraction of the quinone, and even then extraction is never complete as judged by other methods. It is also necessary to shake the system rapidly with the solvent to get effective extraction. This method has been useful, however, as an approach to the determination of both the oxidized and reduced forms of coenzyme Q in mitochondria. It has the advantage over more complete solvent extractions in that the minimum quantity of interfering substances is extracted, thus facilitating the direct spectrophotometric determination of the amount of oxidized quinone in the extract with a minimum of handling which would tend to oxidize any reduced quinone present (19).

This hydrocarbon extraction procedure has also been modified by use of alcohols to improve extraction of quinone, followed by a fractionation of the extract into a hydrocarbon phase and an aqueous phase. This fractionation affords sufficient purification of the extract to allow direct spectrophotometric determination of the quinone in the hydrocarbon phase (38).

Several surveys of coenzyme Q distribution have been made using saponification prior to extraction (25,36). Direct extraction procedures have been used only to a limited extent for survey work (25), but have been used more extensively for determination of coenzyme Q in special circumstances as described above (19,38). Direct solvent extraction of dried insects and microorganisms has also been used (25), but this is a time-consuming procedure involving many repeated extractions and is not generally recommended, unless only a small amount of dried material is available for assay.

IX. SEPARATION OF COENZYME Q FROM IMPURITIES

Separation of coenzyme Q from impurities which interfere with the assay is a fairly simple procedure using column chromatography. separation of closely related homologs of coenzyme Q for separate measurement of each is a more difficult problem, which is best accomplished by reversed-phase paper chromatography or with slightly less precision by use of silicic acid chromatography.

Morton et al. (34) have used water-treated alumina for purification of coenzyme Q. If carried out properly, this adsorbent gives good separation of coenzyme Q from interfering impurities. In our hands, however, we have always found a small loss of coenzyme Q on alumina. This loss is especially great if the alumina is dry. For this reason we have routinely used Decalso* or Florisil† for separation of coenzyme Q since these adsorbents are easy to work with, give adequate separation, and produce a minimum of loss (9,30). For more precise work it is desirable to purify the coenzyme Q by chromatography on a silicic acid supercell column as described by Crane et al. (9). Diplock et al. (14) use extraction with dry acetone at −70°C., followed by chromatography on zinc carbonate paper for simultaneous determination of coenzyme Q homologs and tocopherols.

X. MEASUREMENT OF COENZYME Q

There are four assays which may be used for quantitative determination of coenzyme Q. These are: The spectrophotometric borohydride-reduction assay in which the change in absorbancy at 275 mμ is determined when potassium borohydride is added to a solution of quinone in ethanol; Craven's test, which involves coupling of the quinone with ethylcyanoacetate under alkaline conditions [the basis for the production of a chromophore in this procedure has been discussed by Folkers et al. (17)]; the Dam-Karrer test, which is based on formation of a transient colored derivative after treatment of a quinone having an β-unsaturated side chain with alkali; and the Irrevere-Sullivan test.

1. Specific Assay Methods

A. SPECTROPHOTOMETRIC ASSAY (9)

Reagents. *Ethanol* (absolute).
Sodium or *potassium borohydride* as aqueous solution, 10 mg. in 3 ml. water.
Assay Procedure. The most satisfactory way to use this method is to measure the decrease in optical density at 275 mμ after reducing the oxidized CoQ. Figure 1 shows the ultraviolet spectra of the

---

* *Decalso:* Permutit Co., 50 W. 44 St., New York 36, N. Y.
† *Florisil:* Floridin Co., Talahassee, Florida.

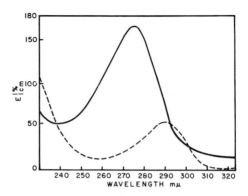

Fig. 1. Ultraviolet absorption spectra of oxidized and reduced coenzyme Q. The solid line is oxidized form and dashed line is the reduced form. The ordinate gives the $E_{1cm.}^{1\%}$ and the abscissa gives wavelength in millimicrons.

oxidized (upper curve) and reduced (lower curve) forms of CoQ. Table I gives the value of the extinction $E_{1\ cm.}^{1\%}$. ox.–red. at 275 mμ. Knowing these values one can calculate the CoQ concentration in a sample from the change in absorbance due to reduction.

From the general similarity between the oxidized and reduced spectra of CoQ, plastoquinone (PQ), α-tocopherylquinone, and vitamin

TABLE I

Spectrophotometric Constants of Coenzyme Q Homologs and Some Related Quinones

Quinone	λ_{max} in ethanol, mμ	$E_{1\ cm.}^{1\%}$	$E_{1\ cm.}^{1\%}$ ox.–red.	Molar extinction coefficient in ethanol
CoQ$_{10}$	275	165	142	14,000
CoQ$_9$	275	172		13,700
CoQ$_8$	275	190		13,800
CoQ$_7$	275	202		13,900
CoQ$_6$	275	240		14,100
Plastoquinone A	255	210	198	15,200
Plastoquinone B	255			
Plastoquinone C	255			
α-Tocopheryl-	262		375	15,100
quinone	269			

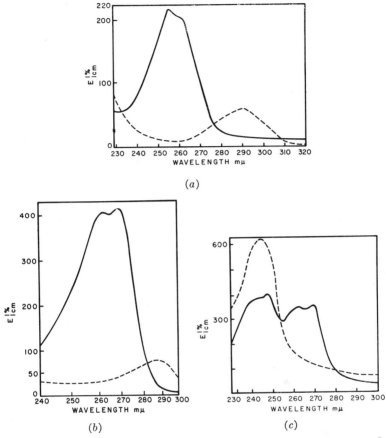

Fig. 2. Ultraviolet absorption spectra of some quinones similar to coenzyme Q. The solid line corresponds to the oxidized form and the dashed line corresponds to the reduced form. The ordinate gives the $E_{1cm}^{1\%}$ and the abscissa gives the wavelength in millimicrons. (a) Plastoquinone. (b) α-Tocopherylquinone. (c) Vitamin K_1.

K, (Fig. 2) it is seen that the presence of more than one of these compounds in a given sample can lead to erroneous results from calculating concentrations of a quinone from oxidation–reduction data.   If such a mixed quinone sample is to be assayed for a particular quinone using the spectral data, one can make an approximate correction for a known interfering quinone by taking the change in absorbance upon

TABLE II

Selective Assays for Terpenoid Quinones

Quinone	Spectrophotometric data λ_{max}, mμ	Isobestic point, mμ	Craven's test λ_{max}, mμ	Dam-Karrer test λ_{max}, mμ	Dam-Karrer test Development time	Irrevere-Sullivan test λ_{max}, mμ
Coenzyme Q$_{10}$	275	238 293 301	620	Shoulder at 550	8 min.	575
Plastoquinone A	255	233 276 308	None	580	55 sec.	575
α-Tocopheryl-quinone	261	282	None	No re-action		585
β-Tocopheryl-quinone	259	280	620	580–600		570
γ-Tocopheryl-quinone	258	279	620			570
δ-Tocopheryl-quinone	257	282	620	520–550		Shoulder at 560
Vitamin K$_1$	269 261 249 241	253 281	None	580, Slow to develop		570–585

reduction at the isobestic point of the oxidation–reduction curve of the interfering compound. For instance, if one has a sample of CoQ and plastoquinone, this may be assayed for CoQ by taking the change in absorbance upon reduction at 275 mμ, and since an isobestic point for PQ occurs at 276 mμ, there will be very little contribution to the drop in absorbance due to PQ. From the absorption curves given for the various quinones one can calculate the $E_{1\,cm.}^{1\%}$ ox.–red. for any wavelength and design an assay to fit the particular situation at hand.

Greater specificity in assaying for CoQ is available in the color tests mentioned below. From Table II it is seen that the Craven test is positive for CoQ but negative for PQ and α-tocopherylquinone, and negligible for vitamin K_1.

B. CRAVEN'S TEST (11,36,41)

Reagents. *Ethyl cyanoacetate.*
KOH, 5% w/v in 95% *ethanol.*
Ethanol, absolute.
Assay Procedure. To x ml. ethanolic solution of quinone containing from 100 to 400 μg. CoQ, add (in the order given): $(2 - x)$ ml. ethanol, 0.5 ml. ethyl cyanoacetate, and 0.5 ml. KOH reagent.

Read optical density at 620 mμ after 6 to 8 min. Begin timing immediately after adding KOH reagent. This can be read against an ethanol blank. Appropriate assay samples without the KOH reagent can be used to correct for extraneous absorbance.

From Table II it is seen that only CoQ, and β, γ, and δ-tocopherylquinone give a positive test. PQ, vitamin K_1, and α-tocopherylquinone do not give a response in this assay; hence this is a valuable assay, since these three compounds are frequently found in biological materials but the β, γ, and δ-tocopherylquinones are much less frequently found.

It is convenient to prepare a standard curve using purified CoQ, from which the concentration of CoQ in subsequent assays can be determined.

The mechanism of color formation has been explained by Shunk et al. (41) to be due to the displacement of a methoxy group by the ethyl cyanoacetate anion.

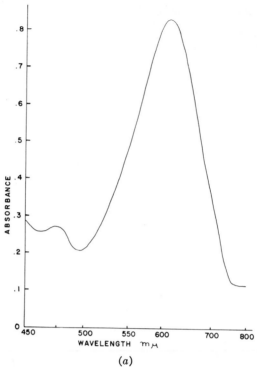

(a)

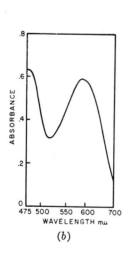

(b)

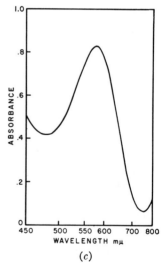

(c)

C. DAM-KARRER ASSAY (12)

Reagents. *Ethanol*, 70%, in ethylene glycol.

KOH, 5%, in methanol–ethylene glycol 1:1 v/v.

Assay Procedure. To x ml. ethanolic sample of quinone containing from 30 to 150 μg. quinone, add $(2 - x)$ ml. ethylene glycol reagent, and 1 ml. 5% KOH reagent.

Read optical density at 580 mμ after 7 min. for CoQ and after 55 sec. for PQ.

This assay is not very specific, as can be seen from Table II.

According to Leiberman the color formation is due to the formation of a mesomeric ion of the quinone in the presence of alkali; see Thompson (ref. 42, p. 147) for an explanation of this.

D. IRREVERE-SULLIVAN ASSAY (20)

Reagents. *Sodium diethyl dithiocarbamate*, 5% w/v, in ethanol, made up fresh every day.

2% w/v alcoholic alkali: 2 g. metallic *sodium* per 100 ml. ethanol.

Ethanol, absolute.

Assay Procedure. To x ml. ethanolic solution of sample, add (in order given): $(2 - x)$ ml. ethanol, 0.5 ml. carbamate reagent, and 0.5 ml. alkali reagent.

Start timing after adding alkali reagent. Read optical density at 575 mμ after 4 min.

Irrevere and Sullivan improved upon the Dam-Karrer assay greatly by incorporating sodium diethyl dithiocarbamate. With this compound present, the color formation is faster and of greater intensity. As an example, two identical samples of CoQ$_{10}$ were assayed: one

---

Fig. 3. Visible absorption spectra of the chromophore of three color tests for coenzyme Q$_{10}$. The ordinate gives absorbance and the abscissa gives the wavelength in millimicrons. (*a*) Craven's test: Cuvette contained 0.4 mg. coenzyme Q$_{10}$, 0.5 ml. ethyl cyanoacetate, 0.5 ml. 5% ethanolic KOH, and ethanol to make the total volume 3 ml. The peak absorbance was recorded 7 min. after adding KOH reagent. (*b*) Dam-Karrer test: Cuvette contained 4.95 mg. coenzyme Q$_{10}$, 1 ml. 5% KOH in methanol–ethylene glycol 1:1, and 70% ethanol in ethylene glycol to make the total volume 3 ml. The peak absorbance was recorded 6 min. after adding the KOH reagent. (*c*) Irrevere-Sullivan test: Cuvette contained approximately 0.2 mg. coenzyme Q$_{10}$, 0.5 ml. sodium diethyl dithiocarbamate, 0.5 ml. alcoholic alkali (as explained in text), and ethanol to make 3 ml. total volume. The peak absorbance was read at 4.5 min. after adding the alkali reagent.

TABLE III

Effect of Diethyl Dithiocarbamate on the Dam-Karrer Reaction

Time, min.	Absorbance at 575 mμ	
	Dam-Karrer reagents only	Dam Karrer reagents + sodium diethyl dithiocarbamate
1	0.24	0.57
2	0.36	0.71
3	0.42	0.84
4	0.43	0.88
5	0.41	0.84
6	0.37	0.82

with the Dam-Karrer reagents only, and one with the Dam-Karrer reagents plus the sodium diethyl dithiocarbamate. The resultant time dependence of color formation (optical density) at 575 mμ is presented in Table III.

From Table II it is seen that the Irrevere-Sullivan assay gives a positive response for many quinones.

The absorption spectra of the solution resulting from assaying CoQ with the Craven's, Dam-Karrer, and Irrevere-Sullivan tests are shown in Figure 3. The absorption maximum which various other quinones give in these color tests are listed in Table II. Also compiled in this table are data on the u.v. absorption maxima, and the isobestic points of the quinones previously discussed.

XI. A DETAILED ASSAY PROCEDURE FOR COENZYME Q

1. Assay of Animal Tissue

A. PREPARATION OF TISSUE

Cut the material up into small pieces; homogenize in a Waring Blendor or a similar blender with about 40 ml. ethanol per 30 g. tissue.

B. EXTRACTION OF COQ FROM HOMOGENATE

Both saponification and direct solvent extraction have been used for the extraction. Both procedures are outlined below.

Saponification.   (*a*) Add to the homogenate the following reagents in preparation for refluxing:

15% w/w potassium hydroxide pellets
10% w/w pyrogallol
150% v/w ethanol

Reflux at a brisk boil for 20–25 min.; cool rapidly.

(*b*) *Separation of nonsaponifiable lipids.* Extract the cooled solution five to eight times with about an equal volume of *n*-heptane or petroleum ether in a separatory funnel.   Enough water should be added to bring the original ethanol concentration down to the range of 50–60%.   Wash the combined organic phases three times with water to remove salt and pyrogallol degradation products.   Evaporate this organic phase (under vacuum and 50–60°C. heat) to dryness and take up the residue in a small amount of ethanol.   The coenzyme Q content may now be determined or the coenzyme Q may be further purified as described in part (*b*) under "Direct Solvent Extraction" (below).

If the level of pyrogallol is less than suggested, a destruction of CoQ can occur.   A comparison was made on the recovery of CoQ from samples saponified with the recommended level of pyrogallol and potassium hydroxide, samples with 0.2% pyrogallol and 20% KOH, and samples treated by the direct solvent extraction method [cf. Table IV].

Direct Solvent Extraction.   (*a*) Add to the homogenate a 3:1 v/v ethanol–ether solution.   For 30 g. tissue, about 200 ml. solution

TABLE IV
Recovery of Added CoQ in Three Extraction Procedures[a]

Conditions of assay	CoQ_{10} added	Per cent recovered
20% KOH, 0.2% pyrogallol	1.86 mg.	11
13% KOH, 10.5% pyrogallol	1.86 mg.	100
Direct extraction 3:1 v/v ethanol/ether	1.86 mg.	61

[a] When methanol was used in place of ethanol in the saponification, a considerable destruction of coenzyme Q_{10} was observed.   Folkers et al.[17] have suggested using methanol in saponification to avoid formation of ethoxy derivatives.   Depending on the type of information desired, one must choose which saponification system to use.

is appropriate. The mixture may be shaken in a glass-stoppered container on a reciprocal shaker for $2^1/_2$ hours or it may be left to stand for 20 hours. After the period of extraction, filter the mixture through a büchner funnel or centrifuge it, and wash the precipitate twice with hot ethanol. Evaporate this combined filtrate or supernatant to dryness as in the above case and take it up in a small volume of ethanol.

(b) *Purification of conezyme Q in the extract.* The extracts from many tissues contain compounds which will interfere with the assay of coenzyme Q. Interference is most often encountered in using the spectrophotometric assay technique. In our experience, the interference is most likely in two forms. First, there are materials which will increase in absorbancy in the 275 mμ region when treated with borohydride or alkali. These materials will cause low values in estimation of coenzyme Q. Interference of this type may be suspected if the isobestic points are not the same as coenzyme Q [cf. Crane et al. (9) and Diplock et al. (14)]. Second, there are other compounds which will decrease in absorbancy at 275 mμ when treated with borohydride or alkali. Obviously, other quinones will interfere in this way when treated with borohydride. Other materials, presumably phenolic, will show a shift in absorbance maximum when treated with alkali alone or with borohydride because of its alkaline nature. To avoid this interference it is necessary to use an alkali blank in which the ethanolic solution of the extract is treated with ethanolic potassium hydroxide solution. We have encountered compounds in the lipids from barley and lightning bugs which show spectral changes in alkali which appear identical to borohydride-induced changes in coenzyme Q.

If interfering compounds are present, it is necessary to purify the coenzyme Q in the extract obtained by the methods outlined above. This purification is most easily accomplished by chromatography of the sample on a small Decalso column. A column containing 40 g. Decalso will be suitable for the extract from 30 g. tissue. Ethanol is carefully removed from the extract by evaporation under vacuum. A small amount of good quality heptane or isooctane is added and again evaporated to remove the last traces of ethanol. Then the sample is taken up in 10–20 ml. of isooctane and transferred to the Decalso column. The flask containing the sample is then washed with small portions of isooctane to effect a quantitative transfer of the sample to the column. The column is then eluted with 200 ml. iso-octane followed by 300 ml. isooctane containing 10% ethyl ether v/v, followed by elution with isooctane containing 10% ethanol v/v. All of the coenzyme Q should be found in the second eluate (10% ether), but the first and third eluates should be checked to make sure of the technique. The coenzyme Q eluted from the column is usually pure enough for spectrophotometric assay. If interfering impurities still persist at this stage, better purification may be achieved using a silicic acid column (9). However, for routine assays it would probably be desirable to use the Craven's test for assay if the chromatography on Decalso does not provide sufficient purification for spectrophotometric assay.

As an alternative to purification by column chromatography, Pumphrey and Redfearn (38) have used phase separation on direct extracts from mitochondria. In special cases this technique will be useful, but for a wide range of materials with variation in lipid impurities we feel the column will give more reproducible results.

C. ASSAY FOR COQ

Any of the assays described previously may be applied to the solution obtained from the above procedures or may be applied directly to the extract.

Each extraction procedure as described above was applied to 30-g. samples of beef heart, one of which had added to it 1.86 mg. CoQ_{10}. The results are shown in Table IV.

In all of these procedures the use of any rubber stoppers or tubing must be avoided, since solvents will extract compounds from the rubber which interfere with the spectrophotometric assay.

For plant material we prefer to use extraction by the saponification procedure followed by assay using Craven's test. This approach reduces interference by plastoquinone and chlorophylls.

XII. PAPER CHROMATOGRAPHY

1. Reversed-Phase Chromatography. Impregnation of Paper with Silicone (29)

A. PREPARATION OF PAPER

Whatman No. 3 MM filter paper is commonly used, although Whatman No. 1 is also suitable. The paper is impregnated with silicone by immersing it in a 5% w/v solution of Dow-Corning Silicone Fluid No. 550 (Dow-Corning Corp., Midland, Mich.) in chloroform for several seconds and allowed to air dry at room temperature.

Streaking of the lipid on the paper will occur as the solvent front advances if the paper is not treated with the silicone or a similar non-polar compound.

B. APPLICATION OF SAMPLE TO THE PAPER

Samples of CoQ in a nonpolar solvent are applied as a small spot in the usual manner. The amount of CoQ per spot should be between 5μg. and 100 μg.

C. DEVELOPMENT OF PAPER

Lester and Ramasarma (29) have described the results of using various combinations of n-propanol and water as developing solvents. 4:1 propanol/H_2O v/v, 3:1 propanol/H_2O, and 7:3 propanol/H_2O are very satisfactory. The authors find that 4:1 propanol/H_2O gives the best resolution for CoQ and plastoquinone.

D. DETECTION OF QUINONES ON THE PAPER

There are two detection methods which give good results for identifying quinones.

(1) The first method, presented by Lester and Ramasarma, consists of dipping the air-dried paper in a freshly prepared aqueous solution of potassium borohydride (0.1% w/v) for about 30 sec. to reduce any quinone to the hydroquinone. The paper is drained briefly and dipped in a 0.1N HCl solution to neutralize any excess borohydride. After draining briefly again, the hydroquinones formed may be visualized by one of two ways.

a. Dip paper for several seconds in an aqueous solution containing 0.25% w/v neotetrazolium chloride and 0.25M potassium phosphate buffer, pH 7.0. After draining the paper, put it into an oven at 80–100°C. for approximately 1–3 min. until purple spots develop on a white background. The time of color development depends on the temperature: near 100°C. the reduction of the dye by the hydroquinone is quite rapid. The lower limit of detection is approximately 5 μg. CoQ.

b.   The hydroquinones produce red spots on a white background when sprayed with a freshly prepared solution of 1 part $FeCl_3 \cdot 6H_2O$ (0.5% w/v in ethanol), 1 part of α,α'-dipyridyl (0.2% w/v in ethanol), and 2 parts H_2O.

(2)   Linn et al. (30) have described a method of detecting quinone structures using leucomethylene blue as the indicator.   They suggest preparing the leucomethylene blue by adding to 100 mg. methylene blue in 100 ml. ethanol, 1 ml. glacial acetic acid and 1 g. zinc dust. Methylene blue is decolorized and can be sprayed on our air-dried paper promptly to avoid reoxidizing the leuco form back to the methylene blue form.   The quinone spots turn blue rather quickly and can be circled.   The rest of the paper gradually turns blue, especially if kept in the light.   The authors find this method easier to use than the prior method of dipping in borohydride.   The lower limit of sensitivity reported by Linn et al. (30) is 1 μg./cm.^{2}.   The method of preparing the leucomethylene blue used in our laboratory consists of adding to 20 ml. aqueous $3 \times 10^{-3}M$ methylene blue, 1 g. zinc dust and 2–3 ml. concentrated H_2SO_4.   The solution is filtered through glass wool after decolorizing, and sprayed immediately on the paper.

2. Vaseline-Impregnated Paper Method

An alternative method of obtaining reversed-phase chromatography is to use a 3% (v/v) of paraffin oil in chloroform solution to dip the paper in instead of the silicone fluid solution referred to above.   In addition to wider availability of the materials, the Vaseline method has certain technical advantages such as its less troublesome u.v. absorption spectrum.   This is a desirable property if one wishes to use paper chromatography as a means of separating CoQ or some other quinone from closely related compounds in fairly large amounts.

The procedures for developing and detecting are identical with those mentioned above for the silicone-impregnated paper method.   Diplock et al. (14) have described the use of zinc carbonate-impregnated paper for separation of coenzyme Q and related compounds.

3. Determination of the Length of the Isoprenoid Side Chain

Paper chromatography by either of the methods described may be used for determination of the length of the isoprenoid side chain on coenzyme Q. The relative R_f of the members of the group decreases with increasing chain length. Unfortunately, the method has not been standardized sufficiently for absolute R_f values to be used for identification. Therefore, precise definition of the coenzyme Q homolog present is based on chromatographic comparison with a series of homologs run in the same system. Since coenzyme Q_{10} and coenzyme Q_6 are now commercially available, it is possible to get a fair estimate of an unknown homolog by chromatographic comparison with these compounds. More precise definition of coenzymes Q_9, Q_8, and Q_7 would best be made by extraction of a sample from tissues known to contain the appropriate homolog [cf. Lester and Crane (25)]. An example of the relative R_f of the coenzyme Q homologs as well as vitamin K_1 and plastoquinones A, B, and C are given in Table V.

TABLE V
Relative R_f Values for Terepenoid Quinones[a]

Quinone	R_f
Coenzyme Q_{10}	0.27
Coenzyme Q_9	0.36
Coenzyme Q_8	0.42
Coenzyme Q_7	0.49
Coenzyme Q_6	0.54
Plastoquinone A	0.25
Plastoquinone B	0.18
Plastoquinone C	0.81
Vitamin K_1	0.59
Q_{263}	0.52

[a] R_f values on silicone-impregnated paper with 4:1 propanol water v/v as described by Lester and Ramasarma (29). These values are relative and cannot be used as absolute because of variations with every chromatogram. Plastoquinone B and C are compounds from spinach chloroplasts with spectra similar to plastoquinone A (13,22). Q_{263} is a quinone from spinach chloroplasts with an absorption maximum at 263 mμ (22). A similar compound has also been reported in chlorobium by Fuller et al. (18).

Plastoquinone C, which has recently been found in plants (13), would probably interfere only with coenzyme Q_6.

Quantitative determination of the amounts of two closely related homologs of coenzyme Q in the same tissue requires a careful separation of the two homologs, followed by application of one of the assay techniques.

For the separation of compounds as closely related as coenzyme Q_9 and Q_{10}, the silicone spots as detected by brief ultraviolet exposure are cut out and eluted into isooctane. The amount in the eluate from silicone-impregnated paper is best determined by Craven's test, since the silicone contains material which interferes with the spectrophotometric assay. Eluates from Vaseline-impregnated paper may be assayed by Craven's test or spectrophotometrically. Isler et al. (21) have described the use of a polyethylene column to separate coenzyme Q_9 and Q_{10} from rat liver. There is some separation of these compounds on silicic acid but not sufficient for accurate quantitative analysis of closely related homologs [cf. Lester and Crane (24)].

XIII. BIOLOGICAL ASSAY OF COENZYME Q ACTIVITY

Restoration of succinic cytochrome c reductase activity in mitochondria from which coenzyme Q has been removed by acetone extraction is the only precise assay for coenzyme Q function. Since other lipid materials act as stimulators or inhibitors of this assay, it cannot be used to assay the amount of coenzyme Q in a crude lipid extract. It may, however, be a useful assay if purified samples of a member of the coenzyme Q group are available or if the coenzymatic activity of other quinones is to be determined.

For this procedure, beef heart mitochondria are prepared as described by Crane et al. (7, 10). The mitochondria are suspended in $0.25M$ sucrose and freeze-dried with the preparation kept frozen at all times until dry. The dried mitochondria are then extracted with acetone. 200 mg. mitochondrial powder is suspended in 20 ml. reagent grade acetone and the suspension is shaken on a reciprocal shaker in a glass-stoppered tube or bottle at about 300 strokes/min. (30-cm. stroke) for 30–90 min. at room temperature (23°C.). The suspension is then centrifuged at low speed and the acetone is decanted. The mitochondrial residue is then placed in a vacuum desiccator until all solvent is removed. The dry residue is then suspended by homogenization with distilled water sufficient to give a protein concentration of 20 mg. protein per milliliter. A glass homogenizer with Teflon pestle is suitable. The resuspended extracted mitochondria are washed once by centrifugation at 50,000 $\times g$ in a Spinco centrifuge and the mitochondrial material which constitutes the sediment is resuspended by homogenization in $0.25M$ sucrose sufficient to make a final protein concentration of 20 mg. protein/ml.

Succinic cytochrome c reductase activity is determined by measuring the reduction of cytochrome c by increase of absorbance at 550 mμ in a spectrophotometer. The reaction mixture contains 80 μmoles potassium phosphate buffer, pH 7.4; 100 μmoles potassium succinate, pH 7.0; 0.4 μmoles potassium cyanide; and 0.2 mg. oxidized cytochrome c (Sigma Chemical Co., St. Louis, Missouri) in a total volume of 1.0 ml. The reaction is started by adding about 0.01 ml. mitochondrial suspension or sufficient to give an increase of 0.02–0.1 absorbance per minute. Test the reagents by using unextracted mitochondria. The coenzyme Q activity of a quinone may then be determined by adding an equivalent amount of extracted mitochondria followed by up to 0.01 ml. ethanolic solution of the quinone to be tested. About 0.1 mg. coenzyme Q may be necessary to obtain maximum activity in this assay. The procedure and specificity of various quinones is described by Ambe and Crane (1). Other extraction procedures, using aqueous acetone systems, have been described by Lester and Fleischer (27).

XIV. DETERMINATION OF UBICHROMENOL AND . UBICHROMANOL

Ubichromenol can be determined by the reduction of ferric salts in ethanol in the presence of dipyridyl as used by Emmerie and Engel (15) for the assay of tocopherol. The products of this reaction are unknown since the ubichromenol is isomeric with the ubiquinone or coenzyme Q. Of course, the ubichromenol must be separated from any tocopherols or hydroquinones before the assay can be applied. Diplock et al. (14) have described the use of zinc carbonate-treated paper for the separation of ubichromenol from tocopherol and the subsequent analysis using ferric chloride dipyridyl reagent. It should also be possible to use silicone-treated paper for this separation.

Ubichromanol has not been detected in natural material, and authentic synthetic ubichromanol has not yet been reported (17). We have used the ferric chloride reagent for determination of the chromanol of hexahydro coenzyme Q_4 (phytyl Q) which was kindly supplied by Dr. Folkers of Merck Sharp and Dohme. If any ubichromanol is present in an extract, it should therefore show an Emmerie-

Engel positive reaction, but we cannot predict the stability or behavior of the chromanols derived from natural homologs of coenzyme Q during chromatography.

References

1. Ambe, K. S., and F. L. Crane, *Biochim. Biophys. Acta*, *43*, 30–40 (1960).
2. Bouman, J., E. C. Slater, H. Rudney, and J. Links, *Biochim. Biophys. Acta*, *29*, 456 (1958).
3. Brodie, A. F., *Federation Proc.*, *20*, 995–1004 (1961).
4. Crane, F. L., unpublished results.
5. Crane, F. L., in G. E. W. Wolstenholme and C. M. O'Conner, eds., *Ciba Foundation Symposium on Quinones in Electron Transport*, J. A. Churchill, London, 1961, pp. 36–75.
6. Crane, F. L., *Plant-Physiol.*, *34*, 546–551 (1959).
7. Crane, F. L., J. L. Glenn, and D. E. Green, *Biochim. Biophys. Acta*, *22*, 475–487 (1956).
8. Crane, F. L., Y. Hatefi, R. L. Lester, and C. Widmer, *Biochim. Biophys. Acta*, *25*, 220–221 (1957).
9. Crane, F. L., R. L. Lester, C. Widmer, and Y. Hatefi, *Biochim. Biophys. Acta*, *32*, 73–79 (1959).
10. Crane, F. L., C. Widmer, R. L. Lester, and Y. Hatefi, *Biochim. Biophys. Acta*, *31*, 476–489 (1959).
11. Craven, R., *J. Chem. Soc.*, *1931*, 1605.
12. Dam, H., A. Geiger, J. Glavind, P. Karrer, W. Karrer, E. Rothschild, and H. Salomon, *Helv. Chim. Acta*, *22*, 310 (1939).
13. Dilley, R. A., L. P. Kegel, and F. L. Crane, *Plant Physiol.*, *37 Suppl.*, xl (1962).
14. Diplock, A. T., J. Green, E. E. Edwin, and T. Bunyon, *Biochem. J.*, *76*, 563–571 (1960).
15. Emmerie, A., and C. Engel, *Nature*, *142*, 873 (1938).
16. Erickson, R. E., K. S. Brown, Jr., D. E. Wolf, and K. Folkers, *Arch. Biochem. Bioyhys.*, *90*, 314–317 (1960).
17. Folkers, K., C. H. Shunk, B. O. Linn, N. R. Trenner, D. E. Wolf, C. H. Hoffman, A. C. Page, Jr., and F. R. Koniuszy, in Wolstenholme, G. E. W., and C. M. O'Conner, Eds., *Ciba Foundation Symposium on Electron Transport*. J. A. Churchill, London, 1961, pp. 100–126.
18. Fuller, R. C., R. M. Smillie, N. Rigopoulos, and V. Yount, *Arch. Biochem. Biophys.*, *95*, 197–201 (1961).
19. Hatefi, Y., R. L. Lester, F. L. Crane, and C. Widmer, *Biochim. Biophys. Acta*, *31*, 490–501 (1959).
20. Irrevere, F., and M. X. Sullivan, *Science*, *94*, 497 (1941).
21. Isler, O., R. Ruegg, A. Langemann, P. Schudel, G. Ruser, and J. Wursch, in Wolstenholme, G. E. W., and C. M. O'Conner, Eds., *Ciba Foundation Symposium on Quinones in Electron Transport*, J. A. Churchill, London, 1961, pp. 79–96.

22. Kegel, L. P., M. Henninger, and F. L. Crane, unpublished results.
23. Kofler, M., in Festschrift Emil Christoph Barell, Hoffman-La Roche and Co. Ltd., Basle, 1946, p. 199.
24. Lester, R. L., and F. L. Crane, *Biochim. Biophys. Acta, 32,* 492–498 (1959).
25. Lester, R. L., and F. L. Crane, *J. Biol. Chem., 234,* 2169–2175 (1959).
26. Lester, R. L., F. L. Crane, and Y. Hatefi, *J. Am. Chem. Soc., 80,* 4751 (1958).
27. Lester, R. L., and S. Fleischer, *Biochim. Biophys. Acta, 47,* 358–377 (1961).
28. Lester, R. L., Y. Hatefi, C. Widmer, and F. L. Crane, *Biochim. Biophys. Acta, 33,* 169–185 (1959).
29. Lester, R. L., and T. Ramasarma, *J. Biol. Chem., 234,* 672–767 (1959).
30. Linn, B. O., A. C. Page, Jr., E. L. Wong, P. H. Gale, C. H. Shunk, and K. Folkers, *J. Am. Chem. Soc., 81,* 4007–4010 (1959).
31. Linn, B. O., N. R. Trenner, C. H. Shunk, and K. Folkers, *J. Am. Chem. Soc., 81,* 1263 (1959).
32. Morton, R. A., in Wolstenholme, G. E. W., and C. M. O'Conner, Eds., *Ciba Foundation Symposium on Quinones in Electron Transport,* J. A. Church-hill, London, 1961, pp. 36–75.
33. Morton, R. A., *Vitamin and Hormones, 19,* 1–42 (1961).
34. Morton, R. A., U. Gloor, O. Schindler, G. M. Wilson, L. H. Choparddit-Jen, F. W. Hemming, O. Isler, W. M. F. Leat, J. F. Pennock, R. Ruegg, U. Schwie-ter, and O. Wiss, *Helv. Chim. Acta, 41,* 2343 (1958).
35. Page, A. C., Jr., P. H. Gale, F. Koniuszy, and K. Folkers, *Arch. Biochem. Biophys., 85,* 474–477 (1959).
36. Page, A. C., Jr., P. H. Gale, H. Wallick, R. B. Walton, L. E. McDaniel, H. B. Woodruff, and K. Folkers, *Arch. Biochem. Biophys., 89,* 318–321 (1960).
37. Pandya, K. P., D. H. L. Bishop, and H. K. King, *Biochem. J., 78,* 35 (1961).
38. Pumphrey, A. M., and E. R. Redfearn, *Biochem. J., 76,* 61–64 (1960).
39. Rowland, R. L., *J. Am. Chem. Soc., 80,* 6130 (1958).
40. Sastry, P. S., J. Jayaraman, and T. Ramasarma, *Nature, 189,* 577 (1961).
41. Shunk, C. H., J. F. McPherson, and K. Folkers, *J. Org. Chem., 25,* 1053 (1960).
42. Thomson, R. H., *Naturally Occurring Quinones,* Academic Press, New York, 1957.
43. Vischer, E. B., *J. Chem. Soc., 1953,* 815.

The Measurement of Carbonic
Anhydrase Activity

ROBERT P. DAVIS, *Albert Einstein College of Medicine, New York*

I. INTRODUCTION

1. General

Carbonic anhydrase is a small metalloprotein widely distributed in animal tissues and in the leaves of green plants. It contains one zinc atom per molecule in a rather firmly bonded structure. Its enzymic function is the catalysis of a normally rapid reversible inorganic hydration reaction whose over-all sequence is

$$CO_2 + H_2O \rightleftharpoons H_2CO_3 \rightleftharpoons H^+ + HCO_3^- \tag{1}$$

While this is among the simplest of enzyme catalyzed reactions, the measurement of carbonic anhydrase activity and the study of the enzyme reaction kinetics have been hampered by the technical difficulty of measuring the rate of a hydration reaction which approaches oxidation–reduction reactions in rapidity. With human erythrocyte carbonic anhydrase, for example, the rate of formation of enzyme-substrate compound is close to that of catalase with methyl hydrogen peroxide as substrate (12). Carbonic anhydrase lacks the convenient colored prosthetic group or coenzyme by which most oxidation–reduction reactions can be readily studied. For carbonic anhydrase, indeed, the role of the zinc atom is not fully understood, since it appears from inhibitor studies (13) not to be the site of CO_2 binding. The metal may actually function to contribute a hydroxyl group or water molecule in the hydration reaction (13). The kinetic and molecular properties of carbonic anhydrase have recently been extensively reviewed (14), and our discussion here will be confined to methods for the measurement of the rate of the enzymic reaction.

There is, unfortunately, no standard method for the measurement of carbonic anhydrase activity. All the methods of value are technically difficult, require at least a moderate amount of custom instrumentation, and contain important assumptions which affect the interpretation of the kinetic data. Since the major chemical features of the catalyzed reaction are the evolution of carbon dioxide gas in the dehydration reaction and the generation of a hydrogen ion in the hydration reaction, it is not surprising that the major methods for measurement of enzymic activity are manometric, electrometric, or indicator techniques. The choice of method to be used depends on the purpose of the experiment. In general, the modern gasimetric methods are most useful for the less stringent requirements of measurement of tissue concentrations and the activity of semipurified enzymic mixtures and for semiquantitative work. For reasons to be discussed below, the same may be said for most simple indicator methods. For precise kinetic work, electrometric methods or the adaptation of indicator methods to rapid-flow techniques must be used.

It is also important to note that in studies with highly purified bovine carbonic anhydrase preparations, peptone must be added in order to maintain enzyme stability (9). This, however, has not been necessary in studies of the human enzyme.

2. Handling of Reagents

Great care must be taken in the preparation of the glassware and reagent solutions in the study of carbonic anhydrase kinetics. All water used should be either doubly glass-distilled or once distilled water which has been passed over a mixed bed of ion-exchange resin— for example, Dowex 50 and Amberlite IRA 400. This step is necessary in order to free the water of metal ions, ammonium ions, and other possible interfering substances. The glassware should be cleaned in a hot nitric acid–sulfuric acid bath and washed very thoroughly with distilled ion-exchanged water. Analytical grade reagents should, of course, be used.

3. Preparation of Substrate Solutions

For studies of the dehydration reaction, sodium bicarbonate may be used, but it should be prepared free of CO_2 in order to remove errors arising from appreciable back (hydration) reaction. For studies of the hydration reaction, a standardized carbon dioxide solution may be simply prepared by bubbling purified carbon dioxide gas through water, with a known partial pressure of carbon dioxide above the solution and a known temperature (mostly simply the reaction temperature); the concentration of CO_2 may be calculated readily from Henry's Law. By taking different volumes of this solution or by using standardized mixtures of carbon dioxide and nitrogen with known partial pressure of carbon dioxide, various final concentrations of substrate solution may be obtained. In order to eliminate loss of CO_2 during the taking up of substrate solution into pipets, syringes, and reaction vessels, the apparatus should be rigged to allow forcing up of the CO_2 solution by brief overpressure rather than by suction.

4. Preparation of the Enzyme

A. AMMONIUM SULFATE FRACTIONATION

The most commonly used method for preparing highly purified carbonic anhydrase from mammalian erythrocytes (12,26) and from plants (15,53,60) has been the second procedure of Keilin and Mann (26), who modified the original procedure of Meldrum and Roughton (42).

One liter of erythrocytes, separated from plasma by centrifugation, is washed with 0.9% NaCl solution and hemolyzed with 0.5 liter of distilled water. The hemolysate is treated in the cold (0°) with a previously cooled mixture of 0.5 liter ethanol and 0.5 liter chloroform. After 15–30 minutes, the denatured hemoglobin is removed by centrifugation. The supernatant solution is filtered and dialyzed for 24 hours against running distilled water.

The enzyme solution is then saturated with ammonium sulfate and the precipitate collected on a Büchner funnel. The precipitate is dissolved in a small amount of water and dialyzed against distilled water until free of ammonium sulfate. Any remaining sediment is now removed by centrifugation.

Ammonium sulfate is added to the supernatant to a concentration of 45% saturation. The precipitate is removed, and the supernatant, containing most of the carbonic anhydrase, is saturated with ammonium sulfate. The enzyme, now in the precipitate, is taken up in distilled water and the solution is dialyzed free of inorganic salt. The enzyme solution is treated three times successively with a suspension of alumina C_γ at pH 6.8 with successive discarding of the centrifuged residue. The colorless supernatant of the alumina treatment is then treated with ammonium sulfate to 50% saturation. The precipitate is discarded and the supernatant fully saturated with ammonium sulfate. The precipitate now contains the enzyme, which is redissolved in water and dialyzed free of ammonium sulfate.

Other methods have been less widely used to prepare carbonic anhydrase from red blood cells (28,30,34,51,52,55), gastric mucosa (26), and plants (58).

B. COLUMN CHROMATOGRAPHY

Lindskog (36) has recently published a newer method for the preparation of carbonic anhydrase from erythrocytes. The initial

step, after washing and hemolyzing the red blood cells, involves denaturation and removal of hemoglobin, chromatography of a hemo-
globin-free lysate of bovine erythrocytes on diethylaminoethyl
(DEAE) cellulose columns, and elution with tris-(hydroxymethyl)-
aminomethane (Tris) buffer, followed by zone electrophoresis on
cellulose columns.   The product shows high specific activity and a
high degree of homogeneity by electrophoretic and ultracentrifugal
analysis.

The initial steps of the procedure comprise sedimenting the red
blood cells, washing with 0.9% NaCl, and hemolyzing with distilled
water.   Following this, hemoglobin is denatured by the Tsuchihashi
procedure (1 vol. of hemolyzed erythrocytes:0.8 vol. 40% ethanol:0.4
vol. chloroform) (56), as in the Keilin and Mann procedure.   The
upper phase of the supernatant of the denatured hemoglobin is dialyzed against distilled water and adjusted with pH 8.0 Tris-HCl
buffer to a final Tris concentration of $0.01M$.   The solution is then
passed through a column (6 cm. diameter $\times$ 40 cm. height) of DEAE-
cellulose previously equilibrated in a cold room with $0.01M$ Tris
buffer at pH 8.0.   The flow rate is 10–15 ml./min.   About 95% of the
protein and an equivalent amount of the enzyme activity are taken
up by the column.   Almost all the carbonic anhydrase can be removed
from the column in high purity by elution with $0.08M$ Tris buffer,
pH 8.0.   The enzymic activity of the eluted fractions parallels the
optical density at 280 mμ.   The active fractions, with almost 100%
recovery and a sixfold purification, can be lyophilized and further
purified by zone electrophoresis, on a column of ethanolized cellulose
in a phosphate–borate buffer system at pH 8.2 and $\mu = 0.05$.   This
procedure yields two forms of carbonic anhydrase, differing only in
slight variation of their electrophoretic mobility.   When the Tsuchihashi procedure is avoided and gentler means employed to remove
hemoglobin, Lindskog obtains almost exclusively one of these forms,
considered by him to be the native enzyme (36,38).   The kinetic
behavior of these types of carbonic anhydrase has not yet been
studied.

II. MANOMETRIC METHODS

1. Apparatus and Procedure

Manometric methods were originally described by Meldrum and
Roughton (42).   The details were elaborated considerably by the

work of Roughton and Booth (48).   Since that time the gasimetric
method of assay of carbonic anhydrase activity has been used quite
extensively (29,30,49,57).   The reaction vessel of Roughton and
Booth is a glass boat-shaped trough of 40–70 ml. capacity.   It is
divided into 2 sections by a central ridge.   The rate of uptake of
carbon dioxide or its evolution is measured manometrically while the
assay mixture is shaken quite vigorously at 0°.   For measurement
of the dehydration reaction, in one compartment of the glass vessel
is placed 2 ml. of a solution containing the enzyme, $0.1M$ Na_2HPO_4,
and $0.1M$ KH_2PO_4, and in the other compartment 2 ml. of a solution
containing $0.2M$ $NaHCO_3$ and $0.02M$ NaOH.   The vessel is attached
to a manometer whose other limb is connected to a compensating
vessel, also shaken vigorously.   The combined vessel resembles a
Barcroft differential manometer.   After temperature equilibration,
the reaction vessel is shaken very rapidly at a constant temperature.
CO_2 evolution is recorded and plotted as a function of time.   Readings are taken at 5-second intervals during the initial period of reaction.

A unique reaction vessel, stirring apparatus and manometric system
have been developed by Keller et al. (27) for studies of the inhibition
kinetics of carbonic anhydrase.

2. Errors and Corrections

In the most stringent work it is necessary to apply several important corrections to the raw data in order to derive truly kinetic information.   Among these corrections are:

1. An estimate of the rate of enzyme inactivation due to extremely
vigorous shaking of the reaction vessel.   The progressive inactivation
of all enzyme preparations, particularly the more highly purified
preparations, may be allowed for by measuring the rate of carbon
dioxide evolution over shorter intervals and extrapolating to zero
time.   This is one of the major defects in the manometric method, for
extremely vigorous shaking is required to assure CO_2 equilibration.
Enzyme inactivation, not always completely reproducible, is in-
evitably encountered.

2. Correction for physical solution of carbon dioxide evolved.
This may be simply done at all recorded pressures from the knowledge
of the volume of reactant mixture and from the Henry's Law constant
at the appropriate temperature.

3. Correction for the degree of buffer activation or inhibition (28,47). The magnitude of this effect has been shown (8) to vary with the degree of purification of the enzyme.

4. The application of a highly derived relationship to correct for the limiting effect of carbon dioxide diffusion.

Formulas have been developed by Roughton and Booth (48) for making these necessary corrections. Generally, except in the most precise kinetic work, the true rate may be given by the equation

$$R = R_m \times R_0/(R_m - R_0) \tag{2}$$

where R_0 is the observed uncorrected initial rate and R_m is the maximal observable rate in the presence of a large amount of enzyme (the rate when CO_2 diffusion is the single limiting factor).

Following application of all of the above corrections, it is essential to demonstrate a linear relationship between the enzymic rate and enzyme concentrations. This, unfortunately, has not been done in most of the studies wherein the manometric method has been applied, or else it has been shown to apply over a severely restricted range of enzyme activity (8,9). As noted above, it has also not been possible in the most accurate work to avoid the extremely vigorous shaking which leads to enzyme inactivation. These have also been major drawbacks in the use of the Warburg apparatus as a tool for the study of carbonic anhydrase activity. In an effort to minimize the above difficulties, Roughton and Booth (49) have recommended the measurement of carbon dioxide uptake at 0°C. by $< 0.024M$ phosphate or veronal buffer in the pH range 7.5–8.5 for the manometric estimation of enzyme activity. Unimolecular velocity constants may be evaluated by the method of Guggenheim (1,24,43). This method also enables extrapolation to initial rates in order to correct for enzyme denaturation secondary to shaking (8) and other time-dependent errors of the method.

III. INDICATOR METHODS

1. Older Methods

The early indicator methods (5,46) are based upon the measurement of the time required for the pH of a reaction mixture to fall several units. The end point is established by a visible color change of an indicator, usually phenol red or bromthymol blue. Because of their simplicity, indicator methods have been used rather widely. They can be criticized, however, because of (1) the lack of corrections for enzyme inactivation at high pH, (2) various diffusion limitations, (3) inhibition by CO_3^{2-}, and (4) the effects of concentrated buffers.

Further limitations are introduced by the use of a rather high concentration of an indicator which quite commonly is itself inhibitory (59) and by the use of a rather broad range of pH over which observations are made. It is over this range particularly that changes in hydrogen ion activity most strongly affect the reaction rate (30,49). As a result, the measured apparent rate is not linearly proportional to the true initial rate. It would be fortuitous to obtain truly kinetic data with only a single point of observation over this broad pH change. Over the wide pH range of study, furthermore, the non-enzymic process changes its reaction mechanism from that of primary hydroxylation of carbon dioxide (direct formation of bicarbonate) to one of simple hydration of carbon dioxide with water (21). No information is available on the pH dependence of the enzymic reaction mechanism, although it may well be a hydroxylation mechanism even at pH 7.0 (13,14).

No allowance is made in the simple indicator methods for the progressive inactivation of the enzyme that may be present, since there is only a single point of observation. No correction, furthermore, is made for the limiting effect of diffusion of carbon dioxide and consequent apparent product inhibition. The inhibitory effect of extraneous buffers is considerable, and carbonate ion may be quite inhibitory to the enzyme (49). The carbonate ion inhibition, however, was not encountered by Maren (39,40) in a modification of the simple indicator method.

These errors, however, are somewhat obviated by the use of veronal buffer. Datta and Shepard (11) have shown that, in an indicator method employing 0.4 mg. % phenol red in a Beckman DK-1 spectrophotometer set at 560 mμ, barbiturate was a much more satisfactory buffer than bicarbonate and could be used at a concentration below $0.0073M$. Tris buffer, however, may prove to be even better as it was non-inhibitory at a concentration of $0.0286M$. These simpler colorimetric methods have been applied successfully by Maren et al. (39,40) in studies of the localization of carbonic anhydrase in various tissues and in kinetic studies and by Lindskog (36) in monitoring the purification of the enzyme. In view of the results of Datta and

Shepard (11), the method of Maren et al. may not have overcome all the major difficulties of inhibitor methods, since barbiturate buffers are still inhibitory at the concentrations used. Under the best of circumstances, simple indicator systems with veronal buffer and phenol red or bromthymol blue suffer from about 20–30% inhibition.

2. Compound Spectrophotometric Assay Technique

A method utilizing a compound optical assay has been published by Cutolo (10) that outwardly appears so simple that a trial of this method appears justified, particularly for the semiquantitative work required by histochemical studies. Experience with this method of assay of carbonic anhydrase is too limited still, but the principle may well be extended logically to other coupled systems enabling the development of an even more accurate analysis for kinetic work.

A. PRINCIPLE

The method basically measures the rate of the hydration reaction of carbon dioxide which leads to the generation of hydrogen ions. The hydrogen ion generation is coupled to the reaction catalyzed by liver alcohol dehydrogenase:

$$\text{Ethanol} + \text{DPN}^+ \rightleftharpoons \text{Acetaldehyde} + \text{DPNH} + \text{H}^+ \qquad (3)$$

Reaction 3 is quite dependent upon hydrogen ion concentration as detailed by Chance and Theorell (6).

A solution of carbonic anhydrase whose activity is to be measured is placed in an alcohol solution containing alcohol dehydrogenase and diphosphopyridine nucleotide. The addition of ethanol causes reaction 3 to move to the right with the appearance of the spectral absorption band of reduced pyridine nucleotide. When this reaction reaches equilibrium, a carbon dioxide solution is rapidly added and hydrogen ion is generated in the hydration reaction catalyzed by carbonic anhydrase. The generation of hydrogen ion forces the alcohol dehydrogenase reaction to the left, with the concomitant disappearance of reduced pyridine nucleotide. The rate of disappearance of reduced pyridine nucleotide is followed in a suitable spectrophotometer by the extinction at 340 mμ. If alcohol dehydrogenase and pyridine nucleotide are in sufficient excess, the generation of hydrogen ions may be rate limiting for this reaction, the rate of which will then be equal to the rate of the carbonic anhydrase reaction.

B. EXPERIMENTAL DETAILS

The assay mixture of the following composition is placed in a quartz spectrophotometric cuvette of 1-cm. path length:

  0.05 ml. of 96% ethanol
  0.05 ml. of a neutralized solution of DPN containing 10 mg. of coenzyme per ml.
  0.02 ml. of a solution of carbonic anhydrase at an analytically convenient dilution
  $4\mu g.$ of crystalline liver alcohol dehydrogenase (510 Racker units)
  1 ml. of $0.05M$ veronal buffer, pH 8.20
  Distilled water to make a final volume of 3 ml.

After a lapse of 2 minutes to permit the formation of reduced pyridine nucleotide, the extinction at 340 mμ is determined. This will have a value of roughly 0.9 optical density units. Then 1 ml. of distilled water saturated with carbon dioxide at known pCO_2 is added rapidly. This operation is best performed in a spectrophotometer cuvette fitted with a Thunberg side tube whose contents are rapidly tipped into the cuvette and mixed before replacement of the cuvette in the spectrophotometer. A stopwatch is started at the time of the addition of the saturated carbon dioxide solution. The value of the extinction is recorded at 30 seconds and at 60 seconds. An appropriate blank is run without the addition of carbonic anhydrase.

A conveniently measurable quantity for expressing the enzyme activity is the value D where

$$D = (0.75\ E_0 - E_{30\ sec}) - (E_{30\ sec} - E_{60\ sec}) \qquad (4)$$

The factor 0.75 is a correction for the dilution of the DPNH by the addition of saturated carbon dioxide solution and E is the optical density at the indicated times. Carbonic anhydrase activity can be expressed as the value.

$$A = (D - D_0)/(0.171) \qquad (5)$$

where D_0 is the blank determination of D and 0.171 is an experimental constant expressing the maximum value of $(D - D_0)$ to which the method can be applied. It is necessary to operate in ranges of enzyme concentration which will give values of $(D - D_0)$ less than 0.171. Cutolo has found that the fractional activity, expressed as percentage of the maximum measurable value ($A \times 100$), is a linear function of the logarithm of the enzyme concentration. The method is most sensitive in the range of enzyme concentration of 10^{-7}–$10^{-8}M$. Although the method awaits development and further study, it is presented in some detail here because of its simplicity and unfamiliarity to English-speaking investigators. It also appears capable of being developed into a true micro method utilizing the fluorescence of reduced diphosphopyridine nucleotide as the indicator. Not enough experience has been accumulated with the method as described to predict feasible modifications, which await development.

3. Rapid Flow Methods

A. PRINCIPLES

The principles of rapid flow methods are well detailed by Roughton and Chance (50). Attempts to use the glass electrode in a flow apparatus have failed, possibly because of adsorption of enzyme onto the surface of the glass with consequent increase in the local enzyme concentration on the electrode (16,17). This is a more significant factor in flow apparatus than in open vessels, in which the enzyme is added shortly before initiation of the reaction and only initial rates are determined, and in which the electrodes may be more thoroughly cleaned between runs.

Photometric methods using indicators to sense changes in hydrogen ion activity have been more satisfactory in flow apparatus (8,9,16,17, 22,36–38). A satisfactory indicator has been found in p-nitrophenol (22), whose pK is 7.0, conveniently (3). The p-nitrophenolate anion is strongly colored ($\epsilon = 18,330$ at 407 mμ), while the acid form has no extinction at this wavelength (3). The construction of an apparatus to adapt a Beckman model DU spectrophotometer to rapid flow photometric work like that required here has been described in detail by Beers (2). This temperature-controlled stop-flow mixing chamber can be adapted for use in several commercial spectrophotometers. This apparatus has also been modified by Lindskog and Malmström (37,38) for their studies of carbonic anhydrase. If the Beckman DU spectrophotometer is used to study reaction kinetics, it may be fitted with a commercial spectral energy recording adapter (Beckman Instrument Co.) for recording of optical density. An adapter for recording percentage transmission may be simply constructed as de-

scribed by Beers (2).   Better still is the device for linear recording
of optical density described by Marr and Marcus (41), for use with
Beckman DU spectrophotometer and a commercial electrometer
amplifier (Keithley Instrument Company) prior to recording.

B. EXPERIMENTAL DETAILS

In the method of DeVoe and Kistiakowsky (16,17) the apparatus is
thermostated at 0.5°C.   Both the hydration of CO_2 and the dehydration of HCO_3^- may be determined.   Buffer, enzyme, and indicator
make up one reaction solution and substrate the other.   The solutions
are best injected simultaneously into a small-bore (2-mm.) capillary
tube, where they are mixed by turbulent flow.   Flow is stopped after
about 1 second with the reaction solution in the observation cell of the
photometer.   Transmittance, at 400 mμ for p-nitrophenol, is measured during the initial 10 seconds of reaction using a phototube,
oscilloscopic display, and photographic recording.   Other display
media, like direct writing oscillographs, are probably quite satisfactory and provide simpler means of data display and analysis.   Initial
pH and initial reaction rates may be calculated simply from the data.
For derivation of equations which aid in the calculations, one may
consult the work of Perrin, appended to the report of the early rapid-.
flow studies of Clark and Perrin (45).   Correction must be made for
the non-enzymic reaction in both directions, bearing in mind the important anionic activation of these reactions (47) and the fact that the
non-enzymic rate may make up as much as one half of the measured
rate.   Correction for the back reaction is generally more important in
measurements of the rate of dehydration than in studies of the hydration reaction (16).

The spectrophotometric data in all the rapid-flow methods yield results in terms of pH vs. time curves, when the apparatus is properly
calibrated with mixtures of known pH at the approximate buffer and
indicator concentrations.   Curves relating ln $[CO_2]$ vs. time may be
constructed from the pH–time curves and the equation derived by
Perrin (45):

$$[CO_2]_t = [CO_2]_0 - [B^-]_0 + \frac{K'[B^-] + [HB]}{K' + [H^+]} \qquad (6)$$

where $[CO_2]_t = [CO_2]$ at any given time, $[CO_2]_0 =$ initial $[CO_2]$,
$[B^-] =$ buffer anion concentration, $[HB] =$ buffer acid concentra-

tion, and K' = apparent dissociation constant of the buffer at the appropriate pH and temperature. The first-order rate constant may be simply calculated from the initial slope of the derived ln $[CO_2]$ vs. time curve.

The flow rate in the reaction chamber should be adjusted so that the rate exceeds the critical value for turbulent flow. Rapid turbulent

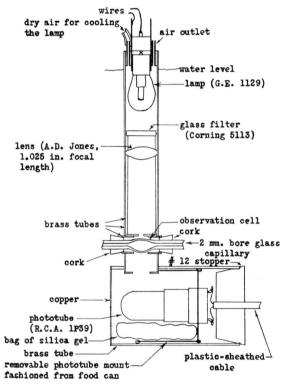

Fig. 1. Photometric apparatus for rapid flow studies of the kinetics of the reaction of carbonic anhydrase. From DeVoe (16), with permission.

mixing of the two solutions will take place as they flow through the capillaries. The mixed solution is driven to a chamber where the measurement can be made (Fig. 1). For water at 0° in a 2-mm. bore tubing, the critical flow rate is about 6 ml./sec. With 5 ml. of solution to be discharged from each syringe in about one second, the downstream flow rate is about 10 ml./sec., thus exceeding the critical value for turbulent flow.

It is also important to avoid an excessively fast flow rate because of the production of cavitation. This cavitation was observed at high flow rates both by DeVoe (16) and by Sirs (54) in their stop-flow systems. DeVoe maintained the internal volume of the reaction system between the mixing point and the photometer observation cell at about 0.5 ml. Under these conditions flow stopped at the detecting element within 50 msec. of mixing. This provides for a negligible unobserved period of reaction. The flow system should allow for flushing and calibration of the mixtures.

IV. ELECTROMETRIC METHODS

1. Principle

There have been a number of attempts to study the kinetics of the reaction of carbonic anhydrase by electrometric techniques (4,55,59). These, like the indicator methods, have involved a broad pH range of observation and are accordingly subject to many of the same criticisms. A rapid recording electromethod has been developed which measures the changes in hydrogen ion activity accompanying the hydration of carbon dioxide in weakly buffered solutions (12,13). This has proved very satisfactory for the measurement of carbonic anhydrase activity free of the accessory assumptions of the gasimetric technique. It also avoids most of the difficulties of static indicator and early electrometric methods. Hydrogen ion activity is measured simply by a glass and calomel electrode system. The electrode signal is fed into an electrometer circuit through a sensitive potentiometer for balancing out the initial signal. The instrument is thus used near the null point for greater accuracy and linearity. Very low buffer concentrations ($0.002M$ phosphate buffer) are used, enabling the direct calibration of the entire apparatus with a known amount of strong acid. One thereby avoids many accessory assumptions in calibrations as well as specific buffer effects, since only initial rates are used. There are fewer assumptions and more consistent results in this procedure than in other methods described previously. The response time of the glass electrode is no impediment since it is generally in the range of 10–50 msec., according to Chance and Love (7) and to Distèche and Dubuisson (18). Important glass electrode effects are ruled out by the linear relation between activity and enzyme concentration and the internal consistency of the results with the method.   Moreover, linear initial rates are maintained over long intervals in individual enzymic rate studies.   In order to assure this, however, it is important to add the enzyme last among reagents except for substrate and to wash the electrode system carefully between runs with large volumes of distilled water.   Under these circumstances adsorption of enzyme to the glass surface of the electrode can be ruled out by the lack of dependence of enzymic rate on the temporal order of experiment.   This, unfortunately, was an important effect in the application of electrometric methods to rapid flow systems as determined by DeVoe (16), evidently because of failure to clean the glass electrode adequately between experimental runs, but was not encountered in the method to be described below.

The reaction cell used in the studies for the development of the electrometric apparatus is a round-bottomed Pyrex vessel of about 175-ml. capacity, mounted in a thermostated bath so that the solution is well below the surface of the thermostating mixture.   The volume of each experimental mixture is 100 ml.   It is possible, however, to adapt this same procedure for very much smaller capacities and probably even micrometric methods.   Stirring of the solutions is provided by a polyethylene or Teflon enclosed permanent magnet driven externally.   Because of instability of the fiber of the calomel electrode, it was necessary in the original experimental design to shut off the magnetic stirrer after 1–2 seconds of the experimental run because of the electrical instabilities of the bridge.   This necessity may be obviated by the use of a salt bridge to an external calomel reference electrode.

The measuring device is basically a very rapid and sensitive automatic recording pH meter.   Changes in hydrogen ion activity of the solutions are measured in glass and calomel electrodes which operate at a temperature range including 0°.   (Beckman Instrument Company, No. 1190–80 and No. 1170, respectively, are quite suitable, although undoubtedly many other electrodes may be used.)   The sensing device is an electrometer amplifier circuit.   For the original work, the impedance of the glass electrode circuit was reduced by an FP-54 electrometer tube in the DuBridge-Brown circuit (19) with an attendant voltage amplification factor of about $1/3$.   Any of the more modern electrometer amplifier circuits, for example, those marketed commercially by Keithley Instrument Co., General Radio Corp., or Applied Physics Corp. (Cary vibrating reed electrometer), are probably satisfactory and avoid many of the problems of the custom adaptation of the DuBridge-Brown circuit. To use the DuBridge-Brown circuit at its balance point, the calomel electrode is connected to one of the e.m.f. terminals of a type K potentiometer, the other being grounded and the galvanometer terminals being shorted. The potential between the glass electrode and the calomel electrode can be compensated by suitably altering the setting of the potentiometer. One may similarly use a packaged electrometer amplifier with the inputs floating and a compensating potentiometer circuit on the input to balance out the initial signal. The output of the DuBridge-Brown circuit can be fed either to a sensitive galvanometer for preliminary balancing or to any of a number of sensitive, rapidly responding recorders.

For the original studies a Model S Speedomax indicating recorder, Type G, (Leeds & Northrup Co.) was used. This instrument was of a constant-speed type, requiring 2 seconds to traverse the chart; it has an input impedance of 0.5 megohm and a sensitivity corresponding to 20 mv. for full scale (about 25 cm.) deflection. Because of the low amplification factor of the DuBridge-Brown circuit, 20 mv. correspond· to about 1 unit on the pH scale. With other combinations of amplifiers and recorders, even smaller full-scale representation may be obtained. The Keithley differential electrometer amplifiers may be used with either 10-mv. potentiometer type recorders or 1-ma. recorders of several varieties. The relevant portions of an experiment extend over not more than 0.2 pH units and the constant speed of the recorder should allow them to be recorded with an effective time constant of about 0.2 to 0.4 seconds.

Another further precaution should be mentioned in connection with the apparatus. Because of its extreme sensitivity it is extremely important to avoid all forms of extraneous pickup. It may be necessary to utilize a Faraday cage under certain laboratory circumstances. This may be simply constructed from copper wire mesh. Another precaution is to avoid ground loops assiduously. This can generally be achieved by trial and error, and is especially important whether one operates with the calomel electrode grounded on the input to the electrometer or with the entire apparatus run floating as a differential electrometer. If an FP-54 tube is used it is best mounted in a sealed brass housing with Drierite or other agent for maintaining low humidity. The surface of the tube may be wrapped in household aluminum foil which is grounded in order to remove the effect of surface charges on the glass on the operation on the tube. A commercial titrigraphic apparatus has been adapted to the study of carbonic anhydrase kinetics (33), but the data are too few to permit full evaluation of its feasibility generally.

2. Experimental Details

All constituents of the experimental solution except the enzyme and substrate are mixed in the reaction vessel and allowed to come to the proper temperature with the magnetic stirrer on. Meanwhile, the potentiometer and the amplifier circuit are balanced, the appropriate volume of the substrate solution forced up into a syringe from a generating vessel, and the automatic recorder allowed to warm up. After the balancing of the initial signal of the pH 7.0 buffer with the slide wire of the potentiometer, the enzyme is added and shortly thereafter the substrate solution is injected rapidly by the syringe. After about 1 or 2 seconds (found empirically to be more than adequate for complete mixing), the magnetic stirrer is stopped if no salt bridge is used to the reference electrode. The change in potential in the glass electrode as the reaction proceeds, a direct function of the activity of the hydrogen ion produced by the reaction sequence

$$CO_2 + H_2O \rightarrow H^+ + HCO_3^+ \qquad (7)$$

is recorded directly and graphically on the recorder. The $0.002M$ phosphate buffer concentration was chosen to make conveniently measurable the pH changes in the initial stages of the reaction. Since the change in e.m.f. is not linearly related to the number of moles of hydrogen ion generated in the reaction, experimental mixtures containing all ingredients except substrate are titrated with a dilute standard acid. The resulting changes of the e.m.f. are thus recorded. The calibrations are then used to convert the e.m.f.–time curves of enzymic and non-enzymic runs with carbon dioxide into hydrogen ion concentration vs. time curves.

Except for slight disturbances at the start of the run lasting no more than one second, linear initial slopes are obtained over a range of at least 0.1 pH unit, after conversion to the hydrogen ion concentration

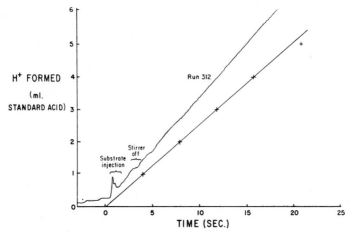

Fig. 2. A typical experimental run at pH 7.00 and 1.5°: substrate concentration 3.78mM; enzyme concentration 2.7 × 10^{-8}M; 0.002M phosphate buffer; added ionic strength 0.001 NaCl; full scale deflection 20 mv. The experimental curve is reduced by calibration with 0.00968M HCl to a plot of ml. standard acid formed against time, from which the slope yields the initial rate, in this case 2.52 μM sec.$^{-1}$. From Davis (12), with permission of the publisher.

scale. This linear rate persists at least 5 to 10 seconds in enzymic runs, depending on the concentration of substrate. The slope of the straight lines is taken as the rate of hydration. Figure 2 shows a typical recorder trace and its conversion to the hydrogen ion concentration scale.

V. HISTOCHEMICAL METHODS

1. Staining Method

A method has been described for the histochemical determination of carbonic anhydrase (32). This method, based on the local precipitation of black cobaltous sulfide, however, has been shown to be invalid (20).

2. Gasimetric Methods

A. WARBURG APPARATUS

The Warburg manometric method has been developed into a micromethod for the determination of carbonic anhydrase activity in animal tissues (1,31,43,44). Magnetic stirrers were used in some studies (44) rather than conventional shaking devices to lessen diffusion errors. The high buffer ionic strengths, long time periods utilized for observation, and general errors of the gasimetric method seriously limit the method for quantitative kinetic work, but the method does have application for less precise quantitation of tissue levels and is less complicated technically than electrometric methods.

B. CARTESIAN DIVER TECHNIQUE

More promising is the use of the Cartesian Diver technique (25, 35) recently used for the analysis of carbonic anhydrase in single cells (23). While technically formidable, the results appear reproducible, and this method appears to be one of the most promising approaches to the histochemical localization of carbonic anhydrase. The enzyme activity was measured in the dehydration reaction

$$HCO_3^- + H^+ \rightarrow H_2O + CO_2 \qquad (8)$$

by the evolution of CO_2 from $1 \times 10^{-4}M$ NaHCO$_3$ at 25° in 0.1M sodium phosphate buffer at pH 7.5. Control experiments are performed simultaneously for measurement of the uncatalyzed reaction and the activity of several known concentrations of carbonic anhydrase. The high ionic strength of the buffer, unfortunately, assures a significant degree of enzyme inhibition in the method as described.

VI. CONCLUSION

While many details in the methods described here have been left to the investigator, this is necessary because of the current lack of a universal assay method for the determination of carbonic anhydrase activity. Local instrumental variations in each investigator's laboratory will determine specific modification of the selected method. The principles discussed above, however, should permit ready construction of the apparatus necessary for the study of carbonic anhydrase in any application.

References

1. Altschule, M. D., and H. D. Lewis, *J. Biol. Chem.*, *180*, 557 (1949).
2. Beers, R. F., Jr., *Biochem. J.*, *62*, 492 (1956).
3. Biggs, A. I., *Trans. Faraday Soc.*, *50*, 800 (1954).

4. Brinkman, R., and R. Margaria, *J. Physiol. (London), 72*, 6P (1931).
5. Brinkman, R., *J. Physiol. (London), 80*, 171 (1934).
6. Chance, B., and H. Theorell, *Acta Chim. Scand., 5*, 1127 (1951).
7. Chance, B., personal communication (1952).
8. Clark, A. M., Ph.D. dissertation, Cambridge University, 1949.
9. Clark, A. M., and D. D. Perrin, *Biochem. J., 48*, 495 (1951).
10. Cutolo, E., *Giorn. biochim., 6*, 270 (1957).
11. Datta, P. K., and T. H. Shepard, II, *Arch. Biochem. Biophys., 79*, 136 (1959).
12. Davis, R. P., *J. Am. Chem. Soc., 80*, 5209 (1958).
13. Davis, R. P., *J. Am. Chem. Soc., 81*, 5674 (1959).
14. Davis, R. P., "Carbonic Anhydrase," in P. D. Boyer, H. Lardy, and K. Myrbäck, eds., *The Enzymes*, 2nd ed., Vol. 5, Chapter 33, Academic Press, New York, 1961.
15. Day, R., and H. Franklin, *Science, 104*, 363 (1946).
16. DeVoe, H., Ph.D. thesis, Harvard, 1960.
17. DeVoe, H., and G. B. Kistiakowsky, *J. Am. Chem. Soc., 83*, 274 (1961).
18. Distèche, A., and M. Dubuisson, *Rev. Sci. Instr., 25*, 869 (1954).
19. DuBridge, L. A., and H. Brown, *Rev. Sci. Instr., 4*, 532 (1933).
20. Fand, S. B., H. J. Levine, and H. L. Erwin, *J. Histochem. Cytochem., 7*, 27 (1959).
21. Faurholt, C., *J. chim. phys., 21*, 400 (1924).
22. Forrest, W. W., Ph.D. dissertation, Cambridge, 1953.
23. Giacobini, E., *Science, 134*, 1524 (1961).
24. Guggenheim, E. A., *Phil. Mag.*, [7] *2*, 538 (1926).
25. Holter, H., K. Linderstrøm-Lang, and E. Zeuthen, "Manometric Techniques for Single Cells," in G. Oster and A. W. Pollister, eds., *Physical Techniques in Biological Research*, Vol. III, Chapter 12, Academic Press, New York, 1956.
26. Keilin, D., and T. Mann, *Biochem. J., 34*, 1163 (1940).
27. Keller, H., W. Müller-Beissenhirtz, and H. D. Ohlenbusch, *Z. physiol. Chem.*, 3, 172 (1959).
28. Kiese, M., and A. B. Hastings, *J. Biol. Chem., 132*, 267 (1940).
29. Kiese, M., *Biochem. Z., 307*, 207 (1941).
30. Kiese, M., *Biochem. Z., 307*, 400 (1941).
31. Krebs, H. A., and F. J. W. Roughton, *Biochem. J., 43*, 550 (1948).
32. Kurata, Y., *Stain Technol., 28*, 231 (1953).
33. Leibman, K. C., D. Alford, and R. A. Boudet, *J. Pharmacol. Exptl. Therap., 131*, 271 (1961).
34. Leiner, M., and G. Leiner, *Biol. Zentr., 60*, 449 (1940).
35. Linderstrøm-Lang, K., *Nature, 140*, 108 (1937).
36. Lindskog, S., *Biochim. et Biophys. Acta, 39*, 218 (1960)
37. Lindskog, S., and B. G. Malmström, *Biochem. Biophys. Res. Comm., 2*, 213 (1960).
38. Lindskog, S., and B. G. Malmström, *J. Biol. Chem., 237*, 1129 (1962).
39. Maren, T. H., *J. Pharmacol. Exptl. Therap., 130*, 26 (1960).
40. Maren, T. H., A. L. Parcell, and M. N. Malik, *J. Pharmacol. Exptl. Therap., 130*, 389 (1960).
41. Marr, A. G., and L. Marcus, *Analyt. Biochem., 2*, 576 (1961).

42. Meldrum, N. U., and F. J. W. Roughton, *J. Physiol. (London)*, *80*, 113 (1933).
43. Mitchell, C. A., U. C. Pozzani, and R. W. Fessenden, *J. Biol. Chem.*, *160*, 283 (1945).
44. Ogawa, Y., and G. Pincus, *Endocrinology*, *67*, 551 (1960).
45. Perrin, D. D., in Appendix to Ref. 9.
46. Philpot, F. J., and J. St. L. Philpot, *Biochem. J.*, *30*, 2191 (1936).
47. Roughton, F. J. W., and V. H. Booth, *Biochem. J.*, *32*, 2049 (1938).
48. Roughton, F. J. W., and V. H. Booth, *Biochem. J.*, *40*, 309 (1946).
49. Roughton, F. J. W., and V. H. Booth, *Biochem. J.*, *40*, 319 (1946).
50. Roughton, F. J. W., and B. Chance, "Rapid Reactions," in S. L. Friess and A. Weissberger, eds., *Technique of Organic Chemistry*, Vol. VIII, Chap. 10, Interscience, New York–London, 1953.
51. Scott, D. A., and J. R. Mendive, *J. Biol. Chem.*, *139*, 661 (1941).
52. Scott, D. A., and J. R. Mendive, *J. Biol. Chem.*, *140*, 445 (1941).
53. Sibley, P. M., and J. G. Wood, *Australian J. Sci. Research*, *B4*, 500 (1951).
54. Sirs, J. A., *Trans. Faraday Soc.*, *54*, 201 (1958).
55. Stadie, W. C., and H. O'Brien, *J. Biol Chem.*, *103*, 521 (1933).
56. Tsuchihashi, M., *Biochem. Z.*, *140*, 63 (1923).
57. van Goor, H., *Enzymologia*, *8*, 113 (1940).
58. Waygood, E. R., "Carbonic Anhydrase (Plant and Animal)," in S. P. Colowick and N. O. Kaplan, eds., *Methods in Enzymology*, Vol. II, Academic Press, New York, 1955.
59. Wilbur, K. M., and N. G. Anderson, *J. Biol. Chem.*, *176*, 147 (1948).
60. Yen, L. F., and P. S. Tang, *Chinese J. Physiol.*, *18*, 43 (1951); through *Chem. Abstr.*, *48*, 10849 (1954).

Polarographic Analysis of Proteins, Amino Acids, and Other Compounds by Means of the Brdička Reaction

OTTO H. MÜLLER, *State University of New York*
Upstate Medical Center, Syracuse

I. INTRODUCTION

1. General

Certain amino acids, polypeptides, and proteins, dissolved in a cobalt-containing buffer of suitable pH, produce a catalytic reaction at the dropping mercury electrode (DME) which has been named "Brdička* reaction" after its discoverer (11). This reaction has gained considerable significance, since it has found application not only in the clinical diagnosis and prognosis of malignancies and other diseases, but also in biochemical studies of native and denatured proteins. The literature in this field has become very extensive; articles may be found in journals of medical specialties as well as in journals of physical, biochemical, and analytical chemistry. While this in itself complicates the task of coordinating the published material, there is an even greater obstacle in the fact that no uniform system is used for recording and evaluating of the data. This is not surprising since the theoretical aspects of this reaction are still not known with any degree of certainty.

Most of the research in this field has been concerned with the development of a polarographic test that would be specific for cancer, hence numerous empirical modifications of Brdička's reaction have been evaluated in terms of this specificity. In general, it was taken for granted that the higher the percentage of positive reactions in known cancer cases and the lower the percentage of positive reactions in non-cancer cases, the better the method. The claims for success for any given method have therefore often shown considerable variation depending on the enthusiasm of the investigator. It is furthermore characteristic of this research that analysts who develop new and "better" methods claim, without giving the experimental evidence, that other available methods were tried but did not prove to be as good as theirs. Thus the reader cannot judge for himself but must either accept the statement on faith or doubt the claims.

* Pronounced almost like "bird-itch-ka" or "brr-ditch-ka."

More thorough investigations of recent years indicate that the polarographic tests are probably no more specific than corresponding nonpolarographic tests, since all of these seem to involve the analysis of similar blood proteins and degradation products. Advantages of the Brdička reaction over other methods therefore lie in something other than specificity for cancer, as for instance: in the simplicity of operation; in the sensitivity, reproducibility, and wide scope of application of the method; and finally in the fact that a permanent record of the analyses is obtained.

Of prime importance in the wider application of the Brdička reaction is a better understanding of the underlying electrode process and of the nature of the substances that give rise to it, as well as a better method of reporting data than has heretofore been customary. Workers interested in clinical diagnosis or prognosis have often been satisfied with reporting currents in millimeters of deflection of a galvanometer with unspecified sensitivity. In addition, the characteristics of their DME were not defined, so that an accurate evaluation of their data for comparison with data obtained by others becomes impossible. Müller and Davis (80) pointed out, 17 years ago, that even with such data comparison was possible, if two empirical measurements of different entities made with the same DME under the same conditions were combined in a ratio, the "protein index." This would then be independent of the characteristics of the galvanometer and DME. However, so far, relatively few applications of this method have been published, but some researchers have incorporated the basic idea into other types of "indexes." Stricks et al. (103), apparently thinking that the purpose of the "index" was to make the method more specific for cancer, went so far as to combine two completely different analyses, one with a DME, the other with a rotating platinum electrode, into a ratio, which they considered more specific than any other. Obviously, the original purpose for the introduction of the "index" is thus lost.

In the writer's opinion, the only satisfactory method for reporting results is in terms of current density, expressed in microamperes per square millimeter (μa./mm.^{2}) of electrode surface (80). This obviously requires the accurate knowledge of the current and of the surface area of the DME, but it is applicable to any single measurement. With the exception of very high, limiting currents, the currents obtained in the Brdička reaction are catalytic currents, proportional to the surface area of the electrode and therefore independent of its drop time. (Thus they are quite different from the diffusion currents of ordinary polarography which are proportional to the ratio of the surface area to the square root of the drop time.) So far there have been only isolated papers published in which the currents were thus reported, but it seems, judging from a recent article (56) that even the Prague school has now recognized the value of this way of reporting data. It is hoped that the present article will further demonstrate the usefulness of the current density values and that this method will find sufficient approval for general acceptance and thus bring more uniformity into published papers.

It will not be the purpose of the present article to review the numerous methods that have been proposed to improve the usefulness of the Brdička reaction for the diagnosis of a variety of diseases, especially cancer. This has already been done in reviews by Brdička et al. (18,19,22,23) and in the comprehensive treatise of Březina and Zuman (25). It will also be impossible to discuss here the ever-increasing number of applications of this reaction to other analyses of proteins. In the fields of physiology, pharmacology, biochemistry, and food chemistry, where they include analyses of body fluids, tissue extracts, or synthetic materials, such applications suggest themselves. Only a minimum of information concerning polarographs, dropping mercury and reference electrodes, and the polarographic method can be given. For further details the reader is referred to readily available texts (31,40,41,60,67,71,75,79,94,100,109).

This article has been written with the following aims:

1. To give the reader sufficient information about the essentials of the Brdička reaction so as to enable him to carry out his own research, if he has some familiarity with polarography.

2. To point out weaknesses and uncertainties in our present knowledge of the Brdička reaction.

3. To suggest promising new uses of the Brdička reaction in protein chemistry.

4. To emphasize the importance of reporting catalytic currents in terms of current density (μa./mm.^{2}).

5. To propose master curves relating current density to concentration for the various substances giving rise to the Brdička reaction.

2. Historical

Brdička discovered the reaction named after him during a study of the reduction of cobaltic salts at the DME (11). He observed a prominent maximum on the second cobalt wave when he buffered the solution of cobaltic salts with $0.1N$ ammonium chloride and $0.1N$ ammonium hydroxide. Figure 1, curve A, illustrates the type of curve obtained under such conditions. The first wave, near -0.2 v.,

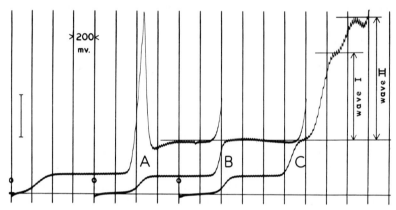

Fig. 1. Polarogram demonstrating the Brdička reaction: (A) Solution of $0.001M$ Co(NH₃)₆Cl₃, $0.1N$ NH₄Cl, and $0.1N$ NH₄OH; (B) solution A containing 0.02% caffeine; (C) solution A containing 0.1 ml. dog plasma. All solutions had a pH of 9.3 and were deaerated with nitrogen gas for 5 minutes. Every curve starts at zero volts (indicated by the small o on the abscissa) vs. SCE. The vertical line at the left indicates 10 μa. in this and other polarograms. The method of measurement of protein waves I and II is shown on curve C.

represents the reduction of cobaltic to cobaltous ions and has no maximum. The second wave, near -1.1 v., is twice as high as the first wave because it involves the reduction of cobaltous ions to the metallic state of cobalt. This second cobalt wave has a high maximum which Brdička ascribed to the adsorption of cobaltous ions at the DME in accordance with the explanation for maxima prevalent at that time. It is important to point out here that, although this explanation has subsequently proved to be erroneous, it has been most fruitful and has served as a basis for most of the theoretical treatment of the Brdička reaction. Today it is known that the cobalt maximum is produced by a marked agitation or streaming of the solution around the mercury drop, which thus transports by convection much larger quantities of the reducible cobalt ions than would reach the electrode by diffusion. This streaming can be easily observed under the microscope if some fine dust particles are suspended in the solution. The reason for this streaming is not yet fully clear; an inhomogeneous electric field has been suggested as the cause.

In polarographic practice it is customary to suppress all kinds of maxima by surface-active materials such as dyestuffs, alkaloids, proteins, etc. Had Brdička used caffeine, he would have obtained curve B of Figure 1 which shows the two cobalt waves (the first one shifted by about 0.2 v. towards more negative potentials) without any maximum. Fortunately, however, Brdička used serum which suppressed the maximum as expected, but which also gave rise to the extra waves seen in curve C of Figure 1. These are generally referred to as waves I and II of the so-called "protein double wave." Wave I looks like an ordinary polarographic wave, while wave II is peaked in the example shown in Figure 1. Depending on the protein concentration and other factors, either may be peaked or overlap so much with another wave as to appear like an ordinary wave. Since protein double waves are not obtained in a cobalt-free buffered solution of serum, they must be cobalt catalyzed. Closer investigation of these waves revealed that the underlying reaction is rather complicated and that it involves a catalytic reduction of hydrogen ions from the buffer.

Catalytic hydrogen waves produced by platinum metals or organic compounds also show peaks which have never been satisfactorily explained. It is difficult to see why a substance that can catalyze the reduction of hydrogen ions at one potential cannot do so, or does so to a much smaller extent, at a somewhat more negative potential. Perhaps all of these catalytic peak curves of polarography will find a common explanation.

Brdička studied the various factors that determine the magnitude of the protein double wave, such as the concentration of protein, cobalt, ammonium chloride, and ammonium hydroxide, by varying only one of these reactants at a time (11). He found that a graph of the height of the protein waves plotted against concentration of reactant would not yield a straight line, but a curve approaching a limiting value with increasing concentration. In further experiments, designed to elucidate the nature of the catalyst, Brdička found that after boiling the serum in neutral ammonium chloride solution and

thus coagulating the protein therein, he could obtain a clear supernatant solution of material which still gave him the "protein double
wave" when polarographed in the cobalt buffer. He therefore concluded that some material, perhaps albumoses, or peptones, or yet
another unknown substance which was not coagulable by heat, was
responsible for the waves (11). A study of amino acids and other
simple substances that might be found in blood was therefore carried
out in the same medium. Glycine, creatine, creatinine, arginine,
leucine, and tyrosine (in concentrations of $5 \times 10^{-4}M$) gave negative
results, but cystine and cysteine gave single waves in buffers of cobaltous salts with peaks at the same potential at which the second
peak occurred in the protein-containing solutions. This reaction was
extremely sensitive (as little as $2 \times 10^{-6}M$ cystine produced a
measurable wave), thus indicating the catalytic nature of the reaction.
On the basis of this evidence and the fact that cysteine-poor proteins,
like gelatine and silk, produce no such catalytic waves, Brdička concluded that these protein double waves are caused by the SH and SS
groups present in the protein (11).

Subsequent papers by Brdička dealt with the various factors affecting the catalytic cysteine wave (12) and with the hydrolysis of proteins which led to the development of a polarographic analysis of
cystine and cysteine in protein hydrolysates (13).

Relatively few applications of this technique were made by others.
In these, some of the interfering substances and other limitations of
the method were studied in some detail. However, in 1937 Brdička
discovered certain differences between normal sera and those from
cancer patients which were revealed by the protein double waves
(16,17). These could be exaggerated by denaturation of the proteins
with potassium hydroxide or by peptic digestion, or they could be
demonstrated in the sulfosalicylic acid filtrates of sera following such
treatment. This discovery gave rise to a large number of publications
which, depending on the inclination of the experimenter, conveyed the
idea that the polarographic cancer test was either very successful or
not specific enough to be useful. Obviously, in retrospect, many of
these early investigations were not done with sufficient care and understanding of polarography so that only gross differences could be recognized. There was little effort made to check the results and procedures of others; investigators preferred to develop their own modifications in the hope of making the tests more specific. After the

polarographic cancer test proved to be no worse nor better than many other cancer tests, some more basic research was done on the nature of the polarographic protein double wave, so that today some fairly valuable information is available. It is by no means enough, details of the mechanism of the reaction still need to be worked out, and the contribution of the various factors has to be so well known that it can be incorporated in an equation which completely defines the catalytic wave of the Brdička reaction.

More recent investigations have been concerned with other sulfur-containing compounds which give catalytic waves similar to those of cysteine. Also, some of the purest available proteins and degradation products of proteins have been investigated in more detail.

The study of polarographically active substances in urine has so far received only scant attention, but there is no reason to doubt that eventually polarographic clearance studies of the active components of blood will be used for the clinical examination of patients. A beginning has also been made in the polarographic study of tissue extracts and of body fluids other than blood.

Although the original microanalysis of cysteine by the Brdička reaction is nowadays largely displaced by polarometric (amperometric) determinations in which the rotating platinum electrode is used, it still serves as a valuable model for the more complicated similar reaction of proteins.   It has the advantage that pure solutions of cysteine or cystine in known concentrations can be readily prepared, while pure proteins are scarce and there is always the possibility that they may be denatured in some way in the alkaline buffer used for the analysis.   Hence it seems worthwhile to discuss the Brdička reaction of cysteine in some detail.

II. FUNDAMENTALS OF POLAROGRAPHY

1. General

For an understanding of the following discussion, a knowledge of some of the polarographic fundamentals is essential.   It should be clear that the polarograms (current–voltage curves) represent the change in flow of current as the dropping mercury electrode (DME) is made more negative with respect to a reference electrode.   In the Brdička reaction, a buffered solution is always used and the currents are fairly large, so that residual and migration currents need not be considered. The potentials are not as well defined as the half-wave potentials of ordinary polarography so that a layer of mercury can serve as reference electrode. The writer nevertheless prefers to use a saturated calomel half-cell (SCE), connected to the test solution by an agar bridge, saturated with potassium chloride. Not only does this provide a saving of mercury, but it also makes the potential recorded on any polarogram directly comparable with those on any other polarogram.

The currents that are involved in the Brdička reaction are catalytic and must be distinguished from the noncatalytic diffusion currents that form the basis for quantitative analysis of ordinary polarography.

2. Diffusion Current

In most reductions in polarography, the currents are controlled by the amount of reducible material that reaches the DME during its short lifetime. This amount, in turn, is determined by the concentration of the material in the solution and by its diffusion coefficient. Hence in noncatalytic reactions one can expect a diffusion-controlled current, directly proportional to the concentration of the reacting material.

Such diffusion currents are defined by the Ilkovič equation, which holds for constant temperature:

$$I_d = 706 \, nD^{1/2}Cm^{2/3}t^{1/6} \tag{1}$$

in which I_d is the diffusion current (in microamperes) when the drop is "ripe," n is the number of electrons involved in the reduction of one molecule of the reducible substance, D is the diffusion coefficient of the reducible substance (in cm.² sec.⁻¹), C its concentration (in millimoles per liter), m the weight of mercury flowing from the capillary per second (in mg. sec.⁻¹), and t is the time (in sec.) necessary for the formation of one drop of mercury before it falls off (the drop time). This means that the weight of each falling drop (in mg.) is given by

$$W = mt \tag{2}$$

and that the surface area of a drop of mercury (in mm.²) when it falls off is

$$A = kW^{2/3} = km^{2/3}t^{2/3} \tag{3}$$

where k is equal to 0.8517 (at 25°C.). The Ilkovič equation can therefore be rewritten as follows:

$$I_d = 706\ nD^{1/2}CW^{2/3}t^{-1/2} = 829\ nD^{1/2}CAt^{-1/2} \qquad (4)$$

or

$$\text{Diffusion current density:}\quad I_d/A = 829\ nD^{1/2}Ct^{-1/2}$$

It can be shown that the weight W is a function of the surface tension of mercury and of the size of the orifice in the glass capillary of the DME (76). The surface tension varies slightly with different solutions and with the voltage applied to the DME. However, at a given applied voltage in a given solution it is constant, and so is the orifice of a given capillary. Hence the drop weight, W, under these conditions is also constant and independent of the effective pressure head, P, that drives the mercury through the capillary. Since the flow of mercury, m, is directly proportional to the driving force, P, one can write

$$m = k'P = W/t \qquad (5)$$

Whenever W is constant, this becomes $P = k''/t$, which shows that the drop time is inversely proportional to the effective pressure head, P. By varying the effective pressure, P, one can determine the nature of a given current. If the current is inversely proportional to the square root of the drop time, or directly proportional to the square root of the effective pressure, then it is diffusion controlled in accordance with the Ilkovič equation.

In the Brdička reaction, the cobalt reductions are noncatalytic and hence the cobalt waves are diffusion controlled and directly proportional to the concentration of the reducible cobalt ion or complex. At a constant cobalt ion concentration, one may expect some change in the height of this wave if the cobalt diffusion coefficient is altered by the formation of a cobalt complex. This will, in general, be correlated with some change in the half-wave potential of the cobalt waves.

3. Catalytic Current

The protein double wave and the cysteine peak are catalytic currents that depend not so much on diffusion processes as on reactions taking place with great rapidity at the electrode surface. They are thus a function of the available surface area. It has already been stated that the weight of each drop of mercury falling from the electrode is constant under a given set of conditions, so that its surface area must also be constant. As a consequence, catalytic currents are independent of the drop time of a given electrode. Thus, by finding the current constant when varying the effective pressure, one can ascertain the existence of a catalytic current.

It should be pointed out, however, that with increasing concentrations of cysteine or protein, these catalytic currents reach certain limits. These limits are diffusion controlled, but in a complicated manner that has not been completely elucidated.

4. Apparatus

A. POLAROGRAPH

The Brdička reaction can be carried out with the simplest of manual polarographic devices (75). However, since in this reaction not a point on a plateau, but a point on the peak of a wave has to be measured, one has to be sure to plot enough points. Since this is quite tedious, a polarograph or similar instrument is definitely advisable. The accurate plotting of the voltage axis is generally not necessary, so that an instrument like the Sargent polarograph model XII is quite adequate.

The galvanometer of the instrument should be calibrated with a known resistance in place of the electrodes.

The application of cathode-ray oscillographs for the rapid plotting of current–voltage curves on the screen of the cathode-ray tube has also been successful (57). While this is worthwhile for the rapid scanning of many samples, one still needs to photograph the picture for a permanent record. Also, the preparation of the sample for analysis is usually so time consuming that the actual time required to take an ordinary polarogram can easily be worked into the analytical procedure in such a way as to become of minor importance.

B. ELECTRODE SETUP AND CALIBRATION

In the writer's opinion, the capillary for the dropping mercury electrode is best mounted firmly and *permanently* on a heavy stand by means of a chuck or similar clamp. The stand is positioned to be as free of vibrations as possible. The capillary is made of glass tubing with uniform bore of 25–35 microns. It is connected to a mercury reservoir by means of clean rubber or plastic tubing so that pressure heads varying from 0 to 80 cm. can be applied.   The DME should have a reasonably short drop time (between one and two seconds) so that the current oscillations occurring with each drop will not be excessive.

A saturated calomel half-cell is mounted near the DME on the same stand in such a way that an agar bridge leading from it dips into an open vessel (also mounted on the stand) containing saturated potassium chloride.   This vessel is greased with vaseline around the top to prevent creeping of the potassium chloride.   A second agar bridge leading from this junction vessel is so mounted that its free end is even with the tip of the DME.   This latter bridge is replaced frequently and removed to a storage vessel between series of analyses. The end of the DME is immersed in distilled water when not in use, and the pressure head is decreased until it ceases dropping.

For analysis by means of the Brdička reaction, the solutions are usually kept in small open beakers which are simply raised on the stand until the DME and the end of the agar bridge dip into the solution.   Immediately thereafter the polarogram is recorded. Between analyses, the DME and bridge tips are washed with a stream of water and dried by wiping with filter or tissue paper.   The polarograms are recorded between -0.8 and -1.9 v.

The calibration of the DME for the Brdička reaction is simpler than that recommended for general polarography (76) unless detailed studies with limiting conditions are contemplated.   One merely needs to ascertain the weight of the drops falling from the DME when it is polarized to the potential at which the catalytic current is measured.   This is done by collecting in a small glass spoon some 10–20 drops while the DME and agar bridge are dipping in a beaker containing one of the cobalt buffers and while a voltage of -1.6 v. is applied.   It does not seem to matter much whether protein is present in the solution or not.   Also the -1.6 v. is not very critical, since some of the catalytic peaks are obtained at slightly different voltages. The collected drops are then transferred to a small filter paper cone, washed with water, transferred to a dry filter paper cone, and then weighed in a small beaker.   The drop weight in milligrams, raised to the $^2/_3$ power and multiplied by 0.8517, gives the surface area in square millimeters.

In some special cases, it may be desirable to free the solution from atmospheric oxygen. This can be done by bubbling through the solution a nonreducible gas such as hydrogen or nitrogen, but it must first be passed through a solution similar to the test solution to avoid any loss of ammonia in the latter. When protein is present, this bubbling causes often an undesirable frothing of the solution. In that case it is best to free the buffer solution first from atmospheric oxygen and then add the protein and bubble just for a few seconds. A special vessel must be used (75) and the tip of the DME and agar bridge are pushed through a rubber stopper which seals this vessel.

C. TEMPERATURE CONTROL

Like all polarographic reactions, the Brdička reaction requires temperature control. However, since the analysis is usually carried out immediately after mixing of the solutions, temperature control at the electrode alone is not of much help. The reagents must also be kept at the same temperature. Therefore, it is best to have a room with constant temperature. Variations of $\pm 1°C$. are still acceptable.

5. Measurement of Catalytic Waves

Brdička originally thought of the peaked cysteine or protein waves as something similar to the ordinary polarographic maxima, such as the cobalt maxima. He therefore was more interested in the "diffusion current" or minimum in current following these maxima, and compared these when studying the effects of components of the solution (11). Since measurements of the minima are not very reliable, especially when the wave is closely followed by another wave with which it overlaps to a certain extent, Brdička changed his procedure and measured the peak values of the catalytic currents (14). As baseline for this measurement one uses the wave height of the final reduction of cobalt to the metallic state which includes all preceding waves, as demonstrated in Figure 1C.

Since all catalytic waves of the Brdička reaction are preceded by the reduction of either tri- or divalent cobalt, and since they are to some extent dependent on the concentration of cobalt and hence on the magnitude of the cobalt wave, only relatively high catalytic currents can be measured. (Although it should be possible to compensate for the preceding cobalt wave and thus measure very small catalytic waves, this has so far not been tried.) At millimolar concentration of trivalent cobalt, one may expect a cobalt diffusion current of about 12 μa., as in Figure 1. In an open vessel, the presence of dissolved oxygen in equilibrium with room air would add about 9 μa. to this. (Oxygen is reduced at more positive potentials than the catalytic wave and its diffusion current and that of the cobalt summate.) Hence there would be no great advantage in the removal of oxygen from the standard divalent and trivalent cobalt buffers which are 1.6×10^{-3} and $1.0 \times 10^{-3}M$, respectively; consequently, most workers carry out their analyses in open vessels. However, at considerably lower cobalt concentrations the removal of oxygen offers definite advantages.

At low concentrations of cysteine or protein, the cobalt maximum may not yet be sufficiently suppressed to permit measurement of the cobalt wave height on the same curve. This can be remedied by the addition of a nonreactive maximum suppressor, but it is often difficult to be sure that this suppressor does not interfere with the catalytic reaction. The writer therefore prefers to record a blank curve of the buffer wherever possible and to use its cobalt wave height as baseline for the subsequent analyses. Such a curve recorded at the beginning and again at the end of a series of analyses also serves as a check on the experimental conditions.

If the cysteine concentration exceeds certain values, one notices that the cobalt wave height begins to diminish, and also that the catalytic cysteine wave shows a second peak as a prewave besides its normal first peak. Obviously, the use of a blank curve under these conditions is faulty, as will be demonstrated later on.

It is not permissible to compare current values measured at a specified applied voltage (e.g., at -1.7 v. vs. SCE) because they would not all be peak values. The potentials at the peak values change considerably (as much as 0.2 v.) with concentration of the cysteine, even if they are corrected for the product of current and resistance. This obviously indicates that the peak potential in catalytic waves has no similar significance as the half-wave potential of diffusion-controlled currents.

III. THE BRDIČKA REACTION OF CYSTEINE

1. Effect of Cysteine Concentration

Of all the simple amino acids and other possible split products of proteins or constituents of serum, Brdička found only cysteine and

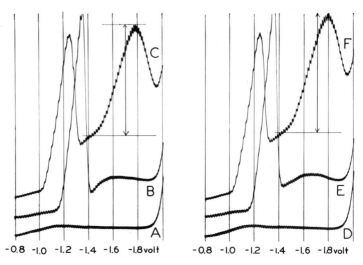

Fig. 2. Polarograms demonstrating the catalytic cysteine wave. (A) 9 ml. cobalt-free buffer (1 ml. $1M$ NH₄Cl + 9 ml. $1M$ NH₄OH) + 1 ml. 10^{-4} M cysteine hydrochloride. (B) 9 ml. TriCo buffer (1 ml. $0.01M$ Co(NH₃)₆Cl₃ + 1 ml. $1M$ NH₄Cl + 8 ml. $1M$ NH₄OH) + 1 ml. 10^{-4} M cysteine hydrochloride. (C) 9 ml. DiCo buffer (2 ml. 8×10^{-3} M CoCl₂ + 1 ml. $1M$ NH₄Cl + 6 ml. H₂O + 1 ml. $1M$ NH₄OH) + 1 ml. $10^{-4}M$ cysteine hydrochloride. (D) 9.5 ml. cobalt-free buffer + 0.5 ml. approximately $10^{-4}M$ cystine. (E) 9.5 ml. TriCo buffer + 0.5 ml. approximately $10^{-4}M$ cystine. (F) 9.5 ml. DiCo buffer + 0.5 ml. approximately 10^{-4} M cystine. Cf. (78).

cystine to give waves catalyzed by cobalt. As may be seen from Figure 2, these two amino acids produce catalytic waves only in buffers containing divalent cobalt salts (henceforth abbreviated as DiCo buffers) and the waves show but a single peak at a slightly different potential than either protein wave, whereas proteins produce a double wave in either DiCo or trivalent cobalt buffers (henceforth abbreviated as TriCo buffers).

It should be pointed out that at relatively very high cysteine or cystine concentrations ($0.01M$), a catalytic wave is obtained even in TriCo buffers. This was first observed by Bergh et al. (8) and has been studied in more detail by Jirsa and Kalous (46), Kalous (52), and Sunahara (106). Since it is only $^1/_{10000}$ as sensitive as the reaction in DiCo buffer, it will not be considered further in this article. Instead, the inactivity of cysteine in TriCo buffer will be used to distinguish cysteine-containing polypeptides and proteins from the simple amino acid.

Concerning Figure 2 it should be mentioned that the waves of cystine and cysteine are identical if the concentration of the cystine is one half the concentration of the cysteine. This must be so because 1 molecule of cystine is reduced at the DME to 2 molecules of cysteine at a potential considerably more positive than the catalytic reaction (not visible on the polarograms reproduced in Fig. 2). Hence at potentials more negative than -0.8 v. (vs. SCE) the electrode reaction is always that of cysteine.

2. Langmuir Adsorption Isotherm

The first attempt at a quantitative interpretation of the cystine currents was made by Brdička in 1934 (14). He studied the effect of cystine concentration on the wave height over the range of 1×10^{-5} to $1.9 \times 10^{-4}M$, in 1×10^{-3} and $2 \times 10^{-3}N$ cobaltous chloride solutions buffered with $0.1N$ ammonium chloride and $0.1N$ ammonium hydroxide. The fact that the waves were peaked was taken as proof that cystine was adsorbed on the cathode surface. As further proof for this assumption was cited the additional fact that the dependence of the height of the current maxima on the cystine concentration reached a limit and could be expressed by Langmuir's adsorption isotherm.

It is interesting to note that the cystine concentration at which this maximum height is reached was $2 \times 10^{-4}M$ at a cobalt concentration of $1 \times 10^{-3}M$. In the solutions with concentrations greater than $5 \times 10^{-5}M$, a second wave appeared ahead of the cysteine maximum. This wave was not discussed by Brdička in this paper nor was it mentioned in subsequent articles and remained forgotten until Müller (74) studied it in more detail.

Brdička assumed that the height h of the maxima was proportional to the surface concentration of cystine, while c was the cystine concentration of the solution. The Langmuir adsorption isotherm applied to this then takes the form:

$$h = z\omega c/(1 + \omega c) \tag{6}$$

where z represents the surface concentration of cystine at saturation, and ω is a specific coefficient. With h expressed in microamperes, Brdička found in his ammonia buffer

$$\text{for } 10^{-3}N \text{ CoCl}_2: \quad \mu a. = \frac{2750 \ (0.74 \times 10^5)c}{1 + (0.74 \times 10^5)c}$$

$$\text{for } 2 \times 10^{-3}N \text{ CoCl}_2: \quad \mu a. = \frac{5500 \ (0.37 \times 10^5)c}{1 + (0.37 \times 10^5)c}$$

These results would indicate that the surface concentration z of cystine is directly proportional, while the specific coefficient ω is inversely proportional, to the cobalt concentration, relationships which were not further discussed by Brdička.

Klumpar (59) investigated the current–cystine concentration relationship from 0.2 to $2.0 \times 10^{-3}M$ at cobalt concentrations that varied from 0.25 to $2 \times 10^{-3}N$, using the same $0.1N$ ammonia buffer as Brdička. The catalytic wave height obtained at constant cystine concentration was not directly proportional to the cobalt concentration, but could be represented by a curve resembling the Langmuir adsorption isotherm. He therefore modified the Langmuir equation as follows:

$$h = A \left(\frac{[\text{Co}^{2+}]}{B[\text{Co}^{2+}] + 1} \right) \left(\frac{[\text{cyst}]}{C[\text{cyst}] + 1} \right) \tag{7}$$

in which A, B, and C are empirical constants. These are obtained from the slopes of straight lines which Klumpar obtained when he plotted the inverse of the wave height against either the inverse of the cystine concentration or the inverse of the cobalt concentration. This equation differs considerably from that proposed by Brdička. It, too, lacks theoretical interpretation, but Klumpar did make the suggestion that kinetic phenomena, rather than adsorption equilibria at the surface of the DME, may determine the magnitude of the catalytic currents.

Brdička and Klumpar's data represent some of the most careful measurements of catalytic cystine waves and may therefore be used to illustrate past shortcomings in the reporting of results involving catalytic currents. Both workers reported currents in millimeters of galvanometer deflection at $1/100$ of full galvanometer sensitivity (which was also stated). One can therefore calculate the actual currents involved. For instance, for 1 and $2 \times 10^{-5}M$ cystine in $1 \times 10^{-3}N$ CoCl$_2$, Brdička obtained 15.7 and 21.3 μa., while Klumpar's data indicate for the same conditions 12.2 and 17.0 μa. (Earlier results of

Brdička cannot be compared because minima were measured.) Thus Brdička's results are about 25–30% larger than Klumpar's. In $2 \times 10^{-3}N$ CoCl$_2$, for a $10^{-5}M$ solution of cystine, the discrepancy is even larger, Brdička obtained a current that was more than 50% larger than Klumpar's.

3. Current Density and Cysteine Concentration

Müller (74) reinvestigated the catalytic cysteine waves, to see if these currents behave like the protein double waves and are a function of the surface area of the DME. The range of cysteine concentrations covered was more than three logarithm units, from 2×10^{-7} to $10^{-3}M$ cysteine, and the concentration intervals were so chosen as to give experimental points about 0.1 logarithm units apart. Each solution was prepared separately so that additive errors were avoided. The analyses were carried out in solutions containing $0.1N$ ammonium chloride and ammonium hydroxide and different concentrations of cobaltous chloride. The series were, furthermore, analyzed with dropping mercury electrodes of different characteristics, at several pressures.

Except for the final limiting wave height at high cysteine concentrations, the catalytic currents were proportional to the surface area of the mercury drop. This means that by expressing the data as current densities, almost identical results were found for different electrodes and drop times. However, the currents were not a linear function of the cobalt concentration, nor did they follow the complex function of the cobalt concentration indicated by Klumpar (59).

4. Second Catalytic Wave of Cysteine

At cysteine concentrations above $2.5 \times 10^{-4}M$, a new wave develops which just precedes the above catalytic wave; apparently it overlaps with it at lower concentrations. It is of a magnitude that still necessitates the assumption of a catalytic wave. However, at cysteine concentrations as high as this, both types of catalytic waves are no longer independent of the drop time of the DME.

The extra catalytic wave at high concentrations of cysteine in DiCo buffer occurs at about the same concentration as the catalytic cysteine wave in TriCo buffer mentioned earlier. This suggests that the two reactions may be caused by similar stable complexes.

(It should be pointed out that in a very dilute DiCo buffer, e.g., $0.5 \times 10^{-4}M$ CoCl$_2$, the extra wave is already obtained at cysteine concentrations of $10^{-6}M$, suggesting that the complex forms whenever the concentrations of cobalt and cysteine approach each other.)

5. Master Curve for Cysteine

Since a master curve for catalytic waves of cysteine in a given buffer can be used for the evaluation of similar data obtained with any other DME, its preparation will be discussed in some detail. It will also serve as an example for all other catalytic waves.

Procedure (for construction of a master curve for the catalytic wave of cysteine in 10^{-3} N cobaltous chloride, 0.1N ammonium chloride, and 0.1N ammonium hydroxide). Weigh out 39.40 mg. cysteine hydrochloride, transfer it to a 25-ml. volumetric flask and make up to the mark with 0.1N HCl. (The HCl prevents the deterioration of the solution.) From this 0.01M cysteine solution, prepare, again using 0.1N HCl, the following more dilute solutions: $2 \times 10^{-3}M$, $1 \times 10^{-3}M$, $2 \times 10^{-4}M$, $1 \times 10^{-4}M$, $2 \times 10^{-5}M$, and $1 \times 10^{-5}M$ cysteine.

Prepare the DiCo buffer as follows: To 25.0 ml. 0.01M CoCl$_2$ solution, add 45.0 ml. 1.0N NH$_4$Cl and 325.0 ml. distilled water. Just before starting the series of analyses, add 55.0 ml. 1.0N NH$_4$OH and shake the solution (kept in a glass-stoppered bottle).

For each analysis, pipet out 9.0 ml. of the DiCo buffer into a 20-ml. beaker, add a fraction of a milliliter of cysteine solution and enough 0.1N HCl to make a total of 10.0 ml. solution. For a blank curve, add 1.0 ml. 0.1N HCl to 9.0 ml. of the DiCo buffer. For even spacing of experimental points, add cysteine solution in the following order: 0.25, 0.30, 0.40, 0.50, 0.60, 0.80, and 1.00 ml. of $1 \times 10^{-5}M$, followed by 0.60, 0.80, and 1.00 ml. of $2 \times 10^{-5}M$, and so on with higher concentrations. Prepare only one solution at a time and analyze it *immediately* after preparation, open to air, because evaporation of ammonia from the open vessel will diminish the polarographic curves at the rate of about 15% per hour. Adjust the galvanometer sensitivity so as to make the resulting curves as large as possible and thus minimize the measuring error.

Some typical polarograms obtained in this fashion are shown in the polarograms reproduced in Figure 3. The top five curves show

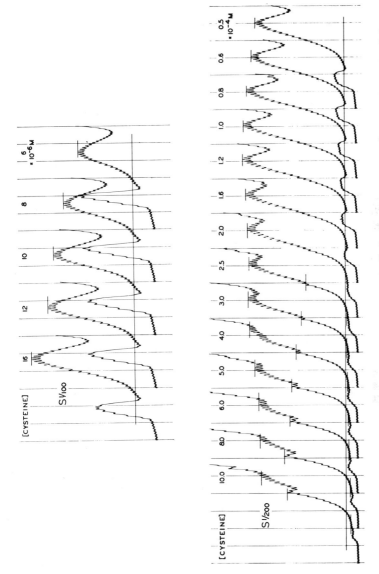

Fig. 3. Effect of varying the cysteine concentration in $10^{-3}M$ DiCo buffer (see text); each curve starts at -0.8 v. vs. SCE and is recorded open to air. Wave heights and cysteine concentrations are indicated. Full galvanometer sensitivity is 2.33×10^{-9} amp./mm.

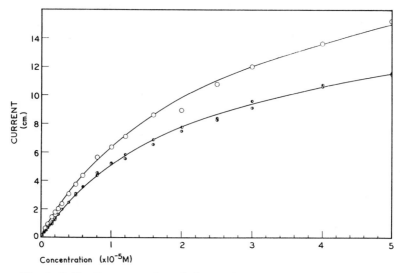

Fig. 4. Calibration curve of catalytic cysteine current in $10^{-3}M$ DiCo buffer (1 cm. = 2.33 μa.) vs. concentration for two different electrodes. ◖ = cystine (plotted as cysteine on the basis $^1/_2$ cystine = cysteine) and ◗ = cysteine, taken with a DME of 1.58 mm.² surface area; ○ = cysteine taken with a DME of 1.99 mm.² surface area.

cysteine waves at relatively small concentrations. These are recorded at $^1/_{100}$ of the maximal galvanometer sensitivity of 2.33×10^{-9} amp./mm. Here the cobalt maximum is still very prominent, hence the horizontal line is drawn to indicate the cobalt wave height which was observed on a simultaneously recorded blank curve. At the higher cysteine concentrations shown in the lower set of curves (at sensitivity $^1/_{200}$), the cobalt maximum is gradually suppressed, but eventually the cobalt wave also is diminished. This can be seen by comparing the short lines drawn in for the cobalt wave heights with the continuous horizontal line which represents the cobalt wave height of the blank at the same galvanometer sensitivity. It may be noticed that near $1 \times 10^{-4}M$ cysteine concentration, the cysteine peak reaches its maximum height. At higher concentrations this peak diminishes slightly, but another wave preceding the cysteine peak becomes noticeable. This second cysteine peak goes hand in hand with the diminution in the cobalt wave height.

The data have been plotted at first in Figure 4 in arbitrary units of

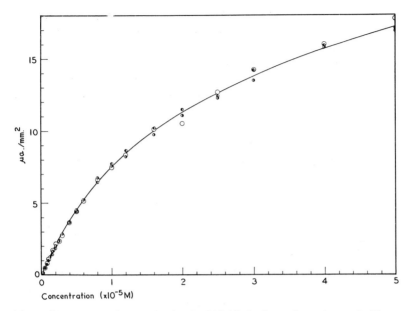

Fig. 5. Master curve for cysteine in $10^{-3}M$ DiCo buffer.   Same data as in Figure 4, plotted as current density vs. concentration.

wave height (in centimeters at sensitivity $^1/_{100}$) vs. concentration, to give typical curves in accordance with the Langmuir equation.   The three sets of data shown in Figure 4 were obtained with cystine and cysteine solutions and with two different electrodes, with surface areas of 1.58 and 1.99 mm.^{2} of the "ripe" drops.   In order to demonstrate the similarity of the data, the cystine concentrations are plotted on the same graph on the basis of $^1/_2$ cystine = cysteine.

The experimental error at cysteine concentrations above $10^{-4}M$ becomes very great, not only because the current then becomes limited, but also because at the high currents obtained, much hydrogen gas is generated at the DME which forces the drops off at irregular intervals.

If the solutions had been exactly prepared, the cystine and cysteine data obtained with the same electrode should have been identical. In the present instance, the results differ by about 10% but not uniformly, suggesting that there may have occurred small errors in the dilutions as well as in the preparation of both the cystine or cysteine and the cobalt buffer stock solutions. This error can be minimized and will usually not amount to more than about 3–4% by duplicate or triplicate analyses and by the use of more accurate pipets.

A much greater and real difference exists between the two different dropping mercury electrodes. Such an error will also appear if the same DME is used at different pressures of mercury. It is obvious that because of this, any standard curves thus prepared can only be used with the same electrode and at the same head of pressure. Breakage of a capillary necessitates recalibration. If the actual current is known in microamperes and the surface area of the drops has been determined, a very simple calculation brings all the data in line and makes it possible to compare the results obtained with different electrodes.

This is demonstrated in Figure 5 in which the cysteine concentration is plotted against current density. Such a master curve is best prepared over the range in which the currents can be most easily measured. Note that here it is possible to average results obtained with several electrodes at different pressures and to gain a fairly reliable curve. Deviations from this curve are essentially due to the preparation of the solutions and clearly indicate the experimental error of the analyses. The concentration of an unknown cysteine solution, similarly analyzed, can then be read directly from the graph, irrespective of the DME used, as long as its surface area and the currents are known in units of mm.^{2} and μa., respectively.

6. Cysteine Determination in Protein Hydrolysates

On the basis of a calibration curve Brdička determined the cysteine content of wool, human hair, serum, serum albumin, and serum globulin, as well as egg albumin in reasonable agreement with published values. Brdička (13) hydrolyzed these proteins as follows:

0.025–0.1 g. of the protein was boiled in 10–25 ml. 5N HCl for 6 hours under reflux. The hydrolysate was made up to 100 ml. with distilled water, filtered, and titrated with NH_4OH to determine its acid content. It was then possible to add the necessary amount of NH_4Cl and NH_4OH to wind up in the final $CoCl_2$ solution with 0.1N NH_4Cl and 0.1N NH_4OH. Brdička estimated his accuracy as ±5%, and he was able to apply his technique to the analysis of cystine in 0.5 mg. of human hair. Brdička also showed that boiling cystine in 5N HCl for 6 hours did not diminish its polarographic activity.

Hydrolysis of glutathione produced a cystine wave 35% higher than expected on the basis of its cystine content, a fact that has not yet been explained. Whether the end product was not all cystine, but some cysteylglycine (which gives a higher catalytic wave than cysteine) was not decided.

7. Cystine in Urine (Cystine Clearance)

The urinary cystine excretion has also been studied by the Brdička reaction. Reed (88) found a considerable increase in the cysteine wave height when diluted urine was left standing in DiCo buffer, reaching a maximum of about three times the starting wave height after one hour. Since added cystine, or cystine in synthetic urine, did not change its wave height, Reed concluded that cystine existed in a free form plus a form from which it is liberated in the DiCo buffer (ammonia–ammonium chloride buffer without cobalt, or cobaltous chloride alone does not have the same effect). In normal individuals, 40–80 mg. free cystine and 60–120 mg. "liberated" cystine are excreted per day. Apparently, acid hydrolysis of the urine produces the same total cystine concentration as the hydrolysis in the DiCo buffer. According to Rosenthal (90), urine from patients with proteinuria must first be deproteinized with acetic acid before a cystine analysis by means of the Brdička reaction is attempted.

Dent et al. (32) used the Brdička reaction for studies of cystine clearance in normal individuals and cystinuric patients. To find the cystine in plasma, these authors dialyzed 0.5 ml. plasma against 2.5 ml. distilled water at 4°C. for 3.5 hours and analyzed 1 ml. of the dialysate in $2 \times 10^{-3}M$ DiCo buffer. Similarly, 1 ml. of diluted urine was analyzed. After feeding cysteine, a large rise in plasma cystine level occurred and the urine cystine increased greatly in both groups of subjects. The endogenous cystine clearance in normal subjects was 2–3 ml. per minute, while it was about 30 times higher in cystinuric patients. In one cystinuric patient tested, the cystine clearance was the same as a simultaneously determined inulin clearance.

8. Substances Interfering with the Catalytic Cysteine Wave

Further application of Brdička's reaction to the determination of cysteine showed that other amino acids could interfere with the analysis. For instance, Sládek and Lipschütz (97) found that the cysteine wave can be completely suppressed by hydrolysates of liver extracts or of stroma from erythrocytes. A study of some amino acids revealed that arginine, β-phenyl-α-alanine, β-phenyl-β-alanine, tryptophane, and histidine had some suppressing effect on the cysteine wave, while urea, cholesterol, lecithin, glucose, and acetic acid, as well as the amino acids glycine, tyrosine, lysine, and α- and β-alanine were without effect. β-Phenyl-β-alanine even gave a catalytic wave of its own in $2 \times 10^{-3}N$ DiCo buffer. Since the relative concentrations of cysteine and addition substances was not stated by Sladek and Lipschütz, some of these experiments were repeated in the writer's laboratory with $10^{-5}M$ cysteine in $10^{-3}N$ DiCo buffer and $10^{-3}M$ added amino acid. Only alanine and methionine had no effect, while the effects of valine, leucine, arginine, lysine, and β-phenyl-β-alanine were moderate (about 10% depression). Serine, threonine, proline, and tryptophane had a more marked effect (about 20% depression), and hydroxyproline depressed the cysteine wave by 40%. Histidine seemed to replace the cysteine wave with its own catalytic wave. It may well be that these amino acids show depressing effects depending on their preparation, storage, and age, and that results obtained with different samples may vary widely. An interference between 2,4-diaminobutyric acid and cysteine will be discussed in Section IV-7-B.

As an example of differences in results may be cited Tropp's analysis of insulin for cystine (114). After hydrolysis with concentrated HCl and HCOOH, this author found consistently values of 7.3–8.3%, i.e., about 30% lower than 12.5%, the value found by Miller and duVigneaud (70) by a colorimetric method. According to Tropp, the height of his cysteine waves was not changed when the analysis was carried out in a synthetic mixture of tyrosine, leucine, histidine, arginine, and glutamic acid. However, Sullivan et al. (104) arrived at a different result with a similar technique. These authors prepared a cystine calibration curve after hydrolyzing known mixtures of cystine and eight amino acids in the same manner as the insulin. With three different insulin preparations they found, by means of the Brdička reaction, 10.9–12.2% cystine in good agreement with 11.0–11.5% obtained colorimetrically. Corrected for moisture and ash, the polarographic data yielded 13.0% and the colorimetric data 12.1%, compared to a value of 12.5% calculated from the total sulfur of the unhydrolyzed samples.

Another method for correcting depressing effects of other substances present, which does not require a knowledge of the approximate composition of the final hydrolysate, was suggested by Stern et al. (102). These authors add known, increasing amounts of cystine to a given quantity of hydrolysate, and analyze the solution after each addition. Taking then a larger quantity of the same hydrolysate in the same amount of buffer, the authors can evaluate the increase in wave height in terms of cystine. An accuracy of $\pm 5\%$ is claimed for solutions containing as little as 12 $\mu g.$ of cystine per milliliter. In this way calibration curves can be prepared for different proteins. It was found that they differed considerably between edestin and casein, but that they could be superimposed for globins from man, horse, sheep, and cattle; the results compared very well with a method in which the cystine is determined as cysteine cuprous mercaptide (5).

According to Kolthoff and Lingane (60), the presence of $0.1M$ nitrate ion eliminates the catalytic cysteine wave (see, however, (10)) while $0.1M$ $(NH_4)_2SO_4$ plus $0.1M$ KCl reduce it more than 20%. Obviously, the presence of reagents that form stable complexes with cysteine, e.g., Ag^+ and Cu^{2+} ions, etc., will also affect the wave.

9. Distinction between Cysteine and Cystine

Since both cysteine and cystine give the same reaction, they can be distinguished only if one is rendered inactive. Brdička (18) found that the addition of potassium iodoacetate in alkaline medium would form a stable complex with cysteine as follows:

$$RSH + ICH_2COO^- \rightarrow RSH_2COO^- + HI$$

Thus the cysteine wave can be eliminated while the cystine wave remains intact.

As an example of this technique, the procedure of Bonting (10) may be cited. This author compared the percentage of SS bonds in the skin from young and adult rats, by treating representative samples either with borate buffer of pH 10 (to get the content of cysteine plus cystine) or with $0.1M$ freshly neutralized sodium iodoacetate in the borate buffer (to get the cystine content alone). After mechanical stirring for 4 hours, the two suspensions were treated twice with trichloroacetic acid, centrifuged, and the clear liquid removed. The residue was hydrolyzed with HCl containing some urea (the latter should decrease the formation of humin which destroys the cysteine). The hydrolysates were then subjected to the Brdička reaction (strangely enough in $0.01M$ $Co(NO_3)_2$ buffer containing $0.1N$ NH_4Cl and $0.1N$ NH_4OH, which according to the above quotation from Kolthoff and Lingane (60) is a poor choice) and the percentage of SS bonds was found to be 79–80 for old and young rat skins, although the total content of cysteine plus cystine decreased by 44% with age.

10. Conclusions about Cysteine Determinations by the Brdička Reaction

From the foregoing may be seen that cysteine analyses by the Brdička reaction are entirely feasible and may be as reliable as other established methods. However, the procedure requires considerable experience in the polarographic technique and is relatively time consuming. For this reason, other methods which have grown out of polarographic studies have become more popular. These are the so-called polarometric or amperometric titration methods in which no actual polarograms are prepared but the current is recorded after each addition of a known amount of titrant to the solution under investigation (31,40,41,60,67,71,75,79,94,100,109). The endpoint of the titration is then determined graphically from the point of intersection of two relatively straight lines and can be very accurate. The titration methods used for the determination of cysteine, cystine, and other thiol compounds cannot be discussed here in detail. They usually employ the rotating platinum electrode instead of the dropping mercury electrode. Depending on the titrant used, they may be classified into argentometric (6,103) and mercurimetric (61) titrations, as well as titrations with p-chloromercuribenzoate (38). The currents measured in these titrations are not catalytic, but depend on diffusion and convection of reducible material.

IV. THE BRDIČKA REACTION OF SIMPLE COMPOUNDS OTHER THAN CYSTEINE

1. General

In his search for the causes of the protein double wave, Brdička found only cystine catalytically active among all the possible components of serum. Yet it gave rise to only one peak, while protein produces two. To learn more about this difference, Brdička (12) studied the tripeptide glutamylcysteylglycine (glutathione) in a DiCo buffer, but found only a gradually increasing current without any peaks in the potential range of the protein double wave. These currents were much smaller than expected on the basis of cysteine content. Letting a $10^{-2}M$ solution of glutathione stand at 62°C. for 5 days produced a marked increase in the wave which now had a peak. Brdička ascribed it to cysteylglycine and concluded that this dipeptide produced a wave about twice as high as that of cysteine (12). However, complete acid hydrolysis of glutathione also produced a cysteine wave that was 35% higher than expected on the basis of its cysteine content so that one must conclude that these early results are connected with a lot of uncertainty.

So far, no systematic study has been made to find out at what point or under what circumstances a single cysteine wave gets transformed into the protein double wave. A step in this direction is the recent study of Sunahara et al. (108) of the octapeptide hormones oxytocin, lysine-, and arginine-vasopressin, which all contain SS groups. They all showed several waves in either DiCo or TriCo buffers that raised a number of questions concerning, but did not settle the problem of, the nature of the protein double waves.

Catalytic waves similar to that of cysteine in DiCo buffers have been observed frequently. Already Brdička had observed that thioglycolic acid shows great activity. To this have been added a large number of sulfur-containing and even sulfur-free compounds which give this reaction to a lesser or greater extent. Some of these compounds even give waves with two peaks, or a mixture of several of them will give two peaks resembling to a certain extent the protein double wave. However, this fact has not helped much to clarify the question of the first protein peak.

2. Acids with a Mercapto Group

A variety of α-mercaptoacetic acids was studied by Fraser et al. (33), who found that all of them showed peaked catalytic waves in the DiCo buffer. Compared to thioglycolic acid (mercaptoacetic acid), thiolactic acid (mercaptopropionic acid) gave a somewhat smaller peak; the presence of two carboxyl groups increased this peak in thiomalic acid (mercaptosuccinic acid), while lengthening the side chain in α-mercaptoglutaric and α-mercaptoadipic acids decreased it progressively. On the other hand, $\alpha\alpha'$-dimercaptoadipic acid produced a peak height of almost twice that of thioglycolic acid, probably because both SH groups are activated by the neighboring carboxyl groups. A greater separation of such groups, as in β-mercapto-propionic and in mercaptomethyl succinic acids, decreases the catalytic activity about a hundred-fold and changes the wave into one with a gradual increase in current without peak.

3. Homocysteine, Isocysteine, and Phenylcysteine

A similar but less pronounced effect is found when one compares the catalytic peak of cysteine with the gradually increasing peakless wave of homocysteine (101). Here the separation between SH and NH₂ groups is increased, with consequent changes in catalytic activity. Isocysteine (116) which represents an α-mercaptopropionic acid with a β-amino group yields a peaked curve similar to cystine but of the same height only at 20 times the concentration of the latter. This indicates that the carboxyl and amino groups must antagonize each other rather than act synergistically in making the SH group catalytically active.

According to Zuman (133) there is a steric effect which produces a lower catalytic wave for the threo form of phenylcysteine than for the erythro form. Both forms are very active in DiCo buffer and show not only a sharply peaked wave at potentials near that of the cysteine wave, but also another peaked wave where the cobalt maximum is usually found.

4. Penicillamine and Substances Linked to Cysteine

If one compares cysteine with penicillamine (86), one finds that the two methyl groups on the same carbon atom as the SH group diminish its catalytic activity by about 50%. On the other hand, when the carboxyl group of cysteine is in a peptide linkage as in cysteylglycine, the catalytic activity is increased so that a larger peaked wave results than with equivalent concentrations of cysteine (12). This peak disappears and in its place one finds a gradually increasing catalytic wave of much smaller magnitude when glutathione is analyzed (12). No definite explanation of this phenomenon has yet been found, since no one has so far studied a variety of peptides in which the NH₂ group of the cysteine forms the peptide linkage. In the meantime it is reasonable to guess that this phenomenon is related to other differences in behavior between cysteine and glutathione. It is believed that glutathione in alkaline solution is in a dynamic equilibrium with a hydroxythiazolidine derivative which eventually changes into a thiazoline by splitting off water (26). Perhaps the need for regeneration of the SH compound from the thiazoline is the reason for the slow rise in the wave and for the decrease in catalytic activity. There has also been speculation whether acetyl cysteine would similarly undergo a rearrangement to a thiazoline (27). Experiments carried out in this laboratory indicate that this is the case, if the polarographic behavior is any criterion. The catalytic wave of acetyl cysteine* in a DiCo buffer showed a gradual increase without any peak and was about one tenth the height of the cysteine wave at comparable concentrations. [See also Sunahara (107).] The wave of unsubstituted thiazoline itself is also similar (62).

5. Effect of Structure on Peak Formation and Potential

The absence of a peak on the catalytic waves does not necessarily imply the same mechanism of the reaction. For instance, Trkal (113), in a study of the Brdička reaction of various sulfur-containing compounds, found thioglycolic acid to give catalytic waves without a peak. This may have had two reasons: First of all, Trkal used a DME with a long drop time which caused large fluctuations in the currents and perhaps hid any existing peaks. Secondly, the peak in this catalysis occurs at a very negative potential (about -1.9 v. vs. SCE), so that the wave tends to overlap with the buffer wave. (With a faster dropping electrode, catalytic waves were obtained in the writer's laboratory which had obvious peaks when the thioglycolic acid concentration exceeded $2 \times 10^{-6}M$.) Cysteamine (β-aminoethyl mercaptan) shows a somewhat smaller activity than thioglycolic acid, and its wave does not produce a distinct peak although it occurs at a more positive potential (-1.7 v.). Thus, the substitution of NH_2 for COOH tends to diminish the catalytic activity. According to Trkal this activity is doubled if the substituent is $N(C_2H_5)_2$ as in diethylaminoethylmercaptan. The wave of this compound is still more positive (-1.6 v.) and shows a peak. However, if the carboxyl group of thioglycolic acid is replaced by an SH group as in ethanedi-

* I wish to express also at this time my thanks to Dr. Clarke for synthesizing a sample of acetyl cysteine for me.

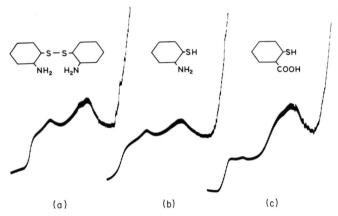

Fig. 6. Polarograms in 1.6 × $10^{-3}M$ DiCo buffer, containing 30% ethanol.
(a) disulfide of o-aminothiophenol, (b) o-aminothiophenol, (c) thiosalicylic acid
(o-mercaptobenzoic acid); all in $10^{-3}M$ concentration.

thiol, the catalytic activity is diminished to about one half, and the
wave resembles a diffusion current although it occurs at a very
positive potential (-1.2 v.).   It is obvious from these results that no
relation exists between activity and potential of the wave or peak.

Aromatic sulfhydryl compounds show varying behavior.   While
thiophenol and benzyl mercaptan are quite inactive (113), thiosalicylic acid does produce a wave (130) (see Fig. 6), although only at
high concentrations (about $10^{-3}M$).   A similarly low activity is
found for o-aminothiophenol and its disulfide (130) which even produces two waves (see Fig. 6), while the para compound is reported to
be inactive (113).   However, inspection of the polarogram of p-amino-
thiophenol published by Trkal reveals a rapidly rising wave *ahead* of
the cobalt maximum, even at concentrations of $10^{-5}M$.   At 5 ×
$10^{-5}M$ this wave is as large as the cobalt maximum and about twice
as large as the diffusion current of 2 × $10^{-3}M$ cobaltous chloride, so
that it must involve a catalytic phenomenon or some stirring at the
electrode.   Further study of this phenomenon is certainly warranted.

6. Effect of Liberation of SH Groups at the DME

A. DISULFIDE REACTIONS

In general, all active thiols will also give catalytic waves when they
are present as the oxidized —SS— compounds.   Just as in the case of

cystine and cysteine (see Fig. 2), the disulfides are reduced to the thiols at the DME at more positive potentials than the catalytic wave and thus behave essentially as if thiols had been present. One interesting difference has been reported for glutathione by Lamprecht et al. (62). While they found the well-known slow rise in current (without maximum) for reduced glutathione, they obtained a peaked wave for SS-glutathione. In view of what has been mentioned earlier, this might indicate that the freshly formed thiol compound has not yet had time to form much of the thiazoline. However, the fact that SS-glutathione had to be 100 times as concentrated in order to produce the same wave height as cysteine indicates that only a small percentage of the reduction product is available for the reaction. A study of the effect of drop time on this reaction should be revealing. The suggestion, made by Lamprecht et al., that SS-glutathione under the conditions of the experiment is not reduced must be rejected in view of the detailed studies of its reduction potentials at the DME by Tachi and Koide (110).

The disulfide bond in α-lipoic acid (6,8-dimercaptooctanoic acid) is reduced at potentials more positive than the catalytic waves so that two SH groups form which cause a very marked catalytic effect in concentrations as low as $10^{-6}M$ (58,105).

B. ETHYLMERCURITHIOSALICYLATE

There may also be catalytic reactions due to SH groups that are liberated from a complex, as is shown by the behavior of sodium ethylmercurithiosalicylate (thiomersalate or merthiolate). Here the sulfur atom is bound to a mercury atom, but the compound is reduced (by reduction of the mercury) liberating the SH or S^- radical, which then shows its catalytic effect (87).

C. BIS-(DIMETHYLTHIOCARBAMYL) DISULFIDE

An interesting, catalytically active compound, the thiol form of which has not yet been studied directly, is bis-(dimethylthiocarbamyl) disulfide $[(CH_3)_2N—CS—S—S—CS—N(CH_3)_2]$. This compound was found to give a wave about one tenth the height of a corresponding cystine solution (112,130).

D. INACTIVE COMPOUNDS

In contrast to these active sulfur compounds, all those in which the sulfur is linked to two carbon atoms seem to be inactive. Examples are: methionine (99,102), djenkolic acid, S-benzyl cysteine (99), thiodiglycol, thiodiglycolic acid, 2-diethylaminoethylsulfide, diallylsulfide, and phenothiazine (113).

E. ACTIVE PRODUCTS FROM INACTIVE COMPOUNDS

The exception to the above rule seems to be compounds that decompose under the conditions of the experiment into active forms. For instance, thiophene-2,5-dicarbonic acid is stable and inactive, while the related compound bis-2,5-chloromethyl thiophene hydrolyzes in the ammonia–ammonium chloride buffer and produces a very active product (113). This reaction seems similar to the alkaline decomposition of mustard gas ($\beta\beta'$-dichlorodiethylsulfide) which, however, requires boiling with concentrated ammonium hydroxide for the hydrolysis (15).

Among other inactive substances that change into active forms upon decomposition in the DiCo buffer may be mentioned *esters*, such as cystine dimethyl ester (62) and cystine diethyl ester (107), or *acetylated compounds*, such as S-acetyl glutathione (62).

F. THIAMINE AND RELATED COMPOUNDS

Extensive studies have also been carried out on thiamine (vitamin B_1) (8,111) and similar compounds. Neither 2-methyl-5-hydroxymethyl-6-amino pyrimidine hydrochloride, nor 4-methyl-5-hydroxyethylthiazole hydrobromide produce a catalytic wave, yet thiamine which contains both of these rings does so in dilute solution (about $10^{-4}M$) (37). Apparently the thiazole ring of the thiamine opens up to produce a thiol form which causes the Brdička reaction (37,111). Air oxidation changes this form into the polarographically inactive —SS— form (111,131,132). In connection with these studies it is interesting that quaternary thiazoles give a catalytic wave while tertiary thiazoles do not (8,130). A variety of quaternary thiazoles, studied by Yamanouchi had similar activity with the exception of benzothiazole methiodide. Disulfide compounds derived from these same active compounds do not show the catalytic wave (130).

7. Active Sulfur-Free Compounds

A. GLYCERALDEHYDE AND DIHYDROXYACETONE

Among the sulfur-free substances that give a catalytic effect in DiCo buffer should be mentioned hydroxyaldehydes and hydroxyketones.

According to Lamprecht et al. (62), glyceraldehyde and dihydroxy-acetone in concentrations of about $10^{-3}M$ produce catalytic waves with very sharp peaks. Since aliphatic aldehydes and ketones, as well as glyceric acid and a Schiff base made from glycine and glyceraldehyde, were all inactive, these authors conclude that in addition to the hydroxyl group the carbonyl group is essential for the catalytic effect.

B. AMINO ACIDS WITH BASIC GROUPS

In the search for substances responsible for the catalytic protein waves, Müller and Elwood (82) isolated material which gave only the first peak of the double wave. Since this material could be liberated by tryptic digestion of protein, Müller (78) had suggested that either arginine or lysine or both might be involved in the reaction. In a subsequent study of amino acids with more than one amino group, Müller and Yamanouchi (85) found that many of these acids behave similarly, although to a different extent, when they are added to DiCo

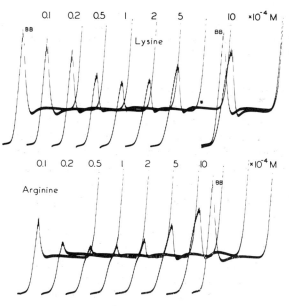

Fig. 7. Polarograms of lysine and arginine in $1.6 \times 10^{-3}M$ DiCo buffer. Concentrations are indicated. *BB* stands for buffer blank.

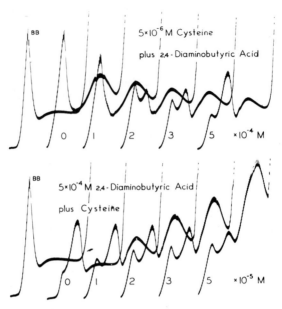

Fig. 8. Polarograms in 1.6 × 10⁻³M DiCo buffer showing effects of 2,4-di-aminobutyric acid on cysteine wave, and vice versa. Concentrations are indicated. *BB* stands for buffer blank.

buffer in increasing concentrations: First, the cobalt maximum is depressed and then a new maximum develops (beginning at about $10^{-4}M$ concentration) that is caused by the amino acid. Since this new maximum appears at about the same potential as the depressed cobalt maximum (see the superimposed curves at the extreme right of the upper polarogram of Fig. 7), it can only be recognized if one increases the amino acid concentration in small steps. The effect decreases in the order: arginine > lysine > asparagine > ornithine > tryptophane > citrulline > glutamine.

In the case of histidine and 2,4-diaminobutyric acid, the new maximum appears at a more negative potential and can be easily distinguished from the cobalt maximum. The presence of cysteine affects the 2,4-diaminobutyric acid maximum and vice versa, as may be seen in Figure 8. A similar interaction between the heights of the cystine and histidine peaks has been described by Shinagawa et al. (96). However, this interaction cannot serve as proof that the same electrode mechanism is involved in both phenomena. On the contrary, the addition of gelatine tends to wipe out the 2,4-diaminobutyric acid maximum without affecting the cyteine wave markedly (85), while the histidine peak is also suppressed by the addition of gelatine (96). Studies still in progress in this laboratory indicate that the "streaming" at the electrode, which is responsible for the cobalt maximum, is also responsible for the 2,4-diaminobutyric acid maximum, but not for the cysteine peak. Such studies are complicated by the fact that during the cysteine maximum, hydrogen gas is evolved, which causes some movement around the electrode, similar to "streaming." A more promising approach to this problem seems to be the labeling of the cobalt in the buffer by means of radioactive Co^{60}. In this way, Shinagawa et al. (96) could show that only the maxima of cobalt and histidine but not the maxima of cysteine or protein were accompanied by the reduction of a quantity of cobalt which reached a peak at the maximum (as required for a maximum caused by "streaming"). For the maximum of cysteine and for the protein double wave, only enough cobalt was reduced to be the equivalent of a diffusion current (as required for a catalysis without "streaming").

This should suffice to demonstrate the great need for some detailed studies on the many compounds mentioned in this section, to find out which are truly catalytic and thus cause the Brdička reaction and which are merely producing an inhomogeneous field which results in "streaming" and thus causes maxima. It may even be that the early cysteine wave which is found in concentrated solutions of cysteine (see Section III-4, Fig. 3) is caused by such a mechanism and thus should not be considered catalytic as required for the Brdička reaction. The same may be said about the peak waves in TriCo buffer which will be considered next.

8. Substances Causing the Brdička Reaction in TriCo Buffer

It has been mentioned earlier that protein seems to be just as active in TriCo as in DiCo buffer, while cysteine must be present in concentrations exceeding $10^{-4}M$ before it shows any effect in TriCo buffer. Yet there are some simple compounds that show essentially the same activities in both buffers. Among such substances with very great activity may be mentioned diethylaminoethylmercaptan and bis-2,5-chloromethylthiophane (active at $10^{-6}M$ concentration) as well as β-aminoethylmercaptan and 2,3-dimercaptopropanol (active at $10^{-5}M$ concentration) (113). Most substances, however, have been found to require a concentration of $10^{-4}M$ or more, similar to cystine, e.g., bis-dimethylcarbamyldisulfide (112). But there are many substances that give no sign of any activity in TriCo buffer even at concentrations of $10^{-3}M$. Among these may be mentioned thioglycolic acid, ethanedithiol (113), dithiodiglycolic acid (112), and the amino acids arginine, lysine, and 2,4-diaminobutyric acid (72).

The literature contains also a report of at least two substances, nicotinamide and nicotinic acid, that give a catalytic reaction in TriCo buffer, but have not yet been reported to give such a reaction in DiCo buffer (8).

The catalytic currents in TriCo buffers are often more complex than those found in DiCo buffers, which makes their explanation more difficult. For instance, in the case of cystine the analysis involves either four (52) or six (106) waves. The suggestion has been made that these involve particularly strong complexes of cystine with trivalent cobalt ions, and that they are in part governed by the rate of the reaction between cystine and the divalent cobalt ions freshly generated at the DME from trivalent cobalt ions (52,106).

V. THE BRDIČKA REACTION OF NATIVE PROTEINS

1. Nature of the Double Wave

A. GENERAL

In his earliest experiments, Brdička (11) had already established the fact that the protein double wave was not specific for any protein. Nearly all proteins tested by him, such as the albumin, globulin, and euglobulin fractions of human serum as well as egg albumin, whey, insulin, beer, etc., gave similar results in DiCo and TriCo buffers. The only proteins failing to give the reaction were gelatine and silk, i.e., proteins with very low cystine content. Hence, Brdička ascribed the double wave to the cystine nuclei in the protein. He also showed that the relationship between the height of the double wave and the protein concentration was not a linear one and that the double wave reached a limiting height. This, coupled with the observation that the effects of cobalt and buffer concentration on the double wave were very similar to their effects on the height of the cystine wave, convinced Brdička that the double wave could be correlated with the cystine nuclei in the protein.

B. CROSSING EFFECT

This explanation remained unchallenged until 1939 when a tremendous general interest in this reaction was created by Brdička's demonstration of the value of the polarographic protein reaction for the diagnosis of cancer (19). Tropp et al. (119) investigated the effects of dilution on a number of protein fractions of horse serum. They found that both parts of the double wave first increased upon dilution before they finally decreased, and that the final decrease was slower for the first peak than for the second peak, so that in very dilute solution the first peak was larger than the second peak. This phenomenon, the "Kreuzungseffect" (crossing effect) was slightly different for the various protein fractions tested and was evaluated as a "protein quotient" representing the ratio of the heights of the second and first peaks. The protein concentration at which this quotient is unity, i.e., when both peaks are of equal height was considered of special value and to be characteristic of the protein analyzed. However, further investigations showed that many proteins do not show such a Kreuzungseffect (117,120). The fact that such an effect exists at all was interpreted to mean that the two peaks had different causes. While the second peak was still ascribed to cystine in the protein, the first peak was believed to be caused by some particular binding (possibly acid amide or diketopiperazine or still another type of binding) of the various amino acids in the molecule.

C. EFFECT OF TEMPERATURE

By varying the temperature, one can demonstrate a Kreuzungseffect for the same protein at different concentrations. The first wave, which practically disappears at 1 °C. and leaves the second wave isolated, grows very much more rapidly with temperature than the second wave (73) and may exceed the latter in height at different temperatures, depending on concentration. Because of this, and because the first wave can be made to overlap with the second peak by a tenfold increase in the ammonia concentration of the test solution, Müller and Davis (80) concluded that the first wave is largely controlled by the activity of free ammonia in the solution, which is increased at higher temperatures. Different rates of growth of the two

waves during denaturation and the isolation of cysteine-poor material
that gives essentially only the first peak, which will be discussed
later on, have also strengthened the idea that substances other than
cystine are responsible for the first wave.

D. LANGMUIR ADSORPTION ISOTHERM

By necessity, studies with proteins are more complicated than
studies with simple amino acids, because most proteins, and certainly
the various plasma fractions, are not pure compounds with exact
molecular weight, but at best are groups of similarly behaving large
molecules. Furthermore, they are easily denatured, so that even the
conditions of the ammonia buffer may be enough to bring about some
changes in the molecule. To minimize this effect, studies on native
proteins must be carried out immediately after mixing of the solutions.

One of the first detailed studies on the catalytic protein waves was
carried out with plasma by Jurka (48), and this was analyzed from the
theoretical standpoint by Brdička (21). Most of the experimental
data could be made to fit a theoretical equation based on the Langmuir
adsorption isotherm given in equation (6).

The catalytic wave height was no longer found directly proportional to the cobalt concentration as in the case of cysteine. The relationship between wave height h and the cobalt concentration, on the
average, was given by

$$h = k_c [Co^{2+}]^{0.74} \tag{8}$$

However, this relationship could be incorporated into the Langmuir
equation as follows:

$$h = \frac{k_\infty [Co^{2+}]^{0.74} \omega c}{1 + \omega c} \tag{9}$$

Here k_∞ represents the surface concentration of protein at the limiting
(infinite) concentration of cobalt, while ω is a specific coefficient and c,
the protein concentration. For Jurka's data, Brdička found $k_\infty =$
6620 and $\omega = 1450$, but what the significance of these figures is was
not discussed. It is doubtful that they have much meaning in this
case. The plasma used came from mixed samples of normal human
blood, which is obviously quite heterogeneous and contains a variety
of proteins, all of which may have somewhat different effects. With-

out the minimum information of at least the total protein concentration and perhaps an electrophoretic analysis, the determination of constants for the Langmuir equation is merely a demonstration of how closely the data adhere to this equation.

E. SIGNIFICANCE OF THE FIRST AND SECOND PROTEIN WAVES

Millar (68) made some definite use of the above relationship during his investigation of five crystalline proteins—trypsin, chymotrypsin, insulin, bovine plasma albumin, and pepsin—at constant cobalt concentrations. He obtained the constants of the Langmuir equation by plotting c/h against c, where h is the height of the catalytic wave and c is the concentration of protein (in mg./ml.). On the whole, fairly straight lines were thus obtained from whose slopes and intercepts the constants z and ω of Langmuir's equation (6) could be calculated. The constant z in this case is equivalent to h_{max}, which is proportional to the mass of protein adsorbed per unit area of electrode surface when the protein concentration is high and the surface is saturated. Millar found an inverse relationship between the z value for either the first or second protein peaks and the volume of the protein aggregate which varied considerably for the five proteins. For the second protein wave he was furthermore able to show a statistically significant relationship between the z values and the ratio of total potential RSH (in μmoles/g. protein) to the volume of the protein aggregate, where "total potential RSH" is the sum of the reported cysteine and half-cystine residues in a given protein. A similar relationship for the first peak was not statistically significant. This would indicate that cystine in the molecule plays a big role for the production of the second peak, and only a questionable role for the development of the first peak of the protein double wave.

2. Evaluation of Catalytic Currents of Proteins

A. CURRENT DENSITY AND PROTEIN CONCENTRATION (in g./100 ml.)

Many analyses of proteins have been described in the literature. They usually demonstrate similar effects, i.e., a nonlinearity between wave height and concentration of the protein and a limiting wave height at high concentrations. As has been pointed out before, the data are unfortunately not presented in a way that makes it possible to compare different proteins and the results of different experimenters. Such comparisons should have been possible ever since Müller and Davis showed that the catalytic wave height is independent of the drop time but is directly proportional to the surface area of a given dropping mercury electrode (80). Thus a report of current densities, i.e., currents expressed in $\mu a./mm.^2$ of electrode surface, becomes generally applicable.

If the current-density method of reporting is not used, some complex analysis of many data is required before results can be compared. For instance, Kalous (54) reported five different standardization curves for five mucoprotein concentrations obtained with three electrodes at different drop times and flow rates of the mercury, which needed to be employed in order to be able to predict the catalytic current at any other drop time and flow rate. It is therefore very gratifying to the writer that in the most recent publication from the Prague school (56) the current-density method of reporting catalytic currents has finally been adopted. Unfortunately, Kalous and Pavliček (56) did not use the value of 0.8517, recommended since 1947 by Müller (75,79,81) for k in equation 3. Instead, they used a value of 0.51, which gives the mean surface area of each drop of mercury exposed to the solution during its lifetime, rather than the maximum surface area of the "ripe" drop. This may result in two sets of values, one 1.67 times greater than the other, being reported in the literature, but it does not alter their significance.

Kalous and Pavliček (56) have measured the current densities of catalytic currents for seven different proteins in TriCo buffer over the range of about 1 to 10 mg./100 ml. and found considerable differences. For characterization of the proteins, they suggest as a polarographic constant B, the current density obtained when the concentration is 5 mg./100 ml. It seems to the writer that analysis over a larger concentration range in which the concentration is expressed in molarity offers more information. This will be illustrated by data obtained with four different proteins.

B. CURRENT DENSITY AND LOGARITHM OF THE PROTEIN
   CONCENTRATION (in g./100 ml.)

The data used as examples were obtained in standard DiCo buffer $(1.6 \times 10^{-3}M \text{ CoCl}_2, 0.1N \text{ NH}_4\text{Cl}, \text{ and } 0.1N \text{ NH}_4\text{OH})$, with dropping mercury electrodes with 1.52 and 1.75 mm.^{2} surface area (when "ripe") (72). The room temperature in a given series was constant but varied from 25 to 26°C. for different series. To cover as large a range of concentrations as possible, approximately 5 g./100 ml. stock solutions of the proteins were prepared in 0.9% sodium chloride solution, which was also used for further dilutions. The stock solution was filtered if necessary and its protein concentration ascertained by Kjeldahl nitrogen analysis. As in the procedure for the cysteine master curve (Section III-5), the stock solutions were then diluted to yield the following concentrations: 1.0, 0.5, 0.1, 0.05, 0.01, and 0.005 g./100 ml. Portions of these solutions (e.g., 0.25, 0.30, 0.40, 0.50, 0.60, 0.80, and 1.00 ml. of 0.005%, followed by 0.60, 0.80, and 1.00 ml. of 0.01% solution, etc.) plus a necessary amount of 0.9% NaCl to make a total of 10.0 ml. final solution were then added to 9.0 ml. of freshly pipetted DiCo buffer (this is kept in a glass-stoppered bottle). The polarogram was recorded *immediately* after thorough mixing, open to air.

Both wave heights were measured and evaluated in terms of surface area, which was determined for each particular DME at an applied voltage of −1.6 v. vs. SCE. In order to get all the data on one graph, the current density was plotted against the logarithm of the concentration of the protein in the solution analyzed. The above sequence of concentrations makes each concentration interval equal to about 0.1 logarithmic unit.

The four proteins thus studied were crystalline trypsin and bovine serum albumin (both Armour products), besides human serum albumin, fraction V, and γ globulin, fraction II (both 99% pure, by electrophoresis). As may be seen from Figure 9, all showed different behavior, but each was perfectly reproducible. It appears as if trypsin produces a Brdička reaction without limit. However, the limiting current simply cannot be reached, because the wave overlaps into a single smooth curve with the buffer wave. A slightly different situation exists with bovine serum albumin. Here, at the highest concentration used (500 mg./100 ml. in the buffer), a limiting height was not yet indicated. However, the increase in wave height with concentration proceeded much more slowly than with the other proteins. Also, at the lowest concentrations, the second wave was so small in comparison with the first wave that it overlapped and could not be measured. The human fraction V definitely tends towards a limit at higher concentrations, while the human fraction II has an obvious limit at a concentration of about 50 mg./100 ml.

Using Kalous and Pavliček's characterization (56), one would find the "polarographic constant B" (at log $C = -2.3$) as follows: human fraction II, 2.0; bovine serum albumin, 2.6; human fraction V, 4.8; and trypsin, 8.0 μa./mm.[2]. These constants are highly arbitrary and do not tell much about the proteins; even their order would change if

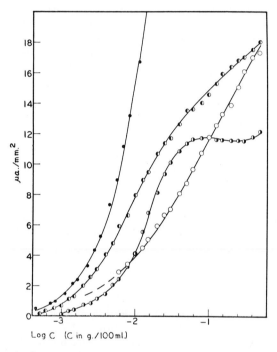

Fig. 9. Graph of current density of *second* protein wave in $1.6 \times 10^{-3}M$ DiCo buffer vs. log protein concentration (in g./100 ml.): ● = crystalline trypsin; ○ = crystalline bovine albumin; ◐ = human albumin (fraction V); ◑ = human γ-globulin (fraction II).

the concentrations were doubled. Compared to this, the presentation of the complete current density–log concentration relationship points out definite differences in behavior. These may be illustrated even better by means of master curves in which the current density is plotted against the logarithm of the protein concentration expressed in moles per liter.

C. MASTER CURVE FOR THE SECOND PROTEIN WAVE

The data of Figure 9, replotted on the basis of molar concentration as in Figure 10, bring out new features of the analysis by means of the Brdička reaction.

For the conversion, the following molecular weights were assumed: trypsin = 24,000 (35), serum albumin (fraction V) = 65,000 (44), and

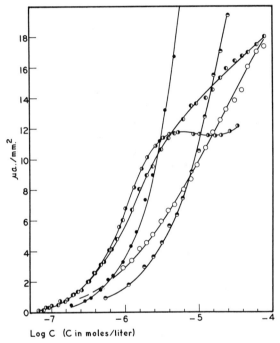

Fig. 10. Master curves of *second* protein wave in $1.6 \times 10^{-3}M$ DiCo buffer vs. log protein concentration (in moles/liter): ● = crystalline trypsin; ○ = crystalline bovine albumin; ◐ = human albumin (fraction V); ◑ = human γ globulin (fraction II). For comparison, the catalytic cystine wave in the same buffer is plotted (as cysteine) on the same scale, as ◓.

γ globulins (fraction II) = 150,000 (44). Small errors in these figures would merely require a slight shifting of the curves to the right or left on the graph of Figure 10. For comparison, data have also been plotted in Figure 10 for cystine. These were obtained in the same $1.6 \times 10^{-3}M$ DiCo buffer, and the cystine data have been plotted as cysteine (as in Figs. 4 and 5) on the basis of $1/2$ cystine = cysteine.

Figure 10 demonstrates a number of surprising phenomena. It may be seen that the activity of the human protein fractions is measurable at $10^{-7}M$ concentration and that it is about the same for both proteins. But, as the concentration increases, the activity of the human fraction II lags behind that of fraction II. Compared to this, the crystalline bovine serum albumin which possibly also starts out with the same activity in the very dilute solution (extrapolation of the curve would point to that) lags even farther behind that of the human fraction V, yet eventually becomes equal to it at high enough concentrations.

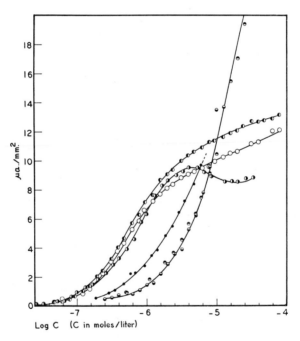

Fig. 11. Master curves of *first* protein wave in $1.6 \times 10^{-3}M$ DiCo buffer vs. log protein concentration (in moles/liter): ● = crystalline trypsin; ○ = crystalline bovine albumin; ◐ = human albumin (fraction V); ◑ = human γ globulin (fraction II). For comparison, the catalytic waves of cystine (plotted as cysteine = ◓) and thioglycolic acid = ◒, recorded in the same buffer, are plotted on the same scale.

D. MASTER CURVE FOR THE FIRST PROTEIN WAVE

If the current density of the first wave of the same four proteins is plotted against the logarithm of their molar concentrations, as in Figure 11, a behavior entirely different from that of the second wave becomes apparent. Notice that the curves for the human fractions V and II and the curve for the crystalline bovine serum albumin practically overlap over a hundred-fold concentration change. This suggests that the same group or structure must be responsible for this in all three proteins and that it most likely is something different from the SH groups which have been held responsible for the second protein wave. A somewhat different behavior is shown by trypsin, but the slopes of all curves of these first waves are similar to those of cysteine and thioglycolic acid which are also plotted in Figure 11 for comparison. (Note that in our experience the cysteine and thioglycolic acid data are identical.)

E. SPECULATIONS BASED ON PROTEIN MASTER CURVES

If one compares the rise in the curves of the human fraction II and of cysteine in Figure 10, one finds a close parallelism. One may therefore speculate that perhaps a fixed multiple of SH groups in each molecule of protein is activated (perhaps five, in accordance with the relatively constant difference of 0.7 logarithmic units). If this reasoning is justified, one would further conclude that human serum albumin also has five activated SH groups at very low concentration, but only about four when the concentration reaches $10^{-6}M$; this gradually diminishes as the concentration increases further and is only one or less when the concentration exceeds $10^{-5}M$. Interestingly enough, at about the same concentration, bovine serum albumin also has only one SH group activated per molecule, while at $10^{-6}M$ only two SH groups seem to be activated in this protein. Whether such speculations will significantly contribute to the problem of available sulfhydryl groups in serum albumin (6,7,43,45), in which at present only one such group is reasonably certain (and that only in mercaptalbumin), is questionable at present.

One may reasonably conclude that further studies of this sort on more-or-less homogeneous groups of proteins should yield additional information about the reaction mechanism. However, attempts to analyze *mixtures* of human fractions II and V by this method have so far not proved very promising in our laboratory.

VI. THE BRDIČKA REACTION OF DENATURED PROTEINS

1. General

Soon after Brdička discovered that polarographic analyses revealed differences between plasma from cancer patients and from normal individuals, he also found that these differences could be magnified by denaturation of the plasma proteins before analysis (16,17). Among the methods of denaturation that have so far been investigated are heat denaturation and treatment with alkali or acid, with ultraviolet light, with x-rays, and with proteolytic enzymes such as pepsin and trypsin, as well as with a variety of chemicals. It is beyond the scope of this article to discuss all of these, especially since the effect, in general, is similar. If such denatured protein solutions are added to DiCo buffer, both parts of the protein double wave grow as a function of time of treatment. This growth is limited, however, and is followed by a gradual decrease in wave height with time. The growth in the height of the catalytic waves has been ascribed to an unfolding of the protein, which thus exposes more polarographically active groups such as SH groups, and the final decrease has been assumed to represent the ultimate hydrolysis of the protein to inactive amino acids or oxidation products. This denaturation of the proteins is often accompanied by a liberation of polarographically active amino acids and polypeptides that are soluble in protein precipitants, such as sulfosalicylic or perchloric acids. The effect of cysteine and similar compounds is eliminated from these soluble filtrate materials by analyzing the filtrates in TriCo buffer. The sulfosalicylic acid-soluble polypeptides are still active in this medium and can thus be determined in isolation. These have also been found in undenatured plasma. Their liberation during denaturation of the plasma proteins is so much greater in plasma from certain patients than from normal individuals that their analysis has become of clinical significance. The nature of the sulfosalicylic acid-soluble polypeptides has been the subject of extensive investigations. It will therefore be discussed in some detail along with the method of alkaline denaturation that seems to have been widely adopted.

2. Alkaline Denaturation of Proteins

In this analysis, originally designed by Brdička (18), plasma, serum, or isolated protein fractions are subjected to mild alkaline digestion

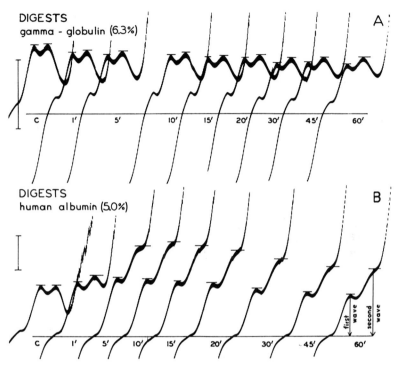

Fig. 12. Polarograms showing the effect of time on the alkaline digest test, in $1.6 \times 10^{-3}M$ DiCo buffer. (*A*) carried out with γ globulin (fraction II); (*B*) carried out with albumin (fraction V). The horizontal line represents the diffusion current of cobalt, obtained during a blank experiment, *C* represents the undigested control. The time of digestion is indicated. Cf. reference 78.

(in 0.2*N* KOH) at room temperature and aliquots of the mixtures are analyzed in DiCo buffer after known intervals of time. The procedure used by the writer is described in detail in Section VIII-2-B in connection with the digest test.

The progress of such an alkaline digestion with time is illustrated by the polarograms reproduced in Figure 12. Note that the two human serum protein fractions (99% pure, by electrophoresis) differ markedly in their behavior during digestion. The albumin fraction V shows a marked rise in both waves for the first 5–10 minutes of digestion, followed by a gradual decline. To distinguish these two phases of the digestion, they have been called the *activation reaction* and the *decay reaction*, respectively.   The γ globulin fraction II shows only a decay reaction.

A. ACTIVATION REACTION

The activation reactions of a number of proteins have been studied in some detail (77).   No activation was found for fractions I, II, and III of human plasma [prepared by method 6 of Cohn's alcohol fractionation techniques (29)].   The α and β globulins present in fractions IV-1 and IV-4 probably do undergo this reaction to a small extent, but their contribution to the activation reaction of plasma is small. Hence, the latter must be ascribed almost exclusively to the albumin, not only in normal plasma where albumin is in excess, but even in pathological plasma where there is more globulin than albumin (78). This conclusion was found to be true in cases of cancer and nephrosis, where fraction V could be isolated from the plasma by the method of Lever et al. (64) and its activation reaction compared with that of the corresponding plasma (72).

Samples of serum albumin from different animals differ considerably in their activation reactions.   To make a roughly quantitative comparison possible, Müller et al. (83) measured the peak height of the second wave attained during digestion and expressed it in per cent of the control value, fully realizing that this involves an error, since there is no linear relationship between catalytic wave height and concentration.   The data of Table I were thus obtained for approximately equal concentrations (4–5 g./100 ml.) of protein at 25° C. These arbitrary percentage values depend considerably on the concentration of the protein (e.g., the activation reaction of human albumin is 185, 160, and 140% for concentrations of 5, 2.5, and 1.25%, respectively).   The very high value for bovine serum albumin results from the fact that the second protein wave is extremely small when this protein is undenatured.   Since the second protein wave is considerably higher in beef *serum* because of the presence of other proteins, the activation reaction for serum is smaller (280%) than for the isolated albumin fraction V (400%).

Notice that most activation reactions have reached their peak after 10–15 minutes.   Human plasma behaves similarly.   This is somewhat shorter than the time given by Brdička (18).   Increased temperature shortens this time, but it also increases the rate of the decay reaction.

TABLE I
Activation Reaction of Serum Albumin (Fraction V) in 0.2N KOH at 25°C.

Source	Peak value (in % of starting value)	Time of digestion needed for peak value (minutes)
Cow	400	10–15
Dog	252	10
Horse	225	5
Sheep	206	15
Man	185	10
Turkey	165	25–30
Pig	150	10–15

The activation reaction of the first wave is small (about 115–120%) and appears to be the same for all the different samples of albumin tested. From this one may conclude that the activation reaction of the first wave is indicative of something common to all albumins, while that of the second wave demonstrates differences existing between different kinds of serum albumin.

B. DECAY REACTION

The decay reaction probably offers a better opportunity to distinguish between similar types of proteins (78). Every protein tested so far has shown the decrease in wave height with prolonged alkaline digestion. When the *logarithm* of this wave height is plotted against time, it is found that a straight line can be drawn through the points

TABLE II
Decay Reaction of Plasma Proteins in 0.2N KOH at 25°C.

Protein	Half life (minutes)	Protein	Half life (minutes)
Human fraction I	300	Albumin fractions (V)	
II	240	Porcine	190
III	130	Turkey	150
IV-1	130	Sheep	120
IV-4	110	Human	110
V	110	Canine	95
Normal human plasma	110–140	Bovine	80
Nephrosis: Human plasma	140	Equine	70
Urine (fraction V)	130–150	Beef serum	75–90

following the activation reaction for the first hour of digestion. From the slope of this line a half life can be calculated for any given protein and compared with other proteins (83). (Since the observed changes are relatively small, the deviation from linearity between wave height and concentration is probably of minor importance.) These half lives are independent of the protein concentration and they are the same for the first and second protein waves. This is of interest since it indicates that the decay reaction involves the molecule as a whole, while the activation reactions of the first and second waves probably deal with different places on the same protein molecule.

In Table II are listed half lives thus obtained for a variety of proteins (83). Notice that the order of half lives in the decay reaction is not the same as the order of the activation reactions of the different albumins in Table I.

It is also of interest that the protein (probably fraction V) isolated from the urine of a patient with nephrosis (with plasma containing 1.6% albumin and 1.7% globulin and with a urinary excretion of 25 g. protein per day) had a half life of 130–150 minutes while the plasma from this patient and fraction V isolated from this plasma (by Lever's method (64)) gave a similar half life of 140 minutes. Thus it appears that the albumin produced at such a high rate in this patient differs only slightly from normal human albumin. Whether variations in the albumin/globulin ratio or in the kind of albumin will account for different half lives observed on plasma samples from a variety of patients, must be determined by future experiments.

3. Filtrate Reactions

A. GENERAL

Polarographic reactions of material left in the filtrate following precipitation of the large protein molecules by sulfosalicylic acid were first observed by Mayer working in Brdička's laboratory (18). Such *filtrate material* produces typical catalytic double waves in TriCo buffer, which have been called *filtrate waves* since their nature is not known with certainty. Following denaturation of plasma proteins by alkali, acid, or heat, the filtrate from many pathological sera yields higher filtrate waves than filtrates from normal sera (18,19,123). This finding has led to the development of a variety of filtrate tests for cancer.

B. NATURE OF FILTRATE MATERIAL PRODUCED BY ALKALINE DENATU-
RATION OF PROTEIN

1. Albumose or Peptone. The filtrate test proposed by Brdička
(19), which has been widely accepted with only minor modifications,
is as follows: 0.4 ml. serum is added to 1.0 ml. 0.1N potassium hydroxide and left to digest at room temperature for 30 or 45 minutes.
At that time the protein is precipitated by the addition of 1.0 ml. of
20% sulfosalicylic acid. After 10 minutes' standing, the solution is
filtered through hard filter paper and 0.5 ml. of the clear filtrate is
added to 5.0 ml. of TriCo buffer ($10^{-3}M$ Co(NH$_3$)$_6$Cl$_3$, 0.1N NH$_4$Cl,
and 0.1N or 1N NH$_4$OH). Brdička found that a high concentration
of ammonium hydroxide does not precipitate the cobalt in trivalent
cobalt solution and is beneficial in making the double wave more
prominent. The 10-minute wait after precipitation before filtration
was recommended because the filtrate waves decrease in height the
longer the filtrate is in contact with the precipitate, probably because
the active material is adsorbed on the precipitate (19,23).

Brdička ascribes the polarographic filtrate wave to the cystine
groups of a protein-like, sulfosalicylic acid-soluble substance because
of its catalytic nature and characteristic shape. Furthermore, he
analyzed completely hydrolyzed filtrate material for cysteine and
found that the ratio of the cysteine content of different hydrolysates
was the same as the ratio of the corresponding filtrate waves (19).
Even more recently (22), Brdička still held the opinion that "the
substance causing the polarographic filtrate wave is a protein degradation product of albumose or peptone character containing cystine
nuclei."

2. Mucoid. However, Brdička's explanation has been challenged
from the start. For instance, Waldschmidt-Leitz (122), after dialyzing the sulfosalicylic acid filtrate, fractionated the filtrate material by
adding different amounts of ethanol. He stated that the precipitate
obtained at 66% ethanol concentration represented the total active
fraction of cancer sera and that it was sulfur free. At higher ethanol
concentrations sulfur-containing breakdown products were precipitated. This fraction was considered similar to *mucoids* because of its
nitrogen and glucosamine content. In infections, the increase in
activity was found in the 66–80% ethanol fraction which contains
sulfur.

On the other hand, Mayer (65) always found sulfur in the 66% ethanol precipitate. By means of alcohol fractionation, this investigator isolated from the sulfosalicylic acid filtrate of heat-denatured human serum a material giving the polarographic double wave. It had an isoelectric point of 3.4 and was found to contain considerable quantities of total sulfur, but none of it in the form of cysteine and only a little in the form of cystine, whether it was from normal or from carcinomatous blood. Since it also contained carbohydrate and glucosamine, Mayer believed that it was a *mucoid-like substance.*

Bergh et al. (8) were intrigued by a large polarographic double wave which they obtained with urine in TriCo buffer and for which they found no suitable explanation. None of the numerous substances suspected, whether they contained sulfur or not, gave catalytic waves of sufficient magnitude. Hence they concluded that the filtrate reaction must involve more than cystine or mucoids. These authors found the filtrate material heat stable and nondialyzable through cellophane, but their attempts at extracting it from urine were not sufficiently successful to get a better analysis.

3. Proteose, Mucoprotein, Acid Glycoprotein, Orosomucoid. Winzler et al. (125) found that precipitation of undenatured plasma protein with trichloroacetic acid left essentially the same amount of filtrate material as the sulfosalicylic acid precipitation. (Since trichloroacetic acid is reducible at the DME, the comparison had to be made on filtrate materials after extensive dialysis.) This demonstrated a similarity between the polarographic filtrate test and such nonpolarographic tests as the "double nitrogen" of Hahn (36), the "albumosemia" of Wolff (128), and the "tyrosine index of serum polypeptides" by Goiffon and Spaey (34). These older tests, depending on differences between trichloroacetic acid as a protein precipitant on the one hand, and phosphotungstic acid, phosphomolybdic acid, or tungstic acid on the other hand, showed essentially the same difference between normal and pathological blood samples as the polarographic filtrate test. It is therefore understandable why the polarographic test is not likely to have any greater specificity for cancer diagnosis than nonpolarographic tests that rely on the same fundamental analysis.

Winzler et al. (125) called the filtrate material *proteose* and found about 50 mg. of proteose nitrogen per 100 ml. in the blood of cancerous rats, while normal blood contained only 3–4 mg./100 ml. This proteose

material was isolated from pooled undenatured rat blood by precipitating the proteins with sulfosalicylic acid and subjugating the
filtrate to dialysis against tap water. The nondialyzable residue was
then dried from the frozen state at low pressure. It showed essentially
the same polarographic activity as material that was precipitated
from the sulfosalicylic acid filtrate with six volumes of ethanol,
following the procedure of Waldschmidt-Leitz (122). The chemical
analysis of the proteose material obtained from *normal* rat blood
revealed that either preparation was low in nitrogen (9%) and high in
sulfur content (6%) on an ash-free basis. The explanation that a
conjugate with sulfosalicylic acid was responsible was abandoned
later (126) when preparations made by precipitation in $0.6M$ perchloric acid (see also (89)) gave the same low nitrogen data but a much
lower sulfur content (1.3%). In agreement with Mayer's earlier

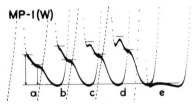

Fig. 13. Polarogram of Winzler's mucoprotein (MP-1) in standard TriCo
buffer, at concentrations of (*a*) 15, (*b*) 20, (*c*) 25, and (*d*) 30 mg./100 ml.; (*e*) is the
buffer blank.

results (65), this material contained much carbohydrate (15%) and
hexosamine (12%) and was consequently called a *mucoprotein* (126).
The mucoproteins were found to be a mixture of three components,
with isoelectric points of 2.3, 3.4, and 4.3, that could be identified by
electrophoresis; they were labeled MP-1, MP-2, and MP-3, respectively (66). The concentration of these mucoproteins is increased
over normal levels in a large percentage of patients with cancer
(127).

A sample of MP-1 (kindly given to us by Dr. Winzler) was analyzed
in our laboratory. It gave a filtrate wave in TriCo buffer (82) which
had a higher first wave at all concentrations tested, as illustrated in
Figure 13. Furthermore, it showed practically no change resulting
from alkaline digestion. Kalous (50) made a similar observation in
electrophoretic studies of plasma subjected to peptic digestion; the

MP-1 concentration remained unaltered in the sulfosalicylic acid filtrate.

This leads to the conclusion that the MP-1 exists preformed in the plasma and does not require protein denaturation for its liberation.

Although MP-1, which is the most important of the mucoprotein fractions, moves with the α-globulin fraction during electrophoresis at pH 8.4, it is most likely left unprecipitated in fraction VI of Cohn's alcohol fractionation procedure (28). The *acid glycoprotein* isolated by Schmid (91) from this fraction VI seems to be identical with the mucoprotein. A sample of this material (kindly furnished by Dr. Schmid) was also tested in our laboratory and showed an almost identical polarographic behavior as the MP-1 sample (see Fig. 13). Winzler, who has discussed the serum glycoproteins in an earlier volume of this book (124) has suggested that the term *orosomucoid* be used for this material.

C. FILTRATES FROM HUMAN PLASMA PROTEIN FRACTIONS AS A FUNCTION OF TIME OF ALKALINE DENATURATION

In order to get a further insight into the nature and significance of the filtrate wave of plasma, filtrates from the same human plasma fractions that had been studied in the activation and decay reactions were analyzed as a function of time of digestion. The proteins were digested in an alkaline medium at room temperature for different lengths of time, precipitated with sulfosalicylic acid, filtered, and the filtrates analyzed in TriCo buffer. The procedure used by the writer is described in detail in Section VIII-2-C in connection with the filtrate test.

Some typical polarograms showing the effect of time of digestion of the filtrate waves of fractions III and IV-1 of human plasma are illustrated in Figure 14. The data obtained with six human plasma fractions (77) are summarized in the graph shown in Figure 15. It is obvious that the behavior of fractions III and IV is markedly different from that of fractions I, II, and V. On the basis of this, one must conclude that only the α and β globulins of fractions III and IV can contribute significantly to that material in the filtrate reaction which increases in polarographic activity upon alkaline digestion. Surprisingly, fraction II, which is known to contain antibodies, fails to contribute to this reaction which becomes so marked in febrile diseases.

Contrary to expectation, serum albumin (fraction V) produced

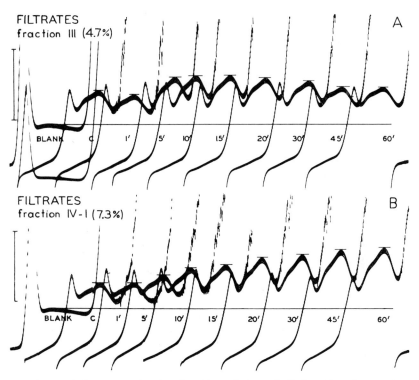

Fig. 14. Polarograms showing the effect of time of alkaline digestion on the filtrate waves of (A) fraction III, and (B) fraction IV-1 of human plasma. The time of digestion is indicated. C represents the undigested control. Cf. (78).

essentially no filtrate wave. This is in direct contradiction with Brdička's findings (20), according to which crystalline serum albumin produces filtrate waves (after either alkaline or peptic digestion) that are indistinguishable from those obtained with carcinomatous sera. Müller (78) did confirm that a filtrate reaction of serum albumin is found after peptic digestion in an acid medium (in contrast to the behavior in alkali), thus demonstrating a definite difference in the polarographic reaction of albumin, depending on the denaturing agent.

In view of these findings, it is difficult to explain the observations of Crossley et al. (30) on filtrates of dog sera. During alkaline digestion of normal sera, these authors found diminishing filtrate waves for

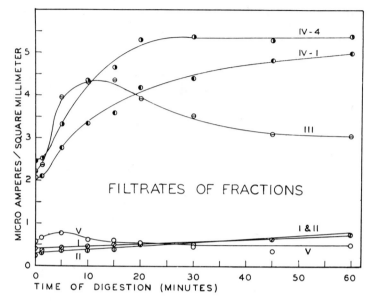

Fig. 15. Effect of time of alkaline digestion on the filtrate values from six protein fractions of human plasma. The solutions used were: fraction I, 4%; fraction II, 6.7%; fraction III, 4.7%; fraction IV-1, 7.3%; fraction IV-4, 4.3%; and fraction V, 5%. Cf. (78).

the first 10 minutes which were followed by an increase up to 60 minutes, while the reverse was true for sera from pneumonia-infected dogs.

Protein fractions were also isolated by Cohn's method 10 (28), as modified by Lever (64), from the plasma of patients with a variety of diseases (72). They consistently gave a negative filtrate test for fractions II and V. Hence, all filtrate test material liberated with time by alkaline digestion has to come from fractions III and IV (fraction I was not tested). These fractionation studies brought out again the fact that fraction VI contains material for the filtrate test that does not have to be liberated by alkaline digestion.

Kalous (51), who obtained essentially similar results, concentrated his efforts on sulfosalicylic acid filtrates from four different glycoproteins, isolated by Schultze et al. (92). The curves obtained were similar to most protein waves except for the sulfosalicylic acid filtrate from serum to which α_1 low molecular weight acid protein (probably

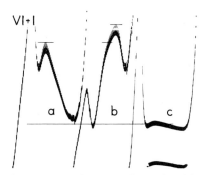

Fig. 16. Human plasma protein fraction VI-1, isolated from a cancer patient, dialyzed against 0.9% NaCl, analyzed in standard TriCo buffer (a) before, and (b) after alkaline digestion for 30 minutes; (c) is the buffer blank.

MP-1) had been added. This had the configuration of the high first wave similar to Figure 13.

The increase in the filtrate material following alkaline denaturation of fraction IV was pursued further by Kalous (53).   By precipitation with either phosphotungstic acid or ammonium sulfate, he isolated from such filtrates, materials that he could redissolve and analyze. Electrophoresis proved that most of the material found in the filtrate from the denatured fraction IV moved with the same velocity in the electric field as component MP-2 of normal plasma.   Kalous therefore concluded that probably α_2 globulins of fraction IV are the source of the material.   Compared to MP-1, this MP-2 material had about twice the polarographic activity in TriCo buffer.   This result is in agreement with earlier work of Kalous and Pavliček (55) in which the α_2-globulin fraction had been isolated from fraction IV by 30–50% saturation with ammonium sulfate, and found to give a polarographic filtrate reaction after alkaline denaturation.

It may therefore be concluded that the filtrate reaction deals with preformed material (MP-1) as well as material liberated by alkaline denaturation (MP-2, from the α_2-globulin fraction).   Additional substances will undoubtedly be found.   For instance, some active material obtained as fraction VI-1 from the plasma of a cancer patient by the method of Schmid (91) gave curves with only one peak in TriCo buffer before digestion (Fig. 16a) and developed a second peak at a more negative potential without affecting the first peak after digestion with alkali (Fig. 16b) (82).

In this connection should be mentioned the fact that such single-peaked waves in TriCo buffer may also be obtained with ultrafiltrates obtained from pooled plasma through a parlodion-covered Giemsa ultrafilter (82). The single peak in these instances occurs at about -1.5 v. (vs. SCE), i.e., near the first peak of the protein double wave, and therefore is of special interest. Further studies have to determine its significance.

D. ENZYMATIC DENATURATION OF PROTEINS

While the preceding denaturation studies have helped to indicate in what protein fractions changes occur during alkaline digestion in the test tube, they tell us nothing about changes that proteins may undergo in the living body. In this respect, polarographic investigations of the effects of proteolytic enzymes should prove more rewarding. However, so far, only scanty information is available.

1. Pepsin Treatment in Acid Medium at 37–40° C. According to Brdička, plasma and serum albumin are denatured in an acid peptic digest and produce higher double waves in DiCo buffer. This denaturation also produces split products from (presumably human) crystalline serum albumin that are soluble in sulfosalicylic acid and give a filtrate wave in TriCo buffer (19). Brdička's findings were confirmed in our laboratory for crystalline bovine albumin and also for human γ globulin (fraction II). The growth of the double wave in DiCo buffer was abrupt and essentially complete in one minute of enzymatic digestion in the case of crystalline bovine albumin (72). A similar growth in the case of human γ globulin was slow, not as extensive, and did not reach a limit in 60 minutes of peptic digestion at 37° C. After 30 minutes' exposure to pepsin, the filtrate waves obtained with crystalline bovine albumin were about 100 times as large as those obtained with human γ globulin, but even the latter material gave waves with a magnitude of 4–5 μa./mm.^{2}.

2. Digestion with Trypsin. The effect of trypsin has been studied sporadically. Jühling et al. (47) found that during the tryptic digestion of fibrinogen, the first protein wave gradually disappears while the second continues to grow. Actually their published polarograms show that both waves grow with time of digestion, but that they eventually overlap to such an extent that the first wave can no longer be measured. In a similar study of the tryptic digestion of insulin, Tropp and Herrbach (118) found a diminution of both protein waves with time of digestion, followed by an increase in the second wave which took on an entirely different shape. Hata and Matsushita (39) found that trypsin had no effect on the polarographic wave of ovalbumin as long as this was in the native state. After ovalbumin is denatured by treatment with alkali, its first wave decreases during the course of tryptic digestion while the second wave increases for 20–40 minutes (depending on pH) before it, too, decreases. These authors also studied sulfosalicylic acid filtrates of these digests and found that there was an increase in both protein waves with time of digestion. A similar observation on the sulfosalicylic acid-soluble portions of tryptic digests of dog sera had been made by Crossley et al. (30), who failed to find measurable differences in the rate of tryptic digestion of normal and infected sera.

Müller and Yamanouchi (84) found that trypsin at 37° C. in a medium of pH 7.1 digests either human or bovine serum albumin, producing increases in the height of the second wave in DiCo buffer without reaching a limit in 5 hours. Apparently the height of the first wave remains unaltered under these conditions. At the same time split products are formed that are soluble in sulfosalicylic acid and produce filtrate waves in TriCo buffer. These increase rapidly in height for the first hour and then remain relatively constant. This behavior and the magnitude of the increases depends to a certain extent on the kind of trypsin used and is not necessarily connected with the activity of the enzyme as determined by standard methods. When γ globulin of human or bovine origin was similarly tested, it was found very resistant to the action of trypsin. At high enzyme concentrations, changes in the wave heights are found, but control experiments have proved that this is caused by self-digestion of the trypsin. Prolonged storage of the γ globulin in the refrigerator (perhaps contamination), or a short alkaline denaturation of the γ globulin renders it susceptible to attack by trypsin (84). Similarly, alkali denatured albumin is also much more labile and gives rise to more sulfosalicylic acid-soluble products than fresh material during tryptic digestion. Since alkali-denatured albumin itself does not give a filtrate wave, this finding is of considerable interest.

An outstanding peculiarity of the filtrate waves of tryptic digests of crystalline bovine albumin in TriCo buffer is the fact that they produce an almost pure first protein peak (82). This single peak grows with concentration, as may be seen from Figure 17. The material

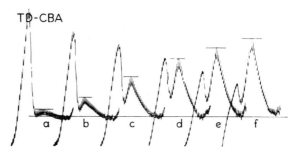

Fig. 17. Tryptic digest (4 hours) of crystalline bovine albumin, precipitated with sulfosalicylic acid, and filtered. Filtrate dialyzed first against phosphate buffer and finally against distilled water (4 days). Dialysate polarographed in standard TriCo buffer in (*a*) 1%, (*b*) 2%, (*c*) 4%, (*d*) 6%, (*e*) 8%, and (*f*) 10% concentrations. Horizontal base line is the diffusion current of cobalt found during the analysis of a blank.

responsible for this is so stable that it produces the same wave when dissolved in the TriCo buffer after having been dried on the steam bath. Because of these results and since trypsin is known to disrupt polypeptide chains near arginine and lysine linkages, Müller (78) suggested that perhaps either of these amino acids, or both, as part of the protein or polypeptide, give rise to the first protein wave. If alkali-denatured albumin is used as substrate for the tryptic digestion, the filtrate material yields a double wave in TriCo buffer. This indicates that trypsin splits off different products from native and denatured albumin (72).

VII. BRDIČKA REACTION IN OTHER MEDIA

1. Nickelous Salts

For completeness' sake, it should be mentioned that a reaction similar to the Brdička reaction can also be obtained in a suitably buffered solution of nickelous salts (24). Cystine and protein yield only a single wave in this solution which is much smaller than in corresponding cobaltous salt solutions. Hence this reaction has not aroused much interest.

2. Glycine Buffer

A similar statement may be made about the finding that catalytic reactions of proteins and cystine can also be produced in cobaltous salts buffered with other than ammonium hydroxide and ammonium chloride. For instance, Kalous (49) prepared cobalt-containing glycine buffers with different buffer capacities and over a pH range of 8.7 to 10.8, and studied the behavior of insulin in this medium. The catalytic polarographic waves obtained could be interpreted in a similar fashion as was done by Millar (69) for varying pH and buffer capacity of ammonium chloride–ammonia buffers.

VIII. PRACTICAL (CLINICAL) APPLICATIONS

1. Polarographic "Indexes"

Although the previous sections have been written to demonstrate the usefulness of the Brdička reaction in typically biochemical problems such as the reactions and characterizations of proteins, enzymes, amino acids, and other substances, the major applications of this reaction have so far been in the clinical laboratory as a diagnostic aid. For this purpose, direct comparison of the unknown with a so-called "normal" on an entirely empirical basis may be adequate, but such a procedure makes it very difficult to compare results obtained in one laboratory with data from another laboratory. Furthermore, the securing of "normal" controls is a nuisance and such "normals" vary among themselves.

To make direct comparisons possible, even with empirical data, Müller and Davis (80) suggested that two polarographic tests be carried out under identical conditions, i.e., the same DME, drop time, temperature, etc., and that then the *ratio* of the values obtained by the two tests be used as an index characteristic of the given unknown. This principle has been incorporated in the *protein index* (80); it has also been applied in several other instances. Balle-Helaers (1) has expressed some of her filtrate data in per cent of the wave height obtained with either native or alkali-denatured sera. In the so-called *glycoprotein index* (4), the height of the filtrate wave is expressed as a fraction of the wave height of electrophoretically isolated α_1 and α_2 globulins *in the same chemical medium*. The *SM index* of Wada (121) is the ratio of two filtrate waves, one obtained after deproteinization with sulfosalicylic acid and the other after deproteinization with methanol.

2. The Protein Index

A. NORMAL VALUE

The protein index is based on the ratio of the polarographic wave heights obtained in two tests, the digest test and the filtrate test. If the current values obtained in both tests are expressed in the same units, then the protein index is filtrate test/digest test, multiplied by an arbitrary constant of 15.

The protein index of normal individuals is 2.4 ± 0.17, with a standard deviation of 0.95 (81). It is independent of age, except for newborn infants, where it is low (129). It is independent of sex, menstruation, and ovulation, but it may rise slightly in a pregnant woman towards term (although it will still remain within normal limits) (81).

Sufficient data for statistical analysis of the protein index of animals have not yet been collected. Compared to man, the normal protein index appears to be about the same in cows (9) and rats, slightly higher in dogs, horses, and monkeys, and somewhat lower in rabbits (81).

In general, values for the digest test will decrease, while values for the filtrate test will increase, in abnormal blood samples. The protein index, being the ratio of the two, will therefore reflect both of these changes and increase even more. In severe cases, protein index values approaching 20 have been reached. Cancer and infectious diseases are known to increase the protein index most markedly, while hepatic disorders (cirrhosis) tend to lower it (see, however, ref. (9)).

The digest and filtrate tests are usually carried out on oxalated plasma; they can be readily adapted to any other protein-containing solution. The procedures used in our laboratory will now be described in some detail.

B. DIGEST TEST

Procedure. Pipet 0.5 ml. of oxalated plasma into a 15 × 125 mm. test tube, add 0.5 ml. of distilled water and 0.25 ml. of $1N$ potassium hydroxide solution and mix thoroughly by shaking. Let stand at room temperature (which should be near 25°C.) in the resulting $0.2N$ KOH medium for exactly 30 minutes (for time studies use shorter intervals of time). Then pipet 0.05 ml. (Kahn pipet graduated in 0.001 ml.) of the protein digest into 10.0 ml. of the standard DiCo buffer ($1.6 \times 10^{-3}M$ CoCl$_2$, $0.1N$ NH$_4$Cl, and $0.1N$ NH$_4$OH) contained in a 20-ml. beaker. This solution is thoroughly mixed by stirring and polarographed immediately, open to air, starting at -0.8 v. (vs. SCE). An undigested protein solution, to which water has been added, serves as control when needed.

Standard DiCo Buffer. This buffer has to be fresh. It is best prepared, just before use, from a stable stock solution and ammonium hydroxide. The stock solution is made up as follows:

  (a)   200 ml. $0.008M$ CoCl$_2$ solution
        plus 100 ml. $1.0N$ NH$_4$Cl solution
        plus 600 ml.   distilled water

or

  (b)   0.3807 g. CoCl$_2 \cdot 6$H$_2$O
        plus 5.35 g. NH$_4$Cl
        made up to 900 ml. with distilled water.

To 90 ml. of this stock solution are then added 10.0 ml. $1.0N$ ammonium hydroxide to make 100 ml. of standard DiCo buffer. This is good for 1–2 hours if kept in a glass-stoppered bottle. It is not advisable to make up more than 100 ml. of the buffer at any one time. (*Note:* The ammonium hydroxide must always be added last to prevent precipitation of the cobalt.)

The time of 30 minutes for digestion was originally chosen because Brdička (18) had found it to produce maximum growth of the protein double wave of normal sera. According to the data presented in Section VI-2-A, this is not quite the case, since the decay reaction has already started. However, since a peak value is probably more difficult to evaluate, the choice of the 30-minute time interval is probably fortuitous.

The results of the digest test need not always be used as part of the protein index. When they are expressed in terms of current density, they can be compared directly with other digest test values. For normal individuals, the current densities of the digest test stay within reasonably narrow limits and they vary even less for a given individual. Statistical analysis of 32 normal individuals yielded a *normal value of the digest test* of 16.7 ± 0.17 μa./mm.^{2} with a standard deviation of 0.97 (81).

On the basis of very few samples analyzed, the following digest test values may be expected in animals (in μa./mm.[2]): 12–14 in the monkey; 8–10 in the horse; 11–13 in the dog; 13–16 in the rabbit; and 10–12 in the rat.

C. FILTRATE TEST

Procedure. Pipet 0.5 ml. of oxalated plasma into a 15 × 125 mm. test tube, add 1.0 ml. of distilled water and 0.1 ml. of 1N potassium hydroxide and mix thoroughly by shaking. Let stand at room temperature (which should be near 25°C.) for 30 minutes (for time studies more samples have to be prepared and each left standing for varying time intervals) and then add 1.0 ml. of a 20 g./100 ml. solution of sulfosalicylic acid. Seal the test tube with a piece of parafilm and mix the contents thoroughly by inverting the tube. The resulting precipitate is left to stand in contact with the filtrate for exactly 10 minutes. Then filter the mixture through a Whatman No. 5 filter paper with a diameter of 55 mm. into a small (12 × 75 mm.) test tube where the filtrate can be kept (sealed with parafilm) for some time before analysis.

This filtrate contains the sulfosalicylic acid-soluble material from a 1% protein solution that has been digested for 30 minutes in 0.063N KOH. Thus the digestion mixture in the filtrate test is not the same as that of the digest test. The reason is that in applying these tests we made every effort to adhere reasonably close to the original tests of Brdička.

When a number of filtrates have been collected they are analyzed as follows: 0.5 ml. of the clear filtrate is added to 5.0 ml. of a TriCo buffer (0.001M hexaminocobaltic chloride, 0.1N ammonium chloride, 0.8N ammonium hydroxide) in a 10-ml. beaker and thoroughly mixed. The mixture is polarographed immediately, open to air, starting at -0.8 v. (vs. SCE).

Standard TriCo Buffer. This buffer is made up in small quantities from the following three stock solutions:

(*a*) 0.01M Hexaminocobaltic chloride: 1.337 g. $Co(NH_3)_6Cl_3$ made up to 500 ml. with distilled water. This solution is quite stable.

(*b*) 1.0N ammonium chloride: 53.5 g. NH_4Cl made up to 1000 ml. with distilled water.

(*c*) 1.0N ammonium hydroxide: If the commercially available ammonia water is quite fresh, about 34 ml. of it, diluted with distilled water to 500 ml. will give an approximately $1N$ solution. Since most stocks which have been on the shelves for some time have lost ammonia, it is best to prepare a slightly more concentrated solution at first and adjust it to $1.0N$ by dilution after its titer against a standard acid has been determined. Frequent checks should be made to be sure of the constancy of this solution, which is best kept in a refrigerator.

The TriCo buffer is prepared by mixing 10.0 ml. portions of stock solutions a and b with 80.0 ml. of stock solution c. With proper precautions against loss of ammonia (storage in a refrigerator and infrequent exposure to the atmosphere) this solution may be kept for several months. On the other hand, the loss of ammonia from an open beaker is so rapid that the 5.0 ml. needed for the polarographic analysis should be pipetted immediately before the filtrate is added.

Like the data for the digest test, the results of the filtrate test can be expressed in terms of current density and compared directly with other filtrate test values. Statistical analysis (of the same 32 normal plasma samples used in the digest test) yielded the following *normal value of the filtrate test:* 2.72 ± 0.18 μa./mm.^{2} with a standard deviation of 1.01 (81).

For animals, one may expect the following filtrate test values (in μa./mm.^{2}): 3–5 in the monkey and dog; 1–3 in the horse, rabbit, and rat.

D. VARIATIONS OF DIGEST AND FILTRATE TESTS

Numerous variations of these tests have been suggested to improve either the accuracy of the technique or increase its diagnostic usefulness. They obviously cannot be considered in detail in this article, but some of the more important aspects will be briefly mentioned.

1. Removal of Oxygen. Analyses at lower concentrations become possible if dissolved oxygen is removed, because one can work at higher galvanometer sensitivities. This advantage is balanced by the extra time lost between preparation of the sample and its analysis, which may cause denaturation of the protein in the buffer. Also, the possibility exists that the ammonia concentration is altered because of the volatility of ammonia, and that solution is lost because of foaming, if protein is present.

2. Maximum Suppressors. These are favored by many who prefer to have the cobalt maximum removed. However, there is always the danger that the maximum suppressor will also affect the catalytic waves. Gelatine, tylose, and caffeine have been frequently used for this purpose.

3. *Concentration of Ammonium Hydroxide.* For the DiCo buffer, almost without exception a $0.1N$ concentration has been used. It is probably the highest concentration possible before the cobalt will precipitate out. However, in the TriCo buffer the situation is different. Here, concentrations of $0.1N$ ammonium hydroxide were originally used by Brdička (18) for studies of ordinary protein digests. However, when the filtrate reaction had been developed, the addition of 0.5 ml. 20% sulfosalicylic acid ($0.8M$) to 5 ml. $0.1N$ buffer essentially neutralized all the ammonium hydroxide so that Brdička went to $1N$ ammonium hydroxide to improve the situation (19). The writer has consistently used $0.8N$ ammonium hydroxide in the TriCo buffer with good results; Winzler et al. (125) found $0.7N$ solutions equally satisfactory. The slightly lower ammonium hydroxide solutions have the advantage that the cobalt maximum is not as large as in the higher concentrations. Hence they are also more easily suppressed by the polypeptides or by maximum suppressors. In this respect it is interesting to note that Stricks et al. (103) were able to suppress their cobalt maximum with caffeine only when part of the buffer had been neutralized by the addition of sulfosalicylic acid.

4. *Use of Volumetric Flasks vs. Pipets.* The procedures described above involve some very careful pipetting of small quantities which requires considerable practice before reproducible results are obtained. In the method of Stricks et al. (103) for the filtrate test, this is avoided by pipetting 0.5 ml. plasma and 1.25 ml. of $0.1N$ KOH into a 5-ml. volumetric flask, where it is left for 30 minutes to digest at 25°C. Then 1.5 ml. 20% SSA is added, the mixture shaken and diluted to the mark, again shaken, transferred to a centrifuge tube, and then centrifuged for about 8 minutes; 1.0 ml. of the centrifugate is added to a mixture of 0.5 ml. of $3 \times 10^{-2} M$ hexaminocobaltic chloride, 0.5 ml. $1N$ NH_4Cl, 1.0 ml. $5N$ NH_4OH, and 1.0 ml. distilled water, which is in another 5-ml. volumetric flask, and diluted to the mark with distilled water. This solution is then polarographed.

5. *Centrifugation vs. Filtration of the Filtrate.* It is generally recognized that the process of filtration removes some of the polarographically active material and that therefore identical procedures

must be used to obtain reproducible results. The use of sintered glass filters has therefore been considered as well as centrifugation of the filtrate. Sekla and Krejčí (93) claim better reproducibility when they centrifugate the filtrate ($\pm 3.9\%$) than wčen they use filter paper ($\pm 8.5\%$); they also get higher filtrate waves with centrifugation than with filtration through either paper or sintered glass filters. [See also Stricks et al. (103) and Ledvina and Coufalova (63).] However, for series analyses it will be difficult in the case of centrifugations to maintain accurate contact times between the precipitate and the filtrate, a factor of considerable importance and easily maintained constant in the case of filtrations.

6. Comparison Standards. In order to avoid the use of a "normal" blood sample as standard of comparison, several other standards have been proposed. For instance, Tropp (115) compared his protein waves to the catalytic wave of a $2.5 \times 10^{-4}M$ cystine solution (when this was prepared in $0.01N$ hydrochloric acid and kept in a refrigerator, it was stable for a long time).

An artificial double wave in TriCo buffer which did not involve any protein was developed by Balle-Helaers (2). This author found that cystamine (the disulfide of β-mercaptoethylamine) gave a single wave in TriCo buffer that could be modified by the addition of tylose (a polysaccharide) to the solution. By a suitable choice of concentrations of these two materials a tylose–cystamine double wave resembling that of protein could be obtained and used as a conveniently prepared standard for comparison. [See also Shinagawa (95).]

More recently, a biochemical standard has been prepared by freeze-drying that can be used to check the Brdička reaction (18).

In view of the fact that it is possible to prepare master curves of proteins in which the relationship of current density to concentration is clearly established, the writer feels that no further need exists for synthetically created reference curves.

3. Polarographic Analysis of Protein Fractions Separated by Paper Electrophoresis

Although this method has so far been used very little, it seems to have tremendous possibilities, not only because it is applicable to micro quantities but also because the electrophoretically isolated fractions can be subjected to further treatment before polarography without removal of the paper. It is particularly interesting in this respect that even fractions that have first been dyed on the paper for identification purposes and then subjected to alkaline denaturation appear to give polarographic results that are fairly quantitative. The status of this application of polarography may be inferred from the following three examples.

Homolka (42) introduced this technique in 1952. He subjected 0.030 ml. of serum to electrophoresis on a 5-cm. wide strip of paper for 24 hours, and then dried the paper at 37°C. To locate the bands, a 1-cm. wide strip was then cut off and developed. The remaining paper was marked accordingly, cut up into 17 suitable pieces, each of which was eluted in a test tube with 0.9% sodium chloride solution. An appropriate amount of TriCo buffer was then added to each eluate and the mixture analyzed polarographically. Spacing the analyses properly on a polarogram, Homolka could draw lines between the peak values of each analysis and thus produce a polarographic electrophero-gram.

Balle-Helaers (3) investigated the polarographic behavior of paper-electrophoretic fractions of 10 mm.^{3} of serum, before and after color-ation, and before and after alkaline denaturation. On the basis of comparisons with spectrophotometric analyses and a biuret test, this author concluded that all the undyed fractions (either before or af-ter denaturation) had a reduced polarographic activity and no satis-factory correlation with the color intensity. In contrast to this, the dyed fractions showed that the alkaline denaturation gave activities essentially proportional to the color intensity of the samples (except for γ globulin).

Kalous (51) applied this technique to a more detailed analysis of the filtrate materials. After removing all sulfosalicylic acid from the filtrate by dialysis, the residue (concentrated by freeze-drying) was placed on filter paper, moistened with pH 4.6 acetate buffer and sub-jected to electrophoresis. Thus 3–5 components could be separated (recognized by staining with bromophenol blue on a separate strip), the appropriate paper sections cut apart, and the fractions eluted in TriCo buffer (53,54). Polarograms recorded with these eluates showed catalytic waves with heights that more or less paralleled the color intensities.

Acknowledgments

Much of the work that has been reported from this laboratory was supported by grants Nos. C-716 and C-2358 from the Division of Research Grants and Fellowships of the National Institutes of Health, U.S. Public Health Service, which are gratefully acknowledged. I also wish to thank Miss Mary Jane Elwood, Miss Patricia Folse, and Dr. Lester H. Gershenfeld for valuable assistance.

For the samples of human plasma protein fractions my thanks go to Dr. Mulford, then of the Division of Biological Laboratories of the Massachusetts Department of Public Health, and for the fractions of animal plasma I am indebted to Dr. Lachat of Armour and Co., Chicago.

References

1. Balle-Helaers, E., *Arch. Belges Med. Sociale, Hyg., Méd. Travail et Méd. Legale, 8,* 401 (1956).
2. Balle-Helaers, E., *Bruxelles-méd., 36,* 339 (1956); *Chem. Abstr., 50,* 10900 (1956).
3. Balle-Helaers, E., *Clin. Chim. Acta, 3,* 51 (1958).
4. Balle-Helaers, E., *Z. anal. Chem., 173,* 105 (1960).
5. Beach, E., S. B. Bernstein, F. C. Hummel, H. H. Williams, and I. G. Macy, *J. Biol. Chem., 130,* 115 (1939).
6. Benesch, R., and R. E. Benesch, *Arch. Biochem., 19,* 35 (1948).
7. Benesch, R. E., H. A. Lardy, and R. Benesch, *J. Biol. Chem., 216,* 663 (1955).
8. Bergh, F., O. M. Henriques, and C. G. Wolffbrandt, *Nature, 142,* 212 (1938).
9. Bodya, K., *Tr. Mosk. Vet. Akad., 21,* 147 (1957); through *Chem. Abstr., 52,* 17455 (1958).
10. Bonting, S. L., Jr., *Biochim. Biophys. Acta, 6,* 183 (1950).
11. Brdička, R., *Collection Czechoslov. Chem. Commun., 5,* 112 (1933).
12. Brdička, R., *Collection Czechoslov. Chem. Commun., 5,* 148 (1933).
13. Brdička, R., *Collection Czechoslov. Chem. Commun., 5,* 238 (1933).
14. Brdička, R., *Biochem. Z., 272,* 104 (1934).
15. Brdička, R., *Collection Czechoslov. Chem. Commun., 9,* 76 (1937).
16. Brdička, R., *Nature, 139,* 330 (1937).
17. Brdička, R., *Nature, 139,* 1020 (1937).
18. Brdička, R., *Acta Unio Intern. contra Cancrum, 3,* 13 (1938).
19. Brdička, R., *Acta Radiol. Cancerol. Bohem. Morav., 2,* 7 (1939).
20. Brdička, R., *Klin. Wochschr., 18,* 305 (1939).
21. Brdička, R., *Collection Czechoslov. Chem. Commun., 11,* 614 (1939).
22. Brdička, R., *Research (London), 1,* 25 (1947).
23. Brdička, R., F. V. Novak, and J. Klumpar, *Acta Radiol. Cancerol. Bohem. Morav., 2,* 27 (1939).
24. Březina, M., in I. M. Longmuir, ed., *Advances in Polarography,* Pergamon Press, Oxford, 1960, Vol. 3, p. 933.
25. Březina, M., and P. Zuman, *Polarography in Medicine, Biochemistry and Pharmacy,* (in Czech) Zdravodnicke Nakladatelstvi, Prague, 1952; (in German) Akademische Verlagsgesellschaft, Leipzig, 1956; (in English) Interscience, New York–London, 1958.

26. Calvin, M., in S. Colowick, A. Lazarow, E. Racker, D. R. Schwarz, E. Stadt-man, and H. Waelsch, eds., *Glutathione*, Academic Press, New York, 1954, pp. 21–25.
27. Clarke, H. T., in S. Colowick et al., eds., *Glutathione*, Academic Press, New York, 1954, p. 30.
28. Cohn, E. J., F. R. N. Gurd, D. M. Surgenor, B. A. Barnes, R. K. Brown, G. Derouaux, J. M. Gillespie, F. W. Kahnt, W. F. Lever, C. H. Liu, D. Mittelman, R. F. Mouton, K. Schmid, and E. Uroma, *J. Am. Chem. Soc.*, 72, 465 (1950).
29. Cohn, E. J., L. E. Strong, W. L. Hughes, Jr., D. J. Mulford, J. N. Ash-worth, M. Melin, and H. L. Taylor, *J. Am. Chem. Soc.*, 68, 459 (1946).
30. Crossley, M. L., R. H. Kienle, B. Vassel, and G. L. Christopher, *J. Lab. Clin. Med.*, 27, 213 (1941).
31. Delahay, P., *New Instrumental Methods in Electrochemistry*, Interscience, New York-London, 1954.
32. Dent, C. E., B. Senior, and J. M. Walshe, *J. Clin. Invest.*, 33, 1216 (1954).
33. Fraser, J. B., L. N. Owen, and G. Shaw, *Biochem. J.*, 41, 328 (1947).
34. Goiffon, R., and J. Spaey, *Bull. soc. chim. biol.*, 16, 1675 (1934).
35. Green, N. M., and H. Neurath, in H. Neurath and K. Bailey, eds., *The Proteins*, Vol. II-B, Academic Press, New York, 1954, p. 1057.
36. Hahn, A., *Biochem. Z.*, 121, 262 (1921).
37. Hamamoto, E., and I. Yamanouchi, *Sbornik mezinárod. Polarog. sjezdu Praze, 1st Congr.*, Pt. I, 77 (1951); *Chem. Abstr.*, 46, 6999 (1952).
38. Hata, T., *Mem. Res. Inst. Food Sci., Kyoto Univ.*, 1, 19 (1951).
39. Hata, T., and S. Matsushita, *Bull. Research Inst. Food Sci., Kyoto Univ.*, 10, 59 (1952); *Chem. Abstr.*, 47, 11274 (1953).
40. Heyrovský, J., and P. Zuman, *Einführung in die praktische Polarographie*, VEB Verlag Technik, Berlin, 1959, in German. The same book has also been published in Czech, Polish, and Hungarian.
41. Heyrovský, J., "Polarographisches Praktikum," in *Anleitungen für die chemische Laboratoriumspraxis*, 2nd ed., Vol. IV, Springer, Berlin, 1960.
42. Homolka, J., *Radiometer Polarographics*, 1, 110 (1952).
43. Hughes, W. L., Jr., *Cold Spring Harbor Symposia Quant. Biol.*, 14, 79 (1949).
44. Hughes, W. L., in H. Neurath and K. Bailey, eds., *The Proteins*, Vol. II-B, Academic Press, New York, 1954, p. 663.
45. Jensen, E. V., in R. Benesch et al., eds., *Sulfur in Proteins*, Academic Press, New York, 1959, p. 75.
46. Jirsa, M., and V. Kalous, *Chem. listy*, 48, 775 (1954).
47. Jühling, L., C. Tropp, and E. Wöhlisch, *Z. physiol. Chem.*, 262, 210 (1939).
48. Jurka, E., *Collection Czechoslov. Chem. Commun.*, 11, 243 (1939).
49. Kalous, V., *Collection Czechoslov. Chem. Commun.*, 21, 1227 (1956).
50. Kalous, V., *Collection Czechoslov. Chem. Commun.*, 21, 1236 (1956).
51. Kalous, V., *Z. physik. Chem.*, Sonderheft 1958, 186.
52. Kalous, V., in I. S. Longmuir, ed., *Advances in Polarography*, Pergamon Press, Oxford, 1960, Vol. 3, p. 924.
53. Kalous, V., in I. S. Longmuir, ed., *Advances in Polaroaraphy*, Pergamon Press, Oxford, 1960, Vol. 3, p. 1067.

54. Kalous, V., *Collection Czechoslov. Chem. Commun.*, *25*, 878 (1960).
55. Kalous, V., and Z. Pavliček, *Collection Czechoslov. Chem. Commun.*, *25*, 3380 (1960).
56. Kalous, V., and Z. Pavliček, *Biochim. Biophys. Acta, 57*, 44 (1962).
57. Kalous, V., and P. Valenta, *Collection Czechoslov. Chem. Commun.*, *22*, 600 (1957).
58. Ke, B., *Biochem. Biophys. Acta, 25*, 650 (1957).
59. Klumpar, J., *Collection Czechoslov. Chem. Commun.*, *13*, 11 (1948).
60. Kolthoff, I. M., and J. J. Lingane, *Polarography*, Vols. I and II, 2nd ed., Interscience, New York-London, 1952.
61. Kolthoff, I. M., W. Stricks, and L. Morren, *Anal. Chem.*, *26*, 366 (1954).
62. Lamprecht, W., S. Gudbjarnason, and H. Katzlmeier, *Z. physiol. Chem.*, *322*, 52 (1960).
63. Ledvina, M., and S. Coufalova, *Clin. Chim. Acta, 6*, 16 (1961).
64. Lever, W. F., F. R. N. Gurd, E. Uroma, R. K. Brown, B. A. Barnes, K. Schmid, and E. L. Schultz, *J. Clin. Invest.*, *30*, 99 (1951).
65. Mayer, K., *Z. physiol. Chem.*, *275*, 16 (1942).
66. Mehl, J. W., J. Humphrey, and R. J. Winzler, *Proc. Soc. Exptl. Biol. Med.*, *72*, 106 (1949).
67. Meites, L., *Polarographic Techniques*, Interscience, New York-London, 1955.
68. Millar, G. J., *Biochem. J.*, *53*, 385 (1953).
69. Millar, G. J., *Biochem. J.*, *53*, 393 (1953).
70. Miller, G. L., and V. duVigneaud, *J. Biol. Chem.*, *118*, 101 (1937).
71. Milner, G. W. C., *The Principles and Applications of Polarography*, Longmans, Green, London, 1957.
72. Müller, O. H., unpublished experiments.
73. Müller, O. H., *Am. J. Physiol.*, *133*, 393 (1941).
74. Müller, O. H., *Federation Proc.*, *8*, 115 (1949).
75. Müller, O. H., *The Polarographic Method of Analysis*, 2nd ed., Chemical Education Publishing Co., Easton, Pa., 1951.
76. Müller, O. H., *Anal. Chem.*, *23*, 1175 (1951).
77. Müller, O. H., *Federation Proc.*, *10*, 95 (1951).
78. Müller, O. H., in T. Shedlovsky, ed., *Electrochemistry in Biology and Medicine*, Wiley, New York-London, 1955, p. 301.
79. Müller, O. H., in A. Weissberger, ed., *Physical Methods of Organic Chemistry* (Technique of Organic Chemistry, Vol. I), 3rd ed., Interscience, New York-London, 1960, Part IV, p. 3155.
80. Müller, O. H., and J. S. Davis, Jr., *J. Biol. Chem.*, *159*, 667 (1945).
81. Müller, O. H., and J. S. Davis, Jr., *Arch. Biochem.*, *15*, 39 (1947).
82. Müller, O. H., and M. J. Elwood, *Federation Proc.*, *13*, 103 (1954).
83. Müller, O. H., L. H. Gershenfeld, and M. J. Elwood, *Federation Proc.*, *11*, 110 (1952).
84. Müller, O. H., and I. Yamanouchi, *Federation Proc.*, *15*, 133 (1956).
85. Müller, O. H., and I. Yamanouchi, *Federation Proc.*, *17*, 115 (1958).
86. Page, J. E., *Analyst*, *73*, 214 (1948).
87. Page, J. E., and J. G. Waller, *Analyst*, *74*, 292 (1949).

88. Reed, G., *J. Biol. Chem.*, *142*, 61 (1942).
89. Robert, B., C. deVaux-Saint-Cyr, L. Robert, and P. Grabar, *Clin. Chim. Acta*, *4*, 828 (1959).
90. Rosenthal, H. G., *Mikrochemie*, *22*, 233 (1937).
91. Schmid, K., *J. Am. Chem. Soc.*, *75*, 60 (1953).
92. Schultze, H. E., I. Göllner, K. Heide, M. Schönenberger, and G. Schwick, *Z. Naturforsch.*, *10b*, 463 (1955), quoted by Kalous (51).
93. Sekla, M., and E. Krejčí, *Casopis lékáru českých*, *93*, 630 (1954); quoted by Březina and Zuman (25).
94. Shinagawa, M., *Polarographic Method of Analysis* (in Japanese), Kyoritsu, 1952.
95. Shinagawa, M., *Bull. Chem. Soc. Japan*, *33*, 272 (1960); through *Chem. Abstr.*, *55*, 656 (1961).
96. Shinagawa, M., H. Nezu, H. Sunahara, F. Nakashima, H. Okashita, and T. Yamada, in I. S. Longmuir, ed., *Advances in Polarography*, Pergamon Press, Oxford, 1960, Vol. 3, p. 1142.
97. Sládek, J., and M. Lipschütz, *Collection Czechoslov. Chem. Commun.*, *6*, 487 (1934).
98. Smetana, J., *Časopis lékáru českých*, *99*, 1410 (1960); through *Chem. Abstr.*, *55*, 15605 (1961).
99. Smith, E. R., and C. J. Rodden, *J. Research Natl. Bur. Standards*, *22*, 669 (1939).
100. Stackelberg, M. von, *Polarographische Arbeitsmethoden*, 2nd ed., W. de Gruyter, Berlin, 1960.
101. Stern, A., and E. F. Beach, *Proc. Soc. Exptl. Biol. Med.*, *43*, 104 (1940).
102. Stern, A., E. F. Beach, and I. G. Macy, *J. Biol. Chem.*, *130*, 733 (1939).
103. Stricks, W., I. M. Kolthoff, D. G. Bush, and P. K. Kuroda, *J.-Lancet*, *73*, 328 (1953).
104. Sullivan, M. X., W. C. Hess, and E. R. Smith, *J. Biol. Chem.*, *130*, 741 (1939).
105. Sunahara, H., *Rev. Polarog. (Kyoto)*, *9*, 165 (1961).
106. Sunahara, H., *Rev. Polarog. (Kyoto)*, *9*, 222 (1961).
107. Sunahara, H., *Rev. Polarog. (Kyoto)*, *9*, 233 (1961).
108. Sunahara, H., D. N. Ward, and A. C. Griffin, *J. Am. Chem. Soc.*, *82*, 6017, 6023 (1960).
109. Tachi, I., ed., *Polarography* (in Japanese) Iwanami, Tokyo, 1954.
110. Tachi, I., and S. Koide, *Sborník mezinárod. Polarog. sjezdu Praze, 1st Congr.*, Pt. I, 450 (1951); *Chem. Abstr.*, *46*, 10012 (1952).
111. Tachi, I., and S. Koide, *Sborník mezinárod. Polarog. sjezdu Praze, 1st Congr.*, Pt. I, 469 (1951); *Chem. Abstr.*, *46*, 10012 (1952).
112. Tachi, I., and S. Koide, *J. Agr. Chem. Soc. Japan*, *26*, 249 (1952).
113. Trkal, V., *Collection Czechoslov. Chem. Commun.*, *21*, 945 (1956).
114. Tropp, C., *Klin. Wochschr.*, *17*, 465 (1938).
115. Tropp, C., *Klin. Wochschr.*, *17*, 1141 (1938).
116. Tropp, C., and F. Geiger, *Z. physiol. Chem.*, *272*, 134 (1942).
117. Tropp, C., F. Geiger, and W. Stoye, *Z. physiol. Chem.*, *277*, 192 (1943).
118. Tropp, C., and W. Herrbach, *Z. physiol. Chem.*, *281*, 50 (1944).

119. Tropp, C., L. Jühling, and F. Geiger, *Z. physiol. Chem.*, *262*, 225 (1939).
120. Tropp, C., and W. Stoye, *Z. physiol. Chem.*, *275*, 80 (1942).
121. Wada, T., *Polarography (Kyoto)*, *3*, 49 (1955); quoted by Kalous, V., *Chemie (Prague)*, *9*, 439 (1957).
122. Waldschmidt-Leitz, E., *Z. angew. Chem.*, *51*, 324 (1938).
123. Waldschmidt-Leitz, E., and K. Mayer, *Z. physiol. Chem.*, *261*, 1 (1939).
124. Winzler, R. J., in D. Glick, ed., *Methods of Biochemical Analysis*, Vol. 2, Interscience, New York-London, 1955, p. 279.
125. Winzler, R. J., D. Burk, and M. Hesselbach, *J. Natl. Cancer Inst.*, *4*, 417 (1944).
126. Winzler, R. J., A. W. Devor, J. W. Mehl, and I. M. Smith, *J. Clin. Invest.*, *27*, 609 (1948).
127. Winzler, R. J., and I. M. Smyth, *J. Clin. Invest.*, *27*, 617 (1948).
128. Wolff, E., *Ann. méd. (Paris)*, *10*, 185 (1921).
129. Yamanouchi, I., personal communication.
130. Yamanouchi, I., *Vitamins (Kyoto)*, *7*, 251 (1954).
131. Yamanouchi, I., *Vitamins (Kyoto)*, *7*, 257 (1954).
132. Yamanouchi, I., *Vitamins (Kyoto)*, *7*, 261 (1954).
133. Zuman, P., *Chem. listy, 52*, 1349 (1958); *Chem. Abstr.*, *53*, 5918 (1959).

AUTHOR INDEX*

A

Abdel-Tawab, G. A., 201, *207*
Abelson, D., 177 (ref. 2), *207*
Abrush, H. I., 236 (ref. 1), *244*
Ahawie, R. I., 266 (ref. 25), *278*
Alberty, R. A., 214 (ref. 6), 215 (ref. 6), *244*
Alcock, N., 29 (ref. 1), 55 (ref. 1), *64*
Alford, D., 323 (ref. 33), *326*
Alkemade, C. T. J., 3, 27 (ref. 46), 33 (ref. 4), *64, 66*
Allan, J. E., 3 (ref. 11b), 15 (ref. 5), 24 (ref. 8), 28, 35 (refs. 11, 12), 40–42, 48, 54, 55 (ref. 5), 56, 59, 62–64, *64, 65*
Allinson, M. J. C., 238 (ref. 2), *244*
Altschule, M. D., 313 (ref. 1), 325 (ref. 1), *325*
Ambe, K. S., 304, *305*
Ambrose, D. A., 75, *144*
Amesz, J., 220, *244*
Ammon, R., 235 (ref. 3), 236 (ref. 3), *244*
Amos, M. D., 55 (ref. 71), *66*
Anders, M. W., 71 (ref. 3), *145*
Anderson, N. G., 314 (ref. 59), 320 (ref. 59), *327*
Andrew, T. R., 56 (ref. 12a), *65*
Armstrong, M. D., 248 (ref. 1), 266, *277*
Arnstein, H. R. U., 254 (ref. 2), *277*
Aronoff, S., 254 (ref. 3), *277*
Ashman, D. F., 179 (ref. 52), *209*
Ashworth, J. N., 378 (ref. 29), *400*
Axelrod, L., 169 (ref. 3), *207*
Axelrod, J., 248 (refs. 4, 5, 7, 23, 24), 249 (refs. 8, 12, 33), 266, 268 (refs. 6, 24), 269 (refs. 23, 24), 272 (ref. 4), 273 (ref. 19), *277, 278*
Ayres, P. J., 189 (ref. 4), 197, 198, *207*, 259 (ref. 9), *277*

B

Baker, C. A., 17, 31, 33 (ref. 13), 34 (ref. 13), 38 (ref. 13), 40, *65*
Baker, R. W. R., 118, *145*
Baldwin, G. B., 212 (ref. 57), *245*
Balfour, W. E., 197, *207*
Balle-Helaers, E., 391, 397, 398, *399*
Baltscheffsky, H., 220 (ref. 17), *244*
Baptist, V. H., 177 (ref. 13), *208*
Barnes, B. A., 378 (ref. 64), 380 (ref. 64), 384 (ref. 28), 386 (refs. 28, 64), *400, 401*
Barrollier, J., 202 (refs. 5, 6), 206, *207*
Bate-Smith, E. C., 72, 133, *145*, 156 (ref. 7), 166 (ref. 7), *207*
Beach, E. F., 355 (refs. 5, 102), 358 (ref. 101), 362 (ref. 102), *399, 402*
Beard, J. W., 224 (ref. 5), *244*
Beaudreau, G. S., 224, *244*
Becker, C., 224, *244*
Beers, R. F., **Jr.**, 317, 318, *325*
Beerthuis, R. K., 71, 88 (ref. 6), *145*
Belcher, C. B., 56 (ref. 13a), *65*
Belleau, B., 253 (ref. 10), *277*
Benesch, R., 356 (ref. 6), 375 (refs. 6, 7), *399*
Benesch, R. E., 356 (ref. 6), 375 (refs. 6, 7), *399*
Bergh, F., 344, 362 (ref. 8), 366 (ref. 8), 382, *399*
Berman, M., 248 (ref. 32), *278*
Bernstein, S. S., 355 (ref. 5), *399*
Beukelman, T. E., 44 (ref. 14), *65*
Bigeleisen, J., 253 (ref. 11), *277*
Biggs, A. I., 317 (ref. 3), *325*
Bishop, D. H. L., 285 (ref. 37), *306*
Blair, A., 248 (ref. 32), *278*
Blatt, J. L., 180 (ref. 54), *209*
Block, R. J., 157, 177, 180, *208*
Blomstrand, R., 125, *145*

* Italic numbers refer to the bibliographies of the different papers.

405

Friedemann, T. E., 201, *208*
Fukushima, S., 31, 33 (ref. 38), *65*
Fuller, R. C., 285 (ref. 18), 302, *305*

G

Gale, M., 176, 194 (ref. 19), *208*
Gale, P. H., 285 (refs. 35, 36), 288 (ref. 36), 289 (ref. 30), 293 (ref. 36), 301 (ref. 30), *306*
Garcia-Hernandez, M., 214 (ref. 24), *245*
Garfinkel, D., 236 (refs. 15, 18), 237 (refs. 15, 18), *244*
Garrod, O., 259 (ref. 9), *277*
Garton, F. W. J., 17, 31, 33 (ref. 13), 34 (ref. 13), 38 (ref. 13), 40, *65*
Gatehouse, B. M., 6 (ref. 41), 12, 23, 24 (ref. 41), 25, 26, 36 (ref. 41), 37 (ref. 41), 38, 48, 55, 59 (ref. 41), 60, 61, *65, 66*
Geiger, A., 295 (ref. 12), *305*
Geiger, F., 358 (ref. 116), 367 (refs. 117, 119), *402, 403*
Gershbein, L. L., 118, *146*
Gershenfeld, L. H., 378 (ref. 83), 380 (ref. 83), *401*
Gerstenfeld, S., 238 (ref. 51), *245*
Giacobini, E., 325 (ref. 23), *326*
Gibor, A., 238 (ref. 34), *245*
Gidley, J. A. F., 3 (ref. 34), 8, 13 (ref. 42), 17 (ref. 42), 28, 54, 55, 59–61, 63, 64, *65, 66*
Gilbert, P. T., 3 (ref. 42a), 27, *66*
Gilford, S. R., 186, 188, *208*, 214 (ref. 75), 215, 216, *246*
Gillespie, J. M., 384 (ref. 28), 386 (ref. 28), *400*
Gillis, J., 42 (ref. 68), *66*
Glavind, J., 295 (ref. 12), *305*
Glenn, J. L., 303 (ref. 7), *305*
Gloor, U., 289 (ref. 34), *306*
Glueckauf, E., 102, *145*, 166
Göllner, I., 386 (ref. 92), *402*
Goiffon, R., 382, *400*
Goodall, McC., 248 (ref. 17), 268 (ref. 17), *278*
Goor, H. van, 312 (ref. 57), *327*

Gordon, E., 269 (ref. 21), 273 (refs. 19, 20), *278*
Gorsuch, T. T., 42, *66*
Gowenlock, A., 189 (ref. 31), 197, 198, *208*
Gower, D. B., 118, *145*
Grabar, P., 383 (ref. 89), *402*
Grant, P. T., 254 (ref. 2), *277*
Grassmann, W., 177, 178 (ref. 32), *208*
Graystone, J. E., 56 (ref. 19), *65*
Greaves, M. C., 55 (ref. 71), *66*
Green, D. E., 280, 303 (ref. 7), *305*
Green, J., 289 (ref. 14), 298 (ref. 14), 301 (ref. 14), 304 (ref. 14), *305*
Green, N. M., 373 (ref. 35), *400*
Gregory, N. L., 80 (ref. 36), *146*
Griffin, A. C., 357 (ref. 108), *402*
Gross, A. M., 169 (ref. 55), *209*
Grove, E. L., 42 (ref. 44), *66*
Gudbjarnason, S., 359 (ref. 62), 361–363 (ref. 62), *401*
Guggenheim, E. A., 313, *326*
Gurd, F. R. N., 378 (ref. 64), 380 (ref. 64), 384 (ref. 28), 386 (refs. 28, 64), *400, 401*

H

Haahti, E. O. A., 71 (refs. 3, 13, 18, 68), 85 (ref. 38), 90, 93 (ref. 20), 95, 96, 103 (ref. 21), 108 (ref. 38), 116, 120 (ref. 38), 122, 124 (ref. 38), 127 (ref. 68), 140, 141 (ref. 15), 144 (ref. 15), *145–147*
Hadjiioannou, S. I., 238 (ref. 40), 239 (ref. 40), 240, 242 (ref. 40), *245*
Hadjiioannou, T. P., 238 (ref. 41), 242, *245*
Hahn, A., 382, *400*
Hahn, J. W., 177 (ref. 13), *208*
Hamamoto, E., 362 (ref. 37), *400*
Hames, G. E., 8, 13 (ref. 59), 15 (ref. 59), 50, 55, *66*
Hamilton, R. J., 70 (ref. 14), *145*
Hanes, C. S., 153 (ref. 41), 157 (refs. 47, 63), 159 (refs. 24, 35, 41), 160, 162 (ref. 24), 166 (refs. 33, 35), 167, 169 (refs. 33, 34), 187, 204, 206, *208, 209*

Leiner, G., 310 (ref. 34), *326*
Leiner, M., 310 (ref. 34), *326*
Leithe, W., 3 (ref. 55), 56 (refs. 56, 57), *66*
LeRoy, G. V., 269 (ref. 28), *278*
Lester, R. L., 280, 284 (ref. 25), 285, 288 (refs. 10, 19, 25), 289 (ref. 9), 298 (ref. 9), 299 (refs. 9, 29), 300, 302–304, *305*, *306*
Lever, W. F., 378, 380, 384 (ref. 28), 386, *400*, *401*
Levine, H. J., 324 (ref. 20), *326*
Lewis, H. D., 313 (ref. 1), 325 (ref. 1), *325*
Lieberman, S., 259 (ref. 35), *278*
Liebhafsky, H. A., 177 (ref. 67), *209*
Linderstrøm-Lang, K., 325 (refs. 25, 35), *326*
Lindskog, S., 310, 311 (refs. 36, 38), 314, 317, *326*
Lindström, O., 61, *66*
Lingane, J. J., 333 (ref. 60), 355, 356, *401*
Links, J., 285 (ref. 2), *305*
Linn, B. O., 282, 283, 285 (ref. 17), 289 (refs. 17, 30), 297 (ref. 17), 301, 304 (ref. 17), *305*, *306*
Lipschütz, M., 353, 354, *402*
Lipsky, S. R., 81 (ref. 32), 95, *146*
Liu, C. H., 384 (ref. 28), 386 (ref. 28), *400*
Lloyd, H. A., 71 (ref. 33), *146*
Lockyer, R., 8, 13 (ref. 59), 15 (ref. 59), 27, 40 (ref. 60), 50, 55, *66*
Lord, S. S., 44 (ref. 14), *65*
Lovelock, J. E., 79, 80, *146*
Ludwig, H., 219 (ref. 35), *245*
Lundegårdh, H., 219, *245*
Luukkainen, T., 85 (ref. 38), 108, 109, 120 (refs. 38, 39), 123 (ref. 39), 124 (ref. 38), 141 (ref. 15), 144, *145*, *146*
L'vov, B. V., 12, *66*

M

McDaniel, L. E., 285 (ref. 36), 288 (ref. 36), 293 (ref. 36), *306*
McDonald, R. K., 269 (ref. 36), *278*

McFarren, E. F., 153 (ref. 45), 154 (ref. 45), 180, *208*
McGregor, R. F., 124, *146*
MacIntyre, I., 29 (ref. 1), 55 (ref. 1), *64*
McMillan, A., 248 (ref. 1), 266 (ref. 1), *277*
McPherson, J. F., 293 (ref. 41), *306*
Macy, I. G., 355 (refs. 5, 102), 362 (ref. 102), *399*, *402*
Mahesh, V. B., 196, 197 (ref. 22), 198, *208*
Malik, M. N., 314 (ref. 40), *326*
Malissa, H., 41 (ref. 62), *66*
Malmstadt, H. V., 17, 53, *66*, 238–240, 242, *245*
Malmström, B. G., 311 (ref. 38), 317, *326*
Mann, J. D., 248 (ref. 7), 266 (ref. 7), *277*
Mann, T., 310, *326*
Mannering, G. J., 71 (ref. 3), *145*
Marcus, L., 214 (ref. 42), 215, *245*, 318, *326*
Maren, T. H., 314, 315, *326*
Margaria, R., 320 (ref. 4), *326*
Margerum, D. W., 59, *66*
Markham, R., 202 (ref. 46), *208*
Marks, V., 226 (ref. 71), 244, *246*
Marr, A. G., 214 (ref. 42), 215, *245*, 318, *326*
Marsh, M. M., 189, *208*
Marsh, W., 226 (ref. 43), *245*
Martin, A. J. P., 72, *146*
Martin, H. F., 86 (ref. 65), 111, 115, 123, *147*
Mason, E. E., 236, *245*
Masuoka, D. T., 266 (ref. 25), *278*
Matheson, A. T., 157 (ref. 47), 167 (ref. 64), *209*
Matsushita, S., 389, *400*
Matt, F., 157 (ref. 59), *209*
Matthews, W., 42 (ref. 44), *66*
May, E. L., 71 (ref. 13), *145*
Mayer, K., 380, 382, 383, *401*, *403*
Mehl, J. W., 383 (refs. 66, 126), *401*, *403*
Meigh, D. F., 202 (refs. 48, 49), *209*
Meijer, J. W. A., 89

SUBJECT INDEX

A

Absorbance(s), automated recording, 213–217, 219–220
terpenoid quinones, 293–294, 296
Absorption spectra, coenzyme Q homologs, 290, 291
metals, 4–9, 47–64
non-metals, 23, 24
Absorption spectroscopy. *See* Atomic absorption spectroscopy.
Acetates, gas chromatography, 110–111, 123, 125, 135
liquid phases, 87, 89, 91, 94, 96
paper chromatography, 197
Acetyl cysteine, 359
Acetylesterase assay, 218
S-Acetyl glutathione, 362
Adenosinetriphosphatase assay, 224–225
Adrenocortical hormones, 124–125
Adsorption isotherm, 345–347, 351, 368–369
Albumin(s), polarography, 369, 371–375, 377–379, 384–385, 388–390
Albumose, 381
Alcohol dehydrogenase, assay, 230, 233–234
and carbonic anhydrase, 315
Aldolase assay, 234
Aldosterone, 125, 197
Alkali metals, 30–31
Alkaline earth metals, 30–31
Alkaloids, 71
Alkoxy derivatives of coenzyme Q, 282–283
Allopregnane, 87, 91
Alumina, 289
Aluminum, absorption spectroscopy, 7, 26, 48
Amines, steroidal, 90, 128, 130

Amino acids, chromatography, gas, 71
paper, 174, 189, 202–206
polarography, 336, 354, 362–365
β-Aminoethyl mercaptan, 359, 366
Aminothiophenols, polarography, 360, 366
Ammonium hydroxide in Brdička reaction, 396
Ammonium pyrrolidine dithio-carbamate, 41, 54
Amperometry, 337, 356
Amylase assay, 242
Amytal, 285
Anaerobes, 284, 285
Anakrom, 80
Analog computers, 236, 237
Androstane, 88, 132
Androstanediols, 134
Androstanediones, 112, 134, 138, 139
Androstaneones, identification, 138, 139
separation, 142, 143
steroid numbers, 132, 134
Androsteneones, 110, 134
Androsterone, 102, 116, 117
derivatives, 109, 111, 120–122
Antimony, absorption spectroscopy, 7, 49
Antimycin A, 285
Apiezon greases, 88
Area measurements, gas chroma-tography, 77–78
Arginine, polarography, 354, 363–364
Argenine-vasopressin, 357
Argon ionization system, 79
Arsenic, absorption spectrum, 24
Arum spadix, 285
Ashing, 42
Asphalt fractions in gas chroma-tography, 88
Astra enzyme assayer, 223–226, 243

Ethylene diamine tetraacetic acid.
   See EDTA
Ethylene glycol adipate (EGA), 93
Ethylene glycol isophthalate (EGIP),
   85, 96
Ethylene glycol succinate (EGS),
   93, 97
Ethylmercurithiosalicylate, 361
Etiocholanone, gas chromatography,
   102, 116, 117
   derivatives, 109, 111, 120–122
Excitation interference, 29–30, 33
Extinction coefficients, coenzyme Q
   homologs, 290
Extraction, coenzyme Q, 286–288,
   296–299
   steroids, 113

F

Feces, spectroscopic analysis, 62
   sterols from, 118–120
Fermentation broth, analysis, 240–241
Ferric chloride, coenzyme Q detection,
   301, 304
Fibrinogen, 388–390
Flame, ionization, 30–31
   detectors, 79–80
   photometry, 23–35, 48–51
Florisil, 289
Flow methods in carbonic anhydrase
   assay, 317–320
Fluoralkyl silicones, 90, 99
Fluorometry, automated, 220
   in chromatogram scanning, 189,
   196–198
Fractionation, carbonic anhydrase, 310
Fructose assay, 229–230
Fungi, quinones from, 283, 284

G

Gallium, absorption spectroscopy, 7, 48
Gas chromatography of steroids,
   69–147
   applications, 117–130
   capillary column, 98–99
   column efficiency, 101–104
   derivative separation, 104–113

detection systems, 79–80, 114–115
   historical, 70–71
   identification methods, 130–140
   liquid phases, 85–97
      choice, 99–101
      non-selective, 86–90
      selective, 90–97
   operating parameters, 73–75
   packed column methods, 79–98
   preparative separations, 141–144
   principles, 72–73
   quantification problems, 113–117
   retention times, 131–137
   steroid numbers, 131–137
   structural correlations, 137–140
   support preparation, 80–85
   terminology, 72–79
Gas Chrom P, 80, 83, 102, 103, 105–107
Gasimetric carbonic anhydrase assay,
   324–325
Gas–liquid chromatography. *See* Gas
   chromatography.
Gastric mucosa, 310
Gitogenin, 129
Glass electrode, 320–321
Glassware cleaning, 309
Gliocladium, 283–284
Gliorosein, 283, 284
Globins, polarography, 355
Globulin(s), polarography, 371–375,
   384, 388
Glucose, assay, 238–240
   metabolic pathways, 248
Glucose-6-phosphate isomerase assay,
   234
Glucosiduronic acid, 266, 268
Glucuronosides of steroids, 117, 120,
   121
Glutamic oxaloacetic transaminase
   assay, 230–232, 242
Glutamylcysteylglycine. *See*
   Glutathione.
Glutathione, cystine analysis, 353
   polarography, 357–359, 361
Glyceraldehyde, 362–363
Glycolytic enzymes, assay, 234
Glycoproteins, 386, 391

Methods of Biochemical Analysis

CUMULATIVE INDEX, VOLUMES I–XI

Author Index

Subject Index